Thu

The Irish in Early Me

CU00798976

The Irish in Early Medieval Europe

Identity, Culture and Religion

Edited by

ROY FLECHNER

and

SVEN MEEDER

Selection and editorial matter © Roy Flechner and Sven Meeder 2016. Individual chapters (in order) © Christopher Loveluck and Aidan O'Sullivan; Elva Johnston; Yaniv Fox; Albrecht Diem; Ian Wood; Caitlin Corning; Mark Stansbury; Rob Meens; Yitzhak Hen; Immo Warntjes; Sven Meeder; Roy Flechner and Sven Meeder; Elizabeth Duncan.

All rights reserved. No reproduction, copy or transmission of this publication may be made without written permission.

No portion of this publication may be reproduced, copied or transmitted save with written permission or in accordance with the provisions of the Copyright, Designs and Patents Act 1988, or under the terms of any licence permitting limited copying issued by the Copyright Licensing Agency, Saffron House, 6–10 Kirby Street, London EC1N 8TS.

Any person who does any unauthorized act in relation to this publication may be liable to criminal prosecution and civil claims for damages.

The authors/have asserted their rights to be identified as the authors of this work in accordance with the Copyright, Designs and Patents Act 1988.

First published 2016 by
PALGRAVE

Palgrave in the UK is an imprint of Macmillan Publishers Limited, registered in England, company number 785998, of 4 Crinan Street, London, N1 9XW.

Palgrave Macmillan in the US is a division of St Martin's Press LLC, 175 Fifth Avenue, New York, NY 10010.

Palgrave is a global imprint of the above companies and is represented throughout the world.

Palgrave® and Macmillan® are registered trademarks in the United States, the United Kingdom, Europe and other countries.

ISBN 978–1–137–43060–1 hardback
ISBN 978–1–137–43059–5 paperback

This book is printed on paper suitable for recycling and made from fully managed and sustained forest sources. Logging, pulping and manufacturing processes are expected to conform to the environmental regulations of the country of origin.

A catalogue record for this book is available from the British Library.

A catalog record for this book is available from the Library of Congress.

Printed and bound by CPI Group (UK) Ltd, Croydon, CR0 4YY

Contents

Abbreviations

AASS	Acta Sanctorum
AU	Annals of Ulster, ed. S. Mac Airt and G. Mac Niocaill, *The Annals of Ulster to A.D. 1131. Pt. 1, Text and Translation* (Dublin, 1983)
Bede, *HE*	Beda Venerabilis, *Historia Ecclesiastica Gentis Anglorum*, ed. C. Plummer, *Venerabilis Baedae Opera Historica* (Oxford, 1896), pp. 3–387; eds. Bertram Colgrave and R.A.B. Mynors, *Bede's Ecclesiastical History of the English People* (Oxford, 1969; revised edition, 1992)
CCCM	Corpus Christianorum Continuatio Mediaevalis (Turnhout, 1966–)
CCSL	Corpus Christianorum Series Latina (Turnhout, 1952–)
CLA	Elias A. Lowe, *Codices Latini Antiquiores. A Palaeographical Guide to Latin Manuscripts Prior to the Ninth Century*, 11 vols. plus supplement (Oxford, 1935–1972)
CLLA	*Codices Liturgici Latini Antiquiores*, ed. Klaus Gamber, 2nd ed., 2 vols., Spicilegii Friburgensis subsidia 1 (Freiburg, 1968), supplemented by B. Baroffio et al., Spicilegii Friburgensis subsidia 1A (Freiburg, 1988)
Columbanus, Letters	G.S.M. Walker, ed. and trans., *Sancti Columbani Opera*, Scriptores Latini Hiberniae 2 (Dublin, 1957), pp. 2–59
CSEL	Corpus Scriptorum Ecclesiasticorum Latinorum (Vienna 1866–)
Einhard, *Vita Karoli*	Einhard, *Vita Karoli Magni*, ed. O. Holder-Egger, *MGH SS rer. Germ.* 25 (Hanover, 1911)
EHD	*English Historical Documents*, 2 vols. (London, 1971–81)
EME	*Early Medieval Europe*
HBS	Henry Bradshaw Society

Jonas, *Vita Columbani*	Jonas of Bobbio, *Vita Columbani discipulorumque eius*, ed. B. Krusch, MGH SS rer. Germ. 37 (Hanover, 1905), pp. 1–294; trans. A. O'Hara and I. N. Wood in *Jonas of Bobbio, Life of Columbanus, Life of John of Réomé, and Life of Vedast*, Liverpool Translated Texts for Historians (Liverpool, 2016)
MGH	Monumenta Germaniae Historica
Auct. ant.	Scriptores: Auctores antiquissimi
Capit.	Leges: Capitularia regum Francorum
Concilia	Concilia. Legum Sectio III, Concilia II, ed. A. Werminghoff (Hanover, 1906–1908); III, ed. W. Hartmann (Hanover, 1984)
DD Kar.	Diplomata Karolinorum
Epp.	Epistolae Merovingici et Karolini Aevi
Epp. Sel.	Epistolae Selectae in usum scholarum
Fontes iuris	Fontes iuris Germanici Antiqui in usum scholarum seperatum editi
Poet.	Poetae Latini aevi Carolini
SS rer. Germ.	Scriptores Rerum Germanicarum in usum scholarum separatim editi
SS rer. Lang.	Scriptores Rerum Langobardicarum et Italicarum, saec. VI–IX
SS rer. Merov.	Scriptores rerum Merovingicarum
SS	Scriptores in Folio
PL	J.-P. Migne (pr.), *Patrologiae Cursus Completus, Series Latina*, 221 vols. (Paris, 1841–1864)
PRIA	*Proceedings of the Royal Irish Academy*
SC	Sources chrétiennes (Paris, 1942–)
Settimane	*Settimane di Studio del Centro italiano di studi sull'alto medioevo* (Spoleto, 1954–)
ZRG Kan. Abt.	*Zeitschrift der Savigny-Stiftung für Rechtsgeschichte: Kanonistische Abteilung*

List of Maps, Figures and Tables

Maps

Figures

Table

Maps

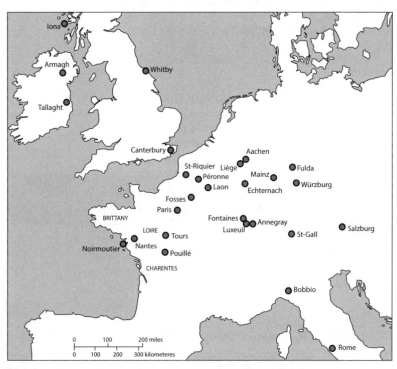

Map 1   From Ireland to Continental Europe in the early Middle Ages

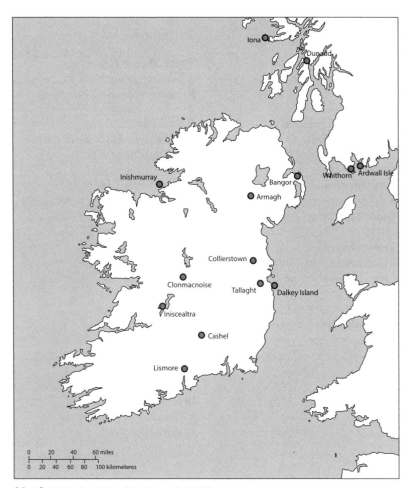

Map 2   Ireland and Argyll in the early Middle Ages

Notes on the Contributors

Caitlin Corning
is Professor of History at George
Fox University in Newberg Oregon.

Albrecht Diem
is Associate Professor at the
Maxwell School of Syracuse
University.

Elizabeth Duncan
researches medieval Gaelic books
and book-production.

Roy Flechner
is Lecturer at the School of History,
University College Dublin.

Yaniv Fox
is Lecturer in Late Antique and
Early Medieval History at Bar-Ilan
University, Israel.

Yitzhak Hen
is Anna and Sam Lopin Professor
of History at Ben-Gurion
University of the Negev.

Elva Johnston
is Lecturer at the School of History,
University College Dublin.

Christopher Loveluck
is Associate Professor and Reader in
Medieval Archaeology, University of
Nottingham.

Sven Meeder
is Lecturer in Medieval History at
Radboud University Nijmegen.

Rob Meens
is Lecturer in Medieval History at
the University of Utrecht.

Aidan O'Sullivan
is Associate Professor of Archaeology
at University College Dublin.

Mark Stansbury
is Lecturer in Classics at the
National University of Ireland,
Galway.

Immo Warntjes
is Lecturer in Irish Medieval
History at Queen's University,
Belfast.

Ian Wood
is Emeritus Professor at the
University of Leeds.

Preface

The present volume is about Irish culture in Europe in the early Middle Ages, focusing in particular on cultural exchanges in Francia. It aims to serve as an introduction to current research in the field and offer critical assessments of the historiography to-date. As such it functions both as a scholarly handbook addressed to experts and a textbook addressed to students seeking guidance as they take their first steps into this field. In chapters that are in the first place informative and accessible to a wide academic readership at all levels, the volume offers a fresh, interdisciplinary perspective on the workings of cross-cultural interaction in the early Middle Ages. We did not ask authors to submit works of original research, yet many chapters offer new and original insights while avoiding issues that would only be of interest to specialists and the use of jargon. Our biggest thanks, therefore, goes to the authors for their stimulating chapters and working within our guidelines.

We would also like to thank the staff of the libraries of Gotha, Padua, Paris and the Vatican for allowing us to reproduce images of manuscripts in their care. We are grateful to the staff of the Ufficio per i Beni Culturali Ecclesiastici della Diocesi di Piacenza-Bobbio for providing us with the image of the funerary stone of Cummian. Drawings of Late Roman Amphorae were made by Dr Amanda Kelly, who kindly allowed us to reproduce them in Chapter 1.

We are indebted to Dr Susan Kelly for her meticulous copy editing of this volume and for her patience with our requirements and queries, which were sometimes sent to her on short notice. We thank Dr Elva Johnston and other members of the organizing committee of the 29th Irish Conference of Medievalists at University College Dublin for hosting a productive workshop with sessions at which a number of contributors presented their chapters-in-progress. Our thanks also go to Professor John McCafferty for helpful comments on the introduction to this volume.

Generous funding towards covering costs associated with the workshop and this volume was received from the College of Arts and Humanities at University College Dublin and the Netherlands Organisation for Scientific Research (NWO), through its support of the *Veni*-project on 'Networks of Knowledge'. We are grateful to both of them.

Introduction: Saints and Scholars

A study of the Irish in continental Europe in the early Middle Ages is invariably a response to centuries of historiography and myth-making that have shaped the way in which a genuine historical phenomenon has been interpreted and reinterpreted by subsequent generations of commentators. Since each generation constructed the past from within its own contemporary concepts much has been clouded by *ad hoc* religious or political agendas that bred teleological narratives. As one generation transmitted its narrative to the other, some notions of the past, be they realistic or exaggerated, have held on more tenaciously than others. One such notion that has been used to tell the story of the Irish abroad is epitomized in the expression *insula sanctorum et doctorum* 'island of saints and scholars', an image which gained currency abroad from the seventeenth century onwards, in no small part thanks to the scholarship of both an Anglo-Irish archbishop of Armagh, James Ussher, and the Catholic Irish Franciscans at Louvain.[1] It has since been used time and time again to refer not only to Ireland itself but to the cultural contribution that the Irish have made overseas. Thus the epithet perpetuated an image of a self-conscious and influential Irish diaspora which continues to resonate strongly to this day. This image is, in part, grounded in hard historical fact, but just as often in little more than fanciful biographies of saintly personalities and romantic antiquarianism of a bygone golden age when religious piety and intellectual endeavour could coexist happily. In separating myth from reality the challenge for the modern historian – and for this very book – is how not to throw the baby out with the bathwater. In other words, one would like to steer away from crippling biographical reverence and engage in some debunking of myths, but at the same time one ought not to be wholly dismissive of past scholarship because we are indebted to it for drawing attention to the phenomenon with which this book is concerned.

Since early modern times, European scholars have emphasized the involvement of Irish holy émigrés in continental religious history between the sixth and eighth centuries as they travelled the mainland to preach their religion of the book. Irishmen were shown to have founded monasteries, bringing with them their native viewpoints and traditions, and making a significant impact on western Europe's monastic landscape. Among the earliest references to the love of learning among Ireland's *doctores* is an account by the eighth-century

1

Northumbrian historian and biblical scholar, Bede, who tells us that Ireland's reputation for scholarship attracted a multitude of students to her many monastic schools.[2] From these centres of learning emanated outstanding works of learning addressing pertinent topics such as ecclesiastical and moral discipline, biblical commentaries, hagiography and computus (the study of the calendar). A good number of these works are known to have reached the Continent, particularly in the eighth and ninth centuries. We know they got there because many survive in continental manuscripts, but even when they do not, their provenance is attested by secondary witnesses. Once on the Continent, these imported texts exerted their influence on literature, science, political culture, religious discipline and legal thought.

This book aims to shed light on Irish influence on European culture and learning by viewing it as a process of cultural exchange. It follows from the conviction that the exertion of cultural influence depends on the participation and agency of more than one party, with the Irish voice being one in a choir of many. For example, the inclusion of a Hiberno-Latin text in a continental manuscript should not immediately be interpreted as proof of an Irish presence in the scriptorium in which the manuscript was written. Rather it invites further questioning, such as: how did the text arrive on the desk of the scribe responsible for this particular codex? From this more questions follow: through how many insular and how many continental hands had it already passed? Was it (still) recognized as Irish? How was the text, if divorced from its original context, understood by its continental audience? Why did the scribe decide to copy this text and what was its relation with the other works in the manuscript? How was this combination of texts subsequently received? Note that these questions primarily concern the continental readership and not the Irish authorship.

The phenomenon of Irish influence in this period is made even more difficult to assess – but also more vital – by the fact that early medieval Europe was a notably international place with impressive long-distance trade routes that connected people (usually the wealthier and more powerful) across ethnic boundaries and facilitated intellectual links throughout the Continent. The Christian church, with its claim to universality, was an important force for stimulating the internationalizing dynamics of western Europe in the early Middle Ages, diluting even further the 'Irish element' within the overall scheme of religious and cultural interaction.

Over the last few decades historians have grown more aware that in order to fully grasp the role and influence of Irish scholarship in the early Middle Ages, it is imperative to study it within its continental context. Major developments in research in the field have directed our gaze to the presence of Irish aspects in the early medieval cultural tradition. These developments are part and parcel of the centrality that several disciplines in the humanities and social sciences – notably those concerned with the modern world – have accorded to cultural identity, cultural appropriation and cultural networks. The present volume aims to bring together the most recent insights, and to make them readily accessible to specialists and students alike.

Historiography: some general trends

A discussion of historiography about the Irish in Europe in the early Middle Ages can be approached from a number of perspectives. The present discussion will address: (i) those periods that scholarship has traditionally covered; (ii) the themes it covered; and (iii) the sway of the national and religious identities of the scholars themselves. Beginning with (i) the division into periods, one may distinguish primarily between a focus on the Merovingian period and on the Carolingian period. The former is characterized by a preoccupation with Columbanus and what has been regarded as 'Columbanian monasticism'.[3] The latter is marked by the biographies of a string of prominent Irish scholars of the so-called Carolingian Renaissance.[4]

As for (ii) themes in historiography, these vary greatly and they can broadly be divided into two: those dealing with events or personalities and those dealing with instances in which texts or actual surviving books have been identified as Irish. Chief among the first category have been, for the early period, the Irish contribution to European monasticism, the political controversies that abbot Columbanus was implicated in (see Chapter 12), and the Easter controversy (see Chapter 6). For the later period historiography has mainly concerned itself with the activities of individual Irish scholars on the Continent who were often associated with the Carolingian court, for example the learning and theological debates of John Scottus Eriugena (d. 877), the political scholarship of Sedulius Scottus (fl. mid-ninth century) and the scientific learning of Dicuil (fl. first half of ninth century) (see Chapters 10 and 12). As for the second category of themes, comprising texts and manuscript production, there has been an interest in anonymous works surviving on the Continent but believed to be by Irishmen, and in particular in works of biblical exegesis and computus. It has also been customary to attribute to the Irish *peregrini* (rightly or wrongly) the introduction of a new genre of normative text, the penitential, and a stricter monastic rule, which in itself can be classified as a form of normative text (see Chapters 4 and 8).

Historians concerned with the presence of Irish scholarship in continental Europe and its consequences have paid much attention to palaeographical and text-critical evidence for the transmission of texts of Irish origin on the Continent and the production of manuscripts in insular or Irish style. Insofar as manuscripts are concerned, the Irish contribution is sometimes bundled together with the Anglo-Saxon or even Breton traditions of book production, and together they form what has come to be recognized more widely as an 'insular' aspect of book production, a topic that continues to form an important strand in the historiography (see Chapter 13). Some, however, have argued that the modern interest in insular manuscripts and the special place that they have often been accorded in scholarship is disproportionate to their relative share in surviving pre-Carolingian Frankish manuscripts: there are approximately 700 manuscripts from the period between 500 and 750, of which about 200 are from Merovingian Francia, and of these only about ten per cent are considered to have been made in insular style.[5] Contacts, mainly (but not only) of a scholarly nature, between Irish and Anglo-Saxon *peregrini* have themselves attracted attention and further contributed to reinforcing the idea of insular culture on the Continent. In certain cases intellectual pedigrees are known (like Alcuin's Irish teacher Colgu), centres of learning in Ireland can be traced (like Ráth Máelsigi, Co. Carlow, where the Anglo-Saxons Ecgberht and Willibrord studied), and the movement of students back and forth across the Irish Sea is documented (commented on by Bede and Aldhelm).[6] Political contacts, like the exile of the Austrasian prince Dagobert to Ireland, are also attested. But the more famous examples – which also have an ecclesiastical dimension – are of contacts between Northumbria and Iona, the influential Irish foundation in Argyll. These include the exile of the Bernician kings Oswald and Oswiu on Iona and the foundation of religious houses in Northumbria, the most famous of which, Lindisfarne, served as a missionary outpost for conversion instigated by Oswald and carried out by the Irish monk bishop Aidan (Áedán).[7] Although the themes of Irish presence in Anglo-Saxon England and of Anglo-Saxons in Ireland are not prominent in the traditional historiographical narrative of the Irish in continental Europe, they are nevertheless essential for understanding the domestic context for *peregrinatio*. Among the more common explanations for the departure of Irish clerics and scholars to the Continent are religious fervour (*peregrinatio pro dei amore*) and, later, the intensification of Viking attacks and settlement, the rise of the ascetic and exclusive *Céli Dé* movement in Ireland, and the centralization of scriptoria in a few major monasteries at the expense of smaller scriptoria and their scribes.[8] Despite its importance, the Irish domestic context for *peregrinatio* has been almost entirely neglected, with one exception.[9] The present volume seeks to redress this neglect with Elva Johnston's contribution (see Chapter 2).

The tendency to view the history of *peregrini* on the Continent in isolation from the Irish at home or in Britain had adverse consequences that led to arbitrary divisions in historiography. Indeed, there has been a marked separation between scholarship relating to the Irish at home and abroad. So much so, in fact, that reading the literature on Irish *peregrini* in continental Europe can have an artificial feel to it because the Irish background of the *peregrini* – or more precisely, their background in Ireland – has been almost entirely ignored. This can sometimes be shown to have been the result of a conscious choice. A case in point is that of the two nineteenth-century champions of Columbanian monasticism, Antoine-Frédéric Ozanam and Charles Forbes René de Montalembert, both of whom can be shown to have been closely familiar with early Irish church history (although the latter author is often dependent on the former). They were familiar, for example, with the important monasteries of Bangor, Clonfert and Clonard, with the *Céli Dé* movement, and with Ireland's foremost saints: Patrick, Brigit and Columba. Nevertheless, they were often very selective – to the point of parsimony – about what they chose to tell their readers about the insular background. There are, however, exceptions to this, like Montalembert's work on Columba, published in English translation in 1866, which gained such currency that it even exerted an influence on Presbyterian Scots.[10] For the most part, however, the Frenchmen's interest was not so much in Ireland or in the insular region *per se*, but in attributing Gallic origins (or at least influence) to Irish saints and monastic culture.[11] For example, although Ozanam mentions the legendary poet Oisín as an example of literature flourishing independently in Ireland, he says that ultimately the 'école irlandaise' was formed under Gallic influence.[12] Likewise, although Montalembert was clearly familiar with St Patrick's *Confessio*, he chose to base most of his biographical account of the saint on Jocelyn's (d. 1214) Life of Patrick, which asserts a Gallic origin for Patrick and makes him a blood relation of the quintessential Gallic saint, Martin of Tours.[13] It is not surprising, therefore, that in discussing Columbanus and what was regarded as his Irish legacy in Gaul, there should be minimal references to his actual Irish background.

One does not get a sense, therefore, that either Ozanam or Montalembert had a genuine interest in understanding *peregrini* in their proper Irish as well as continental context. Stripped of the attributes of identity that they might have brought with them from their homeland, the *peregrini* were made to be reborn *ex nihilo* into their new Frankish environments and were only permitted to retain such cultural attributes that informed their relations with the Franks or Gauls among whom they settled. Paradoxically, therefore, for Irish *peregrini* to be given centre stage in historical studies, their Irish identity had to be suppressed or at the very least severely curtailed. The present volume seeks to curb this tendency not only by examining the domestic background to *peregrinatio* but by repeatedly asking how and whether the Irish component in the *peregrini*'s identity mattered.

The relative isolation in which Irish *peregrini* on the Continent have been studied can be contrasted both with Irish missionary saints in Britain and with Anglo-Saxons in Frankish Europe, whose domestic background has always been prominent in the historiography. The different representations undoubtedly owe something to the greater survival of medieval sources about Anglo-Saxon England than about Ireland, but also to the survival of sources conveying the biographies of the individual personalities. These biographies, usually cast in the form of saints' Lives or hagiography, preserve only cursory factual information about the Irish background of the *peregrini*, or sometimes none at all. Indeed, hagiography is notorious for its use of literary tropes that replicate themselves at the expense of simple descriptive information, a topic that is dealt with here by Yaniv Fox (see Chapter 3). Furthermore, our sources rarely say anything about Irish *peregrini* maintaining contact with their homeland, unlike Anglo-Saxons in Francia and Irish in Britain who are portrayed as continually being involved – either in person but usually indirectly – in the ecclesiastical and political affairs of their homelands or simply keeping in touch with their friends and relations there.[14] In fact, it is to this indirect involvement that we must be grateful for leaving us with trails of correspondence that constitute some of our most important contemporary sources for the period.

It is also true that neither the continental hagiographers, nor the early medieval Irish *peregrini* whose works survive, make mention of any events or personalities that can be corroborated by contemporary sources written in Ireland, which consist mainly of chronicles and hagiography. And so, disappointingly, texts written by or about *peregrini* gloss over the rise and fall of kings, the growth of the great monasteries of Armagh or Clonmacnoise, their dependencies, and sometimes even their mere existence. Incidentally, it has recently been noted that the opposite is also true, namely that sources written in early medieval Ireland very rarely mention *peregrini*.[15]

Historiography: scholars and their agendas

The final (iii) aspect of historiography that will be discussed here is the identities and agendas of modern and early modern scholars. Our current understanding of Irish culture in Europe owes much to the legacy of nineteenth-century intellectuals and the manner in which they chose to synthesize the primary sources that were available to them and to mediate the scholarship of their early modern predecessors. Their work was not free from political and religious partisanship. The Catholic revival of the nineteenth century affected both scholars in Ireland and abroad. Daniel O'Connell's campaign for Catholic emancipation in Ireland, which culminated in the Catholic Relief Act of 1829, has convincingly been argued to have spurred an interest in the early Irish church among Catholic revivalists, mainly in France. Two important exponents of this trend were the aforementioned Ozanam and Montalembert (see Chapter 5). They were, however, not the first to enlist early medieval Irish history in the cause of religion. In Ireland itself there have been both Protestant and Catholic precedents for this. The sixteenth-century Bishop of Ossory, John Bale, and the already-mentioned seventeenth-century Archbishop of Armagh, James Ussher, both claimed that the early Irish church was more akin to Protestantism than Catholicism.[16] This at a time when restrictions on the practice of Catholicism, the breaking-down of patronage ties after the Flight of the Earls in 1607, and the eventual prohibition on Catholic education imposed by the Penal Laws, meant that works on Irish history were often undertaken or published (either in manuscript or print) outside Ireland, most notably in Irish colleges on the Continent.[17] The Irish Franciscan College, St Anthony's at Louvain, was especially prominent in ambitious projects of publishing medieval texts, the most significant among them being the publication in 1645 of 270 Lives of Irish saints in the *Acta Sanctorum* of John Colgan (1592–1658), followed two years later by the publication of source material on Saints Patrick, Brigit and Columba.[18] Then, in 1667, there appeared the *editio princeps* of the collected works of Columbanus by Patrick Fleming OFM, who was killed by Protestants near Prague during the Thirty Years' War. His surviving manuscript was prepared for print by another member of the community at Louvain, Thomas Sheerin.[19] Another Louvain-related work was the compilation of what has become known (thanks to a reference in Colgan's preface to the *Acta*) as the Annals of the Four Masters, which was overseen by Mícheál Ó Cléirigh OFM. Although based at Louvain, he undertook the compilatory work in Donegal between 1632 and 1636, having been sent to Ireland at the instigation of Hugh Ward, Guardian of St Anthony's. However, it only appeared in print between 1848 and 1851 in a seven-volume edition by John O'Donovan.[20]

Probably the most famous work to emerge from the Reformation/Counter-Reformation polemic is Geoffrey Keating's *Foras feasa ar Éirinn* ('Compendium of Knowledge about Ireland'). Completed in the 1630s, Keating's work of Irish ethnogenesis, combining legendary and historical material, also circulated for a long time only in manuscript form, but gained popularity nevertheless. Parts of it were printed as citations in other printed works, like Roderick O'Flaherty's own account of the foundation of Ireland, *Ogygia seu rerum Hibernicarum chronologia*.[21] Keating's text was first printed in English translation by Dermot O'Connor in London in 1723 under the title *A General History of Ireland*. However, it was not until 1902 that the original Irish text began to appear in print by the Irish Texts Society, though the project of preparing the work for print would have started some years before.[22] Hence, although both *Foras feasa ar Éirinn* and the Annals of the Four Masters were produced in the seventeenth century, their appearance in print is very much a nineteenth-century phenomenon and is couched firmly in contemporary political circumstances. As Bernadette Cunningham notes: 'those who sought to recover the medieval past in nineteenth- and twentieth-century Ireland did not do so out of disinterested antiquarianism. They did so in the belief that preserving the memory of the Irish past held the key to the future well-being of the Irish nation'.[23] Based on the foregoing discussion we can already distinguish two phases in the development of historiography *about* the Irish in early medieval Europe: one closely associated with the seventeenth-century Irish Franciscans of Louvain and with Reformation/Counter-Reformation debates, and the other with nineteenth-century Catholic revivalism.

It is tempting to draw an analogy between the diaspora of Irish Catholic scholars before the nineteenth-century Catholic emancipation and the exodus of Irish scholars from Ireland in the Carolingian Renaissance. On the one hand we have a diaspora that was, in part, formed as a consequence of persecution, but also as a consequence of the fading of patronage links with the Gaelic elite, and on the other hand an exodus of scholars in the early medieval period which was, to an extent, a response to the Viking presence and its contribution to the disruption of patronage ties with Irish kings.[24] One wonders if the superficial similarity between the two situations was among the factors that brought seventeenth-century Irish Catholics on the Continent to take an interest in early-medieval Irish cleric-scholars both at home and abroad who were depicted as a leading intellectual and clerical elite. It has already been remarked that the 'impetus to promulgate the image of an island of saints and scholars was most clearly discernible among the Catholic Irish who were educated at universities in continental Europe in the early seventeenth century'.[25] Possibly, however, seventeenth-century Irish expatriates were casting their early medieval compatriots as forerunners in their own image.

The brief discussion of the historiography shows that it is possible to point to three binary divisions of historians. These binaries are: (i) Protestant and Catholic; (ii) writers at home and abroad; and (iii) Irish and non-Irish writers. Although one ought to be careful not to overlook certain commonalities within each binary, there are three general observations that may nevertheless be made. The first is that language is a clear line of demarcation between Catholic and Protestant: some of the former chose to write in Irish, but the latter never did.[26] Secondly, the tendency among non-Irish authors to put less stress on the early medieval history of Ireland itself is certainly more pronounced in comparison with Irish authors who, even when living on the Continent, can be seen to make Ireland their focus. And thirdly, the lives and careers of *peregrini* seem to have been of less concern to Protestant authors. But there were, nevertheless, exceptions. As Richard Sharpe notes with regard to a very specific episode in early Irish history: 'Presbyterian Scots, Irish catholics, and Episcopalians in Scotland, Ireland and England all found their own roots in Celtic Christianity as they imagined it was lived out in the Iona of St Columba, and from 1860 onwards writers of each denomination produced edificatory books that presented Columba and his church in their own idealized image'.[27]

Towards an academization of the debate

In the twentieth century one observes four main themes that dominated scholarship concerning the Irish on the Continent: canon law, biblical exegesis, computus and (again) Columbanian monasticism. We shall take them in turn. Medieval canon law can be said to mark the beginning of the shift towards a more strictly academic debate in the late nineteenth and early twentieth century. What attracted the attention of scholars such as Hermann Wasserschleben, Henry Bradshaw, August Nürnberger, and Siegmund Hellmann, were Irish penitentials and texts of canon law which, ostensibly, seemed to bear the imprint of Irish *peregrini*.[28] The vexing question was whether normative texts with Irish connections which circulated widely on the Continent, like the *Hibernensis* or the *Excarpsus Cummeani*, were compiled in Ireland or on the Continent. Alternatively, could they have originated in Ireland and later been modified on the Continent? This possibility gained support from the fact that some such texts were transmitted in more than one form. Even if the revisers were not Irish, this was nevertheless no trivial point, because the changes that a text undergoes in its transmission can testify to the impact it had and – by association – to the impact that Irish learning had on the ecclesiastical centres associated with copying and revision. Some of these debates have only recently abated with the emergence of a scholarly consensus (albeit not a resolution). So, for instance, it is now commonly accepted that the main text-types of the *Hibernensis* were compiled in Ireland, but that the *Excarpsus* was compiled on the Continent using some Irish material. Penitentials like the *Excarpsus* were among the subjects of an important new study by Rob Meens,[29] which also examined the Irish contribution to medieval penance more generally. Some of its findings are discussed in Chapter 8.

Next we come to biblical exegesis, a topic that is not unconnected to canon law. Irish canon law can be seen to have drawn on biblical exegesis for interpreting law, and exegetical texts were sometimes transmitted together with canon law in the same continental manuscripts. Both types of text circulated relatively widely. Once more, the circulation itself matters because it can be a measure for impact. A debate, or rather controversy, about early medieval Irish exegesis was sparked in 1954 by the publication of Bernhard Bischoff's catalogue which comprised approximately forty pre-ninth-century exegetical texts (many of which were discovered by Bischoff himself), which he believed were either written by Irishmen or influenced by Irish biblical scholarship.[30] In response to initial criticisms and to his own self-correcting ideas, Bischoff published a revised version of his original article in 1966.[31] Bischoff's methods of classification were called to question in 1967 by Edmondo Coccia, who, in a passionate attack, targeted Bischoff not only for his views on exegesis, but also on the contribution of Irish monastic culture to continental monasticism.[32] In time more scholars joined the debate, among them Clare Stancliffe,

Michael Gorman, Michael Herren, and Dáibhí Ó Cróinín.[33] The reaction to Bischoff's work stimulated scholars to restate the evidence in favour of Irish exegesis more firmly. Consequently, the case for early medieval Irish exegesis has not been lost, but merely refined. Herren and Ó Cróinín, for example, urge that no small number of works from Bischoff's list can be tied to Ireland or Irish scholars working outside Ireland with a relative degree of security. In Herren's view, 'at least a handful of Latin works on the Bible can be assigned reliably to Irish origin'.[34] The debate is revisited here in a chapter by Mark Stansbury, who offers a fresh reassessment (see Chapter 7).

The third topic in the order of this discussion is computus, namely the reckoning of the ecclesiastical calendar, a topic that for much of the twentieth century has drawn attention mainly from non-Irish scholars and, as Ó Cróinín said in 2003 concerning key manuscripts pertaining to the study of Irish computistics, 'no native Irish scholar has ever examined them, let alone studied their contents'.[35] From the earliest phases of recorded Christianity, the ecclesiastical calendar has been a vexed issue. It came to be regulated already in the first ecumenical council, held at Nicaea in 325 under the auspices of Emperor Constantine. However, the controversy regarding the Christian calendar, which revolves around the major feast of Easter, was reignited in Gaul in the late sixth and early seventh century, and then in Britain and Ireland in the seventh century. The 'Easter Controversy', as it became known, had different causes in the different places in which it raged, but, to put it crudely, it was broadly the consequence of a clash between conflicting ecclesiastical rites, or practices: those of the Roman, Gallic, or English churches (post 664) on the one hand, and the Irish, British or Breton churches (often referred to by the shorthand 'Celtic') on the other. Ever since the Council of Nicaea, the question of the dating of Easter was steeped with exegetical, scientific, ritualistic and political aspects and implications. As Thomas Charles-Edwards put it: 'if Christianity was to be the religion of the emperor, Christian time should be undisputed'.[36] Insofar as *peregrini* are concerned, the dating of Easter drew attention primarily for its connection with the Irish contribution to the science of *computus*, discussed here by Immo Warntjes (see Chapter 10) and the political as well as exegetical aspects that came into play in Columbanus's disputes with the Gallic episcopate. These are discussed in the chapter by Caitlin Corning (see Chapter 6) and the chapter by Roy Flechner and Sven Meeder (see Chapter 12).

Columbanus brings us to the fourth and final theme, which is Columbanian monasticism. This is another fraught issue which, in

1965, received a new impetus from a study by Friedrich Prinz which tried to systematize the research of this phenomenon, the mere existence of which was about to become controversial. He estimated that, between 590 and 730, monasteries in Gaul and Italy that owed something to the legacy of the Irish abbot Columbanus (d. 615) numbered approximately one hundred.[37] The figure, which suggested a *prima facie* Irish-inspired monastic movement on a significant scale, was based mainly on inferences from hagiography and included also monasteries under the vague heading of 'Irish influence' (*irisch beeinflusste klöster*). Such influence could manifest itself from following a Columbanian or Columbanian-like monastic rule (itself a vexed issue, discussed here by Diem in Chapter 4) to asserting an aspect of Irish identity. Understandably Prinz's hypothesis was challenged and by 1976 a refinement was proposed by Hartmut Atsma.[38] The subject of Columbanian monasticism has been the focus of a major new book by Yaniv Fox who contributes a chapter to the present volume (Chapter 3).[39] Another chapter, by Ian Wood (Chapter 5), judges the phenomenon from a historiographical perspective that goes back long before Prinz, to Ozanam and Montalembert.

Alongside such purely academic endeavours, a debate of both academic and popular import arose regarding the question of quantification and qualification of the participation or isolation of Ireland in the early medieval period, and by extention the scope of Irish influence on European culture. Perhaps buoyed up by then recent political events, Helen Waddell floridly ascribed the salvation of literature to the Irish in her 1927 bestseller *The Wandering Scholars*.[40] Other scholars and novelists articulated similar appreciative narratives on the contribution of Irish saintly and intellectual *peregrini*.[41] But then came dissenting voices, which had in common one simple question, most plainly expressed in the title of Edmondo Coccia's article 'La cultura irlandese precarolingia: miracolo o mito?'.[42] These were perhaps the most extreme versions of what Johannes Duft in the 1950s classified as 'Iromania' and 'Irophobia', arguing that both frequently afflicted medieval as well as modern scholars.[43] The identification of the ailments by Duft did not, however, eradicate them and both sentiments continue to rear their heads from time to time.[44]

The academic interest in Ireland's cultural contribution to Europe was reinvigorated in 1984, as the range of topics and disciplines was expanded with the publication of the first of four volumes of conference proceedings entitled *Ireland and Europe in the Early Middle Ages*, co-edited by Próinséas Ní Chatháin and Michael Richter. The first concentrated on ecclesiastical history, the second (1987) on missions and the uses of the Bible, the third (1996) was devoted to what the editors titled 'learning and literature' and the fourth (2002) to 'texts and transmission'.[45] Some of the contributions in these volumes, and especially the first, became fundamental reading for scholars interested in the activities of the Irish in continental Europe. Nevertheless, many of the contributions did not deal with the Continent at all (but solely with Ireland), and most were written for a highly specialized readership.

Archaeological evidence for trade and communication between Ireland and continental Europe, in particular, tends to escape the gaze of the student of history and advances in this field are often overlooked.[46] The chapter by Chris Loveluck and Aidan O'Sullivan in the present volume aims to remedy this situation (Chapter 1). Other important studies that accrued over the last two decades – mainly journal articles and book chapters – did not have the advantage of appearing in volumes dedicated specifically to the relationship between Ireland and the Continent. Some examples are Rosamond McKitterick's comparison of Irish and Anglo-Saxon missionaries,[47] Roger Reynolds's study of the dissemination and influence of Irish canon law,[48] Rob Meens's work on penitentials,[49] Mary Garrison's work on the Irish at the Carolingian court,[50] and Sven Meeder's work on Irish foundations.[51] This book aims to build on this scholarship and to offer new insights addressing the most pertinent themes regarding the cultural exchange between Ireland and Europe in the early Middle Ages.

Notes

1. For a comment on this expression in early modern times, see Jane Stevenson, 'The Politics of Historiography: or, Novels with Footnotes', in J. Leerssen, A.H. van der Weel and B. Westerweel, eds, *Forging in the Smithy: National Identity and Representation in Anglo-Irish Literary History* (Amsterdam, 1995), pp. 195–206, at pp. 201–2.

2. See for instance Bede, *HE*, III.4; III.27; IV.3; V.10. On monastic education in Ireland, see D. Ó Cróinín, *Early Medieval Ireland 400–1200* (London, 1995), pp. 178–81.

3. A topic familiar to many scholars primarily through the work of F. Prinz, *Frühes Mönchtum im Frankenreich* (Munich, 1965).

4. For names and surviving works by *peregrini* between the late eighth and late ninth centuries, see M. Lapidge and R. Sharpe, *A Bibliography of Celtic-Latin Literature 400–1200* (Dublin, 1985), pp. 169–95. Apart from John Scottus and Sedulius Scottus, these include Murethach Scottus from Auxerre, Dubthach, Magister Fergus and Martin Hiberniensis from Laon.

5. According to an estimate by Ian Wood for insular manuscripts made in Merovingian Francia before 750, based on *Codices Latini Antiquiores*. See his forthcoming 'The Problem of Late Merovingian Culture', in G. Schwedler and R. Schwitter, eds., *Exzerpieren - Kompilieren - Tradieren. Transformationen des Wissens zwischen Spätantike und Frühmittelalter.* We are grateful to Professor Wood for permission to cite the article before publication.

6. Colgu is mentioned in letter 7 by Alcuin (EHD I, no. 192) and in Symeon of Durham's *Historia Regum*, 794 (EHD I, no. 3). On Ráth Máelsigi see D. Ó Cróinín, 'Rath Maelsigi, Willibrord, and the Earliest Echternach Manuscripts', *Peritia* 3 (1984), 17–49. For Anglo-Saxon students in Ireland, see Bede, *Historia ecclesiastica gentis Anglorum,* III.4, III.27, IV.3, and V.10.

7. T. M. Charles-Edwards, *Early Christian Ireland* (Cambridge, 2000), pp. 299–326.

8. The latter is the most speculative since this 'centralisation' is not supported by hard evidence. See K. Hughes, 'The Distribution of Irish Scriptoria and Centres of Learning from 730–1111', in N.K. Chadwick, ed., *Studies in the Early British Church* (Cambridge, 1958), pp. 243–69; J. Contreni and P. Ó Néill, 'The Early Career and Formation of John Scottus', in J. Contreni, *Learning and Culture in Carolingian Europe* (Farnham, 2011), pp. 1–24, at 17–18; S. Hayes-Healy, '"Irish Pilgrimage": A Romantic Misconception', in S. Duffy, ed., *Princes, Prelates and Poets in Medieval Ireland. Essays in Honour of Katherine Simms* (Dublin, 2013), pp. 241–60.

9. T. M. Charles Edwards, 'The Social Background to Irish Peregrinatio', *Celtica* 11 (1976), pp. 43–59.

10. R. Sharpe, *Adomnán of Iona. Life of St Columba* (London, 1995), pp. 96–7.

11. An exception is volume III of C. F. R. de Montalembert, *Les moines d'Occident*, 5th edn, 7 vols (Paris, 1860–77), which devotes an entire chapter (ch. 8) to St Columba and Irish monasticism.

12. A. F. Ozanam, *Études germaniques pour servir à l'histoire des Francs*, 2 vols (Paris, 1847–9), II, ch. 9 (p. 567 in his *Œuvres complètes*).

13. Montalembert, *Les moines d'Occident*, II, p. 458.

14. R. McKitterick, *Anglo-Saxon Missionaries in Germany: Personal Connections and Local Influences*, Vaughn Paper 36 (Leicester, 1991), repr. in her *The Frankish Kings and Culture in the Early Middle Ages* (Aldershot, 1995); L. Von Padberg, *Heilige und Familie: Studien zur Bedeutung familiengebundener Aspekte in den Viten des Verwandten- und Schülerkreises um Willibrord, Bonifatius und Liudger*, Quellen und Abhandlungen zur mittelrheinischen Kirchengeschichte 83, 2nd ed. (Mainz, 1997); J. Story, *Carolingian Connections: Anglo-Saxon England and Carolingian Francia c.750–870* (Aldershot, 2003); J. Palmer, *Anglo-Saxons in a Frankish World, 690–900* (Turnhout, 2009), pp. 66–76.

15. E. Johnston, *Literacy and Identity in Early Medieval Ireland* (Woodbridge, 2013), p. 46.
16. On Bale, see M. McKisack, *Medieval History in the Tudor Age* (Oxford, 1971), pp. 1–25. On Ussher: A. Ford, *James Ussher. Theology, History, and Politics in Early Modern Ireland and England* (Oxford, 2007), pp. 119–32.
17. J. Leerssen, *Mere Irish and Fíor-Ghael. Studies in the Idea of Irish Nationality, its Development and Literary Expression prior to the Nineteenth Century* (Amsterdam, 1986), pp. 254–81.
18. J. Colgan, ed., *Acta Sanctorum Veteris et Majoris Scotiæ seu Hiberniæ*, 2 vols (Louvain, 1645); idem, *Triadis Thaumatugæ seu Divorum Patricii, Columbæ, et Brigidæ. . . Acta* (Louvain, 1647). On the medieval and modern transmission of Irish saints' Lives, see the now classic: R. Sharpe, *Medieval Irish Saints' Lives. An Introduction to the Vitae Sanctorum Hiberniae* (Oxford, 1991). On St Anthony's and the protagonists of the hagiographical project undertaken there, see P. Breatnach, 'An Irish Bollandus: Fr Hugh Ward and the Louvain Hagiographical Enterprise', *Éigse* 31 (1999), 1–30; N. Ó Muraíle, ed., *Mícheál Ó Cléirigh, His Associates and St Anthony's College, Louvain* (Dublin, 2008); P. Ó Riain, 'The Louvain Achievement II: Hagiography', in E. Bhreathnach, J. MacMahon and J. McCafferty, eds., *The Irish Franciscans, 1534–1990* (Dublin, 2009), pp. 189–200.
19. *Collectanea Sacra*, ed. P. Fleming (Louvain, 1667).
20. *Annals of the Kingdom of Ireland, by the Four Masters: from the Earliest Period to the Year 1616*, 7 vols (Dublin 1848–51). But an English translation by Owen Connellan appeared in print already in 1845.
21. R. O'Flaherty, *Ogygia; seu, Rerum Hibernicarum chronologia* (London, 1685). On O'Flaherty and *Ogygia*, see R. Sharpe, *Roderick O'Flaherty's Letters to William Molyneux, Edward Lhwyd, and Samuel Molyneux, 1696–1709* (Dublin, 2013), pp. 1–51, 85–90.
22. The circulation of the work in Irish and English, in manuscript and in print, is discussed by B. Cunningham, *The World of Geoffrey Keating. History, Myth and Religion in Seventeenth-Century Ireland* (Dublin, 2000), pp. 11–13, 201–25.
23. B. Cunningham, 'Transmission and Translation of Medieval Irish Sources in the Nineteenth and Early Twentieth Centuries', in R.J.W. Evans and G.P. Marchal, eds., *The Uses of the Middle Ages in Modern European States: History, Nationhood and the Search for Origins* (Basingstoke, 2011), pp. 7–17, at p. 13.
24. On exile and patronage in early modern times, see B. Cunningham, *The Annals of the Four Masters. Irish History, Kingship and Society in the Early Seventeenth Century* (Dublin, 2014), p. 34.
25. Citation from Cunningham, 'Transmission and Translation', p. 8.
26. Though an interest in the Irish language is attested among some contemporary Protestants. See Leerssen, *Mere Irish*, p. 327.
27. Sharpe, *Adomnán of Iona*, p. 97.

28. F.W.H. Wasserschleben, ed., *Die Bussordnungen der abendländischen Kirche* (Halle, 1851); idem, ed., *Die irische Kanonensammlung* (Giessen 1874; 2nd ed. Leipzig, 1885); A.J. Nürnberger, 'Über die Würzburger Handschrift der irischen Canonensammlung', *Archiv für katholisches Kirchenrecht* 60 (1888), 3–84. H. Bradshaw, *The Early Collection of Canons known as the Hibernensis. Two Unfinished Papers* (Cambridge, 1893); S. Hellmann, *Pseudo-Cyprianus. De XII abusiuis saeculi*, Texte und Untersuchungen zur Gedichte der altchristlichen Literatur 34.1 (Leipzig, 1909).

29. R. Meens, *Penance in Medieval Europe, 600–1200* (Cambridge, 2014).

30. Bischoff, B., 'Wendepunkte in der Geschichte der lateinischen Exegese im Frühmittelalter', *Sacris Erudiri* 6 (1954), 187–281; revised in Bischoff, *Mittelalterliche Studien*, 3 vols (Stuttgart, 1966–81), I, pp. 205–73. An English translation of the revised version is by Colm O'Grady, 'Turning-points in the History of Latin Exegesis in the Early Irish Church: AD 650–800', in *Biblical Studies. The Medieval Irish Contribution*, ed. Martin McNamara (Dublin, 1976), pp. 74–160.

31. Bischoff, *Mittelalterliche Studien, I*, pp. 205–73.

32. E. Coccia, 'La cultura irlandese precarolingia: miracolo o mito?', *Studi medievali* 8 (1967), 257–420. This was largly a response to Bischoff's, 'Il monachismo irlandese nei suoi rapporti col continente', *Mittelalterliche Studien* 1 (Stuttgart, 1966), pp. 195–205. His criticism also extended to Ludwig Bieler's, *Ireland, Harbinger of the Middle Ages* (Oxford, 1963).

33. C. Stancliffe, 'Early "Irish" biblical exegesis', *Studia Patristica* 12 (1975), 361–70 (published in the series *Texte und Untersuchungen zur Geschichte der altchristlichen Literatur* 115); M. Gorman, 'A Critique of Bischoff's Theory of Irish Exegesis: the Commentary on Genesis in Munich Clm 6302 ("Wendepunkte" 2)', *Journal of Medieval Latin* 7 (1997), 178–233; M. Herren, 'Irish Biblical Commentaries before 800', in *Roma, magistra mundi* (Louvain, 1998), 391–407; M. Gorman, 'The myth of Hiberno-Latin exegesis', *Revue Bénédictine* 110 (2000), 42–85; D. Ó Cróinín, 'Bischoff's Wendepunkte fifty years on', *Revue Bénédictine* 110 (2000), pp. 204–37.

34. The citation is Herren, 'Irish Biblical Commentaries', p. 393.

35. Ó Cróinín, *Early Irish History and* Chronology (Dublin, 2003), p. 2.

36. Charles-Edwards, *Early Christian Ireland*, p. 394, and see pp. 391–415 for his lucid discussion of the remaining aspects of the Easter question.

37. The figure is from Prinz, *Frühes Mönchtum im Frankenreich*, map VII A.

38. Hartmut Atsma, 'Les monastères urbains du Nord de la Gaule', *Revue d'Histoire de l'Église de France* 62 (1976), pp. 163–87.

39. Y. Fox, *Power and Religion in Merovingian Gaul. Columbanian Monasticism and the Frankish Elites* (Cambridge, 2014).

40. Helen Waddell, *The Wandering Scholars* (London, 1927), p. 28.

41. For instance Margaret Stokes, *Three Months in the Forests of France: A Pilgrimage in Search of Vestiges of the Irish Saints in France* (London, 1895),

and eadem, *Six Months in the Apennines: Or a Pilgrimage in Search of Vestiges of the Irish Saints in Italy* (London, 1892); see Simon Young, 'On the Irish peregrini in Italy', *Peritia* 16 (2002), pp. 250–55.

42. Which translated as 'Irish pre-Carolingian culture: miracle of myth?'; Coccia, 'La cultura irlandese precarolingia'.

43. J. Duft, 'Iromanie – Irophobie. Fragen um die frühmittelalterliche frühmittelalterliche Irenmission exempliziert an St. Gallen und Alemannien', *Zeitschrift für für Schweizerische Kirchengeschichte* 50 (1956), 241–62. A recent reassessment of the question is by M.J. Enright, 'Iromanie–Irophobie Revisited: A Suggested Frame of Reference for Considering Continental Reactions to Irish Peregrini in the Seventh and Eighth Centuries', in *Karl Martell in seiner Zeit*, ed. J. Jarnut, U. Nonn and M. Richter (Sigmaringen, 1994), pp. 367–80.

44. A popularisation of the 'Iromanic' view is T. Cahill's *How the Irish Saved Civilization: the Untold Story of Ireland's Heroic Role from the Fall of Rome to the Rise of Medieval Europe* (New York, 1995). A recent critical review of Irish literacy, on the other hand, is offered by M. Mostert, 'Celtic, Anglo-Saxon or insular? Some considerations on 'Irish' manuscript production and their implications for insular Latin culture, *c.* AD 500–800', in D. Edel, ed., *Cultural Identity and Cultural Integration. Ireland and Europe in the Early Middle Ages* (Dublin, 1995), pp. 92–115.

45. P. Ní Chatháin and M. Richter, *Irland und Europa: die Kirche im Frühmittelalter = Ireland and Europe: the Early Church* (Stuttgart, 1984); eidem, eds., *Irland und die Christenheit: Bibelstudien und Mission = Ireland and Christendom: the Bible and the Missions* (Stuttgart, 1987); eidem, eds., *Irland und Europa im früheren Mittelalter: Bildung und Literatur = Ireland and Europe in the Early Middle Ages: Learning and Literature* (Stuttgart, 1996); and eidem, eds., *Ireland and Europe in the Early Middle Ages: Texts and Transmission = Irland und Europa im früheren Mittelalter: Texte und Überlieferungen* (Dublin, 2002).

46. A noteworthy exception is the work by J. Wooding, including his article 'Trade as a Factor in the Transmission of Texts between Ireland and the Continent in the Sixth and Seventh Centuries', in P. Ní Chatháin and M. Richter, eds., *Ireland and Europe in the Early Middle Ages: Texts and Transmission* (Dublin, 2002), pp. 14–26.

47. McKitterick, 'Anglo-Saxon Missionaries'.

48. Particularly R.E. Reynolds, 'Unity and Diversity in Carolingian Canon Law Collections: the Case of the Collectio Hibernensis and its Derivatives', in: U.-R. Blumenthal,ed.), *Carolingian Essays: Andrew W. Mellon Lectures in Early Christian Studies* (Washington DC, 1983), pp. 99–135; and idem, 'The Transmission of the Hibernensis in Italy: Tenth to the Twelfth Century', *Peritia* 14 (2000), pp. 20–50.

49. Most recently Meens, *Penance in Medieval Europe*.

50. M. Garrison, 'The English and the Irish at the Court of Charlemagne', in P. L. Butzer, M. Kerner, and W. Oberschelp, eds., *Charlemagne and his Heritage: 1200 years of Civilization and Science in Europe* (Turnhout, 1997), pp. 97–123.
51. S. Meeder, 'The Irish Foundations and the Carolingian World', *Settimane* 57 (2010), pp. 467–93.

1

Travel, Transport and Communication to and from Ireland, *c.* 400–1100: an Archaeological Perspective

Christopher Loveluck and Aidan O'Sullivan

Introduction and context

How did Irish *peregrini*, clerics and manuscripts physically move back and forth between Ireland and the Continent in the early Middle Ages, and did they utilize existing and ongoing economic and trading links between Irish ports and those along the Atlantic coast of Britain, Francia and Iberia? What is the evidence for long-distance maritime trade and exchange between Ireland and continental Europe in the sixth and seventh centuries and afterwards? Can we identify where Irish and other merchant-mariners were sailing to and from in their sea voyages? How might we better exploit archaeological evidence, historical sources and other data towards deepening our understanding of Irish travel, transport and communication to Atlantic Europe, and setting research agendas for the future? This chapter will attempt to deal with these questions and create a sense of how people, goods and ideas were physically moved along the seaways between Ireland and early medieval Europe.

The paper builds on the work of other scholars who have previously traced connections between Ireland and its neighbours, and it follows on particularly from Jonathan Wooding's seminal paper 'Trade as a Factor in the Transmission of Texts'. We do not attempt to reproduce that paper, and the reader is advised to consult it directly for historical references to the movement of merchants and clerics.[1] Rather, in this paper we shall examine the extensive new archaeological evidence for the early Irish medieval economy, trade and exchange. This evidence has accrued during the explosion of

19

developer-led archaeological research in Ireland in recent decades and has highlighted the importance of the Atlantic-facing regions of Europe in helping to drive the social, economic and political transformations of early medieval western Christendom.[2] An archaeological reassessment of links between Ireland, Britain and continental Europe is, therefore, an essential prerequisite to understanding the role and impact of the Irish in early medieval Europe. This role between the fifth and eleventh centuries is assessed within the context of the maritime cultural landscapes of Atlantic Europe and the Channel, and the principal river 'transport corridors' leading into the interior of continental Europe and ultimately to the Mediterranean.[3]

In the first place it is important to emphasize the significant growth and expansion of the early medieval Irish population and economy in the sixth and seventh centuries in the run up to the creation of one of the richest archaeological landscapes in the world.[4] There is abundant archaeological evidence for early medieval settlement expansion from the late fifth to the early sixth century, probably as a response to population growth, with tens of thousands of enclosed settlements across the island. It is also clear that Irish agriculture in the sixth and seventh centuries was innovative and effective, consisting of a sophisticated dairy economy and cereal crops that were processed using corn-drying kilns and horizontal water mills. We also witness an expansionary early Irish church quickly establishing itself as both a political and economic power, and was itself probably investing in agriculture, both through its own estates and through tithes and tributes received from the laity, with a possible focus on grain production and processing. Indeed, it seems apparent that the early Irish economy was creating an agricultural and commodities surplus beyond the needs of subsistence and local lordly-client socio-economic relationships and possibly aimed at long-distance trade. It seems likely, for example, that the early medieval political territory of Brega, whence evidence for increased agricultural activities survives and which was flanked to the east by the Irish Sea coast, was partly involved in agricultural production for long-distance trade across the Irish Sea. At other locations along the Irish coastline there is evidence for imported commodities such as pottery and glass. It may be that these were exchanged for exports in the form of locally produced foodstuffs like butter and flour, as well as other commodities suitable for trade like hides, leather, vellum, livestock and slaves. Trade is typically interpreted in top-down terms, being associated with kings, but it also seems likely that Irish and foreign merchant-mariners were actively involved as agents in this trade, perhaps even as its principal instigators, rather than simply serving elite patrons. We know unfortunately little about the types of vessels being used, and most studies have tended to emphasize that the Irish were using coracle-like vessels built of wood and hides. However, as Wooding has pointed out, the range of terms for ships and boats in Adomnán's Life of Columba, including the words *cimbul*, *curucus*, *nauis*, *longenauis* and *barca*, at least imply that a range of types of seagoing vessels, both native and foreign, could have been seen in Irish coastal waters in the sixth and seventh centuries.[5]

Irish travel and trade in continental Europe, *c*. 400–850

The archaeological evidence for trade with the Continent is principally in the form of imported pottery, of a range of types from the Mediterranean and western Francia. The first form of evidence for trade with the Mediterranean which we shall describe is Phocaean Red Slipware (PRSW) and African Red Slipware (ARSW). PRSW originated in western Asia Minor (modern-day Turkey) and is a type of bowl, of a soft orange-red, pink or brownish-red fabric, covered with a dark-red wash.[6] It broadly dates from the mid-fifth to mid-sixth century and is largely concentrated in the regions between the Black Sea and Sicily.[7] The presence of PRSW in Ireland probably dates from the late fifth to early sixth century, and is found in a range of early medieval Irish settlements, usually of high status, including the probable royal sites at Garranes (Co. Cork) and Clogher (Co. Tyrone), as well as at Mount Offaly (Co. Dublin), and a burial ground at Collierstown (Co. Meath). ARSW was produced in northern Africa from the first to the seventh century and was dispersed largely through the port of Carthage. It was imported into western Britain and Ireland during the fifth and sixth centuries and a single example is known from a *rath*, an enclosed settlement, at Kilree (Co. Kilkenny).[8] It is likely that PRSW was prestigious luxury tableware used during feasting at high-status sites.

Another important indicator of Mediterranean trade connections are the relatively numerous sherds of Late Roman Amphorae (LRA) found in Ireland (and formerly known as 'B-ware'). LRA pottery has been found on at least twenty Irish early medieval sites, including settlements, settlements with burial grounds (so-called 'settlement-cemeteries') and ecclesiastical sites. Various different types are known: LRA1 (formerly known as Bii; see Figure 1.1) is typified by large wheel-made, cylindrical amphorae, probably manufactured in

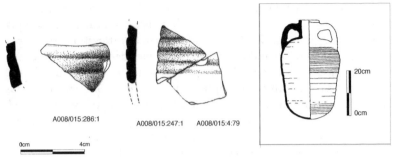

Figure 1.1   Illustrations of the late Roman amphorae (also known as Bii ware) sherds from Collierstown 1 (co. Meath).
Drawing by Amanda Kelly; see note 7

southeast Asia Minor and northern Syria, and has been found in Ireland at such sites as the early medieval royal residence of Garranes (Co. Cork), early medieval monastic settlements at Inishcealtra (Co. Clare), Reask (Co. Kerry), the Rock of Cashel (Co. Tipperary) and the traders' landing place at Dalkey Island (Co. Dublin). LRA2 (Bi) is a type of large, wheel-made, cylindrical amphora produced in the Peloponnese in southern Greece and possibly the Aegean Islands of Chios and Kos. It has been found on at least seven Irish sites, both secular and ecclesiastical, such as the coastal settlement at Colp West (Co. Meath) and Derrynaflan (Co. Tipperary). LRA3 (Biv) is, again, a type of wheel-made amphora from the Aegean or Asia Minor, which is found in southern Britain, but not in Ireland. There are also other LRA types, such as Biii/B misc, and Bv, some of which are known in Ireland. Conflicting interpretations have been suggested for the presence of these LRA. They may have been used for transporting olive oil and/or wine, with LRA1 in particular being associated with the wine trade. However, it is also possible that their usage varied depending on the occasion, sometimes being used for carrying wine, and sometimes for carrying olive oils and other commodities, but without a fixed purpose being attached to a particular type.[9]

The PRSW, ARSW and the LRA found in Ireland and western Britain certainly reflect contacts with the Mediterranean world in the late fifth and early sixth centuries. The distribution clusters of PRSW along the southern and western coasts of Iberia, as well as in southwest Britain and southern Ireland suggest, in particular, a trade route travelling out of the Strait of Gibraltar and up the Atlantic coast in the sixth century.[10] The discovery of a glass flagon from Tintagel (Cornwall), identical to cemetery finds from sixth- or seventh-century

Malaga and Cadiz, further reinforces the existence of a trade route along the Atlantic coast of Iberia to Britain.[11] Ewan Campbell has convincingly argued that this reflects sixth-century trade led by Byzantine merchants in search of tin and lead from southwest Britain, and perhaps gold and copper from southern Ireland. The argument that lead and tin were the targets of trade by Byzantine merchants is supported by isotope analyses of lead found in the Byzantine Mediterranean and emerging historic pollution evidence from Cornwall, in addition to the oft-cited textual evidence for the activities of Byzantine merchants along the coast of Atlantic Europe, who travelled to Mérida (central Spain), probably via the Guadiana estuary and river valley, and to southwest Britain to trade for tin.[12] It has not been suggested, to date, that sixth-century Irish or British mariners were themselves capable of trading all the way down the Atlantic coast to the Mediterranean, and the very limited quantities of Mediterranean imports, such as PRSW, on the Atlantic coast of France certainly do not suggest that such vessels were trans-shipped overland from the Mediterranean coast, along the Garonne and into the Bay of Biscay, via the Gironde estuary.

Yet archaeological evidence certainly indicates direct contacts between the societies living around the Irish Sea and those of western and southern France in the sixth and seventh centuries, via the Atlantic coast, attested in a number of archaeological media, namely, stone sculpture, pottery and glass vessels. For example, Jeremy Knight drew attention to the similarities between incised cross memorials made of stone from the sixth to seventh century from Nantes (Loire Atlantique) and Pouillé (Vienne), with Irish examples at Inishmurray (Co. Sligo) and Ardwall Isle (Dumfries and Galloway).[13] An important source of evidence for trading connections between Ireland and western Francia in particular is the pottery known in Britain and Ireland as 'E-ware' and in western France as cream/white-ware. Significant amounts of E-ware/French white-ware pottery are present particularly along the eastern coast of Ireland and the western coast of Britain, in Cornwall, south Wales and western Scotland. Indeed, archaeological investigations in Ireland in the last decade have increased quantities of E-ware significantly.[14] It seems to have been imported into Ireland between *c.* 525 and 700, so there may be an overlap with some Mediterranean pottery. It is found in a relatively large number of Irish sites, with at least fifty five sites known to have produced it, including early medieval *raths*, crannogs, settlement enclosures and monastic settlements. Although found across a large part of the island, it is particularly concentrated in two areas: the Strangford Lough region in County Down, in northeast Ireland, and in northeastern Leinster, from Dublin, along the Meath coastline to County Louth – effectively the political territories of north Leinster, Brega in particular. E-ware pottery is found in various forms, including jars, beakers, bowls, pitchers and pot lids. It may have been used to transport nuts, spices, honey or dyestuffs and the perforated lids suggest it may also have been used for cooking (the perforations being used to release steam).

The source of this western French white-ware is uncertain, as kilns that produced it have never been found, but the character of the clay would suggest a production area in the lower Charente or Saintonge region. Distributions of this ware also occur in small numbers in Nantes and up the Loire as far as Tours, and several sherds have also been found at Le Yaudet (Côtes-d'Armor) on the northern coast of Brittany.[15] A distribution of glass vessels around the Irish Sea, predominantly cone beakers possibly produced in the Bordeaux region of southwest France, mirrors the distribution of E-ware pottery.[16] Campbell dates the deposition of these artefacts to the sixth and earlier seventh centuries, and sees the Irish Sea distribution of these western French products as the reflection of directional trade networks controlled by merchant-mariners from the Atlantic region of Merovingian France. He arrived at this conclusion thanks to what he saw as the consistent and recurrent nature of the import assemblages of E-ware and glass vessels, which would have been more mixed in terms of goods represented if they had arrived by the more general and opportunistic coastal trade, as suggested by Wooding.[17]

Campbell's view that maritime-merchant initiative came predominantly from the mariners of western France may significantly understate the activities of insular merchants within the maritime exchange networks of Atlantic Europe. Wooding, Jean-Michel Picard and more recently Olivier Bruand have all highlighted the presence of Irish, British/Breton and Anglo-Saxon merchants around the Loire estuary, as far inland as Nantes, predominantly within the context of trade in salt. The Life of Columbanus and the Life of Filibert provide textual 'snapshots' of the presence and some of the activities of these merchant-mariners. Thus, for example, there is a reference in the Life of Columbanus to the saint being taken back to Ireland in the early seventh century via an Irish ship that happened to be at Nantes. The eighth-century Life of Filibert also records the arrival at Noirmoutier of Irish ships with various goods aboard, including a large quantity of shoes and clothes for the brethren.[18] The opportunistic actions of some of these merchant-mariners at Noirmoutier, including the stealing of lead,[19] would suggest that these merchants were more than tied agents of ecclesiastical institutions or secular elites. They appear to have had independence of action for themselves beyond any obligation to any individuals or institutions for whom they may have acted. Indeed, it is probably worth remembering that once a merchant was out at sea he had the option of returning, or not returning, to any patron, depending on whether or not he considered it worthwhile to himself and his crew.

Indeed, Bruand's study of the salt producers of the Loire estuary (at Baie de Bourgeneuf) and the Charente estuary also highlights that most of the salt producers and salt traders along the Loire were free proprietors rather than landless clients of major ecclesiastical institutions. The latter, in many instances, were simply given existing salterns. Merchant-mariners from Ireland and Britain who traded salt in the vibrant trading zone between the Loire and Charente estuaries did not only trade at the beach market at Noirmoutier. They also traded at a host of smaller landing places, some of which are known from textual sources and others are now emerging from archaeological discoveries; for example, the site known as *Portus Castelli* can possibly be identified with Renac.[20] By the Carolingian period, a principal taxation centre and port for the salt trade in the Loire estuary existed at the site of *Portus Vertraria*, which was located somewhere on the Vendée bank of the Loire, close to its estuary, but the exact location of the settlement is still unknown. This *portus* was located at an existing Merovingian royal estate centre, and may represent a Carolingian attempt to tax the salt trade on a more systematic basis than had occurred in the seventh century.[21]

The paramount role of the region between the Charente and Loire estuaries in the Atlantic salt trade during the sixth and seventh centuries could well account for the apparent homogeneity of import patterns of E-ware and glass vessels in Ireland and western Britain. The most likely source area for E-ware is the Saintonge and the lower Charente valley, and much of it could have arrived in vessels involved in the salt trade. This may not only have entailed Irish and British merchants travelling down to the Charente estuary. There is also evidence in the form of the seventh-century, clinker-built coaster vessel known as Port Berteau II, found downriver from Saintes, to show that coastal vessels from the lower Charente valley could also have carried salt and pottery northwards to the Loire estuary trading places, possibly more frequented by insular mariners.[22] Such coastal trade from the Charente to the Loire could also account for the E-ware distribution in the Loire estuary, Nantes and Tours. The targeting of these specific salt-producing regions by Irish and British merchants, which coincided with the primary locus of E-ware production, would negate the need for a paramount role for mariners from western France controlling the insular distribution of imports. Campbell dates the demise of E-ware production to the early seventh century but the evidence of Merovingian gold *tremissis* coinage, struck up until the middle decades of the seventh century and also found in small quantities in Ireland,[23] would suggest that contacts continued with Atlantic France. This is indicated more emphatically in the textually attested actions of Irish and British merchants in the Loire estuary during the late seventh century. The focus of Irish merchants on trading leather goods at Noirmoutier in the later seventh century also highlights the perishable and limited archaeo-logical visibility of most Irish trade in Atlantic France.[24] Finally, there is also the intriguing possibility that Irish merchants were trading for salt, which was not being produced in Ireland but would of course have been an important means of preserving and transport-ing Irish dairy produce, especially butter, between Ireland and the Continent.

On the basis of the archaeological evidence, there appear to have been two main geographical and chronological trade networks in operation between continental Europe and Ireland in the sixth and seventh centuries, as defined by Campbell.[25] The first is a sixth-century network running from the Mediterranean northwards along the west coast of Iberia to the Bay of Biscay, and hence to southern Ireland and southwest Britain. Campbell believes this to have been a maritime network operated by Byzantine merchants in search of metals, such as tin and lead, without any suggestion of maritime travel by Irish or British mariners along the Atlantic coast to the Mediterranean. This ceased to exist in the mid to late sixth century, because of changes in the western Mediterranean economy. The second network was focused on trading links between western Britain and Ireland and the west coast of France, particularly estuar-ies and river valleys of the Gironde (in the sixth century) and the Charente and Loire in the sixth and seventh centuries. Contrary to Campbell's view that this second network was controlled mainly by merchants from western France, it is argued here on the basis of the textual and archaeological sources that mariners from Ireland and western Britain could have played an equal role to any continental mariners in this maritime exchange. Indeed, the textual sources indicate continuity of trade by Irish mariners at the mouth of the Loire long after the end of E-ware production in the early seventh century. What cannot be denied, however, is the huge reduction in the archaeological visibility of evidence for links between Ireland and continental Europe, especially the Mediterranean, after the mid-seventh century.

The latest finds of Mediterranean material around the Irish Sea from the seventh century are all found on sites in western Britain: the later sixth or early seventh-century St Menas *ampulla* brought back from Egypt as a pilgrim's souvenir which was found at the beach trading site at Meols (Wirral);[26] the Byzantine brass censer from Glastonbury (Somerset); the Byzantine ring intaglio from Rhosyr, near Cefn Cwmwd in Anglesey; the Byzantine glass and gold mosaic tessera from Dunadd (Argyll); and also from Dunadd, the mineral orpiment (arsenic sulphide) originating from Vesuvius in the Bay of Naples, which was used to produce a yellow dye for manuscript illumination.[27] The orpiment may have been acquired by the secular rulers of the Dalriadic fortified centre of Dunadd as a gift for the nearby Irish-founded monastic community of Iona. That the orpiment might have been acquired through secular networks for use in a monastic scriptorium rather than directly via ecclesiastical connections is a reminder that we should not assume that ecclesiastical networks were the paramount long-distance networks.

The arrival of Mediterranean goods certainly diminished over the course of the seventh century but the existing maritime infrastructure of mariners and shipping to western France for the salt trade, and the equally archaeologically invisible trade of wine in barrels, continued through the seventh and eighth centuries. This transport infrastructure supported the principal pilgrimage route from Ireland to Rome, which ran along the Loire valley to Nantes and Tours, and hence to the Rhône valley, the Mediterranean, Italy and Rome. Indeed, the route via the Loire valley, the veneration of St Martin of Tours by Irish monastic institutions from the 640s, and subsequent fictitious additions to St Patrick's Lives written between the ninth and eleventh centuries (in the *Vita Tripartita* and the *Vita Tertia Patricii*), including his receiving the tonsure from Martin at Tours, his visit to Auxerre and his visit to Rome, reflects the importance of this 'sacred routeway' to Italy.[28] Further evidence of the presence of Irish travelling along the Loire valley is provided as an aside in the Life of Alcuin, written in the early ninth century, when monks at Alcuin's monastery of St Martin at Tours assume that an Anglo-Saxon visitor at the gates must be British or Irish.[29]

The housing of Irish pilgrims en route to Rome was achieved through the creation of *hospitalia Scottorum* (also written as *hospitalia Scothorum*), and in Rome itself one can assume that pilgrims from Ireland or Scotland had their own *schola peregrinorum*, like the Franks, Frisians, Anglo-Saxons and Lombards. These were ethnically discrete communities of foreigners in Rome which housed pilgrims and also merchants, and by the late eighth century each *schola* also provided a military function in the defence of Rome, in which role they served successfully during the Arab raid on Rome in 846.[30] Whether Irish pilgrims travelled to the eastern Mediterranean is much more debatable for the period between the seventh and ninth centuries. Thomas O'Loughlin and others have argued convincingly that Arculf, supposedly a ship-wrecked Frankish bishop who travelled in Palestine, Alexandria, Constantinople and Rome, was in fact no more than a literary device in the biblical exegesis of Adomnan's *De Locis Sanctis*, which contains an account of his travels.[31] Yet, there was nothing to stop Irish pilgrims using the same Mediterranean shipping and mercantile routeways as the Anglo-Saxon Willibald on his pilgrimage to Jerusalem in the 720s.[32] Likewise, the region of Vesuvius, from which the orpiment at Dunadd originated, was certainly on the route that Willibald took through Italy as he was making his way to the eastern Mediterranean.

Elusive archaeological evidence for Irish influence on continental ecclesiastical sites, 600–850

Despite abundant textual evidence for the impact of Irish churchmen, such as Columbanus, Filibert and Fursa, on the church in Merovingian Gaul, through their foundation of numerous monasteries or influence on Frankish aristocratic foundations, during the seventh century, archaeological excavations have not uncovered any distinctive 'Irish' heritage among the archaeological or architectural evidence. This is true even of the most famous of the Irish foundations, such as the eastern French monastery at Luxeuil, or the Italian monastery at Bobbio, both founded by Columbanus, or the monastery at Noirmoutier, founded by Filibert, or a host of other monasteries across Brittany, Normandy and Picardy.[33] An inscription bearing an Irish name, such as the eighth-century inscription at Bobbio which features in Figure 1.2, is a very rare find indeed. The almost wholesale absence of a distinctive 'Irish' heritage may be, to a significant extent, the consequence of a lack of extensive archaeological excavations at these sites but it is also difficult to know what

Figure 1.2   An eighth-century inscription from Bobbio commemorating 'Cummianus', an Irish bishop
Ufficio per i Beni Culturali Ecclesiastici della Diocesi di Piacenza-Bobbio

to expect of Irish monastic 'signatures' from an archaeological point of view. This is largely because of the wealth of different ascetic and coenobitic traditions of monasticism witnessed in early medieval Ireland itself and because of the near certainty of the use of local artisans and materials in Gaul to construct the major monastic buildings. For example, Sébastien Bully's excavations at the church of St Martin at Luxeuil (Haute-Saône), the most well-known monastery founded by Columbanus, have yielded a sequence of fourth- to sixth-century inhumation graves in sarcophagi, typical of Merovingian central and southern Gaul, replaced by part of the late seventh-century stone church of St Martin, incorporating the crypt-shrine of St Valbert, the third abbot of Luxeuil.[34] The early Christian architecture is typical of Merovingian central and southern Gaul. The major cult centres were also the most frequently renovated and aggrandized following changes in monastic and architectural traditions, as again witnessed in the church of St Martin at Luxeuil, which was rebuilt on a grander scale with side apses, in the ninth century. Such a sequence of dynamic change and rebuilding is seen more emphatically within the occupation sequence of the larger-scale excavations at Landévennec (Finistère), in the west of Brittany. The cult focus developed from a small oratory, cemetery and enclosure, all dated to the sixth century, through its major monumental Carolingian church phases, during which a cloister was added, and finally its Romanesque and Gothic successors.[35]

Very few zones of monasteries beyond their churches and cemeteries have been subject to excavation in France. Bully's excavations at Luxeuil are typical of the parts of monasteries that have been targeted or have been available for excavation. However, Bully and his team have also surveyed and conducted trial excavations at a quarry several kilometres north of Luxeuil, known as the Hermitage of St Valbert. This site was certainly a quarry for some of the stone used for the sarcophagi excavated at Luxeuil and it is possible, although currently unconfirmed, that the quarry could have been the site of a hermitage for Valbert.[36] If so, such a hermitage would not have been unlike the example suggested to have housed St Martin at Marmoutier (Indre-et-Loire).[37] The only major exceptions to the trend of focusing archaeological attention only on the churches and cemeteries are provided by the excavations at Saint-Denis (Seine-Saint-Denis), on the north-eastern outskirts of modern Paris and St Martin of Tours (Indre-et-Loire), although in these cases too the excavations expanded from the church and cemetery foci.[38]

Another notable exception is the small monastery at Hamage (Nord), excavated by Etienne Louis, between 1991 and 2002. The monastery was founded on the south bank of the River Scarpe, a tributary of the Scheldt, by an aristocratic woman, Gertrude, in the 640s. She was probably influenced by St Amandus, a Frankish cleric who had been influenced, in turn, by Columbanus. The earliest phase of occupation at Hamage, attributable to the second half of the seventh century, is characterized by small wooden buildings with earth-fast post-hole foundations of rounded or quadrangular shapes, with a ditched and palisaded enclosure to the south and west, and a church to the north of the monastic enclosure dedicated to St Peter.[39] Louis has noted the apparent similarity between these small cell-like buildings and the small buildings excavated at Whitby (North

Yorkshire), and one may cite even closer parallels between those from Hartlepool (co. Durham), the parent monastery of Hild's foundation at Whitby, and the small seventh-century buildings at Hamage.[40] Given that the founder of Hamage was influenced by St Amandus, and indirectly by Columbanus, and that Hartlepool and Whitby were daughter houses of Aidan's monastery at Lindisfarne, founded according to the traditions of Iona, then it is possible that this mid-to-late seventh-century phase at Hamage could reflect some Irish influence. However, this is not certain. The small buildings were subsequently demolished at the turn of the eighth century with the construction of an additional church, dedicated to St Mary, within the monastic enclosure, with a smaller mausoleum church to its north dedicated to St Eusebia, abbess of Hamage, and the erection of a communal building with multiple rooms and hearths for the women of the Hamage community to the south of the churches. This phase was succeeded in turn by the aggrandizement of the church in the ninth century, with the addition of a cloister, probably reflecting the influence of the Benedictine reforms promoted by the Carolingians.[41] Hence, as at Landévennec, any insular influence was replaced by local and regional continental trends in the eighth and ninth centuries.

However, it is occasionally possible to see greater insular and Irish influence in Brittany at small religious sites. For example at the chapel of St-Symphorien at Paule (Côtes-d'Armor), a small chapel was constructed on a dry-stone and gravel sill in the eighth or early ninth century. The chapel was built adjacent to some springs next to an Iron-Age oppidum, possibly reflecting the Christianization of an earlier cult site. An iron plough coulter was buried at the chapel entrance, a custom attested also in France and the Netherlands between the eighth and eleventh centuries, and a small hoard of silver denier coins of Charles the Bald was buried inside the chapel.[42] The chapel is also associated with a fine copper-alloy bell thought to have been made between *c.* 700 and 900, in Ireland or western Britain. Recent archaeological evidence of bell-casting from Ireland from these centuries, at sites like Clonfad (Co. Westmeath), would make Ireland a likely source for the Paule bell.[43]

Irish/Hiberno-Norse travel, trade and raiding, *c.* 850–1100

During the ninth century, evidence of the presence of Irish merchants on the Atlantic coast of France is much more scarce, but the beach trading sites facilitating the salt trade were still recorded on the

Breton northern banks of the Baie de Bourgeneuf, where trade with unnamed merchants continued, at least until the first Scandinavian attacks along the Loire at Nantes and Tours in the later 840s and 850s.[44] Transport of silver and lead also continued from the mines at Melle (Poitou-Charente), including shipments of lead to the monastery at Saint-Denis in the mid-ninth century.[45] These shipments travelled down the River Charente, probably via the partially excavated river port at Taillebourg (Charente-Maritime). This river port is particularly intriguing, as it seems to have operated as a transhipment point between the seventh and tenth centuries. Pottery sherds, 685 metal finds and the remains of over ten early medieval log boats for river transport suggest that the settlement covered several hundred metres on the right bank of the Charente. Lead finds with an isotopic signature showing an origin at Melle reflect transhipment of lead and probably silver down into the Bay of Biscay. Among the metal finds from the port are six swords of Scandinavian, Hiberno-Norse or Anglo-Saxon types, alongside twenty spearheads and ten axe heads.[46] The swords, in particular, from Taillebourg are likely to have arrived in the Charente-Maritime region carried by Scandinavian or Hiberno-Norse raiders or traders of the later ninth and tenth centuries, but the contexts in which the weapons were deposited are unclear. Their presence marks a transition in the archaeological reflections of relations between Ireland and the Continent between the mid-ninth and tenth centuries. From this time, the physical evidence of Irish contacts with the wider world is represented largely through artefacts with stylistic decoration and forms influenced by Irish and Scandinavian traditions, described as 'Hiberno-Norse'.

Scandinavian raiding was a phenomenon experienced throughout the coasts of Atlantic Europe between the mid-ninth and tenth centuries, including the coastal and riverine towns of western France, the silver mines at Melle, the port-towns of Lisbon, Cadiz and Seville in Iberia, and the western Mediterranean shores of North Africa.[47] This raiding activity also reopened the sea route along the Atlantic coast of Iberia and into the Mediterranean, initially probably for the trade of slaves from northern Europe to Islamic Al-Andalus. From the later ninth century and in the tenth century much of that Atlantic trade, from north to south, was probably facilitated by the major Scandinavian-influenced port-hubs of Dublin (a likely slave-exporting port) and Rouen. Their roles in the trading of slaves to Al-Andalus are supported by textual sources and archaeological finds, and their role as shippers of slaves down the Atlantic coast to Iberia continued into the later eleventh century. Trade in slaves from northern Europe to Al-Andalus and a return trade of goods from Iberia and the Mediterranean was facilitated by Jewish merchants based in Rouen, and the Ostmen of Dublin were buying slaves for resale in the ports of western England, such as Bristol, even at the end of the eleventh century.[48]

From the mid-ninth century there is archaeological evidence attesting trade links between northern Europe and Iberia, in the form of small numbers of silver dirhem coins minted at Cordoba. These are found along the western coast of France, in the long-established trading zone between the Rivers Charente and Loire.[49] These coins could evidence Scandinavian loot from Iberia taken northwards but their use in western France could have been as a medium of exchange for other products, such as salt. From the tenth century, and especially from the middle decades of that century, Dublin and Ireland more broadly were integrated into the wider political and exchange networks of the Scandinavian world looking southwards down the Atlantic coast, northwards to the Atlantic islands and eastwards to the North Sea and Baltic (and hence Central Asia). Under the Guthrifsson dynasty, this even involved political union of the Kingdoms of Dublin and York, between the 920s and *c.* 952. The Hiberno-Norse towns of Dublin, Wexford, Waterford and Cork were firmly implicated in these Atlantic trade routes. Archaeological evidence for the importation of objects includes coin evidence, with some single finds in Ireland coming from York and Norway, but also from Frankish and Carolingian sources, and there are also some coins in Ireland with Kufic inscriptions, suggesting indirect links with the Arab world. There was probably a continued wine trade with western France, particularly Poitou. The recovery of silks from Hiberno-Norse Dublin suggests long-distance trade connections with Byzantium or the Muslim world, and the slave trade probably extended from Scotland across the Irish Sea and southwards to north Africa, as an entry for the year 867 in the so-called Fragmentary Annals suggests by referring to 'Moors' or 'black men' being brought to Dublin by Viking slave traders.[50]

The incorporation of Irish/Hiberno-Norse networks within those of Scandinavian-influenced eastern England resulted in the presence of Irish merchants in the ports and burghal centres of the West Saxon kingdom of England from the mid-to-late tenth century. For example, Irish merchants are recorded in Cambridge in the reign of King Edgar in the 970s.[51] Archaeological indications of trade between Hiberno-Norse Ireland and western Britain in the tenth and eleventh centuries are provided by Scandinavian ring pins and a disc brooch from Chester, and Anglo-Saxon pennies minted at Gloucester but found in Dublin reflect objects taken back to Ireland in the tenth century.[52] In the late eleventh century, there is also evidence for the importation to Dublin of pottery from southwest England. Just as Irish merchants benefitted from incorporation into North Sea and Baltic networks, so did Anglo-Saxon merchants benefit from incorporation within the renewed Atlantic networks to Iberia, pioneered by the mariners of Hiberno-Norse Dublin and Norman Rouen. Materials both probably and certainly obtained from Islamic Iberia were coming into London in the mid-to-late tenth and eleventh centuries, and are present within mercantile archaeological contexts, for example, the silks, figs and grapes (probably eaten as raisins) from Milk Street, London.[53] One of the main export ports of figs and raisins by the later tenth to eleventh centuries was Malaga, in Spain.[54] Other raw materials that arrived via Iberia were gold, mercury, spices and dyes. All were, no doubt, available in Dublin and Ireland's major Hiberno-Norse port towns, and provide the precursor context to the continued growth of Atlantic trade between Ireland, western Britain, western France and Iberia in the central Middle Ages, between 1100 and 1300.

Notes

1. Jonathan Wooding, 'Trade as a Factor in the Transmission of Texts between Ireland and the Continent in the Sixth and Seventh Centuries', in Proinseas Ní Chatháin and Michael Richter, eds, *Ireland and Europe in the Early Middle Ages: Texts and Transmission* (Dublin, 2002), pp. 14–26.
2. Aidan O'Sullivan, Finbar McCormick, Thomas R. Kerr and Lorcan Harney, *Early Medieval Ireland AD 400–1100. The Evidence from Archaeological Excavations* (Dublin, 2014), and Christopher Loveluck, *Northwest Europe in the Early Middle ages, c. AD 600–1150. A Comparative Archaeology* (Cambridge, 2013).
3. Christer Westerdahl, 'The Maritime Cultural Landscape', *International Journal of Nautical Archaeology* 21 (1992), pp. 5–14.
4. O'Sullivan et al. *Early Medieval Ireland,* and see also Wendy Davies, 'Economic Change in Early Medieval Ireland: the Case for Growth', *Settimane* 57 (2010), pp. 111–33.
5. Wooding, 'Trade as a Factor'.
6. I.W. Doyle, 'Mediterranean and Frankish Pottery Imports in Early Medieval Ireland', *Journal of Irish Archaeology* 18 (2009), pp. 17–62, at p. 18.
7. A. Kelly, 'The Discovery of Phocaen Red Slip-Ware (PRSW) form 3 and Bii Ware (LR1 Amphorae) on Sites in Ireland: an Analysis within a Broader Framework', *PRIA* 110C (2010), pp. 35–88, at p. 42.

8. See O'Sullivan *et al.*, *Early Medieval Ireland*, p. 250.
9. Doyle, 'Mediterranean and Frankish Pottery', 40–56; O'Sullivan *et al.*, *Early Medieval Ireland*, pp. 252–5.
10. Ewan Campbell, 'The Archaeological Evidence for External Contacts: Imports, Trade and Economy in Celtic Britain, AD 400–800', in Ken Dark, ed., *External Contacts and the Economy of Late and Post-Roman Britain* (Woodbridge, 1996), pp. 83–96, at pp. 86–8.
11 Ewan Campbell, 'Glass', in Rachel C. Barrowman, Coleen E. Batey and Christopher D. Morris, eds., *Excavations at Tintagel Castle, Cornwall, 1990–1999* (London, 2007) pp. 222–8.
12. Ewan Campbell, *Continental and Maritime Imports to Atlantic Britain and Ireland, AD 400–800* (York, 2007), pp. 127–32.
13. Jeremy Knight, 'Seasoned with Salt: Insular-Gallic Contacts in the Early Memorial Stones and Cross Slabs', in Dark, *External Contacts*, pp. 109–20, at pp. 117–19.
14. E. Campbell, *Continental and Maritime Imports*; O'Sullivan *et al.*, *Early Medieval Ireland*, p. 255.
15. B. Randoin, 'Essai de classification chronologique de la céramique de Tours du IVe au XIe siècle', *Recherches sur Tours* 1 (1981), 103–14; Barry Cunliffe and P. Galliou, *Les Fouilles du Yaudet en Ploulec'h, Côtes-d'Armor, Volume 3: Du quatrième siècle apr. J.-C. à aujourd'hui* (Oxford, 2007).
16. Campbell, *Continental and Maritime Imports*, p. 65.
17. Jonathan Wooding, 'Cargoes in Trade along the Western Seaboard', in Dark, *External Contacts*, pp. 67–82, at pp. 75–6; Campbell, *Continental and Maritime Imports*, pp. 136–8.
18. See Jean-Michel Picard, 'L'Irlande et la Normandie avant les Normands (VIIe–IXe siècles)', *Annales de Normandie*, 2e trim. No.1 (1997), 3–24; and Olivier Bruand, 'Pénétration et circulation du sel de l'Atlantique en France septentrionale (VIIIe–XIe siècles)', *Annales de Bretagne et des Pays de l'Ouest* 115.3 (2008), pp. 7–32.
19. See Olivier Bruand, 'Pénétration et circulation du sel', p. 18.
20. Wendy Davies, *Small Worlds. The Village Community in Early Medieval Brittany* (London, 1988).
21. Bruand, 'Pénétration et circulation du sel'.
22. Eric Rieth, Catherine Carrièrre-Desbois and Virginie Serna, *L'épave de Port Berteau II (Charente-Maritime). Un caboteur fluvio-maritime du haut Moyen Âge et son contexte nautique*, Documents d'Archéologie Françaize 86 (Paris, 2001).
23. Michael Dolley, *The Hiberno-Norse Coins in the British Museum* (London, 1966), pp. 13–14.
24. Wooding, 'Cargoes in Trade', p. 73.
25. Campbell, *Continental and Maritime Imports*.
26. David Griffiths and S. Bangert, 'Ceramic: The St Menas Ampulla', in David Griffiths, Robert A. Philpott and Geoff Egan, *Meols: The Archaeology of the North Wirral Coast* (Oxford, 2007), pp. 58–60.

27. Campbell, *Continental and Maritime Imports*, pp. 78–80; Alan Lane and Ewan Campbell, *Dunadd. An Early Dalriadic Capital* (Oxford, 2000).

28. Jean-Michel Picard, 'Les réseaux martiniens en Irlande médiévale', *Annales de Bretagne et des Pays de l'Ouest* 119.3 (2012), 41–54, at 43–9.

29. See Philippe Depreux, *Les Sociétés occidentales du millieu du VIe à la fin du IXe siècle* (Rennes, 2002), p. 145.

30. W. Levison, *England and the Continent in the Eighth Century* (Oxford, 1946), p. 40. For *hospitalia Scottorum/Scothorum*, see Picard, 'L'Irlande et la Normandie avant les Normands', p. 19; and the Capitulary of the Council of Meaux (845), Canon 40, in W. Hartmann, ed., MGH Conc. III (Hanover, 1984). The *scholae peregrinorum* of Rome are attested principally in the *Liber Pontificalis*'s chapter on the pontificate of Leo III (795–810), ed. L. Duchesne, *Le Liber Pontificalis*, 3 vols. (Paris, 1886–1957), II, p. 6. On the military abilities of the *scholae* see Levison, *England and the Continent*, and Depreux, *Sociétes occidentales*, p. 148.

31. Thomas O'Loughlin, *Adomnan and the Holy Places: The Perceptions of an Insular Monk on the Locations of the Biblical Drama* (London, 2007).

32. Michael McCormick, *Origins of the European Economy. Communications and Commerce, AD 300–900* (Cambridge, 2001), pp. 130–34.

33. Picard, 'L'Irlande et la Normandie'; Michael Richter, *Ireland and Her Neighbours in the Seventh Century* (Dublin, 1999).

34. S. Bully, L. Fiocchi, A. Baradat, M. Čaušević-Bully, A. Bully, M. Dupuis and D. Vuillermoz, 'L'églize Saint-Martin de Luxeuil-les-Bains (Haute-Saône). Première campagne', *Bulletin du Centre d'études médiévales d'Auxerre* 13 (2009), pp. 33–8.

35. Alan Bardel and Ronan Perennec, 'Abbaye de Landevennec: l'évolution du context funéraire depuis le haut Moyen Âge', in Armelle Alduc-Le Bagousse, ed., *Inhumations et édifices religieux au Moyen Âge entre Loire et Seine* (Caen, 2004), pp. 121–58, at pp. 133–52.

36. Bully *et al.*, 'L'églize Saint-Martin de Luxeuil-les-Bains', n. 35.

37. É. Lorans, 'Aux origines du monastère de Marmoutier: le témoinage de l'archéologie', *Annales de Bretagne et des Pays de l'Ouest* 119.3 (2012), pp. 177–203, at pp. 177–79.

38. See Michel Wyss 'Saint-Denis', in Stiegemann, C. and Wemhoff, M., eds., *799: Kunst und Kultur der Karolingerzeit, Beiträge zum Katalog der Ausstellung Paderborn 1999*, (Mainz, 1999), pp. 138–141; and Henri Galinié, ed., *Tours antique et médiéval. Lieux de vie, Temps de la ville, 40 ans d'archéologie urbaine, 30e Supplément à la Revue Archéologique du Centre de la France* (Tours, 2007).

39. Étienne Louis and Joël Blondiaux, 'L'Abbaye mérovingienne et caro-lingienne de Hamage (Nord). Vie, mort et sépulture dans une communauté monastique féminine', in Armelle Alduc-Le Bagousse, ed., *Inhumations de prestige ou prestige de l'inhumation?* (Caen, 2009), pp. 117–49 at p. 119.

40. Étienne Louis, 'A De-Romanized Landscape in Northern Gaul: The Scarpe Valley from the 4th to the 9th Century', in William Bowden,

Luke Lavan and Carlos Machado, eds., *Recent Research on the Late Antique Countryside* (Leiden and Boston, 2004), pp. 479–504, at p. 497; C. Loveluck, 'Anglo-Saxon Hartlepool and the Foundations of English Christian Identity: the Wider Context and Importance of the Monastery', in Robin Daniels and Christopher Loveluck, eds., *Anglo-Saxon Hartlepool and the Foundations of English Christianity. An Archaeology of the Anglo-Saxon Monastery* (Hartlepool, 2007), pp. 186–208.

41. Louis and Blondiaux, 'L'Abbaye mérovingienne', pp. 120–23.

42. J. Le Gall and Y. Menez, *La chapelle de Saint-Symphorien à Paule, Rapport de fouille annuelle 2008*, SRA de l'Archéologie de Bretagne (Rennes, 2008); and Loveluck, *Northwest Europe in the Early Middle Ages*, p. 45.

43. O'Sullivan *et al.*, *Early Medieval Ireland*, p. 140.

44. Davies, *Small Worlds*, p. 100; Galinié, *Tours antique et médiéval*, p. 18.

45. F. Tereygeol, 'Production and Circulation of Silver and Secondary Products (Lead and Glass) from Frankish Royal Silver Mines at Melle (Eighth to Tenth Century)', in Joachim Henning, ed., *Post-Roman Towns, Trade and Settlement in Europe and Byzantium, Vol. 1: The Heirs of the Roman West* (Berlin, 2007), pp. 123–34, at p. 123.

46. Annie Dumont and Jean-François Marioti, eds., *Archéologie et histoire du fleuve Charente. Taillebourg-Port d'Envaux: une zone portuaire du haut Moyen Âge sur le fleuve Charente,* (Dijon, 2013).

47. C. Mazzoli-Guintard, 'Les Normands dans le sud de la peninsula Ibérique au milieu du IXe siècle: aspects du peuplement d' al-Andalus', *Annales de Bretagne et des Pays de l'Ouest* 103.2 (1996), pp. 27–37, at p. 28–9.

48. J. Hillaby, 'Jewish Colonization in the Twelfth Century', in P. Skinner, ed., *The Jews in Medieval Britain. Historical, Literary and Archaeological Perspectives* (Woodbridge, 2003), pp. 15–40, at p. 16; O'Sullivan *et al.*, *Early Medieval Ireland*, p. 275.

49. F. Clément, 'Les monnaies arabes et à legend arabe trouvées dans le Grand Ouest', *Annales de Bretagne et des Pays de l'Ouest*, 115.2 (2008), pp. 159–87, at pp. 160–161.

50. O'Sullivan *et al.*, *Early Medieval Ireland*, p. 275.

51. Henry R. Loyn, *Anglo-Saxon England and the Norman Conquest* (London, 1962), p. 96.

52. David Griffiths, *The Vikings of the Irish Sea* (Stroud, 2010), pp. 133–6.

53. Loveluck, *Northwest Europe in the Early Middle Ages*, pp. 322–5.

54. M. Valor and A. Gutiérrez, *The Archaeology of Medieval Spain 1100–1500* (Sheffield, 2014), p. 126.

2

Exiles from the Edge? The Irish Contexts of *Peregrinatio*

Elva Johnston

Approaches to *peregrinatio*

In a letter to Pope Boniface IV (d. 615), probably written around 613, *peregrinus* and church founder, Columbanus (d. 615), declared that the Irish who inhabited the world's edge were ideal Christians, free of heresy's taint.[1] Rather transparently, Columbanus strongly implies that he, like his fellow countrymen, is a Christian of apostolic mould, preserving the purity of early church belief and practice. For him, those who lived at the edge of the earth were innocent of the errors that flourished closer to its centre, in Burgundy, in Italy and in the very heart of Rome. In this letter, and elsewhere, Columbanus, a man intensely self-conscious of his status as an exile, a *peregrinus*, brews a heady mix of identity, geography and religious orthodoxy. He is a deeply idiosyncratic writer; he also articulates those various factors which led him, and others, to leave Ireland. To find God, he tells us, one must renounce one's native place.[2] Nearly a century later, Adomnán (d. 704), abbot of Iona, wrote a great hagiographical celebration of its founder-saint, Columba (d. 597). The *Vita Columbae* is steeped in the language of exile. Tellingly, not all of it is tied to Iona's first abbot. For instance, Adomnán details the travails of Cormac ua Liatháin, a man who was a contemporary of Columbanus. Cormac is described as unsuccessfully seeking a desert in the ocean, no less than three times, before finally settling for a more mundane religious life.[3] The words which Adomnán uses are loaded: Cormac's desert is the *eremus* or *desertum* of the hermit. It purposefully echoes the ascetic heroism of the Desert Fathers, particularly Anthony of Egypt (d. 356), the contours of whose life had become an inspiration for many western Christians. Both Columbanus and Cormac have come to be seen as iconic *peregrini*, despite the apparently contrasting nature of their experiences. Columbanus succeeded in leaving Ireland permanently, carving out an influential, if controversial, continental career. Cormac, on the contrary, failed to find his transmarine desert and returned to Ireland where, eventually, he came to be revered as a saint. Columbanus speaks to us directly as a self-identified *peregrinus*, although it is left to his biographer Jonas to tease out the implications more fully.[4] Cormac, whose voyages are only known second-hand through Adomnán, is not explicitly called a *peregrinus* at all. Why, then, are both placed on a spectrum of *peregrinatio*?

The major reason is that religious exile, linked with the type of ascetic desert sought in vain by Cormac, features across a variety of texts, either of Irish origin, or emerging from centres with Irish connections such as Bobbio. On the basis of these, it has become commonplace for scholars to situate the experiences of Cormac and of Columbanus within a practice known as *peregrinatio pro Christo* or exile for Christ. They have defined *peregrinatio* as a form of religious renunciation, inspired by the words of Jesus in the Gospels challenging believers to put aside home and family to follow God.[5] Thus, *peregrinus*, a word whose primary classical meaning was stranger, came to be interpreted as referring to a pilgrim or an exile. Among the Irish, *peregrinatio*, the journey of the *peregrinus*, described a life-long exile for the sake of God. By the end of the sixth century, according to this definition, the Irish regarded a permanent overseas *peregrinatio* as the highest form of ascetic renunciation and it inspired many of the Irishmen who left for Britain and the Continent. However, things are not quite so simple. While exile and asceticism are strongly associated in many sources, this association is often indirect and *peregrinatio* may not even be explicitly mentioned, as in the case of Cormac ua Liatháin. Another good example of this type of indirect articulation is the Cambrai Homily, a short text written in a combination of Old Irish and Latin, usually dated to sometime around 700, roughly contemporary with the writings of Adomnán.[6] For the author of the homily, renouncing the world of material attachments, in favour of asceticism, is a form of martyrdom to be equated with the 'red martyrdom' suffered by early Christians. The homily explains that in order to win metaphorical martyrdom the ascetic must separate from the familiar. Scholars have frequently interpreted this as a nod towards *peregrinatio*.[7] Furthermore, the importance of rejecting personal attachments is emphasized in Jonas's Life of Columbanus, written within a generation of its subject's death. It is Jonas who tells us that while exile within Ireland was good, it was surpassed by the superior *peregrinatio* of leaving the island entirely, a formulation which has proved remarkably influential.[8]

Nuances aside, it does seem clear that in the course of the sixth and seventh centuries religious ideals, centred on exile and ascetic martyrdom, coalesced among Irish ecclesiastics. However, it is important to point out that this coalescence was more complex than the standard definition of *peregrinatio* implies. It is noteworthy, too, that *peregrinatio* and *peregrinus* did not always mean exile in the sense which has been discussed, even in Irish texts. Similarly, not all forms of ascetic martyrdom were imagined to involve an exile from home, or, indeed, one which was necessarily permanent. Terminology is sometimes imprecise and scholars should beware of artificially and rigidly defining a concept of *peregrinatio*. In particular, Jonas's hierarchy of *peregrinatio*, culminating in the permanent overseas variety, should not be a straitjacket to the detriment of other possibilities. For instance, an insistence on the life-long nature of *peregrinatio* has led to a fruitless debate about whether Columba can be considered to be a true *peregrinus*. The reason is that he travelled back to Ireland when occasion demanded. Yet, Adomnán is explicit: Columba is a *peregrinus*.[9] Therefore, our understanding of *peregrinatio* needs to be flexible enough to acknowledge the importance of religious exile to Irish ecclesiastics, in a variety of circumstances.

This complexity should not surprise as *peregrinatio* had demonstrably diverse origins and expressions. Furthermore, it did not remain static over time. The *peregrini* of the sixth, seventh, and early eighth centuries can broadly be distinguished from those who came after.[10] The latter were arguably as much encouraged by the possibilities of Carolingian patronage as they were inspired by asceticism. Moreover, as Kathleen Hughes influentially suggested, changes to the religious landscape at home were of equal weight. This included the emergence of the *Céli Dé*, a group of loosely aligned ecclesiastics, who rose to prominence at the end of the eighth century.[11] They praised virtues of *stabilitas*, exhorting monks to remain within their monasteries. The desert could as easily be found at home as in the ocean. However, the *Céli Dé* did not have any noticeable impact on the numbers of Irish clerics travelling abroad. They are most usefully viewed as one end of a spectrum of opinion among Irish ecclesiastics, reflecting changing emphases in ecclesiastical thought.[12] Neither was *peregrinatio* peculiarly Irish, even if Irish practice was influential on how it came to be perceived by their neighbours. The famous English writer, Bede, for instance, presents a very clear vision of *peregrinatio*, one which echoes Irish ideals of exile but is much more interested in the importance of overseas missionary activity, something which is only patchily attested among the Irish.[13] *Peregrinatio* was also geographically diverse. Irish *peregrini* were to be found in Ireland, Britain, on the Continent and among the North Atlantic islands. This chapter will not examine the careers of individual *peregrini* but will instead explore the factors, specific to their experience in Ireland, which inspired them to leave home. The main focus will be on the earliest phases of *peregrinatio* during the sixth and seventh centuries. If life on the edge was so close to Christian perfection, why journey at all? What commonalities catalysed the different trajectories of a Cormac and a Columbanus? What unites the searcher for a lonely desert in the ocean with the founder of monasteries, centrally located in the heart of Europe?

The social and cultural origins of *peregrinatio* in Ireland

The starting point is to identify those influences that shaped the emergence of *peregrinatio*, broadly defined, within Ireland. This area of enquiry has been greatly illuminated by the work of Thomas Charles-Edwards.[14] He has illustrated the extent to which *peregrinatio* echoed native social assumptions. This is underlined by the fact that the vernacular *ailithir* and *ailithre* function as direct semantic equivalents of *peregrinus* and *peregrinatio* although, like them, they predominantly occur within religious literature. However, Charles-Edwards further argues that the Irish words can be usefully considered as part of a wider, and notably rich, semantic field which incorporates legal terms for exile.[15] For Charles-Edwards this suggests that the origins of *peregrinatio* are not only to be located in responses to Christian modes of asceticism. They are also tied to originally native ideas of exile. These, in turn, are encoded in the early Irish law tracts where exile is, primarily, a form of punishment. The Irish penitentials, using the term *peregrinatio*, take a similar position, indicating that the practice was widespread in secular and ecclesiastical society by at least the seventh century. In order to unpick the meanings attached to exile as punishment it is necessary to outline a number of basic features of early Irish society, features which arguably shaped the careers of *peregrini*.

Peregrinatio was concerned with rejecting normal social connections. In striking contrast, the early Irish imagined their world as a network of social communities, structured through an all-encompassing hierarchy of legal status, one which was explicated in minute detail. These communities were composed of groups of people living in a district, bound together in a socio–political framework centred around the local ruler. This basic district was known as a *túath* or petty kingdom.[16] These petty kingdoms were not politically significant on an all-island level but were the lynchpins of Irish society in the local sphere. Their inhabitants were organized through hierarchy, geography, and genealogy, all of which intersected in important ways. The individual was tightly bound into these communal groups. Thus, his or her legal standing, expressed through a legal measure known as honour-price (Old Irish *lóg n-enech*), was not merely a function of personal status. It was also based on how he or she was related to the wider kin group and community.[17] Therefore, each person was effectively locked into a system rooted in deeply embedded genealogical, communal and political ties. *Peregrinatio* was a radical challenge to this interconnectedness.

However, as Charles-Edwards has shown, being disconnected from the wider community was a major disability in early Irish law, one which severely affected an individual's social standing.[18] So, for example, a foreigner, whether from overseas or another Irish kingdom, had limited legal rights. This could be ameliorated through marriage to a native or by submission to the local ruler, but only partially. Moreover, it has been shown that exile, with its attendant legal disabilities, functioned as a form of serious punishment. If an individual committed a particularly reprehensible crime, such as kinslaying or incest, he or she was outcast from the community. This famously could take the form of being set adrift in a boat without a means of steering. The criminal was then left to the seas and God's mercy.[19] While the trope of setting adrift appears in several texts, its earliest extant reflection is in Muirchú's *Vita S. Patricii*, a biography of St Patrick written towards the end of the seventh century. In this Life a criminal bandit, Macc Cuill, attempts to trick Patrick.[20] Macc Cuill eventually submits to the saint and, as a form of voluntary punishment, casts himself adrift in a boat without oars, having shackled his feet and thrown away the key. The destination is left to God. He is providentially washed up on the Isle of Man where Macc Cuill eventually rises to the episcopacy. Muirchú's tale combines a number of suggestive features. Remarkably, Macc Cuill, a foreigner on the Isle of Man, does not lose status but gains it through a fascinating reversal of normal expectations. He transforms from a bandit to a bishop, from a social outcast to society's leader. Indeed, the bishop had the highest honour price of any ecclesiastic according to early Irish law. Yet, although Macc Cuill has been viewed as a proto-*peregrinus* by Charles-Edwards, the language of *peregrinatio* is never employed here or, indeed, elsewhere by Muirchú. On the other hand, the hagiographer is acutely interested in the status of foreigners, given that Patrick himself was one. Nonetheless, a connection can be made between the Macc Cuill episode and *peregrinatio*. Famously in 891, two centuries after Muirchú composed his *vita*, three Irish clerics were washed up on the English coast after crossing the Irish Sea in a rudderless boat. The Anglo-Saxon Chronicle tells us that they did this for the love of God.[21] This is an arresting parallel, although we should be cautious of reading Muirchú in the light of the Anglo-Saxon Chronicle, separated as these texts are by language, date and culture. It seems telling, however, that journeying on the ocean for the sake of God is presented as *peregrinatio* in *Nauigatio S. Brendani* 'the Voyage of St Brendan', a Hiberno-Latin text which may date to the eighth century.[22] These, and other examples, make a compelling a priori case for connecting punishment, exile and voyaging with *peregrinatio*.

At this point it is worth returning to the legal context. The role played by exile within vernacular law has already been outlined. However, this outline needs to incorporate a further important strand, the freedom of movement between kingdoms allowed to those of high status. The general position was that an individual was bound to their kindred and community through blood and through shared space. It was expected that most Irish people would remain living in the same *túath* for the majority of their lives. Extended travel was normally restricted to trade, military matters and marriage alliances between kingdoms. These expectations were so fundamental that the majority were legally classed as *áes trebtha* 'farming people'. They were contrasted with high-ranking professionals such as poets and judges, as well as with kings and clerics, all of whom enjoyed much greater rights of mobility.[23] This freedom to travel was a practical feature in an otherwise decentralized society. But, how did this impact upon *peregrinatio*? Essentially, a high-ranking churchman would expect the right to travel widely. Paradoxically, then, in view of its conceptualization in terms of legal punishment and communal disenfranchisement, *peregrinatio* echoes elite travel privileges. Moreover, the Irish law tracts explicitly give the *peregrinus*, called a *deorad dé*, an outsider or exile for God, the honour price equivalent to a bishop or a local king.

This dual way of legally positioning *peregrinatio*, as shameful punishment or exalted privilege, underlines just how nuanced our readings of it need to be in order to fully appreciate the great debt that it owes to the actualities of Irish society. It was these actualities which inspired Irish ecclesiastics to interpret the ideals of Christian asceticism within a meaningful and familiar frame of reference, one where the breaking of social bonds is envisaged in a culturally specific way. Of course, the shattering of social connections for the sake of God is not uniquely Irish; it was a feature of Christian asceticism everywhere. What was distinctive was the ambivalent and contradictory context in which Irish writers placed this social exclusion, when they depicted *peregrinatio* as both punishment and privilege. Arguably, it is this powerful ambiguity which fostered the creative convergence of originally separate ideals of martyrdom, punishment, submission to God and the providential journey. While this convergence nourished *peregrinatio*, the multitude of influences did ensure that its actual practice varied, producing figures as different as Cormac is from Columbanus. This variety is frequently obscured because continental *peregrini*, such as Columbanus, are viewed as normative rather than being examples of a much wider Irish socio-religious phenomenon.

Geography, exile and identity

This confluence of ideals was further shaped by another significant factor, one which greatly influenced Irish writers from at least the sixth and seventh centuries. It arguably provided an extra impetus towards a specifically overseas *peregrinatio*. This was the question of where to locate Ireland and the Irish within Christian history and Christian understandings of the world. These understandings provided a well-crafted shared framework which encompassed geography, history, and ethnicity. They were based on the Classical geographical tradition, one which was inherited, and developed, by Christian writers. These writers combined the bible with the Classical legacy, re-categorizing the knowledge of antiquity in the process. They put Jerusalem at the centre of the world; they mapped biblical history and Old Testament ethnic divisions onto the Classical geographical model. This was imagined as a globe containing the three continents of Europe, Asia, and Africa, enclosed by the great outer ocean, *oceanus*.[24] The Romans believed that the most civilized peoples lived on the shores of the middle sea, the Mediterranean. As one departed from the centre, people became less civilized and the climate worsened. This ideological geography gave Romans a way to interpret the world and assert their cultural superiority. Roman assumptions were the foundation of how many educated early medieval Christians thought about the geographical landscape. They were popularized between the fourth and seventh centuries by writers such as Augustine, Cassiodorus and Isidore of

Seville.[25] This landscape, as both Irish and English writers noted, placed their islands at the edge, the point where human habitation gave way to the mysteries of the impassable world-encompassing ocean. Indeed, Adomnán's description of Cormac's voyages brilliantly evokes the dangers of this infinite ocean, extending endlessly to the northern horizons. He seems to believe that it marked the boundaries of human possibilities of exploration.[26] But these boundaries were not fixed, no more than the ocean, making it the perfect realm in which to observe the workings of the divine will. This understanding transmuted the providential voyage into an act of trust in God, moving it far beyond concepts of legal punishment. In this sense, the actual journey, the *peregrinatio*, was as meaningful as the destination.

The importance of the encircling ocean was supported by Christian interpretations of the relationship between time and space. They believed that these were intertwined because of their simultaneous creation. These ideas fed into the common belief in an earthly paradise, one which had complex associations with both time and space.[27] It existed beyond time but was also an actual physical place which could be located on a map. Usually, it was situated in the east, being frequently identified with the Garden of Eden. Some, however, believed that it was separated from the ordinary world by the ocean.[28] This strand of interpretation reinforced the sense, already seen in Adomnán, that the ocean flowed at the limits, or even between existences. The clearest distillation of these ideas can be found in *Nauigatio S. Brendani*, a text which provides by far the most extensive early medieval reflection on the nature of the providential voyage undertaken for the sake of God.[29] The author of the narrative portrays *peregrinatio* as both the physical journey to find paradise and the pilgrimage of the Christian through life, the two being symbolically identical. Its central conceit is that the North Atlantic is teeming with monks and hermits who, unlike Cormac ua Liatháin, have successfully found their way to wave-wrapped deserts.[30] The text offers a concentrated idealization of the overseas and life-long exile. Nevertheless, its primary *peregrinus*, the sixth-century Irish abbot Brendan of Clonfert, is only a temporary exile. He returns to Ireland bringing with him the precious insights of his journey, physically manifested as the gemstones of paradise.[31] Thus, the *Nauigatio* presents the complexities of *peregrinatio* in a deceptively simple narrative form. Its *peregrinatio* can be life-long or temporary, it can be eremitical or communal, and it can result in salvation or damnation, such are the dangers of leaving the community and venturing beyond Ireland. Above all, the *Nauigatio* dramatizes the initially ascetic underpinnings of Irish overseas *peregrinatio*, especially that centred on the North Atlantic. Arguably, its portrayal of the ocean as God's laboratory is something which directly emerged from the reception of Christian geography among the Irish.

The North Atlantic locale for overseas *peregrinatio* is sometimes treated as being of less importance than the far better attested world of those Irish clerics who journeyed to Europe. This is not surprising as we cannot trace networks of Irish exiles winding through North Atlantic islands or even begin to establish their influences. However, their experiences of *peregrinatio* help illuminate the broader phenomenon. This is because the push factors to leave Ireland are especially prominent in their cases and the pull factors correspondingly weak. These *peregrini* were not relocating to overseas human societies. Before the settlement of the North Atlantic islands by the Vikings, such social communities, apart from those created temporarily by *peregrini* themselves, simply did not exist. In contrast, the pull exerted by societies in Britain and on the Continent provided, to varying degrees, powerful stimuli to potential Irish exiles, not all of which related to asceticism. For instance, the circle of exiles at Liège, centred around the prolific ninth-century Irish cleric and writer Sedulius Scottus, can hardly be described as being an ascetic colony.[32] Fortunately, however, there is a precious direct witness to these earlier austere *peregrini*. This is the early ninth-century Irish geographer, Dicuil, who gives an important insight into Irish clerical voyagers in his *Liber de Mensura Orbis Terrae*. Dicuil writes of them at their vanishing point; he provides a backwards look into the eighth century, albeit one where he can draw on personal experiences and eyewitness accounts. Dicuil describes Irish clerics as living as hermits on islands, probably to be identified as the Faroes.[33] But, according to Dicuil, the arrival of the Vikings brought an end to their settlements. Additionally, in a famous passage, he depicts an expedition dated *c.* 795 of Irish monks to the then unsettled Iceland. The monks closely observed what they regarded as unusual physical and astronomical data, including the phenomenon of the midnight sun during the Icelandic summer.[34] Indeed, the Icelanders came to believe that Irish monks had settled on the island before them. While the existence of these so-called *papar* may be highly questionable, they do function as a memory of the by then vanished North Atlantic clerical world of the Irish. Their era was likely one of relatively brief duration, when compared to those of other Irish exiles. Cormac's voyage, as recorded by Adomnán, probably lies near its beginning. Dicuil memorializes its end. In the intervening centuries some Irish *peregrini* found their ocean deserts.

The Christian geographical scheme may have had another, less direct, impact, upon the expression of group cohesion among Irish *peregrini*. This is the role that it played in inspiring the Irish to assert their ethnic self-identity. It has already been noted that geography and ethnography were closely linked in Classical and Christian thought. The location of Ireland, at the edge, could be interpreted negatively. It suggested that the Irish were less favoured and less civilized than their continental neighbours. In response, the Irish affirmed their scholarship and Christian orthodoxy, a point which Columbanus makes, not always subtly, in his writings. For him, Irish learning was a font of excellence, not a source of deficiency; it gave him the confidence to speak on matters of doctrine and religious practice.[35] Rhetorically, Columbanus reverses the usual assumption that lands distant from the Mediterranean cradle of Christianity were uncivilized, bleak and doctrinally suspect. Moreover, he offers an unusually personal insight into the dynamic of being an outsider in a foreign society. This dynamic also meant that Irish exiles tended to cluster together in identifiable religious and scholarly networks. For *peregrini* who chose to remain within Ireland, such issues of identity and solidarity were far less important, if at all. These *peregrini*, the *deoraid dé* of the law tracts, even more so than their North Atlantic brethren, are the least prominent group of exiles in academic scholarship. Intriguingly their number may have included women, *peregrinae*, who are otherwise almost entirely absent from the record. It is worth noting Jonas's memorable account of how one such woman inspired Columbanus to seek, firstly, *peregrinatio* within Ireland and, finally, exile overseas.[36] She even remarks that if she had been a man she would have taken the overseas option.

Remembering *peregrini*: absence and social memory

This articulation of Irish identity among overseas *peregrini* apparently contrasts with how they were viewed from home. For, here, there is a surprising *lacuna*, which has long been recognized by scholars, namely the seeming absence of overseas *peregrini* from Irish sources, especially as individuals.[37] The *peregrini* may have emphasized their Irishness but, it seems, their fellow countrymen, who remained in Ireland, were not so impressed. It has already been shown that the concepts of ascetic martyrdom and exile feature prominently in many Irish texts. This is also the case if only sources demonstrably written on the island, such as the vernacular law tracts, are considered. *Peregrinatio* is one of the best-attested phenomena that can be traced through early medieval Irish writings. Moreover, overseas *peregrini* made crucial contributions to Irish intellectual culture. Networks of *peregrini* stimulated the movement of manuscripts to and from Ireland. They physically joined the Irish with their European neighbours, facilitating their contribution to the intellectual life of early medieval Christianity. This is practically demonstrated through the survival of Irish manuscripts in continental libraries; it is also reflected in the long-lasting Irish presence in several European monasteries, such as Bobbio and St-Gall.[38] The close institutional tie between the Irish monastery of Slane and Péronne in northern France is another revealing example of the value attached to these networks by the Irish on both sides of the sea.[39] It seems logical to suppose that Irish exiles gravitated to these centres on account of their known links with home. Yet, as scholars have noted, the medieval Irish chronicles barely commemorate any of the overseas *peregrini*. As these texts provide the preponderance of surviving historical information about specific individuals and churches, this is particularly frustrating.[40] It is worth stressing that this absence does not apply to *peregrini* within Ireland, many of whom may well be among the clerical multitudes whose deaths are recorded. Even among overseas *peregrini* there are some exceptions. Fursa (d. 649), who had significant connections in northern France and was considered the patron of Péronne, is mentioned in the Annals of Ulster. His fame as a visionary, combined with the institutional relationship between Slane and Péronne, are probably the decisive factors.[41] Much later, Dubthach mac Maíle Tuile (d. 869), author of the Bamberg cryptogram, is commemorated in the same text.[42] Nonetheless, the vast majority of overseas *peregrini*, including men as famous as Columbanus, are simply not mentioned.

One way of approaching this seeming evidential gap is through social memory. This can be defined as encompassing the chosen shared histories which join groups of people together. Such histories underpin the formation of communal identity and feed into the elaboration of social practice. Social memory is highly artificial and selective: certain events are memorialized, others are not. In recent years, scholars have become increasingly aware of the crucial role performed by the creation and maintenance of social memory in medieval societies.[43] In early medieval Ireland, ecclesiastics were among the most important custodians of social memory, although this was a function they shared with other groups such as professional poets.[44] The medieval Irish chronicles are an outstanding example of how social memory functions in practice. The ecclesiastical chroniclers chose whom to commemorate and what institutions, secular and religious, to emphasize. Moreover, these choices can be closely mapped onto the interconnected communities, already discussed, which defined Irish life. The overseas *peregrini* did not fit into these structures. This is because the chroniclers' interests are largely confined to people and events within Ireland and, up to a point, the Irish kingdom of Dál Riata in northern Britain. Non-Irish happenings are recorded, but not consistently. A useful example is to contrast the apparent lack of interest in the Irish presence in Anglo-Saxon England in the chronicles with the detailed record provided by Bede in his *Historia Ecclesiastica*.[45] As the earliest stratum of the Irish chronicles ultimately originated from an Iona source, one might expect them to contain many echoes of English developments. Missionaries sent from Iona, after all, made the key contribution to the conversion of Northumbria. Moreover, these missionaries were influential on the subsequent consolidation of Northumbrian ecclesiastical institutions. However, references are extremely limited and without the evidence provided by Bede it is doubtful that historians would now appreciate the foundational contribution of the Irish to this phase of English history. Of course, the chronicles and Bede's *Historia* are different genres of writing. Nonetheless, they are comparable in the sense that the *Historia* is also an articulation of social memory. Bede chooses to remember the Irish in England, while the Irish chroniclers do not.

Does this mean that Irish social memory purposefully excluded the *peregrini*? Answering this sheds further light onto the Irish contexts of *peregrinatio*, especially in structural terms. It is an answer made up of partial observations. As already outlined, the Irish-specific concerns of the medieval chronicles almost certainly account for the lack of *peregrini* in their records. In addition, some exiles may have simply disappeared from knowledge entirely: this is surely the case with many of those *peregrini* who sought ascetic retreats in the North Atlantic. It could even be argued that their lack of commemoration is a marker of their success; they wished to leave Ireland behind them, disappearing beyond the bounds of ordinary society in the process. We know about Cormac ua Liatháin because he failed. But, perhaps, enquiry can be broadened. Irish social memory, particularly before around 800, is deeply concerned with *peregrinatio*. It is why it features, in various guises, in so many texts. These texts ask important questions. What is an exile? What status is proper to a *deorad dé?* How can one become a martyr? Are there deserts in the ocean? These questions go to the heart of *peregrinatio*. They also show a fascination with structure and process, a fascination that shaped the articulation of *peregrinatio* in Irish terms. It is these interests which ensured that *peregrinatio* became part of Irish social memory while individual *peregrini* faded.

Conclusions and contexts

At this point it is worth reconsidering the different elements which have been identified as contributing to the emergence of a distinctively Irish form of *peregrinatio* during the sixth and seventh centuries. How do these fit together into a shared and flexible framework? The first thing to note is that travel is a key unifying element. As already outlined, the Irish conceptualized the act of making a journey in a particular way which aligned it simultaneously with status and with punishment. At the same time, ideas of ascetic martyrdom had gained traction. Together, these provided a rationale for *peregrinatio* within the island. An individual could sever thickly woven communal ties by crossing one of the multitudes of boundaries that divided the many Irish local kingdoms. However, the inspiration to venture further was given an extra push by the Irish reception of the Christian geographical tradition. This helped transform the ocean into a space of ascetic and theological significance. Finally, for those who crossed the seas to Britain and the Continent, a further and highly practical dynamic developed. The likes of Columbanus and, a generation later, Fursa and his family circle established networks which arguably encouraged even more Irish clerics to travel abroad. By the eighth century this had attained a resilient self-sustaining momentum, a momentum which meant that the original ascetic impulses of the earliest *peregrini* came to be less obviously important. If anything, this demonstrates the extent to which Irish networks of *peregrini* flourished through flexibility; they mutated as circumstance dictated, retaining their relevance even as societies and fashions of religious expression changed. And it is this flexibility which defines *peregrinatio*, whether it is the long journey of Columbanus towards fame and Bobbio or Cormac's futile quest across wide Atlantic wastes.

Notes

1. Columbanus, Letter 5, cc. 1–2.
2. Columbanus, Letter 2, c. 6.

3. Adomnán, *Vita Columbae*, 1.6; 2.42; 3.17, ed. and trans. A.O. and M.O. Anderson, *Adomnán's Life of Columba* (Edinburgh, 1961; 2nd edn Oxford, 1991); R. Sharpe, trans., *Adomnán of Iona. Life of St Columba* (London, 1995).
4. Jonas, *Vita Columbani*, 1.3.
5. T. M. Charles-Edwards, 'The Social Background to Irish *Peregrinatio*', *Celtica* 11 (1976), 43–59; Michael Richter, *Ireland and Her Neighbours in the Seventh Century* (Dublin, 1999), pp. 41–7.
6. Whitley Stokes and John Strachan, eds, *Thesaurus Palaeohibernicus: A Collection of Old-Irish Glosses, Scholia, Prose and Verse*, 2 vols (Cambridge, 1903), II, pp. 244–7.
7. C. Stancliffe, 'Red, White and Blue Martyrdom', in D. Whitelock et al., eds, *Ireland in Early Medieval Europe* (Cambridge, 1982), pp. 21–46.
8. Jonas, *Vita Columbani* 1.3. For its influence, see, Charles-Edwards, 'The Social Background'; Richter, *Ireland and Her Neighbours*.
9. Adomnán, *Vita Columbae*, preface; Richter, *Ireland and Her Neighbours*, pp. 49–53.
10. E. Johnston, *Literacy and Identity in Early Medieval Ireland* (Woodbridge, 2013), pp. 49–50.
11. K. Hughes, 'The Changing Theories and Practice of Irish Pilgrimage', *Journal of Ecclesiastical History* 11 (1960), pp. 143–51.
12. W. Follett, *Céli Dé in Ireland: Monastic Writing and Identity in the Early Middle Ages* (Woodbridge, 2006).
13. Bede, *HE*, III.4, III.13, IV.3; Charles-Edwards, 'The Social Background', pp. 45–6.
14. Charles-Edwards, 'The Social Background'.
15. These include *ambue* 'non-native', *cú glas* 'grey dog', *deorad* 'outsider', and *murchoirthe* 'foreigner', literally one thrown up by the sea.
16. F.J. Byrne, 'Tribes and Tribalism in Early Ireland', *Ériu* 22 (1971), pp. 128–66.
17. Fergus Kelly, *A Guide to Early Irish Law* (Dublin, 1988), pp. 1–16.
18. Charles-Edwards, 'The Social Background', 46–53.
19. M.E. Byrne, 'On the Punishment of Setting Adrift', *Ériu* 11 (1932), 97–102; Kelly, *Guide*, pp. 219–21.
20. Muirchú, *Vita S. Patricii*, I.23, ed. L. Bieler, *The Patrician Texts in the Book of Armagh*, Scriptores Latini Hiberniae 10 (Dublin, 1979).
21. Discussed by Charles-Edwards, 'The Social Background', pp. 48–9.
22. There is a large literature on dating this text. D.N. Dumville, 'Two Approaches to the Dating of "Navigatio Sancti Brendani"', *Studi Medievali* 29 (1988), 95–9, influentially suggests the eighth century.
23. Johnston, *Literacy and Identity*, p. 72.
24. N. Lozovsky, *'The Earth is our Book': Geographical Knowledge in the Latin West ca. 400–1000* (Ann Arbor, 2000), pp. 6–8.
25. Lozovsky, *'The Earth is our Book'*, pp. 10–20, 53–5.
26. Adomnán, *Vita Columbae*, 2.42.

27. J. Delumeau, *History of Paradise: The Garden of Eden in Myth and Tradition* (New York, 1995), pp. 42–56; M. Bockmuehl, 'Locating Paradise', in M. Bockmuehl and G.G. Stroumsa, eds, *Paradise in Antiquity: Jewish and Christian Views* (Cambridge, 2010), pp. 192–209.

28. Delumeau, *History of Paradise*, pp. 42–56.

29. T. O'Loughlin, 'Distant Islands: the Topography of Holiness in the *Nauigatio Sancti Brendani*', in M. Glasscoe, ed., *The Medieval Mystical Tradition in England, Ireland and Wales* (Woodbridge, 1999), pp. 1–20.

30. Examples are *Nauigatio* cc. 12, 17, 26.

31. *Nauigatio* cc. 28–9.

32. D. Ó Cróinín, *Early Medieval Ireland 400–1200* (London, 1995), pp. 224–6. (see Chapter 11).

33. Dicuil, *Liber de Mensura Orbis Terrae* c. 15.

34. Dicuil, *Liber de Mensura Orbis Terrae* cc. 11–13.

35. Columbanus, Letter 1, c. 3; Letter 2, cc. 5–6; Letter 3, c. 2.

36. Jonas, *Vita Columbani*, 1.3

37. Johnston, *Literacy and Identity*, pp. 42–58.

38. Ó Cróinín, *Early Medieval Ireland*, pp. 222–4; Richter, *Ireland and Her Neighbours*, pp. 177–80.

39. F.J. Byrne, 'Two Lives of Saint Patrick: *Vita Secunda* and *Vita Quarta*', *Journal of the Royal Society of Antiquaries of Ireland* 124 (1994), 11–12; J.-M. Picard, ed., *Ireland and Northern France AD 600–850* (Dublin, 1991).

40. D. Mc Carthy, *The Irish Annals. Their Genesis, Evolution and History* (Dublin, 2008); N. Evans, *The Present and the Past in Medieval Irish Chronicles* (Woodbridge, 2010).

41. He is commemorated in AU 649. See also, S. Hamann, 'St Fursa, the Genealogy of an Irish Saint — The Historical Person and his Cult', *PRIA* C 112 (2011), pp. 1–41.

42. He is commemorated in AU 869. His career is discussed by D. Ó Cróinín, 'The Irish as Mediators of Antique Culture on the Continent', in P.L. Butzer and D. Lohrmann, eds, *Science in Western and Eastern Civilization* (Basle, 1993), pp. 41–52.

43. J.J. Fentress and C. Wickham, *Social Memory: New Perspectives on the Past* (Oxford, 1992).

44. Johnston, *Literacy and Identity*, pp. 162–9.

45. A.T. Thacker, 'Bede and the Irish', in L.A.J.R. Houwen and A.A. MacDonald, *Beda Venerabilis: Historian, Monk and Northumbrian* (Groningen, 1996), pp. 31–60.

3

The Political Context of Irish Monasticism in Seventh-Century Francia: Another Look at the Sources

Yaniv Fox

It happened at that time, that a certain bishop from the regions of Ireland went to that area, a man by the name of Falvius, who was strong in the grace of sanctity and experienced to the fullest in saintly acts.[1]

This short excerpt is taken from the Life of Sigiramn, an Aquitanian nobleman who in the mid-seventh century established two monasteries in the region of Bourges. The anonymous ninth- or tenth-century Life provides a rather thin, yet probably reliable, factual skeleton, outlining Sigiramn's ancestry, early life and monastic establishments. Other aspects of the saint's Life recounted by the hagiography, such as his ascetic zeal, or his decision to live his life among the paupers of Rome, are somewhat more difficult to verify. Those ideals, at least as they are portrayed in the Life, are quite extraordinary considering Sigiramn's era and social status. More likely they reflect the preferences of his Carolingian hagiographer, who spared no effort to make a wandering beggar of a Merovingian aristocrat.[2]

Sigiramn's decision to spend his days in endless *peregrinatio*, we are told, came about through a meeting with Falvius, a wandering bishop from Ireland, who was passing through the region. Falvius made an indelible impression on the young noble, who immediately joined the bishop's pilgrimage to Rome. Having fulfilled his narrative purpose, Falvius quietly stepped off the stage, and was not mentioned again.

Another story in the same vein is that of Richarius, who was to become the eponymous abbot of Centula, better known by its later

53

name, St-Riquier. In his anonymous eighth-century Life,[3] Richarius is said to have saved the lives of Fichori and Chaidocus,[4] two monks who are said to be Irish, who were accused of casting pagan spells by a crowd of rustics.[5] After the rescue, the two began preaching to Richarius, whereupon he decided to construct a monastery. Much like Falvius, the two Irish monks quickly receded into the background, but only after hearing Richarius's confession and instructing him on the finer points of religious life, thereby providing the impetus for the remainder of the plot.

Readers of Merovingian hagiographies have long been aware of the special literary place such Irish saints occupy. Their arrival in Gaul – as literary characters, at least – was confined almost entirely to the seventh century, a time when the ascetic expertise of the Irish was enthusiastically sought out by the crown and the Frankish elites. So when Irish *peregrini* surfaced now and again in what was, in essence, a quintessential monastic genre, their role was understood by historians as a natural extension of a wider monastic trend.[6] Upon closer inspection, this explanation appears less than convincing. My goal in this chapter is therefore to show how Irish monks were employed in later compositions, and to analyse the complex relationship between the literary portrayals and the historical careers of these enigmatic figures.

The terminology used to describe the continental achievement of the Irish has been a source of endless contention, which I do not intend to re-introduce here. It is clear that there were monks from Ireland working in the Merovingian kingdoms, and that several monasteries were established as a result; it is also clear that the actual number of Irish monks whose existence and accomplishments we may substantiate is very small.[7] The first of these, and also the most famous, was Columbanus, who came to Merovingian Burgundy in 590 or 591 and proceeded to establish three monasteries there and a fourth in Lombard Italy.[8]

Of course, there were other Irish monks of considerable importance. Saint Fursa came to Neustria in the 640s and with the help of its mayor founded Lagny.[9] When he died shortly after, Fursa's patron had him buried at Péronne, which soon received his two brothers, Foillan and Ultán. Those same men were also active in Austrasia, where they later established Fosses.[10] Both monastic groups were to grow in size and importance, weaving themselves into the social and political fabric of Frankish society. The phenomenal success of these movements inspired an outpouring of hagiographical creativity, all of which looked back admiringly at its Irish beginnings.

In this chapter, however, I am primarily interested in less well-known foci of Irish activity, and particularly in the hagiographical treatment of such figures. As I shall show, the factual basis for many of these persons is remarkably meagre, and more importantly, very late. Since Irish monastic founders, wandering bishops, and other ascetics clearly were a popular device in the literary toolkit of the Carolingian hagiographer, they can arguably be said to have served some symbolic function. My goal here is therefore to attempt to explain the employment of Irish characters by Carolingian authors and their desire to amplify or even invent Irish origins for the monastic communities for which they wrote.

Let us then return to Falvius. His brief yet formative role in the Life of Sigiramn was not his only hagiographical appearance – Falvius resurfaces in the Life of Eligius, essentially a Merovingian life, though extensively re-edited during the Carolingian period.[11] Here, too, Bishop Falvius plays a short but decisive role, defending the church against an unnamed heresy. The Life of Eligius reports that during the minority of King Clovis II (d. 658) there appeared in Gaul a heretic from overseas, who began luring the people of Auxerre to his error. In a council convened in Orléans to deal with him, our anonymous heretic managed to confound his accusers. In the end, it was only thanks to the efforts of Bishop Falvius that this villain was defeated.

Had Falvius remained confined to one ninth-century Life, it would have been relatively easy to discount his existence as fantasy. Since he appears twice, we should at least entertain the possibility that we are dealing with a historical figure. Yet even if this were true, the identification of Falvius in the Life of Eligius presents considerable difficulties. Firstly, we really have no way of knowing whether this is in fact the same man who appeared in the Life of Sigiramn. Wilhelm Levison seems to have thought so,[12] although in some of the manuscripts of the Life of Eligius he appears as Salvius, and in others as Flavius. In his edition to the acts of the council of Orléans, Friedrich Maassen suggested that this Salvius was either the bishop of Valence,[13] or of Béarn,[14] but in any event not a wandering Irishman.[15]

Our ability to identify Falvius is further compromised by a glaring chronological discrepancy found in the Life of Eligius. The description of the council in the Life is juxtaposed with Pope Martin I's opposition to Emperor Heraclius's Monothelite initiative.[16] The Life of Eligius reports that the council of Orléans took place 'while these things were happening in Rome', which means that even if the hagiographer was referring to the very beginning of Martin's papacy, the council could not have taken place earlier than 649. At that time

Eligius and Audoin were said to have resided at the Paris court, but this is clearly a mistake, since both men were given episcopal sees no later than 641.[17] While the earliest layer of the Life of Eligius is attributed to the pen of Audoin himself, he could scarcely have made such a mistake, having been personally present at the proceedings. We would then have to agree that the story of the council, and Falvius's role therein, is a part of the Carolingian layer of the Life, whose historical value is questionable. For the purposes of the author of the Life of Eligius, Falvius was probably no more than a convenient literary solution. His inclusion may possibly reflect enduring memories of a historical figure, but more likely, it betrays direct literary borrowing.

The bishop mentioned in the Life of Sigiramn bears striking resemblance to another itinerant bishop – the similarly named Salvius of Valenciennes – whose *passio* places his activities in the reign of Charles Martel.[18] Salvius's hagiography, composed in Charlemagne's day,[19] provides little historical background apart from naming Valenciennes as the bishop's preferred theatre of operations. Much like the bishop in Sigiramn's Life, this Salvius has a young disciple, allowing the hagiographer to explore the mentor-acolyte relationship, and use it to express his own ideas on piety and saintly behaviour. One of these 'teaching moments' takes place when the two chance upon a basilica dedicated to St Martin. Correspondingly, Martin's tomb was the location chosen for the formative scene of the Life of Sigiramn, in which the protagonist took his vows and was tonsured.[20]

The Irish in the cartulary corpus

Another interesting example is Romanus of Mazerolles. Unlike Falvius, Romanus is not a character cast in a hagiography, but a figure securely attested in a will.[21] Ansoald, a seventh-century bishop of Poitiers, took in Romanus, an otherwise unknown Irish bishop, for whom he had restored the ruined monastery of Mazerolles. When Romanus died, Mazerolles was subsumed by Nouaillé and even though Ansoald's will reports that there were some Irish monks living there, we hear nothing more of them. Romanus also appears as a cosignatory on two of Ansoald's documents dealing with the transfer of certain properties to Filibert's monastery of Noirmoutier.[22] Edward James has cast doubt on the authenticity of the documents, and indeed his suspicions seem justified. The list of cosignatories is repeated verbatim in both instances, which is peculiar, given that they were drafted almost a year apart.[23] Since it was ostensibly the same scribe – one Lando – who wrote and witnessed both documents, he could have used the first list as a basis for the second, although we are likely looking at documents that were both drafted much later.

In Lando's charters for Ansoald, Romanus had an associate with an Irish name, Thomeneus (Tómméne), who is thought to have been the same person as Tomianus of Angoulême, a bishop that appears in the canons of the Council of Bordeaux.[24] Angoulême did belong to Ansoald's province, so it would not have been out of place for Tomianus to witness his metropolitan's charter, and indeed on both occasions, Thomeneus signs his name with an appended *minimus episcoporum*. While this identification is not impossible, there are several significant obstacles that make it unlikely. Firstly, reconstructing the list of Angoulême's earlier bishops and determining Tomianus's place on that list is a very complicated task. A ninth-century manuscript containing an episcopal list from Angoulême does not mention Tomianus at all,[25] while the existence of no fewer than twelve of his immediate successors remains highly suspect.[26]

Secondly, Tomianus's Irish origins are never mentioned by contemporary sources. Modern scholars have based Tomianus's Irishness entirely on his name, which is problematic, to say the least.[27] Finally, in order to believe that the two men are identical, we would have to accept the improbable notion that a foreigner could be appointed bishop of a seventh-century Gallic see. Admittedly, there were Irishmen active in Gaul, and particularly in Aquitaine.[28] Yet diocesan bishops like Tomianus were raised to episcopal honours through a network of social connections that was simply not available to a foreigner, no matter how formidable his patron.[29] One can easily imagine hermits, abbots and wandering bishops of Irish background, but a diocesan nomination would come about either through familial prestige, or through the auspices of a very insistent royal supporter. Neither, I believe, applies in the case of a little-known Irish *peregrinus*, making the identification of Tomianus of Angoulême as an Irishman highly unlikely.

Ernest Tardif claims that it is 'very probable' that Romanus should be identified as the Irish priest Rónán from Bede's account of the Council of Whitby.[30] As Ian Wood points out, this connection was neither made by Charles Plummer, who edited the Ecclesiastical History, nor by J. M. Wallace-Hadrill, who wrote a commentary on it.[31] This identification, originally suggested by Jean Mabillon, was based on Rónán's continental education, according to Bede, and on the fact that both Romanus and the Irish Rónán's feasts are held on June 1, which, although hardly conclusive, could be significant.[32] While Rónán learned paschal calculus in Gaul and Italy, his career obviously took him back to Britain, and we have no indication that he ever returned, let alone to Poitiers. Still, there remains the feast day, although as far as I was able to determine, the only Rónán with a feast on 1 June is Ronan of Locronan in the west of Brittany,[33] a sixth-century hermit, whose eleventh-century Life unfolded in the environs of Quimper in Brittany, where he was also buried.[34] Perhaps the confusion stemmed from the presence, in that same chapter of Bede's Ecclesiastical History, of a Kentish priest named Romanus, or with a separate attempt to identify an equally obscure Ronan venerated in Canterbury with Romanus of Caesarea.[35]

Whatever Rónán's actual provenance, Wood poses a very valid question: what would have been the point of fabricating Irish *peregrini*?[36] A possible answer could be that the scribe, whose charters were possibly forged at a later date, never actually mentioned the Irishness of any of the figures involved. It is only Ansoald who called Romanus a *peregrinus ex genere Scottorum*, and we would have no reason to doubt him on this. Jean Marie Pardessus apparently trusted the will of Ansoald, although he, too, expressed grave doubts about the Romanus/Ronan identification.[37] When Lando drew up the charters, he could have taken the name of Romanus from the will, and the name Thomeneus from any of the sources at his disposal. If we discard Tomianus's Irish background, which we probably should, then we are left with one Irish abbot who, while possibly authentic, had a brief and very limited impact on religious life in Poitou.

Irish *peregrini* and their local patrons

Another trait common to all of these figures is that their story, while mostly fictional, is anchored in historical persons. The story of Falvius stretches between two poles – Sigiramn and Eligius – while that of Romanus is securely tied to the figure of Ansoald of Poitiers. Burgundofaro of Meaux serves as another nodal point around which Irish *peregrini* of uncertain quality seem to concentrate. Burgundofaro, or Faro for short, was the son of Chagneric, who appears in the Life of Columbanus as a magnate operating in the region of Meaux, where his son later rose to episcopal dignity.[38] This family also produced Chagnoald of Laon, one of Columbanus's earliest followers, and Burgundofara, abbess of Faremoûtiers. All three were probably related to Audoin of Rouen, whom we have already mentioned, and his brother Ado, founder of the Columbanian house of Jouarre. The crypt of Jouarre houses the remains of Agilbert of Paris, Ado's cousin, who had spent a few years training in Ireland as a younger man. If we are searching for Frankish saints with Irish qualifications, we really need look no further. While it would be difficult to regard Jouarre and Faremoûtiers as Irish in any true sense, their founders, with their impeccable 'Irish' backgrounds, were staples of hagiographical composition.[39]

This is perhaps why, when figures with Irish names like Fiacrius (Fíachrae) or Chillenus (Cilléne) appear in the hagiography, they do so in the context of Burgundofaro's episcopacy. Hildegar, the author of Faro's Life, reports only that he received Fiacrius and Chillenus, who founded the monasteries of Breuil and Aubigny. Interestingly, Hildegar, writing in the second half of the ninth century, claims to have had before him a Life of Chillenus, although this was apparently not the error-riddled Life edited by Albert Poncelet. Separating the facts from later traditions is, however, impossible. The careers of these two men were inflated to include missionary success, episcopal honours, and posthumous miracles. By the time Hildegar was working on his composition, the foundations of Aubigny and St-Fiacre had been swallowed up by the monastery of St-Faron, which would explain Burgundofaro's depiction as the one guiding and supervising the activities of their alleged founders.[40]

The final figure I shall examine here is Fridolin, alleged founder of Säckingen. His tenth-century Life, the dubious product of Balderic of Speyer's attempt to recreate an earlier hagiography he had allegedly seen and memorized, places this saint in Poitiers, around the time of Clovis I's reign.[41] As many have noted, the Life is full of holes, not least of which is the improbability of an Irish mission to Gaul in the very early sixth century. Some, like Prinz and Bieler, were at least willing to consider that the king in question was actually Clovis II, which would have been more in keeping with the timeline of Irish activity in Gaul.[42] Others, like Margrit Koch, were quicker to condemn the Life, providing the usual argument that Ireland's prestige was what drove Balderic to invent an Irish origin.[43] The first problem with identifying Clovis II as the king is that the Life mentions that he had come to hold power over a kingdom spanning 'far and wide', understood by some – though certainly not universally accepted – as a reference to the battle of Vouillé (507).[44] The second is that the hagiographical king exerts his influence over Fridolin's Austrasian foundations, which lay beyond Clovis II's kingdom. This is a valid concern, but it certainly need not constitute a fatal blow to the Clovis II hypothesis.

Säckingen's establishment in the seventh century fits the general chronology, even if, as Friedrich Prinz points out, Fridolin's role in its foundation is much more difficult to ascertain.[45] Poitiers, where he would have begun his mission, had a number of demonstrable

Irish connections. The most important of these was Dido of Poitiers, whose episcopacy coincided with Clovis II's kingship, and therefore also with Fridolin's hypothetical seventh-century career.[46] Dido is famous for his role in the exile of Dagobert II (d. 679), but he also serves as an excellent example of how a Neustrian bishop was able to affect Austrasian politics.[47] Of course, this channel of influence could also explain how Neustrian patronage found its way to Austrasian foundations.

Finally, even if Balderic mistook the king he encountered in the earlier Life for Clovis I, it would not have been the only occasion where the two monarchs were confused. The mid-seventh century re-establishment of Romainmôtier was incorrectly dated to 501 in the tenth-century *Annales Lausonenses*, transforming Clovis II into his eponymous ancestor.[48] This was done ostensibly for the very same reasons: giving the monastery earlier and more illustrious origins. Curiously, it was at Romainmôtier that Wandregisel made an unscheduled stop while *en route* to Ireland. No doubt another hagio-graphical cliché, this decision nevertheless saw him abandon his insular quest to establish the Columbanian house of Fontenelle.[49] In a later rendition of his Life, Ireland was exchanged for Rome, evidence of the factual flexibility of such accounts. The uncertain nature of Balderic's creative process and consequently the historical circum-stances of Fridolin's mission remain obscure, and yet we could possibly accept that at the core of this story lies a small grain of historical truth.

The narrative role of Irish figures

It would perhaps be feasible to provide some general description of the use of Irish *peregrini* in later sources. All of the saints surveyed here had their careers – real or imaginary – in seventh-century Gaul, and all fulfilled the typical roles envisaged for Irish monks: monastic founders and abbots, wandering bishops and missionaries. Chaidoc, Fichori and the Falvius of the Life of Sigiramn may safely be catego-rized as narrative devices, whose role it was to motivate an otherwise sedentary protagonist to action. Sigiramn leaves a promising secular career to pursue a life of begging, but eventually founds two monas-teries in his native city. Similarly, Richarius founds Centula after inadvertently stopping an attempted lynch. If personal confession was traditionally regarded as an innovation brought over by the Irish, it is fittingly employed in Richarius's later Life.[50] The Irish, then, embod-ied the expectations of later hagiographers as upholders of pure ortho-doxy, untainted by ecclesiastical politics. Their imputed impartiality allowed authors to use them, but also to discard them once they had accomplished their task; since they were not attached to any particular see, they made for especially appealing narrative solutions.

Romanus of Mazerolles, Fiacrius and Chillenus were also put to use in later compositions. Assuming the will of Ansoald of Poitiers is authentic, extracting Romanus's name for use in later documents would have been meant to bolster the legitimacy of the various dona-tions to Noirmoutier by inserting a prestigious Irish abbot as witness. So, too, can the mention of Tomianus of Angoulême, if he is indeed identified correctly, although here there is no reason to presuppose any Irish provenance. A proprietary dimension is possibly also what dictated Hildegar's decision to include Fiacrius and Chillenus in Burgundofaro's Life. Since Aubigny and St-Fiacre were integrated into St-Faron not long before Hildegar composed the Life of Faro,[51] claims to landed wealth and ownership of cult centres would have been well served by presenting Burgundofaro as the authority behind these foundations.[52] As Jacques Dubois has pointed out, Fiacrius's episcopal title, present in his tenth-century eulogy, was omitted from the Life of Faro. Perhaps we should understand this as an attempt to provide the bishop of Meaux with clear hierarchical supremacy over the man whose monastery and cult site Bugrundofaro's successor was now claiming.

Of all these men, Fridolin and the Falvius of the Life of Eligius are those that most strain credulity. Still, one characteristic that persists in all of these figures is that they are linked to benefactors that were themselves connected to houses whose Irish origins were seemingly beyond doubt.[53] Eligius and Audoin appear in person in the Life of Columbanus, as does Burgundofaro.[54] Dido and Ansoald of Poitiers had their share of Columbanian ties as well: Dido was likely the dedicatee of the Life of Amatus of Remiremont, while Ansoald was the patron of Noirmoutier.[55] While St-Riquier was not a Columbanian house by any stretch, it was affected by many of the same trends. The *laus perennis* or eternal chant was practised there as in numerous Columbanian houses.[56] More importantly, Richarius was active in England, probably as part of a wider programme set in motion by Dagobert I, which also included the Columbanian bishop Agilbert.[57] At the same time Amandus was operating on Dagobert's behest in Flanders, after a period spent training in Bourges under Sulpicius, who was also bishop when Sigiramn was erecting Millebeccus and Longoretus.[58]

It has not been my intent to argue that Columbanian monasticism served as a platform whence these less-known *peregrini* launched their operations. Rather, it was that hagiographers and charter scribes in later centuries would have found it convenient to link these Irishmen to persons with established credentials. By the time these Lives were being rewritten, Eligius of Noyon, Burgundofaro of Meaux and Richarius of Centula had become household names, especially as part of the culture promoted by the Carolingian court. Audoin's Carolingian Life became the most popular version of his life,[59] and the Life of Eligius took on its current form under a Carolingian editor. Richarius, for example, had his life rewritten by Alcuin of York, who expanded on Richarius's Irish encounter and the time he spent across the Channel.[60] He also rewrote the life of Vaast, whose original Life was probably composed by none other than Jonas of Bobbio, author of the Life of Columbanus.[61] Alcuin knew Salvius of Valenciennes and Amandus, whom he jointly applauds in one of his poems.[62] Proof that these compositions were later read together may be found in such collections as St-Gall, Stiftsbibliothek, MS 563, a ninth- or tenth-century legendary containing the lives of Vaast, Richarius, Amandus and Audoin, among others.[63] Literary techniques and ideas certainly moved between hagiographies, inspiring successive generations of writers who adapted and re-employed them to fit specific needs.

In the examples I have surveyed here, the inclusion of Irish figures either coincided with a reworking of an earlier text or with new compositions that were dependent on older ones. Such appearances were often sudden and brief, and while the reasons for incorporating Irish figures were admittedly varied, they were always used by later authors as a means to an end. Hagiographies employed Irish *peregrini* as narrative catalysts, or to introduce certain religious practices, while the cartulary corpus usually used them as legitimizing agents. Historical lacunae were overcome by weaving Irish *peregrini* into plots that included unanimously respected hagiographical heroes, themselves tied to stories of monastic foundation with strong Irish backgrounds. It is through this marriage of traditions that the evidence we have today came about. Of course, whether such traditions capture some faint factual echo truly remains a riddle.

Notes

1. *Vita Sigiramni abbatis Longoretensis*, c. 9, MGH SS rer. Merov. 4, ed. B. Krusch (Hanover, 1902), pp. 603–25, at p. 611: 'Accidit autem illo in tempore, ut quidam episcopus ex partibus Ybernie adiret istis partibus, Faluius scilicet nomine, qui sanctitatis gratia prepotens atque fultus sanctisque actibus ad plenum erat expertus...'

2. E. Shuler, *Almsgiving and the Formation of Early Medieval Societies, AD 700–1025*, unpublished PhD thesis (University of Notre Dame, 2010), pp. 269–70, and esp. n.1.

3. For dating, see Krusch's introduction to the *Vita Richarii sacerdotis Centulensis primigenia*, MGH SS rer. Merov. 7, ed. B. Krusch (Hanover, 1920), pp. 438–53, at p. 439.

4. For Chaidoc as a Breton rather than Irish name, see F. Lot, 'Nouvelles recherches sur le texte de la Chronique de l'abbaye de Saint–Riquier par Hariulf', *Bibliothèque de l'École des chartes* 72 (1911), 245–70, at p. 264.

5. *Vita Richarii*, c.2, p. 445: 'Fichori ex Hibernia et Chaidocus ex Scottorum patria ueniebant Siccambriam. Vir beatus Richarius fuit eorum obuius, ubi gentiles Pontearii inridebant ei: malefacere adfirm- abant stulti, quod essent dusi; hemaones uocitabant, qui Deum non credebant; eis reputabant, quod segetes tollebant'. For context, see R. Meens, 'Thunder over Lyon: Agobard, the *tempestarii* and Christianity', in C.G. Steel, J. Marenbon and W. Verbeke, eds, *Paganism in the Middle Ages: Threat and Fascination* (Louvain, 2012), pp. 157–66, at pp. 164–65; P.E. Dutton, 'Thunder and Hail Over the Carolingian Countryside', in D. Sweeney, ed., *Agriculture in the Middle Ages* (Philadelphia PA, 1995), pp. 111–137.

6. F. Prinz, *Frühes Mönchtum im Frankenreich: Kultur und Gesellschaft in Gallien, den Rheinlanden und Bayern am Beispiel der monastischen Entwicklung (4. bis 8. Jahrhundert)* (Munich, 1988), pp. 121–51; R. Bornert, 'Les origines du monachisme en Alsace: certitudes acquises, conclusions provisoires, nouvelles hypothèses', *Revue d'Alsace* 134 (2008), 9–77, at p. 13.

7. For a review, see L. Bieler, *Irland: Wegbereiter des Mittelalters* (Olten, 1961), pp. 101–11; L. Gougaud, *Les saints irlandais hors d'Irlande: étudiés dans le culte et dans la dévotion traditionnelle*, Bibliothèque de la Revue d'Histoire Ecclésiastique 16 (Oxford, 1936), esp. pp. 86–92, 98–102, 104–13, 159–64 for saints discussed here.

8. Jonas of Bobbio, *Vita Columbani discipulorumque eius*, MGH SS rer. Merov. 37, ed. B. Krusch (Hanover, 1910), pp. 1–294; D. Bullough, 'The Career of Columbanus', in *Columbanus: Studies on the Latin Writings*, ed. M. Lapidge (Woodbridge, 1997), pp. 1–28.

9. *Vita Fursei abbatis Latiniacensis*, c. 9, MGH SS rer. Merov. 4, ed. B. Krusch (Hanover, 1902), pp. 434–40, at pp. 438–9; S. Hamann, 'St Fursa, the Genealogy of an Irish Saint: the Historical Person and his Cult', *PRIA C* 112 (2012), pp. 1–41.

10. *Additamentum Nivialense de Fuilano*, MGH SS rer. Merov. 4, ed. B. Krusch (Hanover, 1902), pp. 449–51.

11. *Vita Eligii episcopi Noviomagensis*, c. 35, MGH SS rer. Merov. 4, ed. B. Krusch (Hanover, 1902), pp. 663–741, at p. 692: 'Tanta quippe dicendi arte obiectis quaestionibus occurrebat, ut ubi maxime putare- tur adstrictus, ibi quasi anguis lubricus quibusdam foraminibus lapsus eorum se fronti opponeret. Cumque nullo genere a quoquam possit

concludi aut superari, exstitit e nostris quidam per Dei prouidentiam doctissimus episcopus nomine Falvius, qui ita ei in omnibus obuiauit, ut ingens pro hoc fieret et gaudium et expectaculum'; Y. Hen, *Culture and Religion in Merovingian Gaul, AD 481–751* (Leiden, New York, and Cologne, 1995), pp. 196–7.

12. W. Levison's index to MGH SS rer. Merov. 4, ed. B. Krusch (Hanover, 1902), p. 787.
13. *Gallia Christiana*, ed. D. de Saint-Marthe (Paris, 1865), XVI, p. 294.
14. On this identification, see M. Lanore, 'Notice historique et archéologique sur l'église Notre-Dame Lescar', *Revue du Béarn et du Pays Basque* 2 (1905), pp. 16–30, 58–72, 106–21, 145–57, 206–20.
15. *Concilium Aurelianense, a. 639–641*, MGH Conc. aevi Merovingici [511–695], ed. F. Maassen (Hanover, 1893), pp. 207–8.
16. On this, see now S. Esders, 'The Prophesied Rule of a "Circumcised People": a Travelling Tradition from the Seventh-Century Mediterranean", in Y. Hen, O. Limor and T. Noble, eds, *Barbarians and Jews: Jews and Judaism in the Early Medieval West* (Turnhout, forthcoming).
17. E. Vacandard, *Vie de Saint Ouen, évêque de Rouen (641–684)* (Paris, 1902), p. 75; For a 639 departure date, see A. Dierkens, 'Prolégomènes à une histoire des relations culturelles entre les îles britanniques et le continent pendant le haut-moyen âge', in *La Neustrie: le pays au nord de la Loire e 650 à 850*, ed. H. Atsma, 2 vols. (Sigmaringen, 1989), II, pp. 371–94, at pp. 380–1.
18. *Passio Salvii*, c. 12, AASS Iun. 5 (Antwerp, 1709), pp. 196–204, at p. 202.
19. J. Kreiner, *The Social Life of Hagiography in the Merovingian Kingdom* (Cambridge, 2014), p. 269.
20. *Vita Sigiramni*, c. 5, p. 669.
21. J.M. Pardessus, ed., *Diplomata, chartae, epistolae et alia documenta ad res Francicas spectantia*, 2 vols. (Paris, 1843–9), II, p. 239 (no. 438): 'Maciriolas cellula super amnem Vingenam, quam desertam absque cultoribus uel officium redditum inueni, quam postea restaurare et reintegrare fecimus, in qua sanctum Dei peregrinum ex genere Scottorum, nomen Romanum, episcopum, cum suis peregrinis, constitui rectorem et institueram ut ipsi peregrini inibidem perseuerarent'.
22. J. Tardiff, 'Les chartes mérovingiennes de Noirmoutier', *Nouvelle Revue Historique du droit français et étranger* 22 (1898), pp. 763–90, at pp. 786–7.
23. E. James, 'Ireland and Western Gaul in the Merovingian Period', in D. Whitelock, R. McKitterick, and D.N. Dumville, eds, *Ireland in Early Mediaeval Europe: Studies in Memory of Kathleen Hughes* (Cambridge, 1982), pp. 362–86, at p. 379.
24. *Concilium Burdegalense, a.663–675*, MGH Conc. 1, ed. F. Maassen (Hanover, 1893), pp. 215–16, at p. 216: 'Tomianus Aequilesiminus urbis episcopus'; L. Duchesne, *Fastes épiscopaux de l'ancienne Gaule*, 3 vols. (Paris, 1907–15), II, pp. 70–1; S. Kumaoka, 'Autour des évêques de Poitiers au VIIe siècle', *Bulletin de la société des antiquaires de l'ouest et des musées de Poitiers* XII (1998), pp. 185–222, at p. 216.

25. G. Puybaudet, 'Une liste épiscopale d'Angoulême', *Mélanges d'archéologie et d'histoire* 17 (1897), pp. 279–84, at pp. 281–2.
26. Duchesne, *Fastes épiscopaux,* vol., II, p. 70. The *Gallia Christiana* skips over Tomianus entirely. See *Gallia Christiana* vol. 2, p. 982.
27. James, 'Ireland and Western Gaul', p. 378.
28. I.N. Wood, 'The Irish in England and on the Continent in the Seventh Century', The O'Donnell Lectures, Faculty of English, Oxford, 10–11 May 2012, unpublished manuscript, II, pp. 25–6. My thanks to Ian Wood for allowing me an early look at these lectures.
29. On the mechanics of episcopal election, see J. Kreiner, 'About the Bishop: the Episcopal Entourage and the Economy of Government in Post-Roman Gaul', *Speculum* 86 (2011), pp. 321–60, esp. pp. 350–3; B. Dumézil, 'La royauté mérovingienne et les élections épiscopales au VIᵉ siècle', in J. Leemans et al., eds, *Episcopal Elections in Late Antiquity* (Berlin, 2011), pp. 127–44; J. Maxwell, 'Education, Humility and Choosing Ideal Bishops in Late Antiquity', ibid., pp. 449–62. For a more general perspective, C. Rapp, 'The Elite Status of Bishops in Late Antiquity in Ecclesiastical, Spiritual, and Social Contexts', *Arethusa* 33 (2000), pp. 379–99.
30. Bede, *HE*, III.25: 'Erat in his acerrimus ueri paschae defensor nomine Ronan, natione quidem Scottus, sed in Galliae uel Italiae partibus regulam ecclesiasticae ueritatis edoctus'; Tardif, 'Chartes mérovingiennes', p. 775.
31. Wood, 'The Irish in England and on the Continent', II, p. 25 n. 124.
32. J. Mabillon, ed., *Annales ordinis sancti Benedicti* (Paris, 1703), I, p. 474. See also L. Levillain, 'Les origines du monastère de-Nouaillé', *Bibliothèque de l'École des chartes* 71 (1910), pp. 241–98, at pp. 246–7 n. 5.
33. D. Farmer, *The Oxford Dictionary of Saints* (Oxford, 1978), p. 384.
34. *Vita sancti Ronani*, BHL 7336; J.M.H. Smith, 'Oral and Written: Saints, Miracles, and Relics in Brittany, *c.* 850–1250', *Speculum* 65 (1990), pp. 309–43, at p. 330.
35. Bede, *HE,* III.25: 'Observabat et regina Eanfled cum suis, iuxta quod in Cantia fieri uiderat, habens secum de Cantia presbyterum catholicae obseruationis, nomine Romanum'; R.W. Pfaff, 'The Calendar', in *The Eadwine Psalter: Text, Image, and Monastic Culture in Twelfth-Century Canterbury*, ed. M.T. Gibson, T. A. Heslop, and R.W. Pfaff (London, 1992), p. 74; R. Rushforth, *Saints in English Calendars before A.D. 1100*, Henry Bradshaw Society vol. CXVII (London, 2008), Nov. 18.
36. Wood, 'The Irish in England and on the Continent', II, p. 26.
37. Pardessus, Diplomata, vol. 2, p. 239 n. 1.
38. If Chagneric's father is correctly identified as Gundoald, *comes* of Meaux, it then becomes very likely that the family was related to Burgundofaro's predecessor, another Gundoald. On this, see Y. Fox, *Power and Religion in Merovingian Gaul: Columbanian Monasticism and the Frankish Elites* (Cambridge, 2014), pp. 66–7.

39. On this family and their monastic establishments, see Fox, *Power and Religion in Merovingian Gaul*, pp. 65–81.

40. J. Dubois, 'Un pèlerinage au XIIe siècle, le monastère de Saint-Fiacre-en-Brie', *École pratique des hautes études*, 4e section, Sciences historiques et philologiques, Annuaire 1972–1973 (1973), pp. 767–71, at pp. 767–8.

41. Balderic, *Vita Fridolini confessoris Seckingensis*, cc. 9–10, MGH SS rer. Merov. 3, ed. B. Krusch (Hanover, 1896), pp. 351–69, at p. 359.

42. Prinz, *Frühes Mönchtum*, p. 79; Bieler, *Wegbereiter des Mittelalters*, p. 102.

43. M. Koch, *Sankt Fridolin und sein Biograph Balther: Irische Heilige in der literarischen Darstellung des Mittelalters* (Zurich, 1959), p. 112–28.

44. Balderic, *Vita Fridolini*, c. 10, p. 359: 'Ille econtra respondens, dixit, se nichil seu de restauratione ecclesie siue de sacratissimi translatione corporis facturum absque consultu licentiaque pontificis atque regis adiutorio, scilicet Clodouei, qui tunc temporis longe lateque imperialem obtinebat potestatem'; see also the reviews on Koch's thesis in H. Büttner, 'Sankt Fridolin und sein Biograph Balther. Irische Heilige in der literarischen Darstellung des Mittelalters [Margrit Koch]', *Schweizerische Zeitschrift für Geschichte* 10 (1960), 101–2; M.L. Colker, 'Margrit Koch, Sankt Fridolin und sein Biograph Balther: Irische Heilige in der litterarischen Darstellung des Mittelalters', *Speculum* 35 (1960), pp. 468–9.

45. Prinz, *Frühes Mönchtum*, p. 79.

46. Duchesne, *Fastes épiscopaux*, II, p. 84.

47. I.N. Wood, *The Merovingian Kingdoms, 450–751* (London, 1994), p. 236. For the complicated decision to include Poitiers and other Aquitanian *civitates* in the Neustro-Burgundian *teilreich*, see H. Ebling, *Prosopographie der Amtsträger des Merowingerreiches von Chlothar II. (613) bis Karl Martell (741)*, Beihefte der Francia 2 (Munich, 1974), pp. 71–3, 156; and E. Ewig, 'Das Privileg des Bischofs Berthefrid von Amiens (664) und die Klosterpolitik der Königin Balthild', *Francia* 1 (1973), 62–114, at 111 n. 93.

48. See Jaffé's appendix to T. Mommsen, 'Die Chronik des Cassiodorus Senator', *Abhandlungen der philologisch-historischen Classe der königlich sächsischen Gesellschaft der Wissenschaften* 3 (1861), pp. 684–9, at p. 685.

49. *Vita Wandregiseli abbatis Fontanellensis*, c. 9, MGH SS rer. Merov. 5, ed. B. Krusch (Hanover, 1910), pp. 1–24, at pp. 17–18: 'Remotiore loco uolebat inhabitare et arta et angusta uia presidere. Disposuit in Scoccia ambulare'.

50. See L.K. Little, *Benedictine Maledictions: Liturgical Cursing in Romanesque France* (Ithaca NY, 1993), p. 179.

51. Dubois, 'Pèlerinage', p. 768.

52. As does the implied identification of Pipimisium or Pinnevidum as Aubigny, where Faro's wife, Blidechild, supposedly retired. See Hildegar of Meaux, *Vita Sancti Faronis episcopi Meldensis*, c. 106, AASS OSB saec. II, ed. J. Mabillon (Paris, 1669), pp. 606–25, at p. 620;

M. Toussaints du Plessis, *Histoire de l'église de Meaux: avec des notes ou dissertations et les pieces justificatives* (Paris, 1731), I, p. 653.
53. On this, see A. O'Hara, 'Constructing a Saint: the Legend of St Sunniva in Twelfth-Century Norway', *Viking and Medieval Scandinavia* 5 (2009), pp. 105–21.
54. Jonas, *Vita Columbani,* II.21, p. 277.
55. *Vitae Amati,* c. 1, MGH SS rer. Merov. 4, ed. B. Krusch (Hanover, 1902), pp. 215–21, at p. 215; for this identification, see I.N. Wood, 'The Vita Columbani and Merovingian Hagiography', *Peritia* 1 (1982), pp. 63–80, at p. 70.
56. Prinz, *Frühes Mönchtum*, p. 300.
57. *Vita Richarii*, c. 7, p. 448; Wood, *The Merovingian Kingdoms*, p. 170.
58. On this connection, see Y. Fox, '*Ego, Bar-iona*: Jews and the Changing Discourse of Forced Conversion in Columbanian Circles', in *Barbarians and Jews: Jews and Judaism in the Early Medieval West*, ed. Y. Hen, O. Limor, and T.F.X. Noble (Turnhout, forthcoming).
59. P.J. Fouracre and R.A. Gerberding, *Late Merovingian France: History and Hagiography, 640–720* (Manchester, 1996), p. 134.
60. Alcuin, *Vita Richarii confessoris Centulensis*, cc. 2, 8, MGH SS rer. Merov. 4, ed. B. Krusch (Hanover, 1902), pp. 381–401, at pp. 390–1, 393; Wood, *The Merovingian Kingdoms*, pp. 314–15; for Richarius's importance to the Carolingian family, see *Annales regni Francorum* s.a. 800, MGH SS rer. Germ. 6, ed. F. Kurze (Hanover, 1895), pp. 110–11; *Annales Laureshamenses* s.a. 800, MGH SS 1, ed. G. Pertz (Hanover, 1826), p. 38; J. Nelson, 'Opposition to Pilgrimage in the Reign of Charlemagne?', in *Rome and Religion in the Medieval World: Studies in Honor of Thomas F.X. Noble*, ed. V.L. Garver and O.M. Phelan (Farnham and Burlington, VT, 2014), pp. 65–82, at p. 69; E. H. Kantorowicz, *Laudes regiae: A Study in Liturgical Acclamations and Mediaeval Ruler Worship* (Berkeley, 1946), p. 36.
61. See Krusch's introduction to the *Vita Vedastis episcopi Atrebatensis*, MGH SS rer. Germ. 37, ed. B. Krusch (Hanover, 1910), pp. 295–320, at pp. 295–308; *pace* A.M. Helvétius, 'Clercs ou moines? Les origines de Saint-Vaast d'Arras et la *Vita Vedastis* attribuée à Jonas', *Revue du Nord* 391/2 (2011), pp. 671–89.
62. Alcuin, *Carmen XC*, MGH Poetae I, ed. E. Dümmler (Berin, 1881), p. 314: 'Salvius hanc aram, magnus quoque sanctus Amandus / Amplectuntur enim mentibus ambos piis…'.
63. On this, and especially on Salvius of Valenciennes, see Kreiner, *The Social Life of Hagiography*, pp. 260–72.

4

Columbanian Monastic Rules: Dissent and Experiment[1]

Albrecht Diem

Ardo-Smaragdus reports in his *Vita Benedicti Anianensis* how the Carolingian monastic reformer Benedict of Aniane (d. 821) produced a collection of all monastic rules he could find. Benedict did this as part of his endeavor to gain the best possible understanding of the *Regula Benedicti*. Without Benedict of Aniane's efforts, all monastic rules that had been written in the aftermath of Columbanus's arrival on the Continent would have been lost.

This chapter provides an overview of the 'Columbanian' monastic rules that appear in Benedict of Aniane's collection: Columbanus's own rule, the *Regula cuiusdam patris*, the *Regula cuiusdam ad uirgines*, the rule compiled by bishop Donatus of Besançon (d. after 558), and two short rule-fragments that appear at the end of Benedict of Aniane's collection. These texts show how Columbanus's monastic ideals gained currency and were transformed in the Frankish world, but also how contested his legacy was.[2] All the 'Columbanian' rules written after Columbanus's death need to be understood as a response to the original *Regula Columbani*. These responses range from simply changing its grammatical gender, through careful revisions of the text, adaptations and combinations with other rules. Some of them were fierce criticism of Columbanus's monastic ideals as they manifest themselves in his rule and – slightly differently – in Jonas of Bobbio's *Vita Columbani*.

The *Regula Columbani*

It is hard to imagine that the text that Benedict of Aniane inserted into his *Codex regularum* as *Regula Sancti Columbani* represents the program for the monasteries Columbanus had founded himself and for those founded *ex regula Columbani* after his death. The rule lacks all the practical regulations – on the structure of the community, entering the monastery, space and boundaries, interaction with outsiders and guests, and so forth – that one finds in other rules, particularly in the *Regula Benedicti*. Moreover, there are very few connections between this *Regula Columbani* and Columbanian monastic life as it is described in Jonas of Bobbio's *Vita Columbani*. We have to assume that Jonas's notion of the *Regula Columbani* involved much more than just this text – or that the world envisioned by Jonas of Bobbio was no longer the world for which the original *Regula Columbani* was written.[3]

The *Regula Columbani* consists of two parts that are so different that they have been edited as two separate rules.[4] The *Regula monachorum* is a short treatise that begins with chapters on some monastic virtues and vices, followed by a liturgical *ordo* and three chapters on *discretio, mortificatio* and *perfectio*. The text could be read as a guide to how a monk should pursue perfection by submitting himself to communal discipline rather than by performing radical individual asceticism. Obedience to any superior needs to be spontaneous and unconditional *usque ad mortem* 'unto death'; silence is understood as the avoidance of idle chatter and evil speaking; fasting means moderate eating and avoiding satiety and excess; poverty is renunciation of the world and overcoming desire for material things; chastity is the endeavour to become *uirgo mentis* 'virgin of the mind'; *discretio* implies avoiding excess and discerning between good and evil; *mortificatio* is the mortification of the will through submission and humility rather than bodily mortification; and *perfectio* is attained by living in a community under the discipline of the father of the monastery.

There is one fundamental difference between the *Regula Benedicti* and Columbanus's *Regula monachorum*. For Columbanus, intercessory prayer is an integral aspect of monastic liturgy:

> ... first for our own sins, then for all Christian people, then for priests and the other orders of the holy flock that are consecrated to God, finally for those that do alms, next for the concord of kings, lastly for our enemies, that God reckon it not to them for sin that they persecute and slander us, since they know not what they do.[5]

More than the first part of the *Regula Columbani*, the second part, which is edited as *Regula coenobialis*, has certain elements we might consider 'Irish' or 'insular'. It shares many features with insular penitential handbooks, although it focuses exclusively on monks and mostly on transgressions within the monastery. With its long lists of bodily punishments for seemingly minute transgressions (for example, six blows for coughing while chanting) the *Regula coenobialis* has contributed to the reputation of a harsh or even cruel 'Irish' monastic discipline. All its flogging and whipping might cause us to overlook three remarkable aspects of this text that had a strong impact on the future development of western monasticism but also caused differing responses in later Columbanian monastic rules.

(1) The *Regula coenobialis* begins by making a twice-daily ritual of confession as part of the monastic routine along with a bold theological statement: *confessio*, combined with penance, has an effect on eternal salvation:

> 'It has been ordained, my dearest brothers, by the holy fathers that we give confession before the meal and before going to bed, or whenever it is convenient, because confession and penance free from death. Therefore even small things are not to be neglected at confession, because it is written: "He who neglects small things gradually flows downwards" (Ecclesiasticus 19:1).'[6]

The *Regula Benedicti* and the *Regula magistri* describe confession of evil thoughts as the fifth step of humility, but there is no indication that it was to be performed in any regular or ritualized form.[7] The origins of a ritualized confession as part of the monastic routine probably lie in the insular world. We find confessional practices mentioned in several (albeit mostly later) Irish monastic rules. None of them, however, states that confession itself contributes to attaining salvation.[8]

The connection between confession and penance, as well as the integration of confession into general pastoral practice, have, despite a strong interest in penitential handbooks and the practice of penance, barely been investigated. *Confessio*, as it is generally assumed, was always *somehow* part of the practice of penance.[9] Insular and continental penitential handbooks provide remarkably little information about confession in a monastic or pastoral context. Only two of them imply that a priest was involved in confession;[10] some integrate *confessio* in a very general sense into a twelve-step program for gaining salvation that shows great similarity to that of the *Regula Benedicti*;[11] others indicate that *confessio* can simply be understood as *admitting* a transgression[12] or as just one way (among others) in which a sin could come to light.[13] This either implies that *confessio* was indeed such an integral part of penitential practice and pastoral care that it was not worth being explicitly mentioned or – and I consider this more likely – that Columbanus's notion of a regular and ritualized confession, and his idea that confession itself had salutary effect, represented an innovation, and that confessional rituals as part of lay pastoral and penitential practices were a much later development.[14]

Most of the remainder of the *Regula coenobialis* is a long list of transgressions and their precisely determined penances, which includes prayers, floggings and whippings, different degrees of fasting and various periods of penance. These tariffed penances are strangely detached from the requirement of regular confession. It is therefore unclear whether they actually belonged to the confession ritual and whether a voluntary confession had any impact on the severity of penance.

(2) Looking at the list of transgressions, we can detect another remarkable feature of the *Regula coenobialis*. The text is preserved in two different versions, a vaguely coherent shorter version and a long version with rather chaotic extensions, which may have been added at a later stage in response to specific incidents. If we ignore the extensions, the *Regula coenobialis* boils down to two main sets of transgressions: the first are accidents or involuntary acts that may have an impact on monastic rituals, purity and the liturgical conduct of the community, including, for example, forgetting to say 'amen' after grace (six blows), accidentally touching the chalice with one's teeth (six blows), spitting in the church or touching the altar (24 psalms), and, as the worst possible incident, losing the host (one year of penance). One could call these transgressions unprofessional monastic behaviour rather than consciously performed sinful acts. The second set consists of transgressions that have an impact on the social conduct of the community, such as slander, murmuring, disobedience and so on. The *Regula coenobialis* may look like a monastic *Liber paenitentialis,* but it is in fact a handbook which uses tariffed penance as a disciplinary tool for keeping a monastery functioning on a social level and maintaining standards of proper ritual.

(3) The use of tariffed penance itself is the third remarkable aspect of the *Regula coenobialis*. No other continental monastic rule (except the *Regula Donati,* which will be discussed below) determines penance in such a way, although some Irish rules do.[15] Most continental rules stress that punishment has to be determined at the discretion of the abbot or abbess based on specific circumstances, motivation, and willingness to repent.

These aspects in particular – the practice and purpose of confession, the emphasis on ritual and purity, and the rigid tariff-based penitential system – became matters of intense debates within Columbanian monasticism.

The *Regula cuiusdam patris*

The *Regula cuiusdam patris* has not figured in research on Columbanus's legacy, even though it was probably written not long after Columbanus's death and certainly by someone who engaged with

Columbanus's ideas.[16] The text contains numerous traces of both parts of the *Regula Columbani*, but no allusions to the *Regula Benedicti*, which began to spread among Columbanian monasteries less than a generation after Columbanus's death.[17] The first thing that attracts the reader's attention is the number of regulations that impose the sanction of imprisonment or expulsion, two forms of punishment that are applied rarely in other monastic rules.

Lucas Holstenius, who was the first editor of the *Regula cuiusdam patris* in 1661, divided the original text, which lacked any division, into 32 chapters. His division has very much determined the way in which the rule has been read (or rather misread) since.[18] Fernando Villegas produced a critical edition of the *Regula cuiusdam patris* and identified most of the sources that the author quoted or paraphrased, which include extracts from Rufinus's Latin version of the *Regula Basilii*, John Cassian's works, Columbanus's rule, a sermon of Augustine and one allusion to the *Sententiae* of Evagrius Ponticus.[19]

If we disregard the modern chapter divisions, we can instead roughly divide the original text into four thematic blocks. The first addresses behaviour that disrupts the monastic community (disobedience, murmuring, recalcitrance, lying, anger and slander), the second addresses ideals and standards of monastic life (abstinence, manual work, poverty, renunciation of the world, silence, chastity and avoiding greed), the third part discusses the relationship between the brethren and their superiors as well as the latter's responsibilities, and the last part addresses liturgy, liturgical discipline, and the Eucharist.

The *Regula cuiusdam patris* is *not* merely a 'regula mixta' assembled from older monastic texts. Most of it is original, albeit phrased with words and expressions from other sources. Only one of its sources is used in a nearly complete form: the first chapter of Columbanus's *Regula monachorum*, which demands spontaneous, earnest and unquestioning *oboedientia usque ad mortem* towards the superior and condemns every form of hesitation, *murmuratio* or discontent. The author of the *Regula cuiusdam patris* divided Columbanus's chapter on obedience into several fragments that appear in revised order at several different places of the *Regula cuiusdam patris*, and are juxtaposed, expanded, and explained by sections from other monastic authorities, particularly from Cassian's work and the *Regula Basillii*.[20]

One could read the *Regula cuiusdam patris* at least partly as a treatise on the nature of *oboedientia*, critically responding to Columbanus's rule. Very much in line with what Eoin de Bhaldraithe describes as a distinctive Irish approach to obedience,[21] the author of the *Regula cuiusdam patris* deviates from the notion of obedience as a slavish execution of orders and emphasizes that obedience means above all fulfilling the *mandata Dei* (God's commandments). For the author of the *Regula cuiusdam patris* obedience is a monastic virtue and a goal to strive for according to one's capabilities.[22] *Oboedientia* includes a 'horizontal' obedience expressed in the act of serving and loving one another.[23] Moreover, the *Regula cuiusdam patris* strongly emphasizes and details the responsibilities of the superiors and the abbot. They have to partake in this obedience by imposing on their monks only the standards they are willing to follow themselves, by taking care of the physical and spiritual needs of their monks and by acting out of undivided and equal love rather than out of anger. Only a superior who fulfils these criteria may demand the full, unquestioning, spontaneous and joyful obedience that Columbanus expected from his monks. A superior who falls short may be deposed, excommunicated and abandoned. He will burn in hell as a murderer of souls.[24]

All in all, the *Regula cuiusdam patris* develops a notion of *obedientia* and discipline that is not only distinct from that of Columbanus but also far more sophisticated. It may be equally harsh – or maybe even harsher – but it is also far more 'democratic' and cautious with regard to abbatial authority.

One of the reasons for the traditional disinterest in the *Regula cuiusdam patris* is that the rule is far from edifying. Its author seems to have been a very angry person who vigorously expressed a dissenting voice, addressing communities that were disrupted by conflicts, ruled by incompetent seniors and endangered by the corruption of ascetic standards. The rule begins with a vigorous statement against those who submit the *scripturae sanctae* to their understanding (*sensus*) of the rule instead of having their understanding determined by the *scripturae*:

> A good reader should take heed that he does not submit the scriptures to his understanding, but that he submits his understanding to the holy scriptures.[25]

Subsequently, the author of the *Regula cuiusdam patris* elaborates on his own set of biblical quotations and monastic authorities to support *his* interpretation of what may have been Columbanus's original ideas – presumably against the understandings of other followers of Columbanus. It is a document of a battle over monastic ideals and practices in which monks, superiors and abbots may have been found on the right and on the wrong side; they could be expelled but also legitimately leave the community.[26]

Jonas of Bobbio describes several severe conflicts that disrupted Bobbio, Luxeuil and its affiliations after Columbanus's death. When the monk Athala succeeded Columbanus as abbot of Bobbio, some of his monks rose up against him, allegedly because of his ascetic strictness. They left the monastery – not in order to return to the world but to establish a number of communities elsewhere.[27] The monk Agrestius, the main antagonist of Columbanus's successor Eusthasius, also left the monastery and for some time may have gained control over several filiations of Luxeuil.[28] Jonas describes him as a rancorous troublemaker and as a heretic who dared to attack the *Regula Columbani* on such trivialities as making the sign of a cross over a spoon or demanding a blessing when entering or leaving a building of the monastery, which are topics that are indeed addressed in the *Regula coenobialis*.[29]

There are good reasons to relate the *Regula cuiusdam patris* to the conflicts described in Jonas's *Vita Columbani*, and maybe even to Agrestius himself. Some parts of the *Regula cuiusdam patris* can indeed be read as a rejection of certain aspects of Columbanus's rule; others go fundamentally against practices of Luxeuil and its abbots, as they were described and idealized by Jonas of Bobbio, and some could even be related to Agrestius's specific grievances as they were reported by Jonas, albeit in an undoubtedly distorted form.

(1) Different notions of *oboedientia* are not the only deviation from the *Regula Columbani*. Most of the chapters of the *Regula cuiusdam patris* that deal with social transgressions (such as disobedience, disagreement, lying, idle talk, anger and slander) use phrases from Columbanus's *Regula coenobialis* but replace its tariffed penance with imprisonment, a penance given at the discretion of the superior and eventually expulsion.[30] This could be understood as a criticism of a tariffed and mechanical understanding of the *medicamenta paenitentiae*.

Along the same line, but even more fundamental, is another striking difference between the two rules: the *Regula cuiusdam patris* begins by stating that 'the remedy for all disease (of sin) is the bitter chalice of suffering'[31] and ends with stating that the only way of receiving forgiveness for sins is the Eucharist:

> On Sundays one always has to receive the Eucharist as a remedy for sins. But we have to approach the body and blood of our Lord Jesus Christ with all holiness of the heart and the body. Amen.[32]

The question of whether a monk may gain healing through *confessio* and *paenitentia*, as the *Regula coenobialis* proposes, or through the *calix passionis* and through the Eucharist, is certainly not a trivial matter.

(2) The *Regula cuiusdam patris* contains also a number of practical regulations that cannot be tied to the *Regula Columbani* and strongly clash with the description of Columbanian monastic life as it appears in Jonas of Bobbio's *Vita Columbani* and other sources. The text vigorously demands that monks work to sustain themselve and live a life in austerity, a requirement that can be found in several Irish monastic rules as well. They may not own more than what is necessary to feed and clothe themselves and they should give all surplus to the poor. Moreover, the rule attacks corrupted superiors and abbots, who do not follow the standards they impose on others, who do not care of their communities, get entangled in secular matters, and make up their own rules. Monks (implicitly, superiors as well) are strongly discouraged from interacting with female communities, which, on the other hand, have to count on the material support of their brothers, so as not to depend on the outside world.[33]

The Columbanian world as we know it looks different from the one envisioned by the author of the *Regula cuiusdam patris*. Luxeuil's affiliations – male and female alike – were built and endowed by kings, queens, aristocrats and bishops; the monasteries received gifts in exchange for prayer, gained considerable wealth and were keen on protecting it from the greedy hands of any outsider. At least some of them adopted the uninterrupted liturgy of Saint-Maurice d'Agaune (called *laus perennis* by modern historians), which would have made it difficult to sustain themselves through manual work.[34] All Columbanian monasteries belonged to aristo-cratic networks and many of them became hotspots of political power.[35] Clearly none of them could have followed the *Regula cuiusdam patris*.

Many of the criticisms of wrongful abbatial behaviour in the *Regula cuiusdam patris* could easily be applied to Columbanus's successors Eusthasius and Waldebert. Both acted as tireless negotia-tors with kings and the powerful, were constantly on the road, and used Luxeuil merely as their headquarters rather than to fulfil their abbatial duties at their home monastery. Both were deeply involved with Faremoutiers and other female Columbanian communities and spent significant amount of time in the company of their inhabitants.[36]

(3) Finally, there might also be a connection between the content of the *Regula cuiusdam patris* and the criticism uttered by Agrestius himself. Jonas mentions that Agrestius objected to liturgical pomp:

> And he burst out that he knew that Columbanus diverted from the customs of the others and celebrated Mass with an inflation of prayers and collects and that many other superfluous things needed to be condemned along with [their] originator like heresies which were handed down.[37]

A comparison of the liturgical *ordo* laid out in Columbanus' *Regula monachorum* with the section on liturgy in the *Regula cuiusdam patris* shows that its author did indeed significantly cut back on the number of psalms, stating that twelve psalms were to be sung at each nightly Hour, but not at the one Hour at dawn when Mass was to be sung.[38] Columbanus's *Regula* requires that, depending on the length of the night *at least* twelve psalms needed to be sung; certainly twenty-four should be sung at Matins and thirty-six on Saturday and Sunday, which implies that Mass was indeed accompanied by an overwhelming number of psalms.[39]

Did Agrestius perhaps write the *Regula cuiusdam patris*? It is possible that he produced it as a reform manifesto when he had taken control over some of the Columbanian communities. Agrestius was, as Jonas reports, a Burgundian nobleman, who gave away all his possessions when entering Luxeuil. Even Jonas did not deny that Agrestius had become a monk with the right intentions and that he remained a monk until his miserable end. Bruno Dumézil argues that Agrestius imitated Columbanus in his acts, his theological viewpoints (for example, on the Three Chapter Debate) and in his stubbornness,[40] and it is likely that Agrestius did not attack Columbanus, but rather those who monopolized his legacy. Maybe Agrestius, who was denied his own *peregrinatio*,[41] was simply disappointed that Luxeuil had given up so many of its original monastic practices when gaining the protection of the new Frankish rulers Clothar II and Dagobert. If the author of the *Regula cuiusdam patris* was not Agrestius who embodied resistance against Columbanian monasticism in Jonas's *Vita Columbani*, it was certainly someone with similar ideas – maybe one of the monks who supported him, such as Amatus or Romaric, the founder of Remiremont.

To what extent the *Regula cuiusdam patris* can be understood as a call to return to insular monastic roots is yet to be determined and would require a much more systematic comparison with insular monastic texts. Its author was certainly familiar with the language of at least some of these texts. The work contains a number of references to practices we find there as well, including comparatively trivial aspects such as the prohibition on travelling in carts and on horses,[42] and the expression *examinatio carceris*,[43] but also theological ideas such as the combination of love *and* fear of God[44] and the practice of addressing God directly when asking for forgiveness (*ueniam a Deo petere*).[45]

The *Regula cuiusdam ad uirgines*

The *Regula cuiusdam ad uirgines* marks, together with the *Regula Donati* (discussed below), the moment when the text of the *Regula Benedicti* had entered Columbanian monastic discourse.[46] The *Regula cuiusdam ad uirgines* consists of twenty-four chapters (most of them of substantial length) and may have been written as an extension of an already existing rule, possibly Caesarius' *Regula ad uirgines*.[47]

About two-thirds of the text paraphrase the *Regula Benedicti*, but those chapters that make programmatic and theological statements and reflect on the nature of monastic discipline are phrased without identifiable model. There are strong indications that Jonas of Bobbio was involved in its creation. The rule contains more than a hundred similarities in ideas and wording to Jonas of Bobbio's *Vita Columbani*.[48] Many parallels in phrasing appear exclusively in these texts. Particularly the stories Jonas tells in his *Vita Columbani* about the lives and deaths of nuns in Faremoutiers convey in many regards the same ideas as the *Regula cuiusdam ad uirgines*.

The fact that the rule bears the title *Regula cuiusdam ad uirgines* (not *Regula cuiusdam patris ad uirgines*, as it was called in the first edition and ever since) shows that Benedict of Aniane saw the possibility that the author of a female monastic rule may have been a nun or abbess. My tentative ascription to Jonas of Bobbio does not dismiss this possibility. We should assume that the rule was produced in collaboration or at least consultation with the abbess who commissioned the text.

The rule has four core themes: love, motivation, confession and control, and the constant danger of damnation. These themes are ingeniously woven into almost every chapter. With these themes as cornerstones, the author develops, among all monastic rules, the most radical concept of a perfect monastic institution and form of monastic discipline that overcomes human weakness and brings about eternal salvation.

Chapter 5 of the rule provides the theological basis of the rule's concept of love. Every act performed in the monastery – be it an order or a punishment by a superior, a service rendered by an office holder, an interaction between nuns, or a prayer on behalf of others – must be an act of *affectus*, *amor*, *caritas*, *dilectio* and *pietas*. The imperative of love replaces other frameworks of discipline such as obedience, humility and *mortificatio* as we find them in the *Regula Columbani* and in the *Regula Benedicti*. This does not, however, mean that the *Regula cuiusdam ad uirgines* should be considered a more lenient rule than the others. It demands a love that has to determine every act and thought and deploys itself in a system of total control and surveillance that does not allow any physical or mental escape.

A second key theme of the *Regula cuiusdam ad uirgines* is the concern about motivation and the danger of *negligentia*. Motivational terms are spread over the entire *Regula cuiusdam ad uirgines* to the same extent as the terminology of love.[49] The rule establishes an elaborate system of fostering, controlling and disciplining the correct attitude of each member of the community, as it expresses itself in the movement of the body, in the sound of the voice and in the care given to one's work. The rule's objective is thus not simply to control outward behaviour, but to discipline the unreachable inner self: one's thoughts, motivations, dreams and desires that might *lead to* attitudes and actions. Therefore every member of the community is compelled to reveal her entire inner life at least three times a day in a ritual of secret confession:

> Whatever the mind or flesh commits through frailty during the dark time of the night after Compline must be healed through confession after the Second Hour in order to be atoned. But whatever she has committed out of tepidity by deed, look, hearing or thought at daytime, has to be judged at the Ninth Hour after the service is carried out so that she be cleansed. But whatever stain the mind contracts later, after the Ninth Hour, ought to be confessed before Compline.[50]

With this confession ritual, which is extensively explained and theologically underpinned in the first part of Chapter 6, the author expands upon the rule of confession in the *Regula coenobialis*. Confessing one's deeds, as the *Regula coenobialis* demands, is far from sufficient. The truly important things happen inside the mind.

This watertight system of control, motivation, love and confession responds to the awareness of mortal sinfulness that looms inside, beyond outward action, and can only be cured and controlled in a communal effort. As the *Regula cuiusdam ad uirgines* stresses time and again, everything a nun feels or does is a matter of life and death, of eternal reward or everlasting punishment, not only for the individual but also for the entire community. This community, however, plays a crucial role in enabling each individual nun to attain salvation through its prayer and its impartial love. In that sense, the *Regula cuiusdam ad uirgines* is the most coenobitical of all rules. It is astounding how the *Regula cuiusdam ad uirgines* develops this extremely elaborate and radical notion of discipline and community despite the fact that it, to a large extent, merely paraphrases the *Regula Benedicti*.

The *Regula Donati*

The other complete female monastic rule to emerge from the Columbanian world was compiled by Donatus, a former monk of Luxeuil, who became bishop of Besançon.[51] It is an anthology that quotes verbatim large sections from the *Regula Benedicti* (which constitutes roughly forty per cent of the text), Caesarius's *Regula ad uirgines* (roughly thirty per cent) and the *Regula Columbani* (roughly twenty per cent; mostly from the *Regula coenobialis*). The text is divided into seventy-seven chapters and is about half as long as the *Regula Benedicti*, although it is a complete monastic rule tackling all the aspects of monastic life which one would expect of a monastic rule.

Donatus states in his dedication letter that existing rules, despite their great authority, were unsuitable for a number of reasons: the rules of Benedict and Columbanus were written for monks whereas Caesarius's *Regula ad uirgines* was written for a different kind of monastic space (*ob inmutationem loci*), which may be a reference to Caesarius's notion of total enclosure.

It is not clear which of the two rules – the *Regula cuiusdam ad uirgines* or the *Regula Donati* – comes first, but it is likely that both authors held different viewpoints on the role the *Regula Benedicti* should play within their respective monasteries. Such differing viewpoints can also be inferred from other sources related to Columbanian monasticism. Already in the 630s the first episcopal charters issued for Columbanian monasteries consistently refer to a *Regula Benedicti et Columbani* as legal basis for their monasteries.[52] Jonas of Bobbio's *Vita Columbani*, which was written years later, entirely ignores the *Regula Benedicti*. Even in the context of monasteries that already had received episcopal privileges, Jonas mentions only the *Regula Columbani*.

Both the *Regula cuiusdam ad uirgines* and the *Regula Donati* engage with the *Regula Benedicti*, although in very different ways: the author of the *Regula cuiusdam ad uirgines* (thus probably Jonas) does not mention the name Benedict. He thoroughly rewrites the text, and submits its practical regulations to his own monastic ideals. Donatus acknowledges Benedict's authority and not only quotes a large part of the practical regulations of the *Regula Benedicti* but also inserts into his rule most of the theological core of the *Regula Benedicti*, consisting of Chapter 4, on the instruments of good work, Chapter 5, on obedience, and most of Chapter 7, on *humilitas*.

Donatus's fidelity to his sources does not, however, mean that he did not develop his own monastic program. He discreetly mitigated the strictness of Caesarius's and Benedict's rules in many aspects of everyday monastic life, whether it was with regard to enclosure, private possessions, manual labour, fasting or vigils.[53] This mitigation of strictness was probably intended to make his monastery more suitable to his aristocratic constituency. However, he also inserted a large part of Columbanus's tariffed penances and introduced to his rule the notion that a nun can be held in a formal state of penance. Additionally, Donatus introduced the Irish practice of linking prayers with a large number of genuflections.[54]

There is, however, one crucial innovation that the *Regula Donati* shares with the *Regula cuiusdam ad uirgines*. Donatus, in one of the few sections he may have written himself, stipulates that confession be made not only for deeds, but also for words, thoughts and dreams. He further requires three confessions per day, just as the *Regula cuiusdam ad uirgines* does, and leaves no doubt that this is a matter of the greatest urgency:

> Aside from all the other observances of the rule, above all else we admonish both the junior and the senior sisters that they persistently and in ceaseless zeal at every day, every hour and any moment always make confession of [their] thoughts, of every idle word or deed, or of any other commotion of the mind, and that nothing may be concealed from the spiritual mother.[55]

Both rules share, despite their harshness, a certain optimism. Unceasing monastic discipline, strict adherence to the *regula*, the willingness to submit one's innermost thoughts to constant assessment and mutual support through prayer are an effective way to face the ubiquitous danger of eternal damnation. Monasteries thus function as places to organize sanctity and safeguard salvation.

The fragments at the end of the *Codex regularum*

An investigation of responses to Columbanus's rule cannot be complete without addressing the two fragments that appear at the end of Benedict of Aniane's *Codex regularum*.[56] The first one is a slightly rearranged female adaptation of the end of the short version of Columbanus's *Regula coenobialis*. This fragment addresses (among other topics) the required penance for impure dreams and 'being polluted in a natural way' (*naturaliter coinquinata*), which might imply that the reviser of the Regula coenobialis understood menstruation in analogy to nocturnal emissions as a pollution caused by erotic dreams.[57] Simply changing the grammatical gender of the *Regula Columbani*, as the first of these fragments has done, is in itself yet another distinct statement on Columbanus's legacy. It suggests that no substantial revision was deemed necessary, not even for a female community. Donatus wrote his rule because he disagreed on exactly the question of whether Columbanus's or Benedict's rule could be applied word-for-word to female communities.

The second fragment, a sort of treatise addressing a female community, develops a theological argument that moves from the effect of full dedication to God in general to the power of prayer in particular and arrives at the conclusion that continuous prayer expedites the forgiveness of sins, a notion that is very much in line with ideas developed in the *Regula cuiusdam ad uirgines*. It is likely that it had at some point been part of this rule.[58]

Conclusion

The foregoing exploration of the surviving Columbanian monastic rules is not meant to be exhaustive. I hope to have shown that monastic rules need to be taken much more seriously as sources on a vast diversity of heavily contested monastic ideals, practices, notions of discipline and community and the theological grounding of monastic life. In order to recognize this, we need to read them with an eye open for *themes* rather than focus on specific regulations. Comparing the extant 'Columbanian' rules shows, however, another feature that is worth further exploration. Each rule not only expresses different viewpoints, but does so by deploying very different textual techniques, which are important in and of themselves because form should never be separated from content. Columbanus developed his monastic program as a combination of an ascetic treatise on monastic virtues and vices and a list of penances for inner-monastic transgressions. The *Regula cuiusdam patris* is a highly polemical – and rather unpolished – manifesto phrased in the language of older, unnamed, monastic authorities. The *Regula cuiusdam ad uirgines* is a blueprint of a perfect community and is carefully crafted as a drastic revision of the *Regula Benedicti*. The *Regula Donati* is a faithful anthology of respected older monastic rules. The first fragment at the end of the *Codex Regularum* applies an existing rule for monks to nuns by changing the grammatical gender.

The notion of a harmonious, unified and organically evolving 'Columbanian' monastic ideal and a Columbanian monastic *movement* that gradually adopted the *Regula Benedicti* has become obsolete thanks to the work of Clare Stancliffe, Ian Wood, Alexander O'Hara and Yaniv Fox.[59] I hope this article contributes to this new assessment, or perhaps even deconstruction, of Columbanian monasticism by showing that Columbanus's successors may have disagreed about the core of monastic life just as much as they disagreed about politics and power.

Notes

1. I would like to thank Joshua Campbell, Eric Goldberg, Matthieu van der Meer, Alex O'Hara, and Ian Wood for their suggestions and corrections. This chapter has been written as contribution to the Spezialforschungsbereich F 4202 'Visions of Community', funded by the Fonds zur Förderung der wissenschaftlichen Forschung (FWF), the Faculty of History and Cultural Sciences of the University of Vienna and the Austrian Academy of Sciences.

2. On the conflicts arising after Columbanus's death, see the titles on Jonas and Columbanian monasticism listed as suggestions for further reading. See also Chapter 3 in this volume.

3. A. Diem, 'Was bedeutet Regula Columbani?', in M. Diesenberger and W. Pohl, eds, *Integration und Herrschaft. Ethnische Identitäten und soziale Organisation im Frühmittelalter* (Vienna, 2002), pp. 63–89.

4. Columbanus, *Regula monachorum* and *Regula coenobialis*, ed. and trans. G.S.M. Walker, *Sancti Columbani Opera* (Dublin, 1957), pp. 122–69. In Benedict of Aniane's *Codex regularum*, the first part of the *Regula Columbani* (which we call *Regula monachorum*) is titled *Regula coenobialis*; the second part (which we call *Regula coenobialis*) is simply called *Paenitentialis eiusdem*. Most manuscripts use the title *Regula Columbani* for both texts together.

5. Columbanus, *Regula monachorum*, c. 7, ed. and trans. Walker, pp. 130–1.

6. Columbanus, *Regula coenobialis*, c. 1: 'Statutum est, fratres karissimi, a sanctis patribus ut demus confessionem ante mensam, siue ante lectorum introitum, aut quandocumque fuerit facile, quia confessio et paenitentia de more liberant. Ergo nec ipsa parua a confessione sunt negligenda peccata, quia ut scriptum est: Qui parua neglegit paulatim defluit.', quoted from St. Gallen, Stiftsbibliothek, MS 915, p. 173). Walker's edition of this passage (pp. 144–6) is confusing because it conflates different versions of the text.

7. *Regula Benedicti*, c. 7.44–8 (SC 181, p. 484); *Regula magistri*, c. 10.61–65 (SC 105, p. 432).

8. On confession, see *Rule of Ailbe*, cc. 10 and 29, trans. U. Ó Maidín, *The Celtic Monk. Rules and Writings of Early Irish Monks* (Kalamazoo, 1996), pp. 20, 24; *Rule of Ciarán*, c. 16 (ibid., p. 47); *Rule of Cormac Mac Ciolionáin*, c. 6 (ibid., pp. 55–6); *Rule of Carthage*, c. 18 (ibid., p. 67); *Rule of the Céli Dé* (ibid., pp. 86, 88–9); *Rule of Tallaght*, cc. 20–2 (ibid., pp. 105–6); Columbanus, *Paenitentiale* B, c. 30, ed. Walker, p. 180.

9. See, for example, R. Meens, *Penance in Medieval Europe, 600–1200* (Cambridge, 2014).

10. *Canones Hibernenses* II, cc. 3–4, ed. Ludwig Bieler, *The Irish Penitentials* (Dublin, 1963), p. 164; *Canones Wallici*, c. 34, ibid., p. 142.

11. *Paenitentiale Cummeani*, prologue c.6, ed. Bieler, p. 108; *Paenitentiale Silense*, l.5, CCSL 156A, p. 17; *Paenitentiale Cordubense*, l.16, ibid., p. 45.

12. *Paenitentiale Vinniani*, c. 5, ed. Bieler, pp. 74–6.

13. *Paenitentiale Hubertense*, c. 62, ed. Bieler, p. 115; *Paenitentiale Merseburgense*, c. 17, ibid., p. 174.

14. The salutary effect of confession is also implied in his *Paenitentiale* B, c. 30, ed. Bieler, p. 106. Only some later penitenitals, the *Paenitentiale Floriacense*, praef (CCSL 156, pp. 97–8) and the *Paenitentiale Cordubense*, l.190–214 (CCSL 156A, pp. 51–2), describe a detailed confessional ritual; the *Paenitentiale Merseburgense*, c. 43 (CCSL 156, p. 177) mentions the salutary effect of *confessio* on one's deathbed.

15. For example, *Rule of Tallaght*, cc. 46–54, trans. Ó Maidín, *The Celtic Monk,* pp. 113–16.

16. Edited by F. Villegas, 'La "Regula cuiusdam Patris ad monachos". Ses sources littéraires et ses rapports avec la "Regula monachorum" de Colomban', *Revue d'Histoire de la Spiritualité* 49 (1973), 3–36 and 135–44. See also A. Diem, 'Debating Columbanus's heritage: The *Regula cuiusdam patris* (with an English translation), forthcoming in A. O'Hara, *Meeting the Gentes - Crossing Boundaries: Columbanus and the Peoples of Post-Roman Europe* (Oxford, 2016).

17. On the spread of the *Regula Benedicti*, see F. Prinz, *Frühes Mönchtum im Frankenreich* (Darmstadt, 1965), pp. 262–92.

18. L. Holstenius, *Codex Regularum* (Paris, 1661), part 2, pp. 281–92.

19. Villegas, 'La "Regula cuiusdam Patris ad monachos"'. See also A. de Vogüé, *Histoire littéraire du mouvement monastique dans l'antiquité*, 12 vols. (Paris, 2006), X, pp. 287–305. Both overlooked a citation from Augustine, *Sermo* 329, c. 2 (*PL* 38, col. 1455), in *Regula cuiusdam patris*, c. 1.2–3.

20. *Regula cuiusdam patris*, cc. 3.2–3, 3.4, 3.5, 6.1, 29.1, 29.3, 29.4, 29.9.

21. E. de Bhaldraithe, 'Obedience: the Doctrine of Irish Monastic Rules', *Monastic Studies* 14 (1983), pp. 63–84.

22. *Regula cuiusdam patris*, c. 3.1: *Deinde uirtus oboedientiae expetenda est et secundum uires uniuscuisque exercenda est.*

23. Ibid., cc. 3.6–4.1.

24. Ibid., cc. 1.3, pp. 19–20, 23–5.

25. Ibid., c. 1.1: *Caveat lector bonus ne suo sensui optemperet scripturas, sed scripturis sanctis obtemperet sensum suum.*
26. On leaving the community because of an incompetent abbot, see ibid., c. 20.
27. Jonas, *Vita Columbani* II.1, ed. Krusch, pp. 231–2.
28. Jonas, *Vita Columbani.* II.10, ed. Krusch, pp. 252–3.
29. Jonas, *Vita Columbani.* II.9, ed. Krusch, pp. 249–50; Columbanus, *Regula coenobialis*, cc. 1, 3, ed. Walker, pp. 146–8. On Agrestius, see below, 'Further Reading', especially the works by Dunn, Stancliffe, Wood, Dumézil, O'Hara and Fox.
30. Compare Columbanus, *Regula coenobialis*, c. 10, p. 158, lines 23–4 with *Regula cuiusdam patris*, c. 6.1; *Regula coenobialis*, c. 10, p. 158, lines 24–5 with *Regula cuiusdam patris*, c. 7; *Regula coenobialis*, c. 9, p. 154, lines 17–18 with *Regula cuiusdam patris*, c. 81/7, pp. 16–17; *Regula coenobialis*, c. 15, p. 164, line 28 with *Regula cuiusdam patris*, c. 17. p. 2–3.
31. *Regula cuiusdam patris*, c. 1.2: *Calix passionis amarus est, sed omnes morbos penitus curat.*
32. *Regula cuiusdam patris*, c. 32.
33. *Regula cuiusdam patris*, cc. 1.3–4, pp. 12–5, 17–20, 24–5.
34. A. Diem, 'Who is Allowed to Pray for the King? Saint-Maurice d'Agaune and the Creation of a Burgundian Identity', in G. Heydemann and W. Pohl, eds, *Post-Roman Transitions. Christian and Barbarian Identities in the Early Medieval West* (Turnhout, 2013), pp. 47–88, at pp. 79–80.
35. Y. Fox, *Power and Religion in Merovingian Gaul. Columbanian Monasticism and the Formation of the Frankish Aristocracy* (Cambridge, 2014).
36. See, for example, Jonas, *Vita Columbani* II.7–10, ed. Krusch, pp. 240–57; *Vita Sadalbergae*, c. 12, MGH SS rer. Merov. 5, p. 56; *Vita Germani Grandivallensis*, cc. 6–9, MGH SS rer. Merov. 5, pp. 85–7. See also A. Diem, 'Monks, Kings and the Transformation of Sanctity. Jonas of Bobbio and the End of the Holy Man', in: *Speculum* 82 (2007), 521–59, at 552–4; Fox, *Power and Religion*, pp. 141–5.
37. Jonas, *Vita Columbani* II.9, ed. Krusch, p. 250.
38. *Regula cuiusdam patris*, c. 30.3 and 30.5.
39. Columbanus, *Regula monachorum*, c. 7, pp. 130–2.
40. B. Dumézil, 'L'affaire Agrestius de Luxeuil: hérésie et régionalisme dans la Burgondie du VIIe siècle', *Médiévales* 52 (2007), pp. 135–52, at 138–42.
41. Jonas, *Vita Columbani* II.9, ed. Krusch, p. 246.
42. *Regula cuiusdam patris*, cc. 20.2, 21; *First Synod of Patrick*, c. 9, ed. Bieler, p. 54.
43. *Regula cuiusdam patris*, c. 8.7; *Second Synod of Patrick*, c. 22, ed. Bieler, p. 192. The context is, however, different. Here, monastic life is in itself a *examinatio carceris*.
44. *Regula cuiusdam patris*, c. 2.1: 'Primum omnium deum timendum et diligendum est ex toto corde et ex tota anima et ex totis uiribus'. See, for example, *Rule of Cormac Mac Ciolionán*, c. 7, trans. Ó Maidín, *The*

Celtic Monk, p. 56: 'It is no error, and certainly no heresy, to say that the love of God demands fear of him'.

45. *Regula cuiusdam patris*, cc. 10.3, 17.3, 29.2; *Paenitentiale Viniani*, c. 1, ed. Bieler, p. 74; c. 29, p. 84; *Paenitentiale Bigotianum* II, c. 10, p. 222.

46. Printed in *PL* 88, cols 1053–70. The section on the *Regula cuiusdam ad uirgines* is a summary of my previous work on this text. See 'Further Reading'. A new edition with an English translation is in preparation.

47. The *Regula cuiusdam ad uirgines* does not contain traces of Caesarius's rule even though the text was probably available in Columbanian monasteries. There is also hardlly any thematic overlap between both rules, which might indicate that the author of the *Regula cuiusdam ad uirgines* focused on topics that had not been addressed in Caesarius's rule.

48. A list of these parallels will be provided along with the forthcoming edition of the text. Here are some examples of expressions that appear exclusively or almost exclusively in the *Regula cuiusdam ad uirgines* and in Jonas of Bobbio's works: *saniae antidoti, correptione pia, arrogantiae uitio maculata, sine commeatu, ex praesentibus pompis, faleramenta, contumaciae crimen incurrit, damnum neglegentiae, iurgiorum incrementa, uerecundiae metu, pro communi necessitate, de cuius religio non dubitetur, ab omni congregatione obiuregur, moderante scientiae, sub silentii uoce, psalmographi praeconium.*

49. Some examples of positive and negative motivational terms: *tepor, tepescere, tepidits torpentis uitae, moribus grauis, sollers, ingenio fortis, consideratione uigil, non turbulenter, mores languentium, tepescentium ignauiam excitare, corda … excitando erigat, neglegentiae tenebris fuscata, propter negligentias inquirendas, expergistentem sensum uel tepescentem, cum feruor uel cum tepiditate, tarditate uel segnitia culpabiles.*

50. *Regula cuisdam ad uirgines*, c. 6.20–3.

51. Edited by V. Zimmerl-Pannagl on the basis of preliminary work by M. Zelzer, CSEL 98, Monastica 1 (Vienna, 2015), pp. 1–188. The section on the *Regula Donati* section summarises A. Diem, 'New Ideas Expressed in Old Words: the *Regula Donati* on Female Monastic Life and Monastic Spirituality', *Viator* 43 (2012), pp. 1–38.

52. See the foundation charter for Solignac, MGH SS rer. Merov. 4, pp. 746–9; and the Privilege for Rebais, *PL* 87, cols 1134B-37A.

53. Diem, 'New Ideas Expressed in Old Words', pp. 11–31.

54. *Regula Donati*, cc. 11.6, 17.10, 25–32, 33.7–8, 34, 49.9–10, 75.14–16. On genuflections: 34.

55. *Regula Donati*, c. 23. See also c. 19.3–4.

56. Ed. V. Zimmerl-Panagl, CSEL 98, Monastica 1 (Vienna, 2015), pp. 191–240.

57. Fragment from the female *Regula Columbani*, c. 19: 'Et quando praedicatur, si quae uiderint somnium inmundum aut naturaliter coinquinatae fuerint, una cum paenitentibus stare praecipiuntur'.

58. On the treatise *De accedendo ad Deum*, see A. Diem and M. van der Meer, *Columbanische Klosterregeln* (St. Ottilien, 2016), pp. 108-126.

59. See 'Further Reading' below.

5

Columbanian Monasticism: a Contested Concept

Ian Wood

The impact of the Irish on the Continent in the early Middle Ages has long been a contentious issue: the terms 'irophobia' and 'iromania' have even been coined to describe the attitudes of those who deny and those who stress their significance.[1] The debate has raged most bitterly over the question of manuscripts and the transmission of knowledge. It has also touched on Columbanus and the extent and nature of his influence on the development of western monasticism. The division of opinion became prominent in the nineteenth century and it is worth noting the context in which the 'iromaniac' view was first expounded before looking at the difficulty of assessing what Columbanus did or did not contribute to monastic history. Prior to considering the evidence from the nineteenth century, however, it is as well to note earlier awareness of the Irish saint, some of which no doubt fed into the emphasis placed on his importance from the 1840s.

Protestant and Catholic scholars of the Reformation and Counter-Reformation wrote about Columbanus. In the sixteenth century the reformer John Bale, Bishop of Ossory, for instance, made a passing reference to him in his 'De scriptoribus Brytanniae, Scotis et Hybernis', although he was more interested in Columba.[2] Of greater significance was the interest shown by the archbishop of Armagh in the first half of the seventeenth century: James Ussher published what is now known as the fifth of Columbanus's sermons, as well as three poems ascribed to the saint, but which are no longer regarded as being by him.[3] Ussher also discussed some aspects of the rule of Columbanus in *A Discourse of the Religion professed by the Ancient Irish*,[4] a work which set about proving that the early Irish church had more in common with Protestantism than with Catholicism.[5] The *editio princeps* of the saint's works, however, was produced by an Irish

Catholic contemporary of Ussher, Patrick Fleming. Fleming, who was educated at Douai and Louvain, joined the Friars Minor, and went to Rome where he was ordained priest. He returned to Louvain, where he lectured, before being transferred to Prague, to become Guardian of a new college. There he was murdered in 1631, during the Thirty Years' War. His edition of Columbanus's works was published posthumously, in Louvain in 1667, as part of his *Collectanea Sacra*.[6] Ussher and Fleming are an indication that Catholics and Protestants both wished to lay claim to the Irish saint's spirituality.

In 1669, at almost exactly the same time as Fleming's edition of Columbanus's works appeared, Jean Mabillon published the volume of the *Acta sanctorum ordinis sancti Benedicti* devoted to the second century of the Benedictines.[7] Despite the title, the volume included the Lives of several seventh-century abbots, including those of Columbanus and his successors, who were not Benedictine. This was a work that Bruno Krusch dismissed as adding no new codicological information to the editions of Jonas's *Vita Columbani* which were already available in print.[8] Although the edition of Jonas's work may have been textually insignificant, in grouping together the lives of seventh-century abbots who can be placed in a network dominated by the Columbanian foundation of Luxeuil, and in offering a prefatory narrative, Mabillon effectively provided the hagiographical grounds for seeing Columbanus as a key influence on the later Merovingian period.

Despite the riches in Mabillon's collection, the eighteenth century saw no major contribution to the study of Columbanus. The saint received some attention at the start of the nineteenth century, in the writings of two Irish Catholic clergymen, Charles O'Conor and John Lanigan – both of whom came into conflict with the church hierarchy. O'Conor, like Fleming, was as important for his confessional position as for his scholarship: in 1810 he published his *Columbanus ad Hibernos*, which dealt with the issue of the royal veto over the appointment of Catholic bishops in Ireland, something that he supported, and for which he was condemned by Archbishop John Troy.[9] Here O'Conor was making use of Columbanus's name rather more than his writings – and certainly his letter adds nothing to the study of Irish monasticism. For the medieval historian more important is O'Conor's attempt to trace the history of the Irish *peregrini* on the continent, through a study of the Bobbio Missal, the Würzburg Gospels and the Antiphonary of Bangor, in the first volume of his *Rerum Hibernicarum Scriptores*.[10]

Lanigan's early career was spent in Italy: he attended the Irish college in Rome, before teaching at the University of Padua. Following Napoleon's invasion of Italy he returned to Ireland, and for a short time held a chair at Maynooth. He gave up the post, however, following disagreements with the bishop of Cork. His *Ecclesiastical History of Ireland*, which provides a clear statement of his Catholic sympathies, was written towards the end of his life: it was published in 1822, three years before his death. In it he devotes forty pages to Columbanus. Those pages, however, do little more than provide a résumé of Jonas's narrative, with extensive notes. The notes, moreover, are confined to points of fact. Lanigan thought that the achievements of the saint could easily be studied, and that to add any comment on them would take him beyond the concerns of his book, which were essentially to do with Ireland itself.[11] Although those interested in the Irish church may have agreed with Lanigan that information on Columbanus's impact was easily accessible, the wider intellectual world would scarcely have concurred. Telling in this respect is the near silence of Chateaubriand, who has almost nothing to say about either Columbanus or about early Irish spirituality in his *Genie du Christianisme* of 1802.[12] He was far more interested in the oppression of the Irish under Cromwell[13] than he was in what would now be regarded as a Golden Age of Irish Christianity.

In fact, the major accounts of Merovingian history published at the end of the eighteenth and the beginning of the nineteenth century do not have much to say about the Irish saint or his impact: for instance, the abbé de Mably ignores the Irishman, while Gibbon, whose *Decline and Fall* has a substantial chapter on Frankish history, which responds to the work of the French abbé, confines Columbanus to the footnotes.[14] One might be surprised at the Englishman's near silence: it would not have been difficult to present Irish monasticism as an illustration of the religious enthusiasm that Gibbon despised – and indeed the harshness of the rule of Columbanus does draw a comment, but nothing more. After the Revolution, in 1823, François Guizot had nothing to say on Columbanus in his collection of essays on the history of France, which were written as a commentary on Mably's work. He was slightly more forthcoming in his *Histoire de la civilisation en France*, of 1829–32, which calls the saint a model missionary, but otherwise does little other than transcribe Fredegar's account of the conflict between the Irishman and Brunhild.[15] In his history of European civilization, published at the same time, there are no more than passing references to Columbanus.[16] In 1835 Jules

Michelet devoted half a dozen pages to the Irishman and the ecclesiastical reform that he began, but he clearly knew little of Columbanus, whom he erroneously presented as the 'célèbre disciple' of Columba, and he concluded that the Irish monks had no impact on the Continent because the Celts did not understand the Germans: 'Ce défaut de sympathie pour les Germains, pour les travaux obscurs de leur conversion, est la condamnation de saint Colomban et de l'église celtique.'[17]

In fact, modern scholarship on Columbanus had its origins in a precise nineteenth-century context. It can be traced most easily by consideration of Charles Forbes René de Montalembert's *Les Moines d'Occident* of 1860, in which Columbanus and Columbanian monasticism practically explode on the European scene. In Montalembert's account Columbanus earns twice the space dedicated to Benedict.[18] The wider case, that it was Columbanus and the Irish who revived religious life in Europe, had been put marginally earlier by Antoine-Frédéric Ozanam, who is now known primarily not for his historical writing but as the founder of the Société de Saint Vincent de Paul: for his charitable work he was beatified in 1997. Both Montalembert and Ozanam belonged to the same religious circle. Inspired by the author and religious apologist François-René de Chateaubriand, they were part of the Catholic revival of mid-nineteenth-century France, which deliberately turned against the secularism of the Enlightenment. For them the great triumph of religion to be emulated was the Catholic Emancipation Act of 1829, spearheaded by Daniel O'Connell, *Le Liberateur*.[19] O'Connell had shown that a religious revival was possible. Essentially Ozanam (in three major works published in 1847, 1849, 1855, versions of which were available in German and English),[20] and after him Montalembert, transformed what had been a subject of interest to a small number of Irish and ecclesiastical writers into mainstream history.[21] Ozanam and Montalembert set out a case that has regularly been revived – and they did so rather better than most who have followed them, including Christopher Dawson.[22]

The fact that it was French Catholics of the mid-nineteenth century, in the course of their campaign to rejuvenate Christianity, who first presented Columbanus as reviving the religious and cultural life of western Europe, need not invalidate their interpretation. However, the fact that previous generations of scholars had largely ignored the Irishman does suggest that one should look carefully at the evidence, to see whether the emphases of Ozanam and Montalembert or the silences of Gibbon and Guizot can be justified.

The image of Columbanus reviving a moribund church is, of course, set out in Jonas, who claimed that the fervour of religious life had almost been extinguished in Gaul before Columbanus's arrival.[23] This view of Gallic Christianity is, however, scarcely supported by Columbanus's own writings, despite the quality of their Latin, their knowledge of patristic authors, and the vigour in which they express religious enthusiasm. It is simply that Columbanus, apart from decrying Frankish simony, and defending the Irish Easter, provides little detail on the religious life to be found in Francia at the time of his arrival – though he was clearly hostile to the Frankish episcopate and its power. In this historians have tended to follow his views and those of Jonas, although it has become increasingly clear that the episcopate of the early seventh century included figures of significance, who played a major role in the promotion of the cult of saints and in the development of canon law, as is apparent from the collection and development of what is known as the *Vetus Gallica*, which is associated with the diocese of Lyon, and probably with Bishop Etherius, whose successor Aridius, was Columbanus's nemesis.[24] Nor does the Irishman have much to add on religion in Italy, leaving aside his awareness of Gregory the Great, the Tricapitoline crisis, and Arianism at the Lombard court.[25] One could not conclude from the works of Columbanus that he was a contemporary of Gregory of Tours or of Isidore of Seville. Nor could one deduce as much from Jonas.

This takes us to one of the main areas of dispute in Columbanian studies. To what extent is Jonas's picture of the standards of the Frankish church accurate? We have already noted the interest shown in canon law, in the diocese of Lyon. We can, nevertheless, accept that simony was a genuine problem within the Frankish church. Much is made of it in Gregory I's letters to Merovingian royalty and to their leading bishops.[26] In any case episcopal appointment is a regular issue in Gregory of Tours's writings and in the sixth- and seventh-century Frankish councils. In other words, simony was at the centre of debate within the Frankish church before Columbanus's arrival.[27] Beyond the issue of simony, however, the evidence is less clear-cut.

Jonas says that Gaul was in need of the *medicamenta paenitentiae*,[28] by which he may mean the monastic life, rather than penance, to which we will return. No one would deny that in the generations after Columbanus's departure there was a significant increase in the number of monasteries in Francia,[29] some of which were unquestionably 'Columbanian' in that they followed a mixed rule, which included that of Columbanus. That was mapped by Friedrich Prinz, though one would have to say that in charting the influence of Luxeuil he used a whole set of indicators, without distinguishing consistently between unquestionable proof of contact with Columbanus's foundation and rather vaguer points of similarity. For instance, Prinz does not make it easy for anyone trying to track down the number of times the *regula Columbani* is cited in charter material alongside the rules of Benedict and of Caesarius: in fact there are a mere five such citations, not all of which are in charters of unquestionable authenticity.[30] In addition to these references one finds the phrase *regula Columbani* fourteen times in the Life of Columbanus, where some dozen houses other than the saint's own foundations are said to follow his rule.[31] Exactly what is meant by the phrase *regula Columbani* here and elsewhere is unclear, and it may well be something much less specific than a written monastic rule.[32] It is worth remembering that the only rule to survive in Merovingian copies is that of Basil (no manuscript of a rule of Columbanus can be dated earlier than the ninth century).[33] Moreover, while there are a number of other indicators that allow one to talk of a body of likeminded monastic patrons with more or less direct connections to Luxeuil, Prinz had a tendency to categorize monasteries as, in his words, *irofrankisch*. An enthusiasm for monasticism dominated by members of a relatively confined court circle is often the best that one can find in the source material.

There certainly was a major increase in the number of monasteries in Francia after 600. Yet it is worth pausing to consider the numbers: Hartmut Atsma argued for there being 220 monasteries in Gaul at the time of Columbanus's arrival, and 550 by the early eighth century.[34] That may seem an incredible expansion, but take those 220 monasteries, almost all of which were foundations of the century and a half after 450: they may look a good deal less than the number to be found a century later, but compare them with the 100 monasteries known from Italy, or the 86 from Spain.[35] Francia had already been in the grip of monastic fervour by the time of Columbanus's arrival, and although the heyday of the early foundations had passed there is no reason to think that standards in such centres as Lérins and Arles were in catastrophic decline: indeed we have good reason, in the writings of Dynamius of Provence, Venantius Fortunatus and the author of the *Vita Rusticulae*, to think that in some instances they were not.[36] Even Jonas, in his *Vita Iohannis*, seems to acknowledge the continuity of earlier monastic (Lérinian) tradition in Burgundy.

Although some modern scholars allow that there was a thriving tradition of monasticism in late sixth-century Francia, most nevertheless see Columbanus as the figure who effectively established a monastic tradition in the north-east. Yet Columbanus was not even the first founder in the area in which Luxeuil was situated: Jonas himself admits that the Irishman's initial foundation had to be saved by the intervention of an abbot with the British name Carantoc from a neighbouring community.[37] There would, therefore, already seem to have been a monastery of Britons in the Vosges before Columbanus arrived. How many other abbeys do we not know about? And how much more could be said about British/Breton influence?

A second of the contentious issues concerns the Irishness of Columbanus and his monasteries. Most of the insular elements we associate with Columbanus are, in fact, not specifically monastic – this is particularly true of the calculation of Easter. The computus championed by Columbanus had, of course, originated on the Continent, but by his day was confined to Ireland and western Britain.[38] While there would seem to have been a greater interest in calculating the Easter date, and greater skill in so doing, among Irish communities than among their contemporaries,[39] the calculation of Easter was an issue everywhere, as we can see in Gregory of Tours's *miracula*, and in evidence for Rome, Spain and, slightly later, England.[40] Moreover, for all the computistical skill to be found among the Irish, it was not their Easter, but that calculated by Dionysius Exiguus, which would be accepted as orthodox.

There are good reasons for accepting certain liturgical practices as being particularly associated with the Irish, such as blessing with the sign of the cross and genuflecting (as mentioned by Jonas),[41] and also certain prayers and invocations,[42] though in an age when liturgy was not standardized, other groups followed equally individual practices. The emphasis on Irish particularism has tended to obscure the variety to be found across western Christendom – although the recent emphasis on 'micro-Christendoms', following the approach of Peter Brown, has placed regional difference at the forefront of our understanding of early-medieval Christianity.[43]

With the issue of the practice of penance, we have more of a problem, in that sixth-century penitential practice on the Continent seems to have been varied: public penance was not the only practice.[44] Yet the concept of a penitential handbook would seem to have been insular in origin, even if the first examples may have been composed in western Britain rather than in Ireland. Vinnian's penitential is probably the earliest that can be securely ascribed to an identifiable author – and although he would seem to have been active in Ireland, he was probably British by birth.[45] And while the attribution of an apparently earlier text to Gildas is not secure,[46] one might note that the injunction that 'for good rulers we ought to offer the sacrifice, for bad ones on no account'[47] is fully compatible with the views on kings expressed in the *De Excidio Britanniae*. In any case, Columbanus was aware that Vinnian had consulted Gildas.[48] If the penitential tradition did begin in Britain, rather than Ireland, since Gildas would seem to have ended up on the Continent,[49] one should, perhaps, ask whether he, rather than Columbanus, introduced the concept to Francia. The Irishman, however, unquestionably did more to encourage the practice.[50] In addition, he may well have understood penance and monasticism to have been closely related: penitents may have lived a monastic life, as we find in the Life of Columba.[51] This might offer an explanation of Jonas's emphasis on the *medicamenta paenitentiae* introduced by Columbanus.[52]

As for the style of monastic life, Columbanus's rule is distinctive by comparison with the major texts of the fifth and sixth centuries: the rules of Augustine, Caesarius, the Master and Benedict. It has often been noted that on its own it would not have provided enough guidance for a community, and indeed it was soon blended with the rules of Caesarius, Benedict and Basil, and as such became one small element in the tradition of the *regula mixta*.[53] In many ways it is close to a penitential. However, it looks less unusual when compared with the rules ascribed to Lérins by de Vogüé.[54] Not everyone has accepted de Vogüé's dating or his ascription, but the rules would appear to belong to the fifth and sixth centuries, and perhaps to southern France.[55] It would appear, then, that Columbanus's rules derived from the world of fifth-century Gallic monasticism, and that some Frankish monasteries were still adhering to the same monastic traditions.

Most discussions of Columbanian monasticism, however, do not limit themselves to Columbanus's rules, but add to them the depiction of religious life to be found in Jonas. The basic approach is reasonable, in that it is clear that Merovingian Lives could be regarded as *regulae* in their own right: they set out the blueprint of a holy man's view of the monastic life: something that is explicit in the *Vita Patrum Iurensium*.[56] The problem is that the picture of monastic practice that is presented by Jonas may not be an accurate reflection of Columbanus's own practices: Jonas was surely offering what he regarded as the monastic ideal, and associating it with the founding father of Annegray, Luxeuil and Bobbio. That does not mean that he

presents an accurate picture of the monasticism promoted by
Columbanus himself.

There are various points in Jonas's account which may be misleading. One example can be found in Jonas's presentation of the monastic *saepta* ('enclosure') and its sacrosanct nature. According to Jonas,
Theuderic broke the taboo of entering the space reserved for the
monks.[57] This is often regarded as something peculiarly Irish, and it
is linked with the later evidence of royal and episcopal exemptions
from the 620s onwards,[58] and is taken to suggest that Columbanian
communities were initially more withdrawn from the secular world
than were other foundations and that they then provided the model
for greater independence. It is easy to conjure up a picture, on
reading Jonas, of a community isolated in the forest, in which access
to the outside world was restricted.

That Jonas and his contemporaries championed such an idea is
relatively clear. Yet Sébastien Bully's excavations at Luxeuil, which
have revealed the existence of two or even three churches and a vast
number of sarcophagi, some of which would seem to belong to the
period before Columbanus's arrival, have raised considerable difficulties in seeing the monastic community as in any sense isolated: the
basilicas and cemeteries already in existence in Columbanus's time
do not square easily with Jonas's description.[59] And at first sight it is
difficult to see how the community of Luxeuil, to which the Life was
in part addressed,[60] could have taken Jonas's presentation seriously.
This is not just a matter of the supposedly deserted nature of the site,
but also of the monastic *saepta*, and the exclusion of laity. It is,
however, worth looking precisely at what Jonas says, for part of the
problem may be that we do not read his work precisely enough. He
admits the existence of other buildings in the area. The saint only
prohibits entry into the *habitationes famulorum Dei*, presumably
meaning the dormitory or cells, while the *saepta secretiora* that the
king enters is explicitly the *refectorium*.[61] In other words, Jonas's
account implies more than it says, misleadingly and perhaps deliberately so. At Luxeuil there may not have been a great enclosure, at
least in Columbanus's day, but rather a handful of specific buildings
that were out of bounds to those who were not members of the
community. Thus the *Vita Columbani* makes Luxeuil look more
isolated and independent than it was – this was after all a royal foundation (something that Jonas does not admit, but does not deny).
Moreover, the idea that monastic exclusion was a particularly Irish
tradition has been exaggerated by modern scholars, who forget that
there were already monastic immunities before Columbanus arrived,

and that Caesarius sets out restrictions on entry into monastic enclo-sures which are as extreme as anything in Jonas[62] – and, of course, Caesarius's rule was used in the *regulae mixtae* of female houses, as Jonas was well aware.[63]

This leads to the last of the contentious issues, and that is the extent to which what we regard as Columbanian monasticism was really the creation not of Columbanus but of the next generation of (largely) Frankish monastic leaders. It is worth noting here the very slight distribution of the saint's own writings, by comparison with that of the *Vita Columbani*.[64] If we turn to the evidence of monastic rules, it is possible that Columbanus himself was aware of the *Regula Benedicti* before his death.[65] The combination of the *Regula Columbani* and other rules may even have begun in the life time of the saint: but since almost all rules – including those of the Master, Eugippius and Benedict – before the ninth century were essentially *regulae mixtae*, this is no surprise. However, it is absolutely certain that the genera-tions following Columbanus produced the most striking of the surviving *regulae mixtae*: the *Regula Donati*, the *Regula cuiusdam patris* and the *Regula cuiusdam ad virgines*, in all of which the rule of Columbanus was a minor ingredient.[66] And just as his successors created new monastic rules, so too it was they, rather than Columbanus himself, who were responsible for the development of the precise type of monastic immunity to be found in the charter record. What we call Columbanian monasticism was developed largely by Columbanus's Frankish successors.

Downplaying the novelty of Columbanian monasticism is a well-established tradition. One of the most effective examples of it remains Malnory's *Quid Luxovienses monachi* of 1894, where Columbanian monasticism is placed firmly within the broader context of monastic development.[67] Essentially, when the evidence for Columbanus is read alongside the remainder of the documenta-tion for the monastic church of the sixth and seventh centuries, Columbanus is a major and extremely eloquent voice in monastic history, but he is scarcely a bolt from the blue. He comes out of what in origin had been a fifth-century continental tradition, even if some of the practices that he was championing had fallen out of fashion. He is turned into an absolutely pivotal figure by Jonas, who, like all enthusiasts for reform, downplayed elements of continuity. In fact, it is worth noting how limited the support is for the picture of Columbanus's impact presented by Jonas: leaving aside the saint's own writings and the *Vita Columbani*, Columbanus himself only appears in the Chronicle of Fredegar[68] – and, as a heretic, in Bede.[69]

As we have seen, there are only a handful of references to a *regula Columbani* to be found in charters and foundation documents. The impact of the *Vita Columbani* was arguably as great: Jonas is cited in half a dozen other works – in terms of citations a significant number, although the works in question belong to a specific circle of aristo-crats and monastic houses with links to Luxeuil.[70] In other words, the picture of Columbanian monasticism is constructed from a tightly confined body of evidence, impressive in its own right, but not necessarily amounting to the vast network of Columbanian monasticism reconstructed by Prinz, who squeezed every drop of information out of the diplomatic and hagiographical documenta-tion. Prinz provides a single-minded reading of material that can be read in other ways, and which might just as well suggest a rather more diverse pattern of monastic development. It would not be difficult, for instance, to look at the *Nachleben* of the works and deeds Caesarius of Arles (including his sermons, and his conciliar work, as well as his monastic foundations and the composition of his rule): this might well be presented as an indication of influence as extensive as that of Columbanus – yet Caesarius has never been promoted with the same fervour as has the Irish saint. For various reasons (religious in the case of Montalembert, Ozanam and Dawson, nationalist in other cases) scholars since the mid-nineteenth century have been inspired by Jonas's picture to argue that Columbanus marked a major change: the extent of the change, however, remains uncertain.

When all is said and done, the evidence may not be strong enough to decide between the iromaniacs and the irophobes – although the extreme versions of each of the theories will scarcely stand. It may be that progress can best be made not by looking at Columbanus himself, or his foundations, but rather at the world which he entered and the context in which he operated. On the whole, Columbanus is better known than are his Frankish and Gallo-Roman contemporaries – and such contemporaries as are well known, like Gregory of Tours, are rarely brought into play. Merovingian studies tend to create a caesura between the two contemporaries: the Age of Columbanus is presented as beginning after the Age of Gregory of Tours, although in reality they overlap, spiritually as well as chrono-logically. On the whole, those who have argued the case for the Irish revival of spirituality and learning on the continent have been much better acquainted with the evidence for Columbanus himself, and for the Irish context from which he emerged, than with the totality of the evidence for the sixth- and seventh-century monastic church in Gaul and Francia. Yet until we have a clear understanding of the reality of the world in which Columbanus was active, the true extent of his influence as a monastic founder and reformer will elude us.

Notes

1. J. Duft, 'Iromanie – Irophobie: Fragen um die frühmittelalterliche Irenmission exemplifiziert an St. Gallen und Alemannien', *Zeitschrift für schweizerische Kirchengeschichte* 50 (1956), pp. 241–62.
2. John Bale, 'De scriptoribus Brytanniae, Scotis et Hybernis, Centuria decimaquarta', in *Scriptorium illustrium maioris Brytanniae posterior pars, quinque continens centurias ultimas, quas author, Ioannes Baleus Sudouolgius, Anglus, ex Lelando Antiquario, alijsque probis authoribus, non paruo labore collegit* (Basle, 1559), pp. 177–250, at p. 189.
3. James Ussher, *Veterum Epistolarum Hibernicarum Sylloge* (Paris, 1665), pp. 4–11: *Instructio* 5; *Mundus iste transibit*; *Versus ad Hunaldum*; *Versus ad Fedolium*: see G.S.M. Walker, *Sancti Columbani Opera* (Dublin, 1957), pp. 84–7, 183–87, 192–97.
4. James Ussher, *A Discourse of the Religion professed by the Ancient Irish* (London, 1631): chapter 6, 'Of the discipline of our ancient monks, and abstinence from meats', pp. 54–66 , at pp. 62–4.
5. M. Tanner, *Ireland's Holy Wars: The Struggle for the Nation's Soul, 1500–2000* (Yale, 2003), p. 119.
6. P. Fleming's *Collectanea Sacra* (Louvain, 1667): see W. Reeves, 'Irish Library. No. 2. Fleming's *Collectanea Sacra*', *Ulster Journal of Archaeology*, 1st series, 2 (1852), pp. 253–61.
7. L. d'Achery and J. Mabillon, *Acta sanctorum ordinis sancti Benedicti in seculorum classes distributa, saeculum II* (Paris, 1669).
8. B. Krusch, *Ionae Vitae Sanctorum*, MGH SS rer. Germ. 37 (Hanover, 1905), p. 143.
9. C. O'Conor, *Columbanus ad Hibernos* (Buckingham, 1810).
10. C. O'Conor, *Rerum Hibernicarum Scriptores*, 4 vols (London, 1814–26), I, pp. cxxx–cxliii.
11. John Lanigan, *An Ecclesiastical History of Ireland from the First Introduction of Christianity among the Irish to the Beginning of the Thirteenth Century*, 4 vols (1822), II, p. 298.
12. F.-R. de Chateaubriand, *Génie du Christianisme* (originally published Paris, 1802), ed. M. Regard (Paris, 1978), p. 1055.
13. Chateaubriand, *Génie du Christianisme*, pp. 1245–7 n. lvi.
14. See I.N. Wood, 'The Irish in England and on the Continent in the Seventh Century', O'Donnell Lectures, 2012 (forthcoming in *Peritia*): Gibbon's three references to Columbanus occur in the notes to chapter 37 of *The Decline and Fall of the Roman Empire*.
15. F. Guizot, *Histoire de la Civilisation en France*, 6th ed., 5 vols (Paris, 1861), II, pp. 18–23.

16. F. Guizot, *Histoire de la civilisation en Europe* (Paris, 1828), trans. by W. Hazlitt, *History of Civilization in Europe*, 3 vols (London, 1846), II, pp. 113, 114, 117.

17. J. Michelet, *Histoire de France*, 2nd edn, 17 vols (Paris, 1835–67), II, pp. 266–72, see also p. 247. I have not been able to check the original edition of 1833.

18. C.F.R. de Montalembert, *Les moines d'Occident*, 5th ed., 7 vols (Paris, 1860–77), II, Book 9, pp. 3–92 [on Benedict], pp. 451–640 [on Columbanus].

19. On Ozanam and O'Connell, see G. Cholvy, *Frédéric Ozanam. L'engagement d'un intellectuel catholique au XIXe siècle* (Paris, 2003), pp. 586, 626.

20. A. F. Ozanam, *Études germaniques pour servir à l'histoire des Francs*, 2 vols (Paris, 1847–49); idem, *La Civilisation au Cinquième Siècle*, 2 vols (Paris, 1855), trans. A.C. Glyn, *History of Civilization in the Fifth Century*, 2 vols (London, 1868); idem, *La civilisation chrétienne chez les Francs* (Paris, 1849); idem, *Die Begründung des Christentums in Deutschland und die sittliche und geistige Erziehung der Germanen* (Munich, 1845).

21. Montalembert, *Les moines d'Occident*, II, Book 9, pp. 3–92, 451–640.

22. C. Dawson, *The Making of Europe 400–1000 A.D.* (London, 1932).

23. Jonas, *Vita Columbani*, I.5 (p. 161).

24. H. Mordek, *Kirchenrecht und Reform in Frankenreich. Die Collectio Vetus Gallica, die älteste systematische Kanonessammlung des fränkischen Gallien. Studien und Edition* (Berlin, 1975)

25. T. Leso, 'Columbanus in Europe: the Evidence from the *Epistulae*', *EME* 21 (2013), pp. 258–89.

26. R. Markus, *Gregory the Great and his World* (Cambridge, 1997), pp. 171–4.

27. O. Pontal, *Die Synoden im Merowingerreich* (Paderborn, 1986), esp. p. 233.

28. Jonas, *Vita Columbani*, I.5 (p. 161).

29. F. Prinz, *Frühes Mönchtum im Frankenreich* (Kempten, 1965), pp. 121–51: H. Atsma, 'Les monastères urbains du Nord de la Gaule', *Revue d'Histoire de l'Église de France* 62 (1976), 163–87, at 168.

30. J.M. Pardessus, *Diplomata, chartae, epistolae, aliaque instrumenta ad res Gallo-Francicas spectantia*, 2 vols (Paris, 1849), II, pp. 40 (no. 275), 68 (no. 299), 133 (no. 350), 134 (no. 351), 309 (no. 596). See also vol. 1, p. 194, for Faro's supposed privilege for Faremoutiers (n. 226). In addition there is the evidence of *Gesta Abbatum Fontanellensium*, 9, 2, ed. P. Pradié, *Chronique des Abbés de Fontenelle* (Paris, 1999), pp. 108–9. See the comments of J.C. Clark, *The Benedictines in the Middle Ages* (Woodbridge, 2011), pp. 27–30.

31. Jonas, *Vita Columbani*, I.10, 14, 19, 26; II.7, 9, 10, 11, 23 (pp. 170, 175, 176, 190, 210, 243, 248, 249, 252, 253, 255, 256, 257, 281).

32. For the meaning of the phrase *regula Columbani*, see A. Diem, 'Was bedeutet *Vita Columbani*', in W. Pohl and M. Diesenberger, eds, *Integration und Herrschaft. Ethnische Identitäten und soziale Organisation im Frühmittelalter* (Vienna, 2002), pp. 63–89.

33. *CLA* VI, no. 805; XI, no. 1598.
34. Atsma, 'Les monastères urbains du Nord de la Gaule', p. 168.
35. I. N. Wood, 'Entrusting Western Europe to the Church, 400–750', *Transactions of the Royal Historical Society* 23 (2013), pp. 37–73.
36. Wood, 'The Irish in England and on the Continent'.
37. Jonas, *Vita Iohannis*, ed. Krusch, MGH SS rer. Germ. 37 (Hanover, 1905), pp. 326–44.
38. C. Corning, *The Celtic and Roman Traditions. Conflict and Consensus in the Early Medieval Church* (New York, 2006). See also her contribution to this volume.
39. I. Warntjes, *The Munich Computus: Text and Translation. Irish Computistics between Isidore and the Venerable Bede and its Reception in Carolingian Times* (Stuttgart, 2010). See also his contribution in this volume.
40. Corning, *The Celtic and Roman Traditions*, passim.
41. Jonas, *Vita Columbani*, II.9, pp. 249–50.
42. Y. Hen, 'The Nature and Character of the Early Irish Liturgy', *L'Irlanda e gli irlandesi nell'alto medioevo = Settimane* 57 (Spoleto, 2010), pp. 353–80. And see his contribution in this volume.
43. P. Brown, *The Rise of Western Christendom* (Oxford, 1996).
44. C. Vogel, *La discipline pénitentielle en Gaule* (Paris, 1952), p. 203; M. de Jong, 'Transformations of Penance', in F. Theuws and J.L. Nelson, eds, *Rituals of Power from Late Antiquity to the Early Middle Ages* (Leiden, 2000), pp. 185–224.
45. L. Bieler, *The Irish Penitentials* (Dublin, 1963), pp. 3–4.
46. Bieler, *The Irish Penitentials*, p. 3.
47. Praefatio *Gildae de Poenitentia*, 23, ed. Bieler, *The Irish Penitentials*, pp. 62–3.
48. Columbanus, Letter 1, 7 (ed. Walker, *Sancti Columbani Opera*, pp. 8–9).
49. T.D. O'Sullivan, *The De Excidio of Gildas: its Authenticity and Date* (Leiden, 1997), pp. 149–50, lists the debates.
50. See the contribution of Rob. Meens in this volume.
51. For example, Adomnán, *Vita Columbae*, I.21, ed. A.O. and M.O. Anderson, *Adomnán's Life of Columba* (Oxford, 1991), pp. 46–9. I am indebted to Clare Stancliffe for the reference.
52. Jonas, *Vita Columbani*, I.6, 10; II.1, 8, 15, 19, 25 (pp. 161, 170, 232, 245, 265, 273, 290).
53. Clark, *The Benedictines in the Middle Ages* (Woodbridge, 2011), pp. 27–30.
54. A. de Vogüé, ed., *Les Règles des saints Pères*, 2 vols, SC 297–8 (Paris, 1982).
55. J.-P. Weiss, 'Lérins et la 'Règle des Quatre Pères'', in Y. Codou and M. Lauwers, eds, *Lérins, une île sainte de l'Antiquité au Moyen Âge* (Turnhout, 2009), pp. 121–40.
56. I.N. Wood, 'A Prelude to Columbanus: the Monastic Achievement in the Burgundian Territories', in H.B. Clarke and M. Brennan, eds, *Columbanus and Merovingian Monasticism*, pp. 3–32, at p. 4.

57. Jonas, *Vita Columbani*, I.19, pp. 187–93.
58. B. Rosenwein, *Negotiating Space. Power, Restraint, and Privileges of Immunity in Early Medieval Europe* (Ithaca, 1999), pp. 59–73.
59. It is true that the archaeology does not prove beyond doubt that Luxeuil was inhabited at the time of Columbanus's arrival: absolute continuity of habitation is scarcely provable. But if there was an interruption it was very short lived indeed (Bully, personal communication).
60. Jonas, *Vita Columbani*, praef., pp. 144–8.
61. Jonas, *Vita Columbani*, I.19, pp. 187–93.
62. Rosenwein, *Negotiating Space*, p. 41.
63. *Regula Donati*, ed. A. de Vogüé, 'La règle de Donat pour l'abbesse Gauthstrude', *Benedictina* 25 (1978), pp. 219–313.
64. Leso, 'Columbanus in Europe', p. 362. For discussion of the distribution of the *Vita Columbani*, see Wood, 'The Irish in England and on the Continent in the seventh century'.
65. T. M. Charles-Edwards, *Early Christian Ireland* (Cambridge, 2000), pp. 386–8.
66. *Regula Donati: Regula cuiusdam patris ad virgines*, PL 88, cols 1051–70; *Regula cuiusdam patris ad monachos*, ed. F. Villegas, 'La "Regula cuiusdam patris ad monachos": Ses sources littéraires et ses rapports avec la "Regula monachorum" de Colomban', *Revue d'histoire de spiritualité* 49 (1973), pp. 3–36. See Chapter 4
67. A. Malnory, *Quid Luxovienses Monachi discipuli ad regulam monasteriorum atque ad commune ecclesiae profectum contulerint* (Paris, 1894).
68. Fredegar, IV.36, ed. J.M. Wallace-Hadrill, *The Fourth Book of the Chronicle of Fredegar* (Edinburgh, 1960), pp. 23–9.
69. Bede, *HE*, II.4.
70. Wood, 'The Irish in England and on the Continent'.

6

Columbanus and the Easter Controversy: Theological, Social and Political Contexts

Caitlin Corning

Determining the correct date for the celebration of Easter involves important theological and practical considerations. Since there was no universal agreement about the manner in which these considerations should be addressed it is not surprising that the dating of Easter became contentious, causing controversy and conflict in the church for centuries. When Columbanus (d. 615) arrived on the Continent in the late sixth century, he brought with him an older system for dating Easter that was different from the one in use in Rome or the Merovingian churches. Within a few years, the two sides were debating questions of authority and interpretation in an attempt to defeat one another's position or reach a resolution. The controversy between Columbanus and the Merovingian episcopacy reveals in microcosm many of the arguments that would be used throughout the process by which the Irish churches eventually abandoned their traditional method of calculating Easter in favour of the Roman practice.

Background on the Easter Controversy

From as early as the second century, there had been disagreements about how to correctly calculate the date of Easter.[1] This date needed to correspond with the information about Christ's death and resurrection from the Bible. The gospel narratives state that Christ was crucified on, or just after, the Jewish Passover and rose from the dead on the following Sunday.[2] In the Old Testament, the Jews were required to observe Passover on the full moon (*luna* 14) in the first month of spring (Nisan). Therefore, by the third century, most agreed that Easter should be observed on a Sunday following the first full moon of spring. The incorporation of the lunar calendar into the calculations for the date of Easter meant that the celebration would be a movable feast since lunar days do not occur on the same fixed solar dates from year to year. This is because the lunar year is approximately eleven days shorter than the solar. If adjustments are not made, the lunar months move out of sequence with the seasons. The Easter controversy focused on how to correctly use these two calendar systems to determine the date for Easter.

Christians wanted to be able to predict Easter dates into the future, especially as Lent became part of the church calendar. This meant that Christians could not simply wait for a local Jewish community to observe Passover and themselves celebrate Easter the following Sunday since they needed to begin the Lenten fast approximately forty days before Easter. In addition, some Christians argued that the Jews no longer followed the Old Testament instructions for Passover and sometimes observed it twice in one year. By the Council of Nicaea (325), these two factors, combined with the increasing belief that Christians should not rely on Jews to help determine the date of Easter since they had rejected Christ, resulted in the ecclesiastical leaders ruling that churches should use their own calculations to determine the date of the full moon after the equinox and from this, Easter Sunday.

Even with this general agreement, there were issues that led to conflicting Easter dates. One of these was the date of the equinox. From the time of Julius Caesar until the fourth century, Rome believed it occurred on 25th March.[3] However, by the third century, the scholars at Alexandria had recalculated to a more accurate 21st March. If *luna* 14 (the full moon) happened on 22nd March, Alexandria would celebrate on the next Sunday, while those using the 25th March equinox would wait for the next full moon, delaying Easter for over four weeks.

Another disagreement was over the lunar limits within which Easter could fall. *Luna* 14 can occur any day of the week. Since Easter must occur on a Sunday, there needs to be a seven-day span after the full moon for the observance of Easter. For example, if *luna* 14 is on a Tuesday, the following Sunday would be *luna* 19. If *luna* 14 is on a Friday, Easter would be on sixteenth day of the moon. When it came to these lunar limits, some argued that this span should include *luna* 14 since the Gospel of John reports that Christ was crucified on Passover. This group argued for limits of *luna* 14–20. Those at Alexandria believed Easter could not occur on Passover since the Synoptic

Gospels say that Christ was crucified the day after this. Therefore, their limits were *luna* 15–21. The traditional practice in Rome was to have limits of *luna* 16–22. They believed these dates better represented the Gospel story arguing that Christ was crucified on *luna* 14, was in the tomb on *luna* 15 and was resurrected on *luna* 16.

Therefore a complex set of lunar days and solar dates had to be calculated to determine the date of Easter.[4] Differences in the date of the equinox and the lunar range for the Sunday of Easter combined with a number of additional factors meant competing Easter tables listed conflicting dates.[5]

Sources

During the conflict between Columbanus and the Merovingian Church over Easter, the two tables in question were the Victorian table and the *Latercus* 84-year table. Victorius of Aquitaine created his Easter table in *c.* 457 after Pope Leo's archdeacon, Hilarius, who later become pope, requested that he explore the problem of Easter dating and create a more accurate table to be used in Rome.[6] It had a 532-year cycle, placed the equinox on 21 March, and had the traditional Roman lunar limits of 16–22. Using these parameters, Easter was observed between 22 March and 24 April (see Chapter 10). A critical problem with this table was that in some years it listed two possible Easter dates causing confusion about which should be followed.[7] In spite of this, the Victorian table was popular in the Latin West, at least in part because of the perceived papal approval.[8] In addition, it appeared to provide a perpetual Easter table, as the solar dates for Easter repeated every 532 years. The Merovingian churches officially adopted this table at the Council of Orléans in 541.[9]

Columbanus used the *Latercus*, an 84-year cycle attributed to Sulpicius Severus (*c.* 363–420) that may have arrived in Ireland around 430.[10] For years, historians had done their best to recreate this table using details provided by Columbanus, Bede and others from the seventh and eighth centuries. However, in 1985, Dáibhí Ó Cróinín discovered a copy of it in Padua, Biblioteca Antoniana, MS. I. 27 and soon after published his findings.[11] There were scribal errors in the manuscript and initial attempts to recreate the Easter dates proved difficult. Daniel Mc Carthy, who worked with Ó Cróinín on the original reconstruction, was able to make corrections and provided a more accurate reconstruction in 1993.[12] Since then, historians have been able to calculate Easter dates for the fourth through the eighth centuries using the *Latercus* table.[13] This allows them to compare specific years in the Victorian and *Latercus* tables to determine whether either listed a date that would be deemed especially controversial.

The *Latercus* used the older 25th March equinox and had lunar limits of 14–20. Easter could occur between 26th March and 23rd April. Since the supporters of the *Latercus* thought the equinox did not occur until 25th March, they would not celebrate Easter from 22nd to 25th March; dates that were perfectly acceptable in the Victorian table (see Chapter 10). The *Latercus* differs from other known 84-year cycles because it inserts the *saltus lunae* every fourteen years. The *saltus* is when a day is skipped in the age of the moon in order to correspond with astronomical reality. Due to the calculations used by the *Latercus*, the lunar dates listed in the table moved out of sequence with the actual moon by 1.28 days for each 84-year cycle.[14] By Columbanus's time, the *Latercus* was listing lunar days that were inaccurate by at least four days. Therefore, if the table identified a day as *luna* 14 (the full moon), it was actually *luna* 10; a date visibly in error.

Unfortunately for historians, there are few narrative sources that provide details on the Easter controversy between Columbanus and the Merovingian church. In the *Vita Columbani*, Jonas of Bobbio purposely neglected to include any information about it.[15] This is not surprising since by the time he wrote the Life in *c.* 640, the monasteries originally founded by Columbanus had adopted the Victorian table. As with all *vitae*, the purpose of the *Vita Columbani* was to present its protagonist as a saint who was held in favour by God.[16] To report that Columbanus had once supported an Easter table then regarded as incorrect would not have been suitable material for this work. In spite of this, the *Vita* can provide context on Columbanus's relationship with the Merovingian court of Burgundy and the bishops, though, as will be discussed, Jonas also altered this evidence to fit his goals.

Fortunately, there are five surviving letters by Columbanus, four of which discuss the Easter controversy.[17] These letters are invaluable and provide a critical witness in three important ways. First, these letters are the only documents that contain the arguments in support of the *Latercus* table and against the Victorian written by someone who felt the *Latercus* was correct. In all other instances, those who advocated for the Victorian or other tables composed the documents that preserve the arguments in favour of the *Latercus*.[18] Columbanus's letters allow the historian to compare his ideas against the information found in these other sources.

Second, since Columbanus's letters represent a period of over ten years, they reveal the development of his arguments and the modifications in his approaches as the controversy continued. It is not often in the wider history of the Easter controversy that historians have multiple sources by the same person. Given Columbanus's importance in this early phase of the Easter controversy involving Irish churchmen, these letters become even more critical. Finally, because these letters are the only source that details the Easter controversy between the supporters of the *Latercus* and Victorian tables in Merovingian Gaul, they must be used not only to understand Columbanus's opinions but also to reconstruct the arguments of the Merovingian bishops against the *Latercus*.

The controversy as presented in Columbanus's letters

Soon after Columbanus arrived in the Merovingian kingdoms, Easter became an issue. Around 600, he wrote to Pope Gregory the Great (590–604) to ask for papal condemnation of the Victorian table.[19] In this letter, Columbanus attacks the table's legitimacy on three points. First, he argues that by allowing Easter to fall on the 21st or 22nd day of the lunar month, the table supports a 'dark Easter'. By this time in the lunar cycle, the moon rises after midnight so that there are more hours of darkness than moonlight. Since Easter celebrates the triumph of Christ, 'the light of the world', over death, Easter should not be celebrated on a day when light has not conquered darkness. Columbanus then quotes a passage from a document attributed to Anatolius, bishop of Laodicea (d. 283), which states that those who allow Easter to fall on the 21st or 22nd '... not only cannot maintain this on the authority of holy scripture, but also incur the charge of sacrilege and contumacy, together with the peril of their souls'.[20] This issue may have been of special concern to Columbanus because the Victorian table listed Easters on these days in 593–4, 597 and 600.

His second complaint is that this table allows Christ's resurrection to be celebrated before his passion.[21] Since Columbanus regarded 25th March as the date of the equinox and therefore the earliest date for Passover, he did not believe that Easter should be celebrated between 22nd and 25th March. As mentioned, the earliest possible date for Easter in the *Latercus* was 26th March.

His third major accusation against Victorius's table is that its lunar limits (*luna* 16–22) violated the instructions for the week of the Feast of Unleavened Bread as outlined in the Old Testament. In connection with Passover, Jews were to observe this in remembrance of the flight of the Hebrews out of Egypt.[22] Columbanus believed that it should be observed from the 14th to the 20th day of the lunar month. In other words, Passover and the first day of the Feast of Unleavened Bread occurred on the same day. By allowing Easter to fall on *luna* 21–22, not only did this table allow a dark Easter, but Victorius had added two days to his lunar limits never mentioned in scripture.[23]

With regard to the arguments used by the Merovingian bishops against the *Latercus*, Columbanus states their only accusation is that it 'holds Easter with the Jews'.[24] This is an allusion to the fact that the *Latercus* allowed Easter to occur on *luna* 14. In the early church, some Christians had always celebrated Easter on Passover (*luna* 14) no matter the day of the week. This practice, known as Quarto-decimanism, was condemned from the late second century. From that time forward, some argued that *luna* 14, even if it fell on a Sunday, was no longer a viable date for Easter.[25]

Columbanus sees this as a ridiculous claim and argues that allowing Easter to fall on *luna* 14 is not celebrating with the Jews. It is simply following the instructions for Passover and the Feast of Unleavened Bread as outlined in the scriptures. If Christians correctly calculate the date of Easter and it happens to fall on the same day as Passover, this is simply a coincidence. In any case, Passover and Easter belong to God, not to the Jews who rejected Christ. It is God, he contends, who appointed these instructions. Arguing that Easter cannot happen on *luna* 14 is, in effect, questioning God.[26]

Columbanus is clearly disturbed that the pope has not condemned the Victorian table and cannot believe that he would support a dark Easter. He suggests that if it is humility preventing Gregory from rejecting this table for fear of being seen as ruling against earlier popes who supported it, he must remember that 'a living saint can right what by another and greater one has not been righted'.[27] False humility only harms the church.

Columbanus acknowledges that his letter may seem presumptuous, but assures Gregory that rather than writing on his own authority, he is simply asserting the beliefs of numerous church fathers. He states that all the scholars in Ireland have long dismissed the Victorian table as inherently flawed. He notes that Anatolius, whom Jerome praised as a man of great learning, had condemned the practice of dark Easters (*luna* 21–22).[28] Since Victorius allowed these, it remains up to Gregory to choose between Anatolius, and by extension Jerome, on the one hand and Victorius on the other.

This letter reveals Columbanus at his most assured. While he claims humility, he forcefully presents his arguments. This is not a letter that objectively outlines the positives and negatives of the Victorian and *Latercus* tables. Columbanus appears to have believed that his arguments against the Victorian table, his defence of *luna* 14, and his cautions about siding against Jerome would be persuasive enough for Gregory to rule in his favour. He believed he had the obligation to raise these issues with the pope and to remind him of his duty to lead the church into the fullness of truth.[29]

Though Columbanus states that he wrote additional letters to Pope Gregory and also a *brevis libellus* to Aridius, bishop of Lyon (603–15), none of these documents survive.[30] Therefore, there are no sources for this part of the Easter controversy until 603–7 when Columbanus composed his second and third surviving letters. The second letter is addressed to the bishops at the Council of Chalon-sur-Saône (*c.* 603).[31] Columbanus had been asked to appear at this council to discuss Easter, but he refused and instead composed a written response. The third letter was sent to Rome, though the pope is not named.[32] Since there were short papal vacancies in 604 after the death of Gregory the Great, and from 606–7 after the death of Pope Sabinian, historians assume the letter should be dated to one of these periods.

What is new in these two letters is Columbanus's plea that he and his followers be allowed to use the *Latercus* while the rest of the Merovingian church could follow the Victorian table. He pleads with the bishops, 'let Gaul, I beg, contain us side by side, whom the kingdom of heaven shall contain'.[33] In the third letter, he reminds the pope of the debate between Polycarp, bishop of Smyrna (d. 167), and Pope Anicetus (*c.* 158–67).[34] According to tradition, the two could not come to an agreement on the correct dating of Easter but decided to let each celebrate according to their own tradition rather than fracture the unity of the church.

In the past, statements such as these were interpreted by some historians as demonstrating that the Irish supporters of the *Latercus* did not regard diversity in Easter dating as a problem, but instead viewed it as part of the normal multiplicity of practices in the church. For example, Kathleen Hughes in her magisterial *The Church in Early Irish Society* presented the idea that the Irish 'expect[ed] diversity' while the continental church did not. In fact, she argued that only the supporters of the Roman tables saw Easter dating as 'not a matter of church discipline, but almost as a matter of faith'.[35]

More recently, historians have emphasized that the Irish did regard Easter dating as a matter of significant concern and were not supportive of diversity in this area.[36] In light of this, these passages have been reinterpreted. First, Columbanus states in both letters that he has appended his earlier letter to Pope Gregory.[37] As discussed, it clearly condemns the Victorian table. Second, although he assumed his readers would be familiar with his arguments, he does restate his main claims against Victorius's system. To the bishops at Chalon, he reminds them that the Victorian table celebrates Easter before the equinox, uses the unlawful *luna* 21–22, and violates the arguments of Anatolius. Columbanus adds that he regards Victorius as having little authority for he wrote after the great Fathers of the church.[38] To the pope, he again emphasizes that Anatolius condemned the lunar limits later adopted by Victorius.[39]

In Columbanus's second letter, he focuses on the need to submit to God and to seek together for the truth.[40] He does suggest that both traditions could be followed, but only so long as 'both traditions are good'. Otherwise, 'whatever agrees better with the Old and New Testament should be maintained'.[41] Columbanus's arguments against the Victorian table suggest that he was confident the *Latercus* would prevail if both sides humbly searched for the truth.

Columbanus's shift from requesting a condemnation of the Victorian table to simply requesting that his monastic foundations be allowed to use the *Latercus* most likely arose from the political realities he faced in *c.* 603. In his second letter, he calls upon the bishops to protect rather than persecute his foundations.[42] He is concerned with the divisions this quarrel is causing and seems troubled that he might be forced to leave Burgundy.[43] He realized, at this point, that there was little chance the Merovingian bishops would adopt the *Latercus*. His only option to ensure that his foundations were not forced to use the Victorian table was to attempt to compromise with the bishops.

No record of the Council of Chalon survives. However, given that Columbanus wrote to the papacy after this, it can be assumed that the bishops were not open to his compromise. Therefore, when he wrote to the papacy in 604/606–7, he wanted the pope to rule that he was outside the jurisdiction of the Merovingian bishops. It is in this context that he mentions the story of Polycarp and Pope Anicetus.[44] For the sake of unity, Pope Anicetus agreed that two Easter traditions could be used. How much more should the pope allow Columbanus to do the same when his Easter table had the support of Anatolius and Jerome? In addition, towards the end of this letter, he reminds the pope of the ruling of the second ecumenical council of Constantinople (381) that churches in heathen lands should follow the traditions of the Fathers.[45] By referring to this canon, Columbanus was trying to demonstrate that there was historic precedence for his contention that he should not be subject to the authority of Merovingian bishops, but instead should be allowed to continue to follow the tradition of the Irish churches.

By 607, Columbanus and the Merovingian bishops had been debating Easter for over a decade. Historians recognize that Columbanus must have had royal support in order to ignore the continued opposition by the episcopacy. While Easter was a serious theological issue, politics often influenced the ways in which specific ecclesiastical leaders or institutions could respond. Determining the exact role the Merovingian royal family in Burgundy may have played in the controversy is difficult. Columbanus never refers to the king so his letters provide little help. In addition, historians know that in the Life of Columbanus, Jonas has manipulated events in this period to reflect the political situation *c.* 640 when the Life was composed. In 613, Chlothar II, king of Neustria (584–629), over-threw Brunhild and her descendants. To justify this, Chlothar and his court encouraged the belief that Brunhild and her descendants were hopelessly corrupt. By the time Jonas wrote the Life, Chlothar and his successors had been patrons of the Columbanian houses for almost thirty years. Therefore it is not surprising that Jonas tried to distance Columbanus from Brunhild and her grandson Theuderic (595–613), but portrayed the saint as prophesying the eventual triumph of Chlothar.[46]

Despite the attempts by Jonas to downplay the support Columbanus initially received in Burgundy from the royal family, it is clear that there was a close and influential relationship. It is probable that Luxeuil and Columbanus's other monasteries in Burgundy were royal foundations.[47] Even in the Life, Jonas includes the information that before they turned against Columbanus, Theuderic sought spiritual advice from the saint and Brunhild looked to Columbanus to bless Theuderic's children.[48]

One of the best examples of the importance of royal support can be seen at the Council of Chalon. It is important to keep in mind that many bishops held their positions because of royal patronage. Brunhild was influential in the election of a number of bishops including Aridius of Lyon, who presided at the council meeting.[49] In addition, Theuderic's approval would have been needed to call a church council.[50] It is only possible to speculate why the king allowed Easter to be discussed at this meeting. He may have been pushing for the compromise position Columbanus proposes as a way to solve the ecclesiastical dispute.[51] In any case, in addition to Easter, the bishops at Chalon also discussed the fate of Desiderius, bishop of Vienne (d. 607). Desiderius appears to have offended Brunhild, who responded by arranging for his denunciation and exile by the bishops.[52] Therefore, Desiderius, who had angered Brunhild, was condemned on various charges and exiled. Columbanus, who did not even bother to attend the meeting, seems to have faced no sanctions. Given the patronage Columbanus received from Theuderic and Brunhild, it is possible the bishops knew that there was little possibility of enforcing any condemnation.

Although not a problem in 603, Thomas Charles-Edwards has suggested that the controversy between Columbanus and the episcopacy in Burgundy eventually contributed to the saint's exile from Burgundy seven years after Chalon.[53] Jonas reports that Columbanus was exiled because he refused Brunhild's request to bless her illegitimate great-grandchildren. She then turned the court and episcopal hierarchy against him.[54] Charles-Edwards, however, points out that in 610, Theuderic had to surrender territory to his brother, Theudebert (595–612), king of Austrasia. In light of this weakness, he may have needed to ensure the support of the secular and ecclesiastical nobility. Theuderic may have decided that Columbanus was too divisive and so needed to be removed from the court.

The last letter in which Columbanus mentions Easter was written to his own communities after his exile in 610.[55] Much of the letter is concerned with reminding his monks that those who follow Christ will face tribulation and persecution. He encourages them to remain humble, at peace and united. In a section addressed to Athala, whom Columbanus thought might succeed him as abbot, he warns that the community may become divided over Easter. In fact, he thought that cracks were already beginning to appear and urged Athala to stand firm. He worried that his enemies would use Easter to divide the community and that without his presence, his monks might abandon the table he held to be correct.

End of the controversy in the Columbanian communities

Historians do not know when the Columbanian houses finally abandoned the *Latercus*. One possibility is that they did so soon after Columbanus's death in 615. It must be remembered that the leaders of the Columbanian monasteries, such as Eustasius and Athala, were closely linked to the Merovingian aristocracy.[56] Therefore, they would have used the Victorian table before joining one of Columbanus's monastic foundations. Perhaps some of the monks had supported the *Latercus* more out of loyalty to their founder and less because of a conviction that it represented the correct method for calculating Easter.

Despite Columbanus's protests, there were strong arguments in favour of the Victorian table. First, it did have wide support. Insofar as church unity is concerned, this is an important factor. Not only had this table been approved by a Merovingian church council, it was the one used in Rome. Second, supporters of the Victorian table could point to the fact that it did agree with the Biblical narrative. As mentioned, according to the Gospel of John, Christ was crucified on *luna* 14, was in the grave on *luna* 15, and resurrected on *luna* 16. Therefore lunar limits beginning with the sixteenth day of the month, as advocated by Victorius, reinforced the concept that Easter is a celebration of Christ's resurrection, not his death. It also allowed for a clearer separation of Jewish and Christian practice by avoiding Easter on *luna* 14.

If Columbanus's monasteries did not abandon the *Latercus c.* 615, the other possibility is that they did so shortly before 628.[57] Jonas reports that a council was held at Mâcon (626/7) to hear complaints against the Columbanian houses.[58] If these monasteries were still using the *Latercus*, this could explain, at least in part, why the bishops met. However, Jonas's account of the specific accusations is vague and historians can only speculate if Easter was an issue.[59] If the Columbanian houses had been using the *Latercus* as late as 626/7, they must have changed soon thereafter because in 628, Pope Honorius (625–38) granted a privilege to Bobbio, one of the houses founded by Columbanus in northern Italy.[60] Honorius's interest in the Easter controversy is attested in a letter he wrote to Irish clergy in which he argued against the *Latercus*.[61] Since it is doubtful that Luxeuil and Bobbio would have been using different Easter tables and it is unlikely that Honorius would have granted a privilege to Bobbio at a time when it actively condemned the Victorian table, most historians see this as a *terminus post quem non* for the abandonment of the *Latercus* by the Columbanian monastic houses.[62]

Conclusion

Easter dating was a critical issue that caused divisions between Columbanus and the Merovingian church in the first part of the seventh century. Each group believed that the opposing side's table violated key Christian concepts associated with this feast. Columbanus's four letters allow the historian to chart a progression in his response to the Easter controversy from his initial confidence that the papacy would condemn the Victorian table, to his suggestion of a compromise where both tables would be used and, finally, his anxiety that his own monks might adopt the Victorian table. Throughout this, Columbanus's ability to continue to use the *Latercus* in the face of mounting episcopal opposition rested heavily on his ability to maintain royal support and patronage.

Columbanus's letters also are important because they reveal the similarities and differences in the arguments and approaches used as the controversy developed in the British Isles. For example, Cummean and Bede both report that the supporters of the *Latercus* from Iona also referenced Anatolius in support of their Easter calculations.[63] On the other hand, Bede states that the supporters of the *Latercus* at the Synod of Whitby (664) claimed the table reflected the traditions handed down by the Apostle John.[64] Columbanus never used this argument. It is possible that this claim was not utilized until the late 620s when the supporters of the Victorian table in Ireland argued that Rome and rest of the church viewed Victorius's calculations as correct. Appealing to the authority of St. John may have been a way to legitimize use of the *Latercus* in the face of this assertion.

Unfortunately, due to the vicissitudes of time coupled with the fact that the Columbanian communities did not want to preserve the memory of their founding saint supporting an Easter table that was eventually rejected by the rest of the church, it is not possible to fully reconstruct all the phases of this conflict or establish for certain when his foundations fully embraced the Victorian table. However, Columbanus's letters do provide invaluable contemporary evidence and preserve the arguments presented by one of the most ardent supporters of the *Latercus* table.

Notes

1. For surveys of the Easter Controversy see Bonnie Blackburn and Leofranc Holford-Strevens, *The Oxford Companion to the Year* (Oxford, 1999), pp. 791–828; Bede, *The Reckoning of Time*, ed. and trans. Faith Wallis (Liverpool, 1999), pp. xxxv–lxiii; Thomas Charles-Edwards, *Early Christian Ireland* (Cambridge, 2000), pp. 391–415; George Declercq, *Anno Domini: The Origins of the Christian Era* (Turnhout, 2000); Leofranc Holford-Strevens, *History of Time: A Very Short Introduction* (Oxford, 2005), pp. 44–63; Alden Mosshammer, *The Easter Computus and the Origins of the Christian Era* (Oxford, 2008).

2. The Synoptic Gospels (Matthew, Mark and Luke) disagree with the Gospel of John. The Synoptic Gospels report that Christ observed Passover with his disciples before being arrested and killed. John states that the Passover had not occurred when Christ died (John 18:28; 19:13, 31).
3. Bede, *On the Nature of Things and On Times*, ed. and trans. Calvin Kendall and Faith Wallis, (Liverpool, 2010), p. 22.
4. For a history of lunar calendars to the early eighth century see Leofranc Holford-Strevens, 'Paschal Lunar Calendars up to Bede', *Peritia* 20 (2008), pp. 165–208.
5. See also Immo Warntjes's chapter in this volume.
6. Hilarius succeeded Leo as pope in 461. Victorius of Aquitaine, *Cursus Paschalis*, ed. Theodor Mommsen, *Chronica Minora*, MGH Auct. ant. 9 (Berlin, 1892), pp. 667–735. See also Declercq, *Anno Domini*, pp. 82–95 and Mosshammer, *The Easter Computus*, pp. 239–44.
7. Blackburn and Holford-Strevens, *The Oxford Companion to the Year*, pp. 793, 808–9.
8. Bede, *On the Nature of Things*, p. 24.
9. Council of Orléans, c. 1, *Concilia Aevi Merovingici 511–695*, ed. Friedrich Maassen, MGH Conc. 1 (Hanover, 1893), pp. 86–99, at p. 87.
10. Daniel Mc Carthy, 'On the Arrival of the *Latercus* in Ireland', in Immo Warntjes and Dáibhí Ó Cróinín, eds., *The Easter Controversy of Late Antiquity and the Early Middle Ages*, Studia Traditionis Theologiae 10 (Turnhout, 2011) pp. 48–75.
11. Daniel Mc Carthy and Dáibhí Ó Cróinín, 'The "Lost" Irish 84-Year Easter Table Rediscovered', *Peritia* 6–7 (1987–88), pp. 227–42.
12. Daniel Mc Carthy, 'Easter Principles and a Lunar Cycle Used by Fifth Century Christian Communities in the British Isles', *Journal for the History of Astronomy* 24 (1993), pp. 204–24.
13. See Blackburn and Holford-Strevens, *The Oxford Companion to the Year*, pp. 870–5; and Caitlin Corning, *The Celtic and Roman Traditions: Conflict and Consensus in the Early Medieval Church* (New York, 2006), pp. 183–90.
14. Immo Warntjes, 'The Munich Computus and the 84 (14)-year Easter Reckoning', *PRIA* 107C (2007), pp. 31–85, at 36.
15. For an excellent analysis see Clare Stancliffe, 'Jonas' Life of Columbanus and his Disciples', in John Carey *et. al.*, eds., *Studies in Irish Hagiography: Saints and Scholars* (Dublin, 2001), pp. 189–220.
16. For a discussion on hagiography see Thomas Head, *Medieval Hagiography: An Anthology* (New York, 2000), pp. xiii–xxv.
17. Transcriptions and translations of these letters can be found in G.S.M. Walker, *Sancti Columbani Opera*, Scriptores Latini Hiberniae 2 (Dublin, 1957), pp. 2–37.
18. For example, there is a letter (*c.* 632) by the Irish ecclesiastic Cummean written to convince Iona and others to abandon the *Latercus*. He conveys the arguments by the *Latercus* supporters, but only to counter

them. Cummian, *Cummian's Letter De Controversia Paschali*, eds. and trans. Maura Walsh and Dáibhí Ó Cróinín (Toronto, 1988).

19. Charles-Edwards, *Early Christian Ireland*, p. 368.
20. Columbanus, Letter 1, pp. 4–5.
21. Columbanus, Letter 1, pp. 4–5.
22. The dating of this feast is complicated by the fact that some Old Testament passages imply that it should last seven days including Passover (*luna* 14–20), while other passages state that it should start the day after Passover (*luna* 15–21). For example, Num. 28:16–17 and Deut. 16:1–4.
23. Columbanus, Letter 1, pp. 6–7.
24. Columbanus, Letter 1, pp. 6–7.
25. Eusebius, *Historia Ecclesiastica*, 5:23–24; Blackburn and Halford-Strevens, *The Oxford Companion to the Year*, p. 791.
26. Columbanus, Letter 1.
27. Columbanus, Letter 1.
28. Ibid, p. 8–9. Columbanus quotes from and refers to *De ratione paschali*. Historians disagree whether this is an actual work by Anatolius or an insular 'forgery'. In either case, Columbanus thought it was an authentic text. For the text and arguments that this is by Anatolius see Daniel Mc Carthy and Aidan Breen, *The Ante-Nicene Christian Pasch. De Ratione Paschali: The Paschal Tract of Anatolius, Bishop of Laodicea* (Dublin, 2003). For arguments that it is a forgery see Mosshammer, *The Easter Computus*, pp. 130–61.
29. Damien Bracken, 'Juniors Teaching Elders: Columbanus, Rome and Spiritual Authority,' in Éamonn Ó Carragáin, ed., *Roma Felix: Formation and Reflections of Medieval Rome* (Aldershot, 2007) pp. 253–76.
30. Columbanus, Letter 2, pp. 16–17; Letter 3, pp. 22–23.
31. Columbanus, Letter 2, pp. 12–23.
32. Columbanus, Letter 3, pp. 22–5.
33. Columbanus, Letter 2, p. 17.
34. Eusebius, *Historia Ecclesiastica*, v.24.
35. Kathleen Hughes, *The Church in Early Irish Society* (Ithaca, New York, 1966), pp. 104, 108. Other historians argued that Easter was not the true issue of dispute. Instead, it was one of authority. For example John McNeill, *The Celtic Churches: A History, AD 200–1200* (Chicago, 1974), p. 109.
36. Charles-Edwards, *Early Christian Ireland*, pp. 407–11.
37. Columbanus, Letter 2, pp. 16–17, and Letter 3, pp. 22–23.
38. Columbanus, Letter 2, pp. 16–19.
39. Columbanus, Letter 3, pp. 24–5.
40. Columbanus, Letter 2, pp. 14–15; Bracken, 'Juniors Teaching Elders', pp. 167–71.
41. Columbanus, Letter 2, pp. 18–19.
42. Columbanus, Letter 2, pp. 16–17.
43. Columbanus, Letter 2, pp. 18–19.

44. Columbanus, Letter 3, pp. 24–5.
45. *First Council of Constantinople*, Canon 2, ed. C. H. Turner, *Ecclesiae occidentalis monumenta iuris antiquissima, canonum et conciliorum Graecorum interpretationes latinae*, 2 vols in 9 parts (Oxford, 1899–1939), II.3, pp. 401–72.
46. Charles-Edwards, *Early Christian Ireland*, pp. 350–66; Corning, *The Celtic and Roman Traditions*, pp. 34–36; Alexander O'Hara, 'The *Vita Columbani* in Merovingian Gaul', *EME* 17.2 (2009), 126–53; Ian Wood, *Merovingian Kingdoms, 450–751* (London, 1994), pp. 194–5.
47. Wood, *Merovingian Kingdoms*, p. 195; Ian Wood, 'Jonas, the Merovingians, and Pope Honorius: *Diplomata* and the *Vita Columbani*', in Alexander Murray, ed., *After Rome's Fall: Narrators and Sources of Early Medieval History* (Toronto, 1998), pp. 99–120, at pp. 106–8.
48. Jonas, *Vita Columbani*, i.18.
49. Wood, *Merovingian Kingdoms*, pp. 133–4.
50. Yaniv Fox, 'The Bishop and the Monk: Desiderius of Vienne and the Columbanian Movement', *EME* 20.2 (2012), 176–94, at 176–7.
51. In Book 2 of the *Vita Columbani*, Jonas relates that Chlothar, though a supporter of the Columbanian foundations, gave approval for a church council to be held at Mâcon (*c.* 626/7). No explanation is given for the king's support of this church council (Jonas, *Vita Columbani*, ii.9).
52. Wood, *Merovingian Kingdoms*, pp. 104–6, 131–3.
53. Charles-Edwards, *Early Medieval Ireland*, p. 317.
54. Jonas, *Vita Columbani*, i.18–20.
55. Columbanus, Letter 4, pp. 26–37; Stancliffe, 'Jonas' *Life of Columbanus*', pp. 203–4.
56. Jonas, *Vita Columbani*, i.20, ii.1.
57. Charles-Edwards, *Early Medieval Ireland*, pp. 364–9; Stancliffe, 'Jonas' *Life of Columbanus*', pp. 206–7.
58. For additional analysis of this council see Charles-Edwards, *Early Medieval Ireland*, pp. 364–7; and Corning, *The Celtic and Roman Traditions*, pp. 48–55.
59. Jonas, *Vita Columbani*, ii.9–10; Stancliffe, 'Jonas' *Life of Columbanus*', pp. 205–8.
60. Jonas, *Vita Columbani*, ii.23; Wood, 'Jonas, the Merovingians, and Pope Honorius', pp. 118–20.
61. Bede, *HE*, ii.19.
62. Charles-Edwards, *Early Christian Ireland*, p. 367.
63. Cummian, *Letter*, pp. 84–87 and Bede, *HE*, iii.25
64. Bede, *HE*, iii.25; Damian Bracken, 'Rome and the Isles: Ireland, England and the Rhetoric of Orthodoxy', *Proceedings of the British Academy* 157 (2009), pp. 75–97, at 94–7.

7

Irish Biblical Exegesis

Mark Stansbury

The books of the Bible are the holy texts of Christianity, yet for those trying to understand them in western Europe during Late Antiquity and the early Middle Ages they were fraught with difficulties. First, the texts were full of names, places, plants, animals, objects and customs that would have ranged from the exotic to the utterly unfamiliar in the eyes of contemporaries. Second, aside from the usual problems in manuscript transmission, there were also puzzles and inconsistencies within the texts themselves. Third, as Christians of that period saw it, the books of the Bible conveyed truth in a variety of ways. At its most basic level, the Bible's account of historical events – from the creation of the world to Paul's time in Rome – was entirely true. Yet these and other passages could also express truth elliptically rather than directly, and understanding this required special skills and knowledge.[1] Finally, of course, the books of the Bible referred to each other: the New Testament interpreted passages from the Old Testament and the letters of the New Testament expanded on the teachings of the Gospels.[2] Works of biblical exegesis written during our period aimed to clarify these obscurities and reveal the meanings of the texts.[3]

Most exegesis in our period must have been oral, either among individuals or in groups. These could have been formal occasions, such as a classroom discussion or hearing a homily, or informal ones such as private conversations. Scholars of exegesis today study written exegetical texts, some of which had their origins in these oral explanations and many of which, in turn, must have informed oral explanations. Although 'commentary' is the English catch-all description for a work of biblical exegesis, in fact *commentarius* is only one of several Latin titles used for such works, which include *explanatio, expositio, quaestiones, glossa*, and so on. To judge from their contents, it is difficult to see that there was any expectation that, for example, an *explanatio* had different aims than an *expositio*. Written exegetical

116

works in our period often follow the order of the biblical text upon which they are commenting by considering the text in small sections (often two to three modern verses long). Since there were no standard ways of referring to biblical passages, the text of the biblical passage being analysed usually stands before the commentary in the manuscript and is called the lemma (pl. lemmas or lemmata). The commentary itself could vary in length from a synonym to clarify the meaning of a single word to an expansive consideration of a longer passage. Exegetical works are often concerned with single books of the Bible, though at times groups of books are treated, such as the Minor Prophets or the Pauline letters. This would also have corresponded with the manuscripts of the Bible, among which pandects, or complete Bibles, were rare. Some exegetical works also considered parts of individual books or topics, such as the Hexameron (the six days of creation) or the miracles found in the Bible. Much early-medieval exegesis is not 'original', which is to say that the writers of exegetical works often took their material from previous writers. This great diversity in exegetical works was no doubt partly due to the considerable diversity in the aims, audiences and authors of these works.

The exegetical works of the early Middle Ages were studied by theologians, but held very little interest for historians throughout much of the early-modern and modern periods. This began to change at the end of the nineteenth century with the work of the Benedictine historians Germain Morin and André Wilmart and then in the middle of the twentieth century with the work of Ceslas Spicq, Beryl Smalley and Friedrich Stegmüller, which provided overviews of the field.[4]

Irish exegesis and its study

The first sustained engagement with the Bible in Ireland must date from the process of Christianization, the beginnings of which are commonly dated to the fifth century. The earliest extant exegetical works by Irish writers date from the seventh century, though the Psalm commentary of Columbanus may have been still earlier. Scholars born in Ireland and who lived on the Continent continued to write exegetical works through the ninth century. Most of the manuscript evidence for Irish exegesis comes through transmission on the Continent in continental scripts (though often with indications of earlier insular scripts) and the manuscripts are preserved in continental libraries. One salient characteristic of the surviving exegetical work is the amount written in the vernacular. From a theological point of view Irish scholars are especially important for the role they played in using and transmitting works by Pelagius and for transmitting a Latin version of Theodore of Mopsuestia's Psalm commentary.

The term Irish exegesis is used in two ways, however. It can mean exegesis composed by students of the Bible from Ireland or it can mean a distinctive Irish approach to explaining the Bible. From the early modern period there was never doubt that writers from Ireland composed exegetical works and James F. Kenney's *Sources for the Early History of Ireland*, published in 1929, gave an overview of the material that remains indispensible today.[5] The question of a distinctive Irish exegesis was raised by several scholars writing during the middle of the twentieth century. These included Smalley in her *Study of the Bible in the Middle Ages*, Paul Grosjean in his 1955 article 'Sur quelques exegetes irlandais du viième siècle', and most influentially by Bernhard Bischoff in his article 'Wendepunkte in der Geschichte der latein-ische Exegese im Mittelalter', first published in 1954 and revised for publication in the first volume of Bischoff's collected articles, *Mittelalterliche Studien*, in 1966.[6]

As many have observed, Bischoff's article was not only about a turning point, but it also represented a turning point in the study of its subject. One early response to the issues raised by 'Wendepunkte' was 'Early "Irish" Biblical Exegesis,' an especially important article by Clare Stancliffe published in 1975. In it Stancliffe pointed out how interrelated early medieval biblical commentaries could be and questioned not only Bischoff's assumptions but the term 'Irish exegesis' as well.[7] Bischoff's work was continued in Joseph Kelly's two-part 'Catalogue of Early Medieval Hiberno-Latin Biblical Commentaries' published in *Traditio* in the late-1980s. Kelly presented Bischoff's conclusions as largely accepted, remarking that 'Discordant voices were and remain few'.[8] He also increased the thirty-nine works in Bischoff's list to 114. A series of articles published in the late 1990s called into question both Bischoff's methodology and his attribution of specific works as Irish and certainly added both more voices and more discord to the debate. Throughout this period the work of Martin MacNamara investigated both the textual and theological affiliations of many Irish texts, both exegetical and biblical. In the 1990s, the Brepols publishing house started a subseries of the Corpus Christianorum, the Scriptores Celtigenae, dedicated to new editions of Latin exegetical, homiletic, and theological works. (For biblio-graphical details and a more complete survey, see Further Reading.)

'Wendepunkte' point-by-point

Because Bischoff's article has become central to the study of Irish exegesis, and especially to the identification of new works as Irish, it is worthwhile reviewing its methodology and conclusions. The article is in two parts. The first part is a discussion of biblical exegesis in the early Middle Ages and the relationship of Irish exegesis to it, ending with a set of criteria for establishing an unattributed work as Irish, which Bischoff called *Symptomen* or symptoms. The second part of the article provides a detailed catalogue of works along with Bischoff's comments and reasons for their Irish attribution. This structure was surely one of the reasons for the article's great influence: it not only provided a framework for studying an understudied field, it also provided a roadmap for future scholars to begin working on previously unpublished texts. The first part of the article begins with an introduction giving an overview of exegesis in the early Middle Ages (pp. 205–7), which is followed by an excursus on the glosses from the school of Archbishop Theodore at Canterbury (pp. 207–9), then comments on the Irish school of exegesis (pp. 209–13), a discussion of the Ps. Jerome commentary on Mark (pp. 213–15), a discussion of 'Irish symptoms' (pp. 215–22) and finally discussion of the ways that the *Bibelwerk* (the Irish 'reference Bible') embodies many of these symptoms (pp. 222–24).[9]

Bischoff began by arguing that exegesis of the patristic age ended with Gregory the Great (d. 604) and Isidore of Seville (d. 636). After a century, Bede (d. 735), Ambrosius Autpertus (d. 784), Alcuin (d. 804) and Carolingian theologians up to Iohannes Scottus (d. 877) drew from this well. Patristic exegesis, and those who relied on it, was, more or less, formed by the Alexandrian school of Origen (d. 254), which focused on allegorical explanations. Some Irish scholars, as early as the seventh century, exhibited the influence of the Antiochene school, which focused on historical explanations, through translations of Theodore of Mopsuestia. But it seems that these translations and the Irish works based on them were confined to Ireland and to a small circle of scholars, so that they were not able to have a visible influence on the biblical scholarship of the Carolingians and Anglo-Saxons, which was, in general, fairly uniform. 'When I dare talk about turning points in this apparent uniformity, this is primarily based on previously unexploited material, from which we can see that from the seventh until the early ninth century there were several directions, and that there is basic evidence that the development of biblical scholarship took another course.'[10]

Bischoff then immediately explains why the uniformity is apparent: he cites as non-allegorical Bede's commentary on Acts and its *Retractatio*, as well as his *Thirty Questions* on Kings and the *Eight Questions*. This then begins an excursus on the school of Theodore and Hadrian at Canterbury, which reinforces the point about the different directions that exegesis could have taken. In collaboration with Michael Lapidge, this excursus would later become *Biblical Commentaries from the School of Theodore and Hadrian*, published in 1994. Compared to the Canterbury School, Bischoff argued, Bede's work was a decisive return to the older tradition of Latin exegesis. And despite the fact that Bede could have used the glosses of Theodore and Hadrian in many of his works, it remained independent of them. Bede's primary aim was allegorical exegesis.

In the first section Bischoff sets up his approach by arguing that all early medieval exegesis descends from one or the other of two schools: the school of Antioch, which represented literal exegesis, and the school of Alexandria, which represented allegorical exegesis, an idea that Smalley had stressed in *The Study of the Bible*. Thus, Bischoff implied, all later allegorical interpretation must originate from those who followed the Alexandrine school and all subsequent literal interpretation from the Antiochene.[11] This way of categorizing medieval exegesis is problematic for several reasons.

First, although these schools may have had a reality in the Greek East of the fourth century, by the seventh to ninth centuries, these would have been all but unknown in the Latin West. Indeed, the Latin exegetical writers of the seventh, eighth and ninth centuries never mention them, nor do they claim allegiance to one or the other of the schools. Of much more importance during our period, for example, would have been contemporary theological debates such as the Three Chapters controversy, which involved Theodore of Mopsuestia, but was not based on whether his exegesis was literal or allegorical.

Second, looking at commentaries this way ignores the purpose and the audience of a commentary. It is quite clear that different commentaries were written with different audiences and different purposes in mind, and one might suspect that the degree to which literal explanations are offered might be more related to this than adherence to a school. Bischoff's own example of Bede's *Retractatio* on Acts, for example, is not due to adherence to an exegetical school but to his seeing the sixth-century bilingual Greek-Latin *Codex Laudanus* of Acts (Oxford, Bodleian Library, MS Laud. Gr. 35; *CLA* II.215). In the letter to Acca of Hexham prefaced to the *Expositio in*

Lucam, Bede tells the bishop that his commentary is written not for the learned (*doctoribus*) but for the squeamish readers (*fastidiosis lectoribus*) so common in their day.[12]

Third, there is no work of exegesis that is interested in only one sense of scripture. Indeed, according to Jerome, the goal of commentary was entirely different. In the preface to his commentary on Jeremiah, Jerome wrote of the 'ignorant slanderer' (he meant Pelagius) who had apparently criticized him for borrowing too much of his interpretation. Jerome writes that this critic, when reading Jerome's commentaries on Paul's letter to Ephesus, 'was snoring so much that he did not understand the laws of commentaries, in which many opinions of different writers are included, both tacitly and explicitly with the authors' names, so that it is the choice of the reader to decide which ought to be especially chosen'.[13] So, for Jerome, at least, rather than trying to adhere to one interpretive school or another, the role of a commentary was to offer divergent opinions for the reader's choice. Finally, while biblical commentaries are more likely to contain a mixture of both literal and allegorical interpretation, Bischoff gives us no criteria for classifying a given work of exegesis other than the impression it creates.

Bischoff then argued that: '[t]he names of the great Anglo-Saxons Bede and Alcuin (...) who established Anglo-Saxon learning in Francia, also overshadowed the memory of another exegetical school, the Irish'.[14] He went on to paint a picture of early Christian Ireland as offering sanctuary for 'several heretical and apocryphal texts that seem to have been destined to disappear on the Continent', citing works by Pelagius, Theodore of Mopsuestia, and other apocryphal texts (p. 210). This section of his argument is taken largely from his *Habilitationsschrift* written at Munich and completed in 1943.[15] In another argument taken from his *Habilitationsschrift*, Bischoff says that the Irish ground was prepared to receive these texts because there was a learned class (the *filid*) and that the Bible was of special importance.

In fact, in many ways, 'Wendepunkte' represents the fulfilment of a suggestion Bischoff made in his *Habilitationsschrift* (p. 28): 'Just as the investigation of grammatical literature has resulted in a significant increase in the Irish contribution, so we ought next to inspect biblical-exegetical literature (which is mostly anonymous) for Irish characteristics (*Züge*), such as, for example, the use of Pelagius (since Zimmer), in addition to questions about *locus, tempus, persona,* answers with "*non difficile*" etc.'

In the second part of this section Bischoff argued that for Ireland in the seventh century we are on firm ground with the following works:

1. The biblical glosses in Usserianus Primus (Dublin, Trinity College, MS 55);
2. Lathcen *Egloga* (= Bischoff's B5), a set of excerpts from the *Moralia* of Gregory the Great;
3. Ailerán *Mistica interpretatio* (B25) and the short Kanones poem (B12). The *Mistica interpretatio* is a treatise that gives the deeper meaning of the genealogy of Christ;
4. Pseudo-Augustine, *De mirabilibus sacrae scripturae* (B38) (a study of several miracles in the Bible);
5. A Reichenau commentary on the Catholic Epistles (B35).

If these are the earliest attributable commentaries, it is interesting that Lathcen and Ailerán are squarely within the tradition of allegorical exposition and literally follow the fathers: Gregory's *Moralia in Job* and Jerome's Hebrew names, respectively. And far from concentrating on the literal interpretation of the Bible, Lathcen's *Ecloga* pays special attention to Gregory's allegorical interpretation.[16] The Reichenau commentary on the Catholic Epistles, which was used by Bede, likewise cites the fathers and Bischoff himself described it in the catalogue as 'primarily a moral interpretation in short sentences'.[17] Pseudo-Augustine's *De mirabilibus* alone seems to stand out, but even here, as Austin Cagle has recently argued, the relationship between miracles and the natural world is more complicated than it appears on the surface.[18]

Perhaps the most interesting aspect of this section is what Bischoff does not do. He does not analyse these Irish works and ask what features they share or identify a common approach to exegesis. Oddly, these securely Irish works play very little role as touchstones in the remainder of the article. Perhaps his point is that the other, anonymous, commentaries represent a turning point in Irish exegesis, but then this would give us two Irish schools – the one represented by the early works Bischoff lists here and the one with texts that share Irish symptoms. Following this, Bischoff briefly argued for the Irish provenance of a commentary on Mark's Gospel.

The fifth section is perhaps the most significant because it contains Bischoff's method for attributing otherwise unattributed works as Irish. He began by noting that it is an exception to be able to assign the name of an Irish author to a work attributed as Irish through internal evidence.[19] He then wrote: 'In most of the works contained in the following catalogue it was finding rarely-used sources and the observation of conspicuous features that first drew the attention until finally, as I believe, discerning a sort of family resemblance became possible.'[20] This is perhaps the weakest point in Bischoff's argument. It is clear that he has established a body of exegetical works, and once this corpus was established, Bischoff then asked what other features this corpus had in common. Once these had been identified – his Irish symptoms (*irische Symptomen*) – then they could be used to test unattributed works. If a work met the criteria and was otherwise unattributed, then it could be put in the family portrait. The main problem is that Bischoff does not ask whether these criteria are also met by other texts. To show that Irish texts share features does not mean that other non-Irish texts do not also share them. Thus, they cannot be used as a way to identify non-attributed texts unless it is possible to show that securely non-Irish texts do not meet these criteria. As we shall see, this is a problem.

This fallacious way of reasoning is common and goes under several names, such as 'clustering illusion' or the 'Texas sharpshooter fallacy'. But one of the best explanations comes from the Dubner Maggid, Jacob ben Wolf Kranz of Dubno in the present-day Ukraine, who died in 1804. As a famous storyteller (*maggid*) Jacob was known for the parables that always seemed to fit the situation he was illustrating. When asked to explain his ability to do this, the *maggid* naturally told a parable. In the parable, the son of a nobleman returns from the military academy to see the side of a barn filled with targets, each with a single shot at the bulls-eye. When he asked to see the remarkable marksman, a small child told him that Narele, the town fool, who was responsible for the performance, did not shoot at the targets. Instead, he shot first and then drew the circles.[21]

Perhaps the most sympathetic summary of Bischoff's symptoms was given by Kelly:

> These elements were rarely unique to the Irish and were often borrowed from the Latin Fathers, but the Irish used them so frequently that they could be considered Irish characteristics. These included *inter alia* a fondness for rudimentary questions, the citation of the *tres linguae sacrae* (Hebrew, Greek, Latin), the use of the phrase *non difficile* to characterize a question, the adoption of procedures from ancient grammarians, open references to heterodox writers (such as Pelagius) and non-canonical gospels (such as that to the Hebrews), an interest in genealogies, and the determination of a book's *tempus, locus, et persona*.[22]

But even applying these criteria is not straightforward: Are all equally important? How many must be met for a text to qualify as Irish? If more criteria are met is the text more Irish?

Perhaps more tellingly, there are texts for which no Irish connections have been argued and that still have many of Bischoff's symptoms. One example is the anonymous *Glosa Psalmorum ex traditione seniorum*, a psalm commentary edited by Helmut Boese.[23] Boese argued in the preface of his edition that there is no evidence of any Irish influence and attributes the commentary to southern France in the first half of the seventh century. Yet we see that the preface begins with *tres linguae sacrae* in question-and-answer format. The commentary on Ps. 28:9 refers to the *uita theoretica*. The commentary on Ps. 57:8 describes water flowing from the mountains after winter as a reference to natural phenomena. The commentary on Ps. 86:1 discusses the grammatical structure of the verse and refers to *grammatici*. Finally, one could argue that it has a great interest in literal exegesis. In other words, we can see a work for which no Irish connections have been argued, but which fulfils several of Bischoff's criteria.

We might also ask what the reaction of contemporaries was. Did they notice Irish exegesis as distinctive? We can take two examples to address this question. The first is from Jonas's Life of Columbanus and has to do with the troublesome monk Agrestius, who plagued most of the abbacy of Eustasius, Columbanus's successor at Luxeuil. Near the end of his life, Agrestius and his supporters tried to persuade Chlothar II to condemn Columbanus's monastic rule. Chlothar demurred and instead decided to call a council in Mâcon, presided over by Treticus, Bishop of Lyon. At the council, Jonas tells us, Agrestius asked for three practices to be condemned: signs of the cross repeated over spoons, asking for a blessing when entering or leaving the monastery and the multiplication of prayers and collects during the Mass. After Eustasius had answered the objections by citing biblical passages, Jonas tells us that: 'Agrestius, thrown into confusion by these responses and ones like them, added the offense of babbling, falsely accusing them of tonsuring the head differently, writing another script, and differing from the customs of all.'[24]

The relevant point here is what Agrestius does not mention: exegesis. At a moment when he seems to be grasping for any possible objection to the practices of the Luxeuil monks, exegesis is not mentioned. Now this episode in the Life is difficult to interpret: one could argue, for example, that Agrestius is complaining about practices instituted by Columbanus which had been changed under his successor. But at any case, exegesis is not mentioned.

Another episode connected with the missionary activity of St Boniface has been explored recently by Sven Meeder.[25] Meeder examined Boniface's objections to the Irishman Clemens, which included a laundry list of complaints, including that he denied and contradicted the canons of the church, that he rejected the writings of the Fathers and that he claimed he could be a bishop even though he had two children.[26] Meeder argues that a list of *capitula* in the third section of a Würzburg florilegium (Würzburg, Universitätsbibliothek, MS Mp.th.q. 31, fol. 54v, from the late-eighth or early-ninth century) also concerns Clemens and Aldebert, who were both condemned as heretics. Capitulum 23 is of special interest to us, because it condemns those who say that 'everything written' (*omnem scriptum*) should be interpreted historically, i.e. that none of the figurative senses existed.[27] The language of the *capitula* is problematic, and it is unclear whether the reference is to everything written or specifically to the Bible. In addition, no Irish biblical commentary would have been described as so literal as to be heretical.

To sum up, Bischoff's introductory section is open to serious objections, primarily on two grounds: first, his classification of biblical commentaries as following one of two schools, either as literal or allegorical exegesis; second, the way he derived his *Symptomen*: rather than looking at all exegesis and picking works that shared features, he started with the shared features and worked backward – he shot first, and drew the target second. By looking at the *Glosa Psalmorum ex traditione seniorum*, we can see one example of a text that has Irish symptoms, but seems not to be Irish. Finally, there seems to be no contemporary notice of Irish exegesis as a distinct or idiosyncratic phenomenon. Eustasius's critic Agrestius did not mention biblical exegesis in connection with his complaints. While the heretical practice of interpreting the entire Bible literally, which is condemned in the Würzburg florilegium, is possibly associated with Clemens, it seems at the very least to be associated with the two heretics and more likely to be a more general accusation.

Current and future research

Despite its flaws, Bischoff's 'Wendepunkte' article has been important in encouraging scholars to work on texts that otherwise would, in all likelihood, never have been published. Indeed, his great accomplishment is much the same as the one performed by the scribe who first attributed *De mirabilibus sacrae scripturae* to St Augustine. In both cases, interesting texts were given a context that encouraged their preservation and study. Perhaps the most significant step in publishing the texts identified by Bischoff was the establishment of the Scriptores Celtigenae, which published its first volume in 1996 and had published seven volumes by June 2014, five of them exegetical works.[28]

Much of the work stimulated by 'Wendepunkte' focused on using Bischoff's symptoms to identify texts as Irish. It is unfortunate that 'Wendepunkte' did not stimulate a parallel effort to investigate non-Irish exegesis. This has meant first, that Bischoff's characterization of non-Irish exegesis has been tacitly accepted by those studying Irish exegetical works, even though it is extremely broad and lumps together works that have a wide range of aims and audiences. Second, it has meant that the background against which Irish exegesis is intended to stand out is still under-investigated. In order to establish clearly whether Irish exegesis is distinctive, we must first establish clearly what it is distinctive from. Thus clarity for one requires clarity for the other.

It is odd that one of the most obvious sources for establishing whether there was a distinctive Irish exegesis has also been largely ignored, namely the extensive biblical glosses in Latin and Old Irish. The first and still most valuable collection of these glosses is the 700-page first volume of *Thesaurus Palaeohibernicus* in 1901. If the goal is to establish whether there is a distinctive Irish method of clarifying biblical texts, then surely this must be one of the first places to start. Since the nineteenth century these glosses have been mined as a resource for the Irish language, but their contents largely ignored. Because of their treatment as largely linguistic forms, the relationship between the Irish and Latin glosses has also been obscured. Because Bischoff set out to study only Latin exegesis these glosses did not come within his purview. This is certainly understandable from a practical point of view, yet there are good arguments for widening the point of view now. First, many of the sets of glosses are a mix of Latin and Irish, and all are explaining the Latin texts of the Bible. Indeed, if there is a typically Irish way of dealing with biblical texts we might expect it to be most clearly expressed in these texts, which are presumably composed by and intended for Irish speakers.

Besides practicalities, one further reason for not considering glosses and commentaries together is that they are different genres with different ways of explaining a text. This is misleading. Both are texts that have as their objectives the clarification of the meaning of a target text. Often, however, this distinction is more about the layout of the two texts on the page rather than the contents. For example, if a set of glosses were printed in lemmatized form (as the *Glosa Seniorum* is), then the appearance is often indistinguishable from a commentary. Likewise, if the elements of a commentary were divided and printed or written alongside the target text, the result would also often be indistinguishable from a set of glosses. In addition, as Best showed, glosses such as those in Milan, Bibliotheca Ambrosiana C. 301, were copied as a unit, just as commentaries are.[29]

One of the arguments Bischoff explicitly makes is that Anglo-Saxon exegesis overshadowed Irish exegesis on the Continent, which seems to imply an opposition, even a degree of animosity. Yet not only did scholars from both islands have much in common, several exegetical works have glosses not only in Old Irish, but in Anglo-Saxon as well, a feature that they share with some computistical works. Perhaps these glosses are one indication that exegetes writing in Old Irish and Old English had a great deal in common in the study of the Bible as well. It is perhaps worth pursuing from the viewpoint of the social circumstances that would have brought these communities together and especially the relationship between Latin and both vernaculars in the study of exegesis.[30]

One consequence of following Bischoff's symptoms has been to characterize exegetical works in a very broad and often very imprecise way as 'primarily allegorical' or 'primarily literal'. As we have seen, this is open to many objections, not the least of which is viewing the commentary as a homogenous unit, while they are often assemblages collected in nuggets from here and there. For example, in explaining any given passage an author might include the allegorical meaning of one writer, the historical sense of another, explanations of unusual Latin words from a glossary, Hebrew words from Jerome, etc. The basis for such selection can be a fixed aim in the exposition or it can be purely practical. Perhaps one profitable route to examine exegetical works would be to exploit this and to examine the exegesis of the individual passages that make up a commentary. For example, one could compare such basic features as how the text was divided into lemmata as well as the sources of the interpretations of individual passages across a range of commentaries. This approach would allow the building up a mosaic of affiliations over a range of exegetical work.

The study of exegesis as a way to gain insights into wider religious, political and cultural issues is comparatively recent and the study of Irish exegesis as distinctive is more recent still. Perhaps the most promising future direction is one that pursues suggestions made by Stancliffe in 1975: 'The commentaries we have been considering do not witness to an isolated native phenomenon, but rather form one part of the exegetical activity common to all those countries in the Latin West which still looked back to the work of the great Church Fathers.'³¹ In order to understand what went on in Ireland, we must also understand what went on in the wider world.

Notes

1. To take one example, the Israelites' seizure of Egyptian gold and silver described in Exodus 12:35–6 expressed a historical truth, but Augustine showed it expressed another truth as well, namely God's permission for Christians to adopt useful pagan knowledge (*De doctrina christiana* 20.40). It is worth noting that in our period there was no systematic explanation of these different sorts of meaning.
2. See, for example, 2 Tim. 3:16–17: 'omnis scriptura diuinitus inspirata et utilis ad docendum ad arguendum ad corrigendum ad erudiendum in iustitia ut perfectus sit homo Dei ad omne opus bonum instructus'.
3. The more general term for the study of meaning in texts is hermeneutics.
4. For early knowledge of Irish exegetes see, for example, J. Sichard, ed., *Sedulii Scotti Hyberniensis, in omnes epistolas Pauli collectaneum* (Basle, 1528) and C. O'Conor, *Scriptores rerum Hibernicarum* (Buckingham, 1814), vol. 1 pt. 2, pp. cxxv–vi. For the view of exegesis, see Christopher Ocker, 'Medieval Exegesis and the Origin of Hermeneutics' *Scottish Journal of Theology* 52 (1999), pp 328–45.
5. James F. Kenney, *The sources for the early history of Ireland: Ecclesiastical. An introduction and guide* (New York, 1929).
6. B. Smalley, *The Study of the Bible in the Middle Ages* (Oxford, 1964), p. 35; Paul Grosjean, 'Sur quelques exegetes irlandais du viième siècle', *Sacris Erudiri* 7 (1955), pp. 67–98; B. Bischoff, 'Wendepunkte in der Geschichte der lateinischen Exegese im Frühmittelalter' *Sacris Erudiri* 6 (1954), 189–279, revised in his *Mittelalterliche Studien* 3 vols (Stuttgart,1966–81), I, pp. 205–73; trans. C. O'Grady, 'Turning-Points in the History of Latin Exegesis in the Early Middle Ages', in M. McNamara, ed., *Biblical Studies: The Medieval Irish Contribution*, Proceedings of the Irish Biblical Assoc. 1 (Dublin, 1976), pp. 74–160.
7. C. Stancliffe, 'Early "Irish" Biblical Exegesis', *Studia Patristica* 12 (1975) (= *Texte und Untersuchungen zur Geschichte der altchristlichen Literatur* 115, ed. Elizabeth Livingstone), pp. 361–70.
8. J. F. Kelly, 'A Catalogue of Early Medieval Hiberno-Latin Biblical Commentaries', *Traditio* 44 (1988), pp. 537–71, at p. 538.
9. The page numbers are from the revised version published in *Mittelalterliche Studien*.
10. 'Wendepunkte', p. 206: 'Wenn ich im Widerspruch zu dieser schein-baren Einförmigkeit sogar von Wendepunkten zu reden wage, so geschieht es hauptsächlich auf Grund bisher unerschlossenen Materials,

aus dem sich erweisen läßt, daß es auch in der Zeit vom VII. bis ins frühe IX. Jahrhundert verschiedene Richtungen gegeben hat, und daß Ansätze dafür vorhanden waren, daß die Entwicklung der Bibelwissenschaft einen anderen Verlauf nahm'.

11. The Alexandrine or allegorical 'school' is often represented by Origen (d. 254) and Athanasius (d. 393); the Antiochene or literal by Diodore of Tarsus (d. 390), Theodore of Mopsuestia (d. 428), and Nestorius of Constantinople (d. 450). For the early view of the two schools' influence, see Smalley, *Study of the Bible in the Middle Ages*, pp. 1–26. For a more nuanced view, see H.-J. Vogt, 'Unterschiedliche Exegese der Alexandriner und der Antiochener. Cyrillische Umdeutung Christologischer Texte des Theodor von Mopsuestia', in G. Schöllgen and C. Scholten, eds, *Stimuli. Festschrift für E. Dassmann* (Münster, 1996), pp. 357–69.

12. Bede, *In Lucae Euangelium expositio*, ed. D. Hurst, CCSL 120 (Brepols, 1960), p. 7.

13. Jerome, *In Hieremiam prophetam,* ed. S. Reiter, CSEL 59 (Vienna, 1913), p. 4: 'ut nuper indoctus calumniator erupit, qui commentarios meos in epistulam Pauli ad Ephesios reprehendendos putat nec intellegit nimia stertens uaecordia leges commentariorum, in quibus multae diuersorom ponuntur opiniones uel tacitis uel expressis auctorum nominibus, ut lectoris arbitrium sit, quid potissimum eligere debeat, decernere, quamquam et in primo eiusdem operis libro praefatus sim me uel propria uel aliena dicturum el ipsos commentarios lam ueterum scriptorum esse quam nostros'. See R. Starr, 'The Flexibility of Literary Meaning and the Role of the Reader in Roman Antiquity', *Latomus* 60 (2001), pp. 433–45.

14. 'Wendepunkte', p. 209: 'Die Namen der großen Angelsachsen, Bedas, und Alcuins, der, von Karl dem Großen eingeladen, die angelsächsische Wissenschaft in das Frankenreich verpflanzte, haben auch das Gedächtnis einer anderen exegetischen Schule überschattet, der irischen'.

15. *Die lateinische Bildung der keltischen Völker im Frühmittelalter. Grundlagen und Eigenart* (Munich, 1943), pp. 28–31.

16. C. Kannengiesser, *Handbook of Patristic Exegesis* (Brill, 2006), p. 1359.

17. 'Wendepunkte', p. 266: 'Vorwiegend moralische Erklärung in kurzen Sätzen'.

18. A. Cagle, *Nature, Miracles, and Governance. Identifying a Platonic Metaphysic in* De Mirabilibus Sacrae Scripturae, MA Thesis, NUI Galway 2013.

19. 'Wendepunkte', p. 215: 'Daß der aus inneren Gründen gesicherten Bestimmung eines Werkes als irisch durch die Nennung des irischen Autors das Siegel aufgedrückt werden kann, ist freilich eine Ausnahme'.

20. 'Wendepunkte', p. 215: 'Bei der Mehrzahl der im folgenden Katalog enthaltenen Werke war es die Feststellung gewisser seltener benützter Quellen und die Beobachtung auffälliger Merkmale, die zuerst die Aufmerksamkeit wachriefen, bis sich schließlich, wie ich glaube, der Blick für eine Art Familienähnlichkeit schärfte'.

21. Peninnah Schram, ed., *Stories within Stories from the Jewish Oral Tradition* (Aronson, 2000), p. 154.

22. Kelly, 'A Catalogue of Early Medieval Hiberno-Latin Biblical Commentaries', p. 537.

23. Anonymus, *Glosa Psalmorum ex traditione seniorum,* Teil 1, ed. H. Boese (Herder, 1992).

24. 'His et horum similibus responsis confusus Agrestius, addit garrulitatis noxam, calumniatur capitis comam aliter tondi, alium caracterem exprimi et ab omnium mores disciscere', Jonas, *Vita Columbani,* II.9 (p. 251). See M. Stansbury, 'Agrestius et l'écriture de Luxeuil', in J. M. Picard, ed., *Autour du scriptorium de Luxeuil,* Les Cahiers Colombaniens 2011 (Luxeuil, 2012), pp. 68–74.

25. S. Meeder, 'Boniface and the Irish Heresy of Clemens', *Church History* 80 (2011), pp. 251–80.

26. Meeder, 'Boniface', 257 n. 14 (see also Chapter 12 in this volume).

27. Meeder, 'Boniface', 280: 'De eo quod dicunt omnem scriptum histo-rialiter debere intellegi', and translation on p. 263.

28. The exegetical works published to date are: Anonymus, *Liber de ortu et obitu patriarcharum,* ed. J. Carracedo Fraga, CCSL 108E (Brepols, 1996); Anonymus, *Expositio evangelii secundum Marcum,* ed. M. Cahill, CCSL 82 (Brepols, 1997); Anonymus, *Pauca problesmata de enigmatibus ex tomis canonicis,* ed. G. MacGinty, CCCM 173 (Brepols, 2000); Anonymus, *Liber questionum in euangeliis,* ed. J. Rittenmueller, CCSL 108F (Brepols, 2004); Anonymus, *Expositiones Psalmorum duae sicut in codice Rothomagensi 24 asseruantur,* ed. L. De Conninck, CCCM 256 (Brepols, 2012); Anonymus, *Psalterium Suthantoniense,* ed. P. Ó Néill, CCCM 240 (Brepols, 2012). Among those in preparation are Augustinus Hibernicus, *De mirabilibus Sacrae Scripturae,* Marianus Scottus, *Marginalia in Epistolas S. Pauli,* and the anonymous *Commemoratio Geneseos, Commentarius Vindobonensis in Matthaeum, Eclogae Tractatorum in Psalterium, Expositio in Canticum canticorum, Expositio quattuor Evangeliorum, Historica investigatio Evangelii secundum Lucam,* and *Pauca problesmata ex Novo Testamento.*

29. R. I. Best, *The Commentary on the Psalms with glosses in Old-Irish preserved in the Ambrosian Library (MS. C 301 inf.). Collotype facsimile, with Introduction* (Dublin, 1936)

30. See J. E. Cross 'On Hiberno-Latin Texts and Anglo-Saxon Writings', in T. O'Loughlin, ed., *The Scriptures and Early Medieval Ireland. Proceedings of the 1993 Conference of the Society for Hiberno-Latin Studies on Early Irish Exegesis and Homiletics,* Instrumenta Patristica 31 (Brepols, 1999), pp. 69–79.

31. Stancliffe, 'Exegesis', p. 366.

8

The Irish Contribution to the Penitential Tradition

Rob Meens

In memory of Raymund Kottje

In the introduction to the collected works of Columbanus, G.S.M. Walker wrote: 'Auricular confession and private penance, so characteristic of subsequent devotion, took their origin from the practice of Luxeuil; and there is scarcely one European penitential which does not show some trace of Irish influence.'[1] It was with this citation that the late Raymund Kottje opened his contribution to the edited collection *Ireland and Europe*, published in 1982, a contribution that still provides an excellent overview of the dissemination of Irish penitential books on the European mainland.[2] The present chapter should be regarded as an update to and reassessment of Kottje's essay. Although carefully qualifying Walker's statement by drawing attention to some form of Iromania in Walker's views (see Introduction), Kottje fully endorsed Walker's assertion that a radical new departure in the pastoral practice of hearing confession, assigning penances and reconciling sinners had its roots in Ireland. This Irish pastoral practice was then disseminated throughout Europe by means of Irish, and later Anglo-Saxon, *peregrini* and missionaries, radiating from the earliest known Irish foundation, the monastery of Luxeuil, founded in the late sixth century by the Irish abbot Columbanus. The manuscripts of Irish penitential books, the dissemination of which Kottje charted with great precision, revealed the activities of centres of Irish influence on the European mainland, such as Brittany, St-Gall or Bobbio. Kottje subscribed to the then prevailing view that the Irish invented a new form of penance, which differed from the late antique formal ritual of public penance by which sinners were first separated from and later reconciled to the Christian community in an elaborate liturgical setting. This new insular form of penance was less formal and less public and therefore it came to be considered as private penance. For Walker and Kottje the Irish invented private penance.

Now, it is undeniable that in the insular world in the sixth century a new sort of text developed: the handbook for confessors, or the *libri paenitentiales*. These books were indeed transmitted to the European mainland by Columbanus and his followers and blossomed in the Carolingian age. This indicates that something was indeed changing and that 'the Irish' – to use a shorthand for churchmen stemming from an array of different ecclesiastical traditions that were connected to, but certainly not confined to, Ireland – contributed to a period of transforming penance. Yet, to view this as the invention of private penance is to my mind teleological. Even if Irish penitential books contributed to the development of private penance in later centuries, for which there is no convincing evidence, there is no reason to assume that penance as it was practiced in Ireland in the early period was seen as private. Actually there is no notion of private penance in any early insular source. Moreover, I think that the idea that there was a single form of public penance in the late antique and early medieval world that was then replaced by private penance is misleading. There are many indications that penance could take many shapes and forms in the period before the year 600.[3] In other words: the distinction between public and private penance is much too simplistic and does not correspond with the complex reality of the past. In this contribution I will first briefly review what recent research has contributed to the knowledge of the transmission of insular penitential books on the Continent, before assessing what was new about Irish ways of dealing with sinners and what impact the Irish might have had in Francia.

Insular penitential texts

The Irish penitentials have been edited and translated in 1963 by Ludwig Bieler for the series *Scriptores Latini Hiberniae*, which remains the standard edition to this day, although not all of the texts edited there can be regarded as Irish.[4] It is more accurate to employ the term 'insular' in relation to most of these texts because, as we shall see, many of the texts in question are difficult to pin down geographically with precision and they are all in various ways interconnected. The pattern of connections suggest a world of intense contacts between Ireland, Wales and Cornwall, and possibly we should include Brittany here as well, since Finnian, the author of an early penitential book, may have been from Brittany and clusters of early text are found in admittedly later manuscripts that stem from this region. The best-known penitentials generally labelled Irish are those attributed to Finnian, Columbanus and Cummean. These works are preserved in a handful of manuscripts, all written in ecclesiastical centres on the European mainland, and in particular northern France, southern Germany (Salzburg, St-Gall), northern Italy (Bobbio) and Burgundy. Kottje was able to identify a number of manuscripts of the so-called Second Synod of St. Patrick that Bieler had not known, but the most important discovery in this field since Bieler's edition has been Ludger Körntgen's, who established that a penitential preserved in the Biblioteca Ambrosiana in Milan was not a ninth-century reworking of the seventh-century Irish penitential of Cummean, but rather its source.[5] This text, which he named the *Paenitentiale Ambrosianum*, was probably composed in the sixth century in the insular world. It was known in Ireland in the seventh century when Cummean used it to compose his work on penance.

A late ninth-century penitential which I edited twelve years ago as the *Paenitentiale Vindobonense C* contains a group of ten canons, the direct sources of which could not be identified. These canons mostly relate to matters of priestly purity and have some connection to additions found in simple Frankish texts of this kind of the eighth and ninth centuries. These additions stem mostly from insular sources. The unidentified canons from the *Vindobonense C* show a remarkable resemblance to two Irish penitentials, the *Paenitentiale Bigotianum* and the Old Irish Penitential, in that they censure several forms of contact with women. The first canon, for example, assigns a period of seventy days of fasting as penance for a priest (*sacerdos*) who has been defiled by milk of a woman (*lactum mulieris*, perhaps to be read as *tactum*, defiled by a female touch). Another one prescribes forty days of penance for touching a woman's breasts.[6] The correspondences with the *Bigotianum* and the *Old Irish Penitential* suggest that these ten canons were not the product of the imagination of the ninth-century compiler of the *Vindobonense C*, but were adopted from an earlier insular source for which they are the sole witness. This would mean that what we have here is a trace of an otherwise unknown insular penitential.

Penance in the insular world

Apart from these two texts, there is nothing substantial to add to Kottje's discussion of the dissemination of Irish penitentials in his article of 1982. There has been some debate about the Irish nature of particular texts, notably the Penitential of Finnian and the *Bigotia-num*, as well as about the Penitential of Columbanus, but in general his views are still valid.[7] Where things have been moving a lot is in the interpretation of what penance actually was and the context in which it was applied. The sharp dichotomy between private and public penance that historians took for granted for a long time has been called into question by scholars such as Mary Mansfield, Mayke de Jong and Sarah Hamilton, who stressed the diversity of penitential practice.[8] The distinction between two major forms, one public and the other private, existed mostly in the minds of bishops worrying about the proper ways of doing penance in the Carolingian age, but does not reflect actual behaviour.[9] The question of who was affected by views on sin and penance as expressed in penitential books has also provoked much discussion. Franz Kerff and Sandy Murray questioned the prevailing view that penitential books were widely used in a pastoral setting.[10] They argued that penitential books did not reach parish priests, but that their use was generally confined to bishops, who employed them foremost in the legal context of an episcopal court. Their minimalist views have, however, incited a response from David Bachrach and myself, among others.[11] For Ireland the question about the uses of penance in a secular setting has been discussed by Colman Etchingham, who argued that the rules that we find in penitential books did not apply to the laity in general, but only in the case of the *manaig*, the dependants of monastic institutions living under a quasi-penitential regime. Catherine Swift, however, following up suggestions by Thomas Charles-Edwards, sees much more room for priests judging sinners in a local context.[12]

What then are we to make of the situation in Ireland before *peregrini* set out for Francia and beyond and, so we may suppose, took their penitential books and practices with them? A group of sixth-century texts generally regarded as precursors of penitential handbooks and edited as such by Bieler, provide information on the earliest instances of ecclesiastical discipline in the British Isles. These are known by their modern titles as the Preface of Gildas on Penance, the Excerpts from a Book of David, the Synod of North Britain and the Synod of the Grove of Victory. It is not always clear, however, whether these texts address monks, clergy or the laity. Some, like the Preface of Gildas, have a strong monastic outlook, while others, like the Excerpts from a Book of David, mostly address clerical failings but also, to a certain extent, censure lay behaviour. These texts seem to reflect a world in which monastic and episcopal forms of authority coexisted and penance was mostly used as a tool for enforcing ecclesiastical discipline rather than as a means for helping individual sinners distressed about their salvation.[13]

The *Paenitentiale Ambrosianum* has a much clearer pastoral outlook. It has a strong monastic flavour, as demonstrated, for example, by its structure, which is based on the eight principal vices originally formulated by Evagrius of Pontus and subsequently promulgated in the West by John Cassian. The *Ambrosianum* prescribes a specific protocol for dealing with sinners in which the sinner is first urged to do penance for his sins and if he does not comply with this advice, disciplinary tools, such as exclusion from the table, are to be applied in order to put pressure on him. Such an exclusion from a communal meal fits a monastic or clerical community. This monastic outlook notwithstanding, the text addresses bishops, priests, virgins, widows, clerics and laypeople. The canons that are specifically addressed to laymen, however, do not display the same careful protocol for approaching sinners. The other early insular penitential, the one composed by Finnian, is also characterized by a rather sophisticated approach to sin as is demonstrated, for example, by censuring sinful thoughts rather than deeds. Once more, such a nuanced approach seems to have been reserved for the clergy. For laymen and laywomen sinful intentions were less serious because, as Finnian puts it, 'he is a man of this world, his guilt in this world is lighter but the reward in the world to come is less.'[14] In dealing with the sexual life of the married, Finnian sets a high standard. The text not only forbids any form of sexual activity outside of marriage, it also denies remarriage, and prescribes continence if a marriage does not bring forth children because, according to Finnian, she is an *uxor sterilis*, 'barren wife'.[15] The fact that no penances are prescribed in relation to these rules about marriage indicates that this actually was more of a model for a Christian marriage rather than rules that were being enforced in practice.

Both these penitentials, Finnian's and the *Ambrosianum*, envisage laymen and laywomen doing penance for their sins. It is hard to imagine, however, that at such an early stage there existed some kind of regular form of lay confession in the insular world in the sixth century. It has been suggested that the laymen addressed in these penitential books were closely bound to the monastery and were in fact almost exclusively dependent monastic tenants. Yet there might be another group of lay people targeted in these texts. Since many canons targeting laymen are concerned with forms of violence and with adultery, namely with acts that were of high social relevance, and since, when knowledge of them became public, they required some form of public satisfaction, one may infer that ecclesiastical penance could function as an alternative means of settling conflicts between laypeople. This interpretation is corroborated by the content of these canons. Finnian, for example, rules that a layman who struck his neighbour and caused some form of bleeding, should not only fast for forty days, but should also compensate his neighbour by giving him a certain amount of money, whereas no compensation is required from a cleric committing the same offence. That priests or monks were in a position to negotiate in specific conflicts is suggested by the Life of Columba. Adomnán, the author of the Life, relates how a certain Librán, after having killed a man, did penance on Iona and was reconciled with his victim's kin through negotiations by Columba himself (this is a case I have discussed elsewhere).[16] That the *Ambrosianum* might have functioned in a similar context is suggested by its discussion of a man having sex with a virgin or a widow. In such a case the culprit should do penance for a year and seek reconciliation with the woman's family by paying the bride-price as established in the law.[17] Hence, in cases of lay people, reconciliation with the offended party apparently was part of the penitential process.

While the author of the *Ambrosianum* remains unknown and the author of Finnian's penitential a shadowy figure at best, the author of a third important insular penitential is a well-known historical personality. Columbanus is not only the protagonist of a Life written by Jonas of Bobbio, but a good many of the texts he wrote himself have also been preserved, and these texts can serve as a corrective to Jonas's often tendentious account. Columbanus composed a penitential book probably from loose files.[18] In the form in which it has been preserved, it also contains material added after Columbanus's death in 613. Columbanus probably composed the work after he left Ireland, so in a strict sense this is not an insular text, although one may nevertheless choose to regard it as such because of its insular inspiration. In this work Columbanus clearly envisaged three groups of sinners: monks, clerics and laymen. There is an interesting difference in the way sins with serious social consequences are dealt with in regard to these three groups. Whereas clerics and lay people are always required to compensate the offended party, monks are not. A cleric or layman who killed his neighbour must first go into exile and after his return he should seek reconciliation with the victim's parents and assume the role of their son, fulfilling their wishes.[19] For Christians living in the world reconciliation with an offended party seems to have been of greater importance in the penitential process than for monks living in the seclusion of their monasteries. There is also a remarkable correspondence between the sections devoted to monks, clerics, and the laity in Columbanus's penitential. The earlier insular texts speak about the laity only in the specific context of sins that have clear social repercussions: violence, theft and adultery. Columbanus, however, adds an entire range of other transgressions and actually addresses the same offences regardless of whether he is dealing with monks, clerics or the laity. He is the first, for example, to assign a specific penance for masturbation, drunkenness or participating in pagan festivals in a lay context.[20] Although the penances for lay men and women assigned by Columbanus are lighter than those for monks and clerics, in principle Columbanus demanded that lay people model their life on that of the monk.[21] This raises the question how Columbanus envisaged his penitential being used. Jonas speaks about Columbanus's attraction of a great many converts. Particularly the *medicamenta paenitentiae*, 'the remedies of penance', would have drawn many to his new foundations.[22] One can imagine that Columbanus's penitential was being employed in relation to aristocratic families who sought close contact with the charismatic holy man. To judge by his penitential, Columbanus set high standards for members of such circles who wished to be associated with his foundations. His confrontation with Theuderic II and Brunhild demonstrates that he was willing to uphold such demands even when confronted with royal anger.[23]

The last influential insular penitential written in Latin was composed by Cummean, possibly the same person who around the year 633 wrote a famous letter to the abbot of Iona regarding the proper date of Easter. As already mentioned, Cummean's penitential was based on the *Ambrosianum*, a fact that explains its monastic outlook. It is hard to establish which sinners are addressed by this work. It contains rules for all Christians, although the severity of penance is adapted to the sinner's position in society.[24] Some canons seem more geared towards a monastic environment, such as the canons censuring monastic vices of *acedia* (languor), *tristitia* (sadness) or *iactantia* (vainglory), but it is also striking that these more monastic vices are dealt with very briefly. Other clauses discuss the life of the married and therefore address laymen and laywomen. Often, however, Cummean does not distinguish clearly between clerics, monks or laypeople. His penitential is similar to Columbanus's work in that it seems to demand the same conduct from these three groups. Yet, it is often unclear to which group exactly its clauses are addressed, which might suggest that again this text functioned in a context where such distinctions were rather fluid, as for example in a situation where laypeople associated themselves closely with a monastic centre.

The uses of Irish texts on the Continent

If we try to draw some conclusions from this brief discussion of Irish penitential texts, it seems safe to conclude that all of the fully developed penitentials – namely, of Finnian, Columbanus, Cummean and the *Paenitentiale Ambrosianum* – have a strong monastic component. They all deal with sinning monks, clerics and lay people. There is, however, a certain contrast between sins attributed to monks and those attributed to clerics and laypeople. Whereas the former are concerned mainly with controlling the vices as a means of attaining perfection, the latter are concerned with diffusing social tensions and seeking reconciliation between conflicting parties. There is no reason to suppose that these books were used in the context of secular priests hearing confession. All elements indicate that they functioned in a context to which monks were central and clerics and laity more peripheral. Three groups of lay folk seem to be particularly acknowledged: monastic tenants, people entangled in serious social conflicts who sought ecclesiastical mediation and finally aristocrats in search of close ties with holy men. Some of these categories could, of course, overlap.

Is it useful to see this opening up of monastic penitential practices and, in particular, the recourse to ecclesiastical mediation in resolving complicated social conflicts, as 'private penance' as opposed to public penance? I think not. Nobody at the time thought in such categories. It is only modern historians searching for the origins and legitimation of current practices who labelled these forms of penance as 'private penance'. It is striking that Columbanus ran into trouble on several issues with Merovingian bishops, but that penance was never an issue. This indicates that continental bishops did not see his handling of sin, confession and penance as something radically new. Columbanus brought insular texts with him when he arrived on the Continent which must have guided his dealings with sinners but they do not appear to have disturbed ecclesiastical authorities in Gaul or northern Italy.

If we want to investigate what happened to Columbanus's rulings regarding sinners, we can look at a particular family of eight penitential texts which can be labelled the 'simple Frankish penitentials'.[25] These texts drew upon Columbanus's penitential, which was their main source, but combined its regulations with conciliar legislation. The unproblematic way in which rulings from a handbook for confession were combined with canons pronounced by late antique conciliar meetings or the Merovingian provincial synod of Auxerre, suggests that such regulations were not regarded as fundamentally different. To the canon adopted from Columbanus regarding manslaughter by a cleric, the 'simple Frankish penitentials' add a canon from the council of Ancyra regarding accidental killings.[26] Another canon from this council which discusses several forms of divination was also included in this group of texts.[27] A canon forbidding festivities on 1st January was adopted from the council of Auxerre.[28] It is striking that these texts rely mainly on that section of Columbanus's penitential which is concerned with sins committed by the clergy. They seem to be intended particularly to discipline clerics, although the fact that many of the canons do not specify whether the sinner is of clerical or lay status, recalls the fluidity that we observed in such matters in insular penitentials. As such, the 'simple Frankish penitentials' linked up with two movements in the Merovingian church aiming at a renewal of Christian life: one initiated by Columbanus and another, somewhat earlier Burgundian reform movement, which culminated in two major councils in Mâcon (581–3 and 585) and the diocesan synod of Auxerre (shortly after 585).[29]

The clauses from the 'simple Frankish penitentials' were often combined with those of Cummean and of Theodore, the seventh-century archbishop of Canterbury. Theodore's work is extant in five traditions, which probably reflects a somewhat different genesis compared to that of the other penitential books. The existing versions appear to have originated from pupils' reports of the archbishop's teachings. Bede speaks highly of the school that Theodore and his companion Hadrian established in Canterbury and it is likely to have been in this context that the different traditions of his penitential sentences, often mixed with other authoritative statements, originated.[30] These three traditions – comprising the 'simple Frankish penitentials', Cummean, and Theodore – were first combined in a highly influential work known as the *Excarpsus Cummeani*. There is evidence to suppose that this penitential book was composed in the northern French monastery of Corbie in the second quarter of the eighth century and that the Anglo-Saxon missionary and church reformer Boniface was somehow implicated in the enterprise.[31] The *Excarpsus* was often transmitted together with the influential canon law collection known as the *Vetus Gallica*, a text that was reworked in

Corbie in the same period. The combination of this penitential book with a canon law collection stresses one of its main characteristics: a concern for ecclesiastical hierarchy and authority.

The *Excarpsus* is not the only penitential book written in the eighth century which demonstrates a concern for authority. Other books combining the same set of sources, the so-called tripartite penitentials, demonstrate by the ways in which they present their material a similar concern. Most of them originate from the region of northern France, where apparently such concerns for authority were rife. A remarkable number of penitential books composed in the second half of the eighth century combine different traditions. Sometimes, as in the Tripartite St-Gall Penitential which was written in northern France in the late eighth century, these different traditions would be presented alongside one another. This work, for example, contains a series of canons based on the 'simple Frankish penitentials', followed by a series of Theodorian canons and finally a series of sentences adopted from Cummean's penitential.[32] The author of a penitential known as the *Paenitentiale capitula iudiciorum* who drew on the Tripartite St-Gall penitential, made the differences between the three traditions even more clear by juxtaposing them for each offence. For the case of manslaughter and murder, for example, he first presented three sentences from the simple Frankish penitentials, which he named *iudicium canonicum* 'a canonical judgment', followed by nine from Theodore and four from Cummean.[33]

The rich diversity in penitential judgments that thus became evident by works as the *Paenitentiale capitula iudiciorum*, could also raise eyebrows. The *Excarpsus Cummeani* had already left out some canons because they did not conform with the stricter outlook of other traditions. Thus the compiler, for example, left out Cummean's relatively lenient approach towards boys having sex with animals, an offence for which Cummean had assigned a penance of one year. Instead, the compiler included only Theodore's canon sentencing such a sinner to fifteen years of penance.[34] Other compilers building on the *Excarpsus*, for example the author of the *Paenitentiale Vindobonense B*, written in Salzburg at the end of the eighth century, reintroduced a number of canons that the *Excarpsus* had left out.[35] The variety in approach that transpires in these texts and the increasing number of penitential books that were written in the later eighth century, mainly in the northern and eastern regions of the Frankish kingdom, testifies to a lively interest in penitential matters in the second half of the eighth century. The manuscript transmission of some of these new texts is remarkably rich. The *Excarpsus Cummeani* is extant in over twenty manuscripts dating from the eighth and ninth centuries, and eight extant manuscripts contain the *Paenitentiale Capitula Iudiciorum*.[36]

The increase in the production of these texts and in their dissemination that we can observe from the second half of the eighth century, contrasting strongly with the more limited manuscript transmission of the Irish penitential books, must surely be related to the programme initiated by the Carolingian kings and their court to promote religious life in their kingdom, an effort that is known as the Carolingian Renaissance or Carolingian Reforms. These new penitentials were more clearly aimed at influencing lay behaviour, unlike the Irish texts that as we have seen were reaching out to the laity, but were always geared towards the life of monks and clerics. The catalogues of religious practices that were condemned as being pagan or superstitious, or the detailed discussion of the life of the married, are a case in point.[37] We also have evidence in episcopal statutes as well as in priests' examinations that priests were supposed to possess penitential books, and inventories of country churches do indeed show that such was the case.[38] This all seems to suggest that the practice of confessing one's sins and doing penance for them was no longer radiating from specific monastic centres out towards the laity in the forms that we have discussed above, but that from the second half of the eighth century confession and penance became more and more a part of regular Christian life; a Christian life that became to an ever larger extent ruled by written codes in this period. It was in this period that, in the words of Julia Smith: 'ideologues at the Carolingian court set out to establish a comprehensive code of conduct for the laity and a firm place for them within the Christian church'.[39] Texts were increasingly concerned with the formation of a Christian: how he had to behave and how he was involved in ecclesiastical ritual. As a consequence, important social events, such as baptism, marriage and funeral rites, were more and more given a scripted liturgical form. The concerns of Charlemagne for the proper forms of baptism, for example, led to an explosion of texts that discuss the liturgy of baptism.[40] In the field of penance we see a similar increase in texts that were attempting to help priests in their task. The Carolingian stress on authority had the consequence of restricting the hearing of confession to the priesthood, more so than it had been before. Liturgical *ordines* were, moreover, added to penitential books, defining the proper liturgical forms for this ritual.

The Carolingian stress on authority and hierarchy also led to a discussion of the nature of the authority of penitential handbooks themselves. This came to a head in the five Carolingian reform councils of 813, which were convened in Mainz, Châlons, Tours, Reims and Arles at the behest of the aging emperor in order to debate the state of the Frankish Church. Three of these councils debated the authority of the texts with which a penitent was to be judged.[41] In the same three councils the bishops agreed that Christians who had sinned in public were to perform public penance.[42] What exactly should be understood in this context as 'public' is a moot point, but it is arguable that it regarded those sins to which the laity was particularly susceptible, according to early insular penitential books: adultery, murder and other forms of behaviour that caused social tensions. In the penitentials of insular origin which we have discussed, some form of compensation to the offended party was part and parcel of the process of penance. In the early Carolingian penitentials that adopted many canons from their insular predecessors the aspect of compensation is no longer apparent. This might indicate that in the second half of the eighth century, when confessing your sins was becoming part of the regular Christian life in the Carolingian world and consequently the range of sins for the laity had been significantly expanded, reconciliation with the offended party had become less prominent in the practice of penance. This called for a renewed stress on the public aspect of doing penance, at least in certain areas of the Carolingian world, and it was in this period, I would argue, that secret penance and its public counterpart were born. Insular texts and attitudes certainly contributed to this process, as did Columbanus and his foundations of Luxeuil and Bobbio, but, nevertheless, Walker's statement which prefaces this paper is in need of some qualification.

Notes

1. G.S.M. Walker, ed., *Sancti Columbani Opera*, Scriptores Latini Hiberniae 2 (Dublin, 1957), p. xxxiii.
2. R. Kottje, 'Überlieferung und Rezeption der irischen Bußbücher auf dem Kontinent', in H. Löwe, ed., *Die Iren und Europa im früheren Mittelalter* (Stuttgart, 1982), I, pp. 511–24, at p. 511.
3. R. Meens, *Penance in Medieval Europe, 600–1200* (Cambridge, 2014), pp. 12–36.
4. L. Bieler, ed. and trans., *The Irish Penitentials*, Scriptores Latini Hiberniae 5 (Dublin, 1963).
5. L. Körntgen, *Studien zu den Quellen der frühmittelalterlichen Bußbücher*, Quellen und Forschungen zum Recht im Mittelalter 7 (Sigmaringen, 1993), pp. 7–86, with an edition of the text on pp. 257–70.

6. Canons 1 and 5, ed. R. Meens, '"Aliud Benitenciale": The Ninth-Century *Paenitentiale Vindobonense C*', *Mediaeval Studies* 66 (2004), 1–26, at 22, and see the discussion on 7–9.

7. On Finnian, see L. Fleuriot, 'Le "saint" breton Winniau, et le pénitentiel dit "de Finnian"?', *Études Celtiques* 15 (1976–1978), 607–14; P. Ó Riain, 'Finnian or Winniau?', in P. Ní Chatháin and M. Richter, eds, *Irland und Europa: Die Kirche im Frühmittelalter / Ireland and Europe: The Early Church* (Stuttgart, 1984), pp. 52–7; D. Dumville, 'Gildas and Uinniau', in M. Lapidge and D. Dumville, eds, *Gildas. New Approaches* (Woodbridge, 1984), pp. 193–205, at p. 198; and P. Ó Riain, 'Finnio and Winniau: A Return to the Subject', in J. Carey, J. Koch, P.-Y. Lambert, and P. Mac Cana, eds, *Ildánach, ildírech. A Festschrift for Proinsias Mac Cana* (Andover, 1999), pp. 187–202. For the *P. Bigotianum*, see W. Follett, *Céli Dé in Ireland. Monastic Writing and Identity in the Early Middle Ages* (Woodbridge, 2006), pp. 67–9, and Meens, *Penance in Medieval Europe*, p. 61; for the discussion of the Penitential of Columbanus, see M. G. Muzzarelli, 'Il penitenziale di Colombano nella storiografia recente', in M.C. De Matteis, ed., *Ovidio Capitani: Quaranta anni per la storia medioevale* (Bologna, 2003), pp. 141–55.

8. M. Mansfield, *The Humiliation of Sinners. Public Penance in Thirteenth Century France* (Ithaca and London, 1995); M. de Jong, 'What was Public about Public Penance? *Paenitentia publica* and Justice in the Carolingian World', in *La giustizia nell'alto medioevo II (secoli IX–XI) = Settimane* 44 (Spoleto, 1997), pp. 863–904; S. Hamilton, *The Practice of Penance, 900–1050* (Woodbridge, 2001).

9. Meens, *Penance in Medieval Europe*, pp.118–123.

10. F. Kerff, 'Mittelalterliche Quellen und mittelalterliche Wirklichkeit. Zu den Konsequenzen einer jüngst erschienenen Edition für unser Bild kirchlicher Reformbemühungen', *Rheinische Vierteljahrsblätter* 51 (1987), 275–86; idem, 'Libri paenitentiales und kirchliche Strafgerichtsbarkeit bis zum Decretum Gratiani. Ein Diskussionsvorschlag', *ZRG, Kan. Abt.* 75 (1989), 23–57; A. Murray, 'Confession before 1215', *Transactions of the Royal Historical Society*, 6th series 3 (1993), pp. 51–81.

11. R. Meens, 'The Frequency and Nature of Early Medieval Penance', in P. Biller and A.J. Minnis, eds, *Handling Sin: Confession in the Middle Ages*, York Studies in Medieval Theology 2 (Woodbridge, 1998), pp. 35–61; D. S. Bachrach, 'Confession in the Regnum Francorum (742–900)', *Journal of Ecclesiastical History* 54 (2003), pp. 3–22.

12. C. Etchingham, *Church Organisation in Ireland A.D. 650–1000* (Maynooth, 1999); C. Swift, 'Early Irish priests within their localities', in F. Edmonds and P. Russell, eds, *Tome: Studies in Medieval Celtic History and Law in Honour of Thomas Charles-Edwards* (Woodbridge, 2011), pp. 29–40. See T.M. Charles-Edwards, 'The Pastoral Role of the Church in the Early Irish Laws' in J. Blair and R. Sharpe, eds, *Pastoral Care Before the Parish* (Leicester, 1992), pp. 63–80. The topic is

not directly addressed in T.M. Charles-Edwards, *Early Christian Ireland* (Cambridge, 2000).
13. Meens, *Penance in Medieval Europe*, pp. 40–5.
14. P. *Vinniani* c. 6, ed. Bieler, *Irish Penitentials*, p. 76.
15. P. *Vinniani* c. 41, ed. Bieler, *Irish Penitentials*, p. 88.
16. R. Meens, 'Penance, Shame and Honour in the Early Middle Ages', in J. Wettlaufer and B. Sère, eds, *Shame between Punishment and Penance. The Social Uses of Shame in the Middle Ages and Early Modern Times*. Micrologus Library 53 (Florence, 2013), pp. 89–102, at pp. 91–4.
17. P. *Ambrosianum*, II c. 2, ed. Körntgen, *Studien*, p. 260.
18. T. M. Charles-Edwards, 'The Penitential of Columbanus', in M. Lapidge, ed., *Columbanus. Studies on the Latin writings*, Studies in Celtic History 17 (Woodbridge, 1997), pp. 217–39.
19. P. *Columbani B* cc. 1, 13, ed. Bieler, *Irish Penitentials*, pp. 98, 102.
20. P. *Columbani B* cc. 17, 22–24, ed. Bieler, *Irish Penitentials*, pp. 102–4.
21. A. Diem, *Das monastische Experiment. Die Rolle der Keuschheit bei der Entstehung des westlichen Klosterwesens*. Vita Regularis. Ordnungen und Deutungen religiösen Lebens im Mittelalter 24 (Münster, 2005), pp. 247–8.
22. Jonas of Bobbio, *Vita Columbani abbatis discipulorumque eius*, I.10, ed. B. Krusch, MGH SS rer. Merov. IV, p. 76.
23. Jonas, *Vita Columbani*, I.18–19, ed. Krusch, pp. 86–90.
24. Charles-Edwards, 'Penitential of Columbanus', p. 218.
25. They are easily available in the edition by R. Kottje for the Corpus Christianorum, see *Paenitentialia minora Franciae et Italiae saeculi VIII–IX*, ed. R. Kottje, CCSL 156 (Turnhout, 1994), pp. 1–60; for a brief discussion of these texts, see Meens, *Penance in Medieval Europe*, pp. 77–80.
26. P. *Burgundense* cc. 1–2, ed. Kottje, pp. 5–9; cf. P. *Columbani B* c. 1 and Council of Ancyra c. 22 (23), ed. C.H. Turner, *Ecclesiae occidentalis monumenta iuris antiquissima canonum et conciliorum graecorum interpretationes Latinae* (Oxford, 1907), II.1, pp. 110–11.
27. P. *Burgundense* c. 25, ed. Kottje, pp. 33–37; cf. Council of Ancyra c. 23 (24), ed. Turner, *Ecclesiae occidentalis monumenta*, pp. 112–13.
28. P. *Burgundense* c. 34, ed. Kottje, pp. 49–53; cf. Council of Auxerre, ed. C. de Clercq, *Concilia Galliae A. 511-A. 695*, CCSL 148A (Turnhout, 1963), p. 265.
29. See R. Meens, 'Reforming the Clergy: A Context for the Use of the Bobbio Penitential', in Y. Hen and R. Meens, eds, *The Bobbio Missal. Liturgy and Religious Culture in Merovingian Gaul*, Cambridge Studies in Palaeography and Codicology 11 (Cambridge, 2004), pp. 154–67.
30. Bede, *HE*, IV.2, ed. B. Colgrave and R. Mynors, *Bede's Ecclesiastical History of the English People*, 2nd edn (Oxford, 1992), pp. 332–4. For a discussion of Theodore's penitential, see Meens, *Penance in Medieval Europe*, pp. 89–96.
31. For its origin in Corbie, see L. Körntgen, 'Der *Excarpsus Cummeani*, ein Bußbuch aus Corbie', in O. Münsch and T. Zotz, eds, *Scientia*

Veritatis. Festschrift für Hubert Mordek zum 65. Geburtstag (Ostfildern, 2004), pp. 59–75. For its connection to Boniface, see R. Meens, 'Aspekte der Christianisierung des Volkes', in F. J. Felten, J. Jarnut, and L. von Padberg, eds, *Bonifatius. Leben und Nachwirken (754–2004)* (Wiesbaden, 2007), pp. 211–29.

32. For a study and edition of this text, see Meens, *Tripartite boeteboek*, pp. 73–104 and pp. 326–53.

33. Meens, *Tripartite boeteboek*, pp. 436–8.

34. *P. Cummeani*, II cc. 6, 8 and X cc. 5, 16, ed. Bieler, *Irish Penitentials*, pp. 114, 128; *P. Theodori* U I,2,3 and 15,d., ed. P.W. Finsterwalder, *Die Canones Theodori Cantuariensis und ihre Überlieferungsformen*, Untersuchungen zu den Bußbüchern des 7., 8. und 9. Jahrhunderts, 1 (Weimar, 1929), pp. 290–1, included as *Excarpsus*, III c. 10, II c. 4, ed. H.J. Schmitz, *Die Bussbücher und das kanonische Bussverfahren. Nach handschriflichen Quellen dargestellt*, (Düsseldorf, 1898), pp. 613, 609.

35. Meens, *Tripartite boeteboek*, 105–37 and Meens, 'Kanonisches Recht in Salzburg am Ende des 8. Jahrhunderts. Das Zeugnis des *Paenitentiale Vindobonense B*', *ZRG Kan. Abt.* 82 (1996), pp. 13–34.

36. F. Asbach, 'Das Poenitentiale Remense und der sogen. Excarpsus Cummeani: Überlieferung, Quellen und Entwicklung zweier kontinentaler Bußbücher aus der 1. Hälfte des 8. Jahrhunderts', unpublished Inaugural-Dissertation, University of Regensburg (1975), and L. Mahadevan, 'Überlieferung und Verbreitung des Bussbuchs "Capitula Iudiciorum"', *ZRG Kan. Abt.* 72 (1986), 17–75; see also Meens, *Penance in Medieval Europe*, pp. 110–12 and appendix on pp. 229–30.

37. For penitentials as sources for 'magic' and sexuality, see D. Harmening, *Superstitio. Ueberlieferungs- und theoriegeschichtliche Untersuchungen zur kirchlich-theologischen Aberglaubensliteratur des Mittelalters* (Berlin, 1979); V. Flint, *The Rise of Magic in Early Medieval Europe* (Oxford, 1991), pp. 41–2 and passim; P. Payer, *Sex and the Penitentials. The Development of a Sexual Code, 550–1150*, (Toronto, 1984).

38. Meens, *Penance in Medieval Europe*, p. 114.

39. J. Smith, 'Religion and Lay Society', in R. McKitterick, ed., *The New Cambridge Medieval History II: c. 700–c. 900* (Cambridge, 1995), pp. 654–678, at p. 654.

40. S. Keefe, *Water and the Word. Baptism and the Education of the Clergy in the Carolingian Empire*, 2 vols. (Notre Dame, 2002); see also the discussion on the creed documented in S. Keefe, *A Catalogue of Works Pertaining to the Explanation of the Creed in Carolingian Manuscripts* (Turnhout, 2012). O. Phelan, *The Formation of Christian Europe. The Carolingians, Baptism and the* Imperium Christianum (Oxford, 2014).

41. Council of Tours c. 22, Council of Chalon c. 38 and the council of Reims c. 16: ed. A. Werminghoff, MGH Conc. II.1 (Hanover and Leipzig, 1906), pp. 289, 281, 255.

42. Chalon c. 25, Arles c. 26, Reims c. 31: ibid., pp. 278, 254, 256.

9

The Liturgy of the Irish on the Continent

Yitzhak Hen

What type of liturgy did the Irish *peregrini* on the Continent celebrate? This is a fascinating question that can shed some fresh light on
the liturgical history of both Ireland and Francia in the early Middle
Ages. In order to address this question, one has to deal first with
three interrelated issues that will, eventually, provide a clearer picture of the liturgical scene. These are: (i) what type of liturgy was
practised on the Continent when the Irish *peregrini* first arrived there?
(ii) What type of liturgy were they familiar with in their homeland?
And (iii) how did these two liturgical traditions interact with each
other once the Irish settled on the Continent? Only then will a better
understanding of the liturgy used by the Irish on the Continent
emerge. Let us, then, have a closer look at each of these issues.

The Gallican liturgy of Merovingian Francia

Ever since the publication of Jean Mabillon's *De liturgiae gallicana*,[1] the
liturgy of early medieval Gaul has been classified as 'Gallican'. But
whereas 'Gallican' for Mabillon meant 'Merovingian' (and this is
how 'Gallican' is used throughout the present paper), at the hands of
later liturgists 'Gallican' became a confusing and misleading term
applied to miscellaneous liturgical traditions from northern Italy,
Frankish Gaul, Visigothic Spain and north Africa, all of which were
assumed to be mere derivatives of the Roman rite and therefore represent parallel developments in a linear liturgical evolution.[2] However, this process of liturgical formation has rightly been called into
question in recent years, and modern scholarship has revealed how
profoundly creative and dynamic were the various sub-divisions of
the western rite.[3]

As far as the liturgy of early medieval Gaul is concerned, very little
can be said with certainty about its formation in Late Antiquity and

146

the early Merovingian period, mainly because of lack of evidence. Nevertheless, even from the little evidence that survives in the sermons of Avitus of Vienne and Caesarius of Arles, the writings of Gregory of Tours, the poems of Venantius Fortunatus, and the abundant hagiographical compositions from the period, late antique early Merovingian Gaul appears to have been a rich and dynamic period of liturgical activity.[4] This activity continued well into the seventh and the eighth centuries, as attested by a remarkable series of liturgical manuscripts that were compiled, partially-composed for the first time, or simply copied, by men and women in various religious communities throughout the Merovingian kingdoms.[5]

Two principal characteristics of the Merovingian liturgy – diversity and eclecticism – are also the reasons because of which any attempt to delineate the nature of that liturgy is extremely precarious. The high degree of diversity that characterized the Merovingian rite reflected not only differences in local customs and usages, but also different ideals and standards on the part of the composers and celebrants.[6] This diversity was considerably enriched by eclecticism. Merovingian liturgy was constantly under a variety of external influences, most notably Roman, but also Mozarabic (Visigothic), northern and southern Italian, and Anglo-Saxon. Consequently many prayers and customs, which originated outside Francia, were embedded in the Frankish rite.[7] In turn, the Frankish liturgy itself influenced the liturgical development and creativity of Visigothic Spain, Anglo-Saxon England, northern Italy and even Rome.

Hence, both the diversity and the eclecticism of the Frankish rite make it nearly impossible to draw clear-cut boundaries between what is Merovingian and what is not. And yet, some observations can be made. First, the language and style of the Merovingian prayers are rather rhetorical and effusive. The verbosity and peculiar style of Merovingian liturgists is most clearly manifested in the elaborate episcopal benedictions *ad populum* ('to the people'), which – unlike the Roman benedictions, which were short, formulaic, and succinct – are prolonged with florid language, colourful images and ideas, and sometimes even opaque theology. No wonder that Pope Zacharias described them as vainglorious and strongly advised Boniface to refrain from using them.[8]

Secondly, the Merovingian church developed a distinct calendar of liturgical celebrations that diverged in some aspects from the liturgical calendar of Rome. For example, Rogation days, that is, prescribed days of prayers and fasting, which are a special innovation of the Merovingian church, were celebrated in Gaul before Ascension Day.[9] Similarly, the feast of the *Cathedra Petri* ('The Throne of Peter', that is, the commemoration of the day in which the Apostle held his first service in Rome) in Gaul was followed by the feast of the Assumption of the Virgin Mary.[10] Moreover, it was normal practice in Merovingian Gaul to have the 'kiss of peace' before the Eucharistic prayer, and it may well be that the episcopal benediction was given immediately after the *Pater Noster* and before communion.[11] One can add to these celebrations specific feasts in honour of typical Merovingian saints, such as Symphorianus, Leodegarius, or Genovefa,[12] who gave the liturgical calendar a very local character.

Thirdly, it was common in Merovingian Gaul to have three readings from the bible during the celebration of a Mass – one from the Old-Testament Prophets, one from the Gospels, and one from the Epistles, whereas in the Roman rite there were only two lessons, one from the Epistles and one from the Gospels.[13] And finally, most Merovingian sacramentaries that survive contain a huge variety of votive and private Masses for various occasions, which clearly indicate that each and every celebrant could pick and mix whatever he deemed appropriate, or even compose some prayers of his own if he were capable of doing so.[14] Although a certain Frankish *canon missae* – that is, a succession of short prayers that were supposedly recited in each celebration of the Mass – evolved during the Merovingian period,[15] there was no uniformity, and no compliance with the rite of Rome was ever imposed or even demanded. This flexible and non-binding liturgical world was the world that welcomed the Irish *peregrini* on the Continent and, as we shall see, it was not significantly different from the liturgical world with which the *peregrini* were familiar in their homeland.

The early Irish liturgy

To outline the nature and character of the early Irish liturgy is a very perplexing task. Not much has survived from early medieval Ireland as far as the liturgical evidence is concerned, apart from a stash of fragments, many of which are in palimpsest form,[16] and three larger compilations: the Antiphonary of Bangor,[17] the Stowe Missal,[18] and the so-called Irish Palimpsest Sacramentary.[19] And yet, although these liturgical compositions were written in what palaeographers usually label 'Irish script',[20] there is no way to ascertain their Irish origins, and paradoxically most of them were actually copied in either Anglo-Saxon England or on the Continent.[21]

The so-called Irish Palimpsest Sacramentary, for example, was copied, most probably, in the third quarter of the seventh century, in Northumbria, by a scribe trained in the Irish tradition.[22] Similarly, the Irish origin of the seventh-century Antiphonary of Bangor is nothing more than an intellectual guesswork.[23] Nothing in the Antiphonary of Bangor suggests that it was actually copied in Ireland and not in a continental centre where some Irishmen resided, and although it contains some references to Bangor and Saint Comgall, we cannot be sure it reflects the liturgy celebrated in Ireland at the turn of the seventh century. In fact, we cannot be sure it reflects any liturgical practice, since it appears that no service whatsoever could be performed from the miscellaneous liturgical collection of this idiosyncratic compilation. The same ambiguous picture emerges from a quick look at the various Irish liturgical fragments that survive.[24] The odd one out in that respect, as we shall see, is the Stowe Missal. Hence, not only is the evidence for the early Irish liturgy relatively scant and dispersed, it is also extremely fragmentary and ambiguous.

This fundamental disadvantage, coupled with a strong sense of local patriotism, combined with a dose of romanticism, led in the past to some crackpot theories on the origins, development and nature of the early Irish liturgy, arguing its distinctiveness and impact on the liturgy of the early medieval west. Frederick E. Warren's monumental survey of the early Irish liturgical sources, which was published in 1881,[25] had clearly set the tone for subsequent studies.[26] According to him, the bits and pieces of the Irish liturgical books that survive clearly indicate that a separate and unique liturgical tradition, which he dubbed 'the Celtic Rite', emerged in early medieval Ireland. This conviction, one should stress, accorded extremely well with the general vision of early medieval Ireland that characterized nineteenth- and early twentieth-century scholarship.

Over the last thirty years or so there has been an immense proliferation of scholarly interest in issues relating to the early history of Ireland, which resulted in a better understanding of the period.[27] It is by now commonplace to deny that early medieval Ireland could have been anything like 'a Dark Age Hippy colony inhabited by gentle gurus doing their own Christian thing far removed from the stultifying influence of sub-Roman bishops and their dioceses'.[28] In more than one respect, early medieval Ireland was integrated into the history of western Europe, and the notion of an independent 'Celtic Church' was justly taken to task. Consequently, the nature of the so-called Celtic Rite had to be re-evaluated and redefined.

By breaking free from Warren's shadow and shedding off the romanticism and prejudice that characterized most studies of the early Irish liturgy, modern scholarship has been able to rise to the challenge and provide a more accurate re-assessment of the early Irish liturgy.[29] A new wave of studies clearly showed that there is no evidence whatsoever for a separate, distinctive, Irish rite, and that in all probability the early Irish used a form of the Gallican liturgy that was common to most of the early medieval west.[30]

Central to every evaluation of the early Irish rite was a careful examination of the so-called Stowe Missal, which is the sole early medieval Irish compilation whose Irish origin is secure.[31] Copied most probably at Tallaght in the last decade of the eighth century or the first quarter of the ninth century, the Stowe Missal is the smallest liturgical book that came down to us from the early medieval west.[32] It contains fifty-six folios, written in bold, angular, rather large Irish minuscule, by at least five scribes. Eleven more folios, containing excerpts from the Gospel of John were added at the beginning of the codex, written in rounded Irish minuscule and copied shortly after the original manuscript. Soon afterwards the entire text was thoroughly corrected and revised by Máel Cáich and a number of other scribes, probably at the monastery of Lothrae (Lorrha, Co. Tipperary).[33] It was then that the last section of the Stowe Missal, which contains a short treatise on the Mass and three short spells, all in Irish, were added at the end of the manuscript.

The liturgical section of the Stowe Missal is conspicuous in its brevity and limited range of prayers. This liturgical economy, together with the manuscript's modest and compact features suggests that it was not produced for an important church or high ecclesiastic, but was rather intended as a private service-book, a *uade mecum*, which a priest could easily carry with him and find therein all the necessary liturgical material to execute his pastoral duties.[34] As such, the Stowe Missal is indeed a unique piece of liturgical evidence, but one has to remember that it reflects only a limited, local and extremely selective liturgical situation, and must not be taken to represent the entire Irish (or, as was once thought, Celtic) rite.

The nature of the liturgical pieces in the Stowe Missal is extremely revealing. Although some have argued in the past that the basic liturgy of the Stowe Missal is that of the Roman rite,[35] a careful examination of the texts themselves in light of modern scholarship reveals how overwhelmingly Gallican the rite of the Stowe Missal is. Measuring the Stowe Missal by a Gallican yardstick will clarify that point.

Edmund Bishop had already noted 'the Irish eclectic, or tinkering, method in liturgy',[36] and indeed, many of the Stowe Missal's prayers could be traced, with minor changes and variations, in other Gallican sacramentaries, such as the Bobbio Missal, the *Missale Gothicum*, the *Missale Gallicanum Vetus*, the *Missale Francorum*, or the Old Gelasian Sacramentary, but also in the so-called *Sacramentarium Veronense* or in the Spanish *Liber Ordinum* and *Liber Mozarabicus Sacramentorum*.[37] To these one can add the Stowe Missal's *canon missae*,[38] whose earliest versions, as we have just seen, were copied in Merovingian Gaul and were part of the so-called Gallican tradition.

Moreover, the litany, which is part of the Stowe Missal's *ordo missae*, lists only thirteen names of pan-Christian saints, such as Mary, the Apostles, and the Evangelists, with no mention of distinct Irish saints.[39] It was only at a later stage, when revising and adapting the Stowe Missal for his own use, that Máel Cáich added to the litany and to the *memento* of the *canon missae* names of distinct Irish saints.[40] These additions clearly reflect the local Irish predilections of Máel Cáich and his circle, but it also points to the possible Gallican sources he used, for he also added the names of Martin and Hilary. This Gallican tendency was strengthened by the *Deprecatio sancti Martini pro populo*, which was also incorporated into the *ordo missae*.[41] Finally, the style and language of the Stowe Missal point unmistakably to the Gallican tradition. The Stowe Missal's prayers are not only longer than those known to us from Roman liturgical texts, such as the *Sacramentarium Veronense*, but also much more vivid and flamboyant, with a tendency for metaphor and biblical expression.[42]

From all the evidence adduced above, it appears that the Stowe Missal complies with most of the characteristics of the Gallican tradition, and if indeed it reflects the liturgy of early medieval Ireland, then the early Irish liturgy may well be classified as Gallican. Such a conclusion, however, must not be taken to imply that the early Irish liturgy was a mere derivative of the Gallican rite, or that Irish liturgists simply copied whatever they had found in their continental and Anglo-Saxon sources. The compiler (or compilers) of the Stowe Missal picked various prayers that they found in their Gallican sources, arranged them according to their own peculiar needs, changed and altered their language whenever they felt it was necessary and even added new prayers of their own.[43] Combing through the leaves of the Stowe Missal one can really appreciate how creative and innovative were the original compilers and Máel Cáich in preparing this small liturgical book and adapting it for their own use.[44] Hence, although relying heavily on Gallican prayers and traditions, the Stowe Missal is a remarkable product of an experimental age of liturgical activity in Ireland.

Irish on the Continent

Given the fact that the liturgy celebrated in early medieval Ireland was, as far as we can tell, an offshoot of the Gallican tradition that evolved in the early Medieval west, it is only logical to assume that the Irish *peregrini*, who made their way to the Continent in the late sixth, seventh and early eighth centuries were familiar with the Gallican rite long before they embarked on their journey. What they found on the Continent was quite similar to what they were used to, and they therefore had no difficulty fitting into the liturgical scene that they found. In other words, the Irish *peregrini* did not experience a 'liturgical shock' when they heard their Frankish contemporaries at prayer.

The best evidence for the smooth liturgical integration of the Irish *peregrini* into the continental Gallican orbit, is provided by the liturgical *libelli* they had brought with them from Ireland.[45] Shortly after their arrival, these *libelli* were no longer needed, since a huge variety of elaborate and up-to-date sacramentaries and other liturgical compositions were available on the Continent. These newly formed liturgical compilations served the liturgical needs of the Irish on the Continent better than the small *libelli* they had brought with them, which then became redundant, and subsequently were palimpsested or simply discarded.[46] Such a scenario explains not only the fragmentary state of our evidence, but also the fact that most of the Irish liturgical fragments known to us were all associated, in one way or another, with centres on the Continent with a large Irish presence.

To sum up, there were no major differences between the liturgy celebrated in early medieval Ireland and that celebrated on the Continent. The Irish *peregrini*, one may assume, continued to use the liturgy they were familiar with, enriching it with local prayers and customs. After all, the very same liturgical tradition embraced both early medieval Ireland and Merovingian Gaul, so that continuity rather than rift and estrangement must have been the order of the day. There is at least one Irish *peregrinus* who would definitely have agreed with this conclusion. In a short treatise commonly known as *Ratio de cursus qui fuerunt eius auctores* ('An Account of the *liturgical rite*: who were its authors?'), which was composed by an Irishman on the Continent sometime before 767, the author delineates the various liturgical traditions of the early medieval church.[47] According to him, the Irish liturgy was brought from Gaul to Ireland by Germanus of Auxerre and Patrick, and was taken back to the Continent by Irish *peregrini*.[48] This, our author believes, was the liturgy celebrated by Columbanus and his followers, 'and if you do not believe me', he concludes, 'you can find it all in the Life of the blessed Columbanus and the blessed Abbot Eustatius, and in the *dicta* of the blessed abbot Athala of Bobbio'.[49] This, as the foregoing discussion has demonstrated, is also the picture that emerges from the liturgical evidence.

Notes

1. Jean Mabillon, *De liturgia gallicana libri tres* (Paris, 1685); reprinted in *PL* 72, cols 99–447. On Mabillon and his contribution, see Yitzhak Hen, 'Key Themes in the Study of Medieval Liturgy', in Alcuin Reid, ed., *T&T Clark Companion to Liturgy* (London, 2015), pp. 73–92.

2. On the so-called Gallican liturgy, see William S. Porter, *The Gallican Liturgy*, Studies in Eucharistic Faith and Prayer 4 (London, 1958). For further bibliography, see Cyrille Vogel, *Medieval Liturgy: An Introduction to the Sources*, trans. and rev. William G. Storey and Niels K. Rasmussen (Washington DC, 1981), pp. 275–7.

3. See, for example, Vogel, *Medieval Liturgy*, pp. 273–89. See also Éric Palazzo, *A History of Liturgical Books from the Beginning to the Thirteenth Century*, trans. Madeleine Beaumont (Collegeville, 1998).

4. See Yitzhak Hen, *The Royal Patronage of Liturgy in Frankish Gaul to the Death of Charles the Bald (877)*, HBS, Subsidia 3 (London, 2001), pp. 21–41.

5. On these manuscripts, see Yitzhak Hen, *Culture and Religion in Merovingian Gaul, AD 481–751* (Leiden, New York and Cologne, 1995), pp. 43–60; idem, *The Royal Patronage of Liturgy*, pp. 21–41; Philippe Bernard, *Du chant romain au chant grégorien (VIe-XIIIe siècle)* (Paris, 1996); Matthieu Smyth, *La liturgie oubliée: la prière eucharistique en Gaule antique et dans l'Occident non romain* (Paris, 2003).

6. See Hen, *Culture and Religion*, pp. 82–120; idem, 'Unity in Diversity: the Liturgy of Frankish Gaul before the Carolingians', in Robert N. Swanson, ed., *Unity and Diversity in the Church*, Studies in Church History 32 (Oxford, 1996), pp. 19–30.

7. See, for example, Yitzhak Hen, 'Rome, Anglo-Saxon England and the Formation of the Frankish Liturgy', *Revue Bénédictine* 112 (2002), pp. 301–22.

8. See Boniface, Letter 87, ed. Michael Tangl, MGH Epp. sel. 1 (Berlin, 1916) p. 198. On these episcopal blessings, see Eligius Dekkers, '"Benedictiones quas faciunt Galli". Qu'a voulu demander saint Boniface?', in A. Lehner and W. Berschin, eds, *Lateinische Kultur im VIII. Jahrhundert. Traube-Gedenkschrift* (Saint-Ottilien, 1989), pp. 41–6.

9. See Joyce Hill, 'The *Litaniae maiores* and *minores* in Rome, Francia and Anglo-Saxon England: Terminology, Texts and Traditions', *EME* 9 (2000), pp. 211–46.

10. See *Missale Gothicum*, XX.148–56, ed. Els Rose, CCSL 159D (Turnhout, 2005), pp. 410–13, and see Rose's comments on pp. 236–44.

11. See Hen, *Culture and Religion*, pp. 69–70.

12. *Missale Gothicum*, LXI.414–18 and LXIII.425–31, ed. Rose, pp. 507–9 (Symphorianus), 512–5 (Leodegarius); *Le lectionnaire de Luxeuil*, no. 16, ed. Pierre Salmon, Collectanea Biblica Latina 7 (Rome, 1944), pp. 23–4 (Genovefa).

13. On the so-called Gallican reading system, see *Le lectionnaire de Luxeuil*, ed. Pierre Salmon, pp. lxxxvii–xcii; Vogel, *Medieval Liturgy*, pp. 299–304, esp. pp. 303–4.

14. See Hen, *Culture and Religion*, pp. 121–53.

15. On the Frankish *canon*, commonly and incorrectly known as the Roman *canon*, see Hen, 'The Liturgy of the Bobbio Missal', in Yitzhak Hen and Rob Meens, eds, *The Bobbio Missal: Liturgy and Religious Culture in Merovingian Gaul* (Cambridge, 2004), pp. 140–53, at pp. 150–2.

16. These fragments are listed in *Codices Liturgici Latini Antiquiores*, ed. Klaus Gamber, 2nd ed., 2 vols., Spicilegii Friburgensis subsidia 1 (Freiburg, 1968), supplemented by B. Baroffio et al., Spicilegii Friburgensis subsidia 1A (Freiburg, 1988) [hereafter cited as *CLLA*], nos. 101–177, 211, 216. See also Michael Lapidge and Richard Sharpe, *A Bibliography of Celtic Latin Literature, 400–1200* (Dublin, 1985), nos. 505–91, 785–821, 1275–85, pp. 130–50, 210–21 and 337–41 respectively; James F. Kenney, *The Sources for the Early History of Ireland, I: Ecclesiastical* (New York, 1929), rev. by Ludwig Bieler (Dublin, 1966), pp. 687–732.

17. Milan, Biblioteca Ambrosiana, MS C 5 inf.; *CLA* III, no. 311; *CLLA*, no. 150. For an edition, see Frederick E. Warren, ed., *The Antiphonary of Bangor*, HBS 4 (London, 1893) [facsimile] and HBS 10 (London, 1895) [introduction and text].

18. Dublin, Royal Irish Academy, MS D II 3; *CLA* II, no. 268; *CLLA*, no. 101. For an edition, see George F. Warner, ed., *The Stowe Missal*, HBS 31 (London, 1906) [facsimile] and HBS 32 (London, 1915) [introduction and text].

19. Munich, Bayerische Staatsbibliothek, MS Clm 14429, fos 1–61, 64–71 and 73–82; *CLA* IX, no. 1298; *CLLA*, no. 211. For an edition, see Alban Dols and Leo Eizenhöffer, eds, *Das Irische Palimpsestsakramentar im Clm 14429 de Staatsbibliothek München*, Texte und Arbeiten 53–4 (Beuron, 1964).

20. On the Irish system of script, the starting point is Julian Brown, 'The Irish Element in the Insular System of Scripts to *c.* AD 850', in Heinz Löwe, ed., *Die Iren und Europa im früheren Mittelalter* (Stuttgart, 1982),

pp. 101–19; idem, 'The Oldest Irish Manuscripts and their Late Antique Background', in Próinséas Ní Chatháin and Michael Richter, eds, *Ireland and Europe in the Early Middle Ages* (Stuttgart, 1984), pp. 311–27; both papers were reprinted in J. Bately, M. Brown and J. Roberts, eds, *A Palaeographer's View: Selected Writings of Julian Brown*, (London, 1993), pp. 97–124 and 125–39, respectively.

21. David N. Dumville, *A Palaeographer's Review: The Insular System of Scripts in the Early Middle Ages* (Osaka, 1999), esp. pp. 17–40 and 121–4. See also Marco Mostert, 'Celtic, Anglo-Saxon or Insular?', in Doris Edel, ed., *Cultural Identity and Cultural Integration: Ireland and Europe in the Early Middle Ages* (Dublin, 1995), pp. 92–115. See Chapter 13.

22. On this sacramentary, see Dold and Eizenhöfer, *Das Irische Palimpsestsakramentar*, pp. 1*–128*; Leo Eizenhöfer, 'Zu dem irischen Palimpsestsakramentar im Clm 14429', *Sacris erudiri* 17 (1966), 355–64; Bernhard Bischoff, *Die südostdeutschen Schreibschulen und Bibliotheken in der Karolingerzeit*, 2 vols. (Wiesbaden, 1974–80), I, pp. 243–4 and II, pp. 242–3; Hen, 'Rome, Anglo-Saxon England, and the Formation of the Frankish Liturgy'.

23. On the Antiphonary of Bangor, see Michael Curran, *The Antiphonary of Bangor and the Early Irish Monastic Liturgy* (Dublin, 1984); Jane Stevenson, 'The Antiphonary of Bangor', *Peritia* 5 (1986), pp. 430–7.

24. See Yitzhak Hen, 'The Nature and Character of the Early Irish Liturgy', in *L'Irlanda e gli Irlandesi nell'alto medioevo* = *Settimane* 57 (2010), pp. 353–80, at 358–9.

25. See Frederick E. Warren, *The Liturgy and Ritual of the Early Irish Church* (Oxford, 1881); reprinted with a lengthy new introduction by Jane Stevenson (Woodbridge, 1987); reprinted again (without Stevenson's introduction) with a short preface and updated bibliography by Neil X. O'Donoghue (Piscataway NJ, 2010).

26. See also Louis Gougaud, *Christianity in Celtic Lands: A History of the Churches of the Celts, their Origin, their Development, Influence and Mutual Relations*, trans. Maud Joynt (London, 1932; reprinted with an introduction by Jean-Michel Picard, Dublin, 1992), pp. 313–38; Mark Schneiders, 'The Origins of the Early Irish Liturgy', in Próinséas Ní Chatháin and Michael Richter, eds, *Ireland and Europe in the Early Middle Ages: Learning and Literature* (Stuttgart, 1996), pp. 76–98; Smyth, *La liturgie oubliée*, pp. 114–24.

27. For some recent surveys of early medieval Ireland, see Thomas M. Charles-Edwards, *Early Christian Ireland* (Oxford, 2000); Dáibhí Ó Cróinín, *Early Medieval Ireland, 400–1000* (London and New York, 1995); and the various papers in idem, ed., *A New History of Ireland, I – Prehistoric and Early Ireland* (Oxford, 2005).

28. Alfred J. Smyth, 'The Golden Age of Early Irish Monasticism: Myth or Historical Reality?', in Brendan Bradshaw and Dáire Keogh, eds, *Christianity in Ireland: Revisiting the Story* (Dublin, 2002), pp. 21–9, at p. 21.

29. See Neil X. O'Donoghue, *The Eucharist in Pre-Norman Ireland* (Notre Dame, 2011); Yitzhak Hen, 'The Nature and Character of the Early Irish Liturgy'.

30. O'Donoghue, *The Eucharist in Pre-Norman Ireland*, esp. pp. 199–200; Hen, 'The Nature and Character of the Early Irish Liturgy'.

31. A few later short liturgical texts were also added to manuscripts with secure Irish provenance, but they are too patchy to give any coherent picture. See *Missa de visitatione infirmorum*, in Dublin, Trinity College, MS 59 (A. IV. 23) [The Book of Dimma], fos 52r–54r; *CLA* II, no. 275; *CLLA*, no. 145; for an edition, see Warren, *The Liturgy and Ritual of the Celtic Church*, pp. 167–71. *Missa de infirmis*, in Dublin, Trinity College, MS 60 (A. I. 15) [Book of Mulling]; *CLA* II, no. 276; *CLLA*, no. 141, fos 49v–50r; for an edition, see Warren, *The Liturgy and Ritual of the Celtic Church*, pp. 171–3. Dublin, Trinity College, MS 52 [Book of Armagh], fos 19r and 52v respectively; *CLA* II, no. 270; *CLLA* 146; for an edition, see Warren, *The Liturgy and Ritual of the Celtic Church*, pp. 173–4.

32. The volume of literature on the Stowe Missal is enormous and cannot be listed here. For some important studies, see Warner, *The Stowe Missal*, pp. vii–lviii; Kenney, *The Sources for the Early History of Ireland*, no. 555, pp. 692–9; Smyth, *La liturgie oubliée*, pp. 114–19; Sven Meeder, 'The Early Irish Stowe Missal's Destination and Function', *EME* 13 (2005), 179–94; O'Donoghue, *The Eucharist in Pre-Norman Ireland*, esp. pp. 61–71; Hen, 'The Nature and Character of the Early Irish Liturgy', pp. 361–73.

33. Warner, *The Stowe Missal*, pp. xxxvi–xxxvii; Pádraig Ó Riain, 'The Shrine of the Stowe Missal Redated', *PRIA* 10C (1991), 285–95, at pp. 294–5.

34. Kenney, *The Sources for the Early History of Ireland*, p. 699; Meeder, 'The Early Irish Stowe Missal's Destination and Function'; Hen, 'The Nature and Character of the Early Irish Liturgy', 361–73.

35. See, for example, Thomas O'Loughlin, *Celtic Theology: Humanity, World and God in Early Irish Writing* (London and New York, 2000), p. 131.

36. Edmund Bishop, *Liturgica Historica: Papers on the Liturgy and Religious Life of the Western Church* (Oxford, 1918), p. 166.

37. See Warner, *The Stowe Missal, passim*.

38. Warner, *The Stowe Missal*, pp. 3–19.

39. Warner, *The Stowe Missal*, p. 3.

40. Warner, *The Stowe Missal*, p. 14 and pp. 15–16. See also Edmund Bishop, 'The Litany of Saints in the Stowe Missal', in idem, *Liturgica Historica*, pp. 137–64.

41. Warner, *The Stowe Missal*, p. 6.

42. See, for example, Warner, *The Stowe Missal*, pp. 19, 22, 23. See also Hen, 'The Nature and Character of the Early Irish Liturgy', pp. 368–9.

43. Warner, *The Stowe Missal*, pp. 21–2, 125–6.

44. Hen, 'The Nature and Character of the Early Irish Liturgy', esp. pp. 370–2.

45. On the fact that these were *libelli missarum* and not fragments of sacramentaries or antiphonaries, see Hen, 'The Nature and Character of the Early Irish Liturgy', pp. 373–5.

46. See Yitzhak Hen, 'Liturgical Palimpsests from the Early Middle Ages', in George Declercq, ed., *Early Medieval Palimpsests*, Bibliologia 26 (Turnhout, 2007), pp. 37–54.

47. *Ratio de cursus qui fuerunt eius auctores*, ed. K. Hallinger, in *Corpus consuetudinum monasticarum, I: Initia consuetudinis Benedictiae* (Siegburg, 1963), pp. 83–91, and see there the introduction on pp. 79–81. See also Peter Jeffrey, 'Eastern and Western Elements in the Irish Monastic Prayer of the Hours', in Margot E. Fassler and Ralf A. Baltzer, eds, *The Divine Office in the Latin Middle Ages: Methodology and Source Studies, Regional Developments, Hagiography* (Oxford, 2000), pp. 99–143, at pp. 131–4; Dominique Barbet-Massin, *L'Enluminure et le sacré: Ireland et Grande-Bretagne, VIIe–VIIIe siècles* (Paris, 2013), pp. 449–87; Yitzhak Hen, *The So-Called 'Ratio de cursus qui fuerunt eius auctores' and the Liturgy of the Early Medieval West* (forthcoming).

48. *Ratio de cursus qui fuerunt eius auctores*, ed. Hallinger, pp. 86–90.

49. *Ratio de cursus qui fuerunt eius auctores*, ed. Hallinger, p. 90.

10

Computus as Scientific Thought in Ireland and the Early Medieval West

Immo Warntjes

Christianity dominated western European intellectual thought between the fall of the Roman Empire in the fifth century and the so-called Renaissance of the twelfth century. Intellectuals were members of religious orders and the centres of learning and teaching were monasteries and cathedral schools, not the secular institutions of Late Antiquity or the universities of the later Middle Ages. The subjects of study were also different, and this is especially apparent in what nowadays is called science. From an early medieval Christian perspective, science was expected to serve two principal purposes. The first was to provide a thorough understanding of God's creation as manifested in nature and the second was to establish the liturgical calendar based on the date of Easter, which depended on both the Julian and a lunar calendar. It was this second and ostensibly more modest objective that was the source of deep and acrimonious intellectual, theological and political conflict in this period. For despite its focus on a practical aim, calendrical calculations nevertheless had important theological underpinnings and far-reaching doctrinal as well as political consequences.

In order to rise to the challenges underlying such calculations it was necessary to draw upon mathematical and astronomical models. However, only the most basic data from such models were transmitted to the emerging Latin West with the consequence that new concepts and terminology had to be articulated. Eventually, a new discipline was created, known as 'computus'. This was the science of time-reckoning in particular and of the mechanics of the cosmos in general.[1] In the early medieval period, science can largely be equated with computus in the Latin West.

Computus has its roots in Late Antiquity, and quickly developed on the periphery of the former Western Roman Empire, in Visigothic

Spain in the sixth and early seventh, in the insular world in the seventh and early eighth centuries. The few late antique texts that survived in this transition period were the scaffolding for what was to become a most vibrant intellectual endeavour, which, together with the study of grammar and exegesis, formed the three central pillars of Christian learning. The new concepts and definitions that computus required were, to a large degree, developed independently in different regions, resulting in numerous distinctive regional characteristics within this discipline, principally Visigothic, Irish and Anglo-Saxon. As a result, computus makes an ideal subject for the study of regional influences on Frankish culture and of the transmission of ideas that help to uncover intellectual and monastic networks. Tracing the transmission of scientific ideas through space and time remains a major task for future research. This chapter will outline the influence of Irish scientific thought on the Continent in the early Middle Ages, which is best approached under four thematic headings: tables, texts, scholars and manuscripts. The order in which these themes will be addressed here corresponds to the chronology of influence.

Continental Easter tables and Ireland

When the Western Roman Empire collapsed in the first half of the fifth century, one zone in particular remained a stronghold of chronological studies, Aquitaine and the neighbouring Narbonensis, roughly coterminous with modern-day southern France. At that time, the old Roman 84-year Easter reckoning, known as the *Supputatio Romana*, grew increasingly out of sync with the visible moon phases, thereby necessitating the creation of new tables.[2] The two most influential Easter tables that originated at this time can be traced to Aquitaine. These are the *Latercus* and the Victorian. Both, however, would eventually be surpassed in the Latin West during the sixth, seventh and eighth centuries by a third table whose roots may go back to the late fourth century. This was the Alexandrian, also known in the Latin West as the Dionysiac. The tables principally differed on three counts: (i) their lunar limits for Easter Sunday, (ii) the earliest date they allowed for the Easter full moon and (iii) their Julian calendar limits. For convenience, the differences are tabulated in Table 10.1.

The principles underlying the first table, the *Latercus*, remained obscure until 1985, when Dáibhí Ó Cróinín discovered the only known Easter table of this reckoning in a tenth-century manuscript now in the Biblioteca Antoniana in Padua (see Figure 10.1).[3] Like the *Supputatio Romana*, the *Latercus* is based on an 84-year luni-solar

Table 10.1   Easter tables and their principal differences

	Lunar limits for Easter Sunday	Earliest Easter full moon	Julian calendar limits for Easter Sunday
Latercus	14–20	21 March	26 March–23 April
Victorius	16–22	20 March	22 March–24 April
Alexandria/ Dionysius	15–21	21 March	22 March–25 April

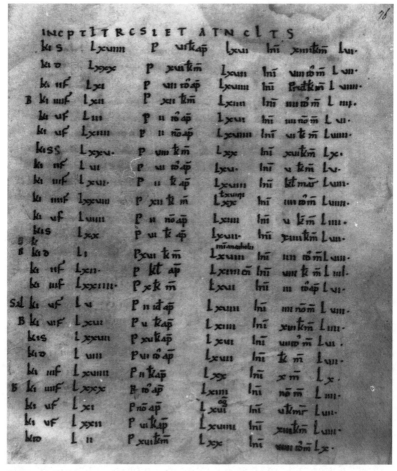

Figure 10.1   Padua, Biblioteca Antoniana, MS I 27, 76r. The columns are: bissextile years (corrupted); weekday of 1 January; lunar age of 1 January; Julian calendar date of Easter Sunday; its lunar age; Julian calendar date of the beginning of Lent; its lunar age.

cycle, but the two differ on both the lunar and Julian calendar limits for Easter Sunday.[4] The Padua manuscript also confirmed Sulpicius Severus's (d. *c.* 425) authorship of the *Latercus*, which was first attributed to him in a seventh-century letter by Aldhelm of Malmesbury to the Briton king Geraint, but heavily disputed since the seventeenth century.[5]

The second table discussed here emerged on the scene in the midfifth century as Rome's continued adherence to the *Supputatio Romana* — which the papal see staunchly defended against Eastern practice — was being undermined by the inaccuracies of this reckoning.[6] Unlike the *Latercus*, which seems to have been a private initiative, this table was commissioned by Pope Leo from Victorius of Aquitaine.[7] The Victorian table can be distinguished from the *Supputatio Romana* and the *Latercus* by its 19-year (rather than 84-year) lunar cycle. Furthermore, it was designed for perpetual use and so it covered the entire 532-years of its luni-solar cycle (lunar cycle of 19 × solar cycle of 28 = 532 years).

The third and final reckoning in this discussion, the Alexandrian, was originally composed in Greek and is named after its place of origin. But since it was popularized in the Latin West through Dionysius Exiguus's translation from 525, it is also known as the Dionysiac.[8] Like the Victorian reckoning, it is based on a 19-year lunar cycle. However, not only was it composed earlier than the Victorian, but its Greek-eastern origins were in fact the cause for the papacy's decision to commission an alternative table that would maintain consistency with Roman dogma. Alexandrian lunar limits for Easter Sunday were based on the passion data as suggested by the Synoptic Gospels, while Rome favoured Johannine resurrection chronology. (In)famously, Pope Leo accepted the Alexandrian date in 455, which, two years later, led Victorius to include 'Greek' alternatives (not necessarily coinciding with the actual Alexandrian dates) in his table, a practice he was heavily criticized for in subsequent centuries.[9] Eventually, Rome adopted the Dionysiac reckoning, but only as late as the 640s, while other parts of Italy, especially those re-conquered by the Byzantine Empire, had already followed Dionysius since earlier in the sixth century.

Although all these Easter reckonings were either devised or translated on the Continent, we are about to see that Ireland played a pivotal role in their transmission. Dan Mc Carthy has plausibly argued that Sulpicius's *Latercus* reached Ireland around the time of Palladius, who was famously sent 'to the Irish believing in Christ' by Pope Celestine in AP 404 = AD 431 (AP = years from the passion and AM = years from the creation of the world were the dominant linear timelines before the eighth century, when AD = years from the incarnation of Christ became popularized).[10] It was undoubtedly the only reckoning followed in Ireland when reliable historical records begin to appear in the sixth century. Our best witness is Columbanus, who left Ireland for the Continent as *peregrinus* in *c.* 590.[11] It is impossible to determine whether the *Latercus* had enjoyed popularity in Gaul similar to its popularity in Ireland in the fifth and early sixth centuries, but in 541 the synod of Orléans decreed that the Victorian reckoning was to be followed throughout the Frankish kingdoms.[12] It can therefore be said that Columbanus reintroduced the *Latercus* into Gaul, a reintroduction that sparked a major controversy, but also generated a lively intellectual debate (see Chapter 6).

The decision of the Frankish clergy to make the Victorian reckoning mandatory cannot have gone unnoticed in neighbouring Ireland. Columbanus's letters suggest that at least the generation of Irish scholars that preceded him had received, studied and rejected the Victorian system. But with the Roman mission to Anglo-Saxon England in 597, the pressure on the Irish church increased. Like the Irish, the Britons also followed the *Latercus*, and the newly arrived Roman clergy quickly discovered that their practices were at odds with those of the natives. This caused considerable tension, not only because of the underlying theological and technical issues (see Chapter 6), but also since these differences soon became symbolic identifiers of the rivalling *gentes*.

In the 620s, alerted by both the missionary experience in Anglo-Saxon England and the Columbanian encounter in Gaul and Italy, the papacy started a campaign to impose the Victorian reckoning on the Briton and Irish 'heretics', as they had become labelled.[13] Only the southern Irish clergy is known to have responded positively in the early 630s (as attested by an important letter by a certain Cummian, of whom little is known).[14] The southern Irish followed the Victorian reckoning for about seventy years, right up to the year 700,[15] adjusting it to suit the needs of the seventh century. However, the northern clergy and the Britons remained faithful to the *Latercus* throughout the seventh and, in case of the Britons, well into the eighth centuries.

Cummian's letter is important not only for the testimony it affords on reform among the southern Irish clergy, but for recording the intricacies of the debate – both conceptual and technical – that raged between clerics and eventually brought about the change. It allows us to see how the controversy stimulated the acquisition and

application of scientific knowledge, subsequently creating a sophisticated scientific discourse that remained unrivalled in the Latin West
for the next two centuries.[16]

The southern Irish review and adjustment of the Victorian Easter
table is best illustrated by the surviving manuscript witnesses. A good
example is the Victorian table for 700–771 transmitted in the manuscripts Paris, Bibliothèque nationale de France, MS Lat. 4860 (see
Figure 10.2), fos 147v–148r, and Vatican, Biblioteca Apostolica
Vaticana, MS Reg. Lat. 586, fos 9r–10v, which was modelled on the

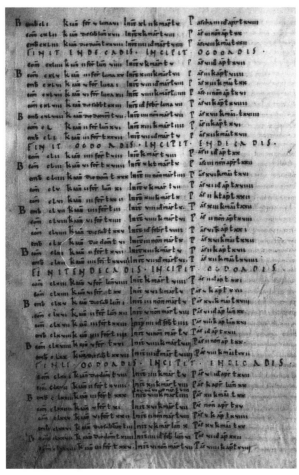

Figure 10.2 Paris, Bibliothèque Nationale de France, MS Lat. 4860, fol. 148r. The columns
are: bissextile years; common and embolismic years; AP; weekday of 1 January; its lunar age;
Julian calendar date of the beginning of Lent; its lunar age; Julian calendar date of Easter
Sunday; its lunar age.

structure of the *Latercus* (as witnessed by the Padua manuscript) exactly (plus AD and common and embolismic years). Under the influence of the *Latercus*, it introduced data for the Lenten fast previously absent in the original form of the Victorian table, as represented in the second oldest surviving computistical manuscript, Gotha, Universitätsbibliothek, MS 75 (see Figure 10.3). This adjustment arguably took place in a milieu that had followed the *Latercus* previously, which is likely to have been southern Ireland. Another important feature of the Victorian table for 700–771 is the deliberate

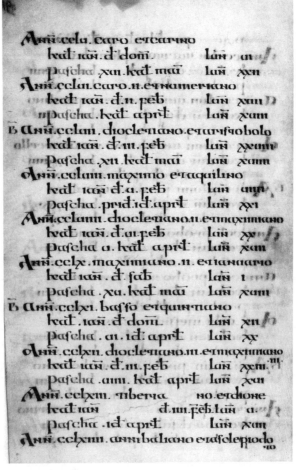

Figure 10.3   Gotha, Universitätsbibliothek, MS 75, fol. 91v. The data presented are: bissextile years; AP; consuls; weekday (feb- is a misreading of feria) of 1 January; its lunar age; Julian calendar date of Easter Sunday; its lunar age.

omission of double dates; it recorded only the 'Latin' *luna* 22 and no longer the *luna* 15 ascribed by Victorius to the 'Greeks'. For the year 740, it contains an interesting note: 'Up to this point, the Greeks and the Latins celebrate Easter at the same time, that is for fifty years.'[17] This observation results from a faithful comparison between Victorian and Dionysiac data (rather than from an analysis of Victorius's double dates; Victorius's 'Greek' *luna* 15 is not identical with Dionysiac *luna* 15). Frankish scholars had learned the tools of comparing the two reckonings from their Irish sources, where comparisons between the Victorian and the Dionysiac reckonings are well attested.[18] The best example comes from the prologue to a now lost Victorian Easter table covering the century 699 to 799. The prologue shows that in this table, the three major linear timelines – counting years from the creation of the world, the passion of Christ and the incarnation – were aligned. Achieving this alignment is a challenging task of considerable complexity.[19] Such tools certainly played an important role in the adoption of the incarnation era, which we still follow today, in eighth-century Francia.[20] After their Irish phase, the Easter reckonings were more refined than before and with their reintroduction to the Continent immensely advanced the scientific knowledge in the Frankish kingdoms.

Another important witness for Irish influence is Northumbria, where Irish clergy controlled monasteries and exerted considerable influence from the 630s at least. It is in Northumbria that we find a forceful illustration of the impact of Rome's turning to the Dionysiac reckoning: in 664 a decision was taken at the synod of Whitby to abandon the *Latercus* of the northern Irish churches and expel the traditionalist Irish clergy from Northumbria. Thereafter, according to Bede, Anglo-Saxon England became Dionysiac. Following the synod of Whitby the question of introducing Dionysius spread to Ireland and the Irish communities in Britain, in the area of present-day Argyll. Abbot Adomnán of Iona converted to Dionysius in the late 680s, with most churches in northern Ireland (including Armagh) following suit, but not Iona itself or its dependencies. This change in the north of the *regiones Scottorum* made the southern Irish churches reconsider their position. By the first decade of the eighth century, Dionysius seems to have been unanimously accepted, though not without resistance from adherents of Victorius. Finally, in 716, the last stronghold of the *Latercus* in the *regiones Scottorum*, Iona, gave in.[21] And so, just when the Dionysiac table had to be recalculated for the next 95-year period of 722 to 816, it was dominant in much of Europe, namely Rome and Italy, the *regiones Scottorum*, Anglo-Saxon England, and among the missionaries in

Frisia. Visigothic Spain had fallen to the Arab conquest, the Frankish clergy still supported their native Victorius, while in Wales the *Latercus* continued to hold currency.

A recalculation of data was necessary, because the Alexandrian reckoning was traditionally designed as a 95-year table, introduced by Dionysius Exiguus in the Latin West. This period was not cyclic, but the data of every fourth year (those designated as bissextile (leap-) years in the original table) had to be recalculated, as Dionysius explains in his Prologue. The first extension of Dionysius's table was achieved by a certain Felix Gillitanus (and surely others independently) in around 626 (Dionysius's final year).[22] No information survives on how Rome and the Italian monasteries dealt with the question of extending the Dionysiac table at its next occurrence in 721. All evidence that has survived comes from the insular world and Frisia. Ceolfrith's letter to the Pictish king Nechtan of *c.* 710 famously states that recalculating the 95-year period posed no obstacle to Anglo-Saxon intellectuals; in fact, expertise was such, according to Ceolfrith, that producing correct data for the entire 532-year cyclic period had been achieved.[23] Bede backs this up by providing the details in *De temporum ratione* of 725, which may have had a Dionysiac 532-year Easter table attached.[24] Unfortunately, these statements cannot be corroborated by the existing manuscript witnesses. The earliest full 532-year Dionysiac Easter table comes from the end of the eighth century.[25] And there are numerous texts compiled in the early eighth century showing some monastic communities struggling with this task.[26] Still, we may assume that most succeeded in the end.

Our best witness is the famous Easter table of Willibrord. This, it will be noted, is the oldest Dionysiac Easter table that has survived (especially, there is no known surviving copy of Dionysius's original covering 532–626, with the final nineteen years of the preceding Cyrillian table prefixed). Early in his career, Willibrord was educated in the Dionysiac system by one of the best specialists in the field, Wilfrid, the advocate of the Roman/Dionysiac party at the synod of Whitby. He then left his native Northumbria to increase his knowledge in Ireland, studying under Ecgberht in the monastery of Ráth Máelsigi. Ecgberht was the very man who in 716 converted the congregation of Iona, the last stronghold of the *Latercus*. Accordingly, Willibrord was trained by two expert supporters of the Dionysiac system. When he left Ireland for his mission to Frisia in 690, he had to bring the essentials of this reckoning, since neighbouring Francia, his support base, was still following Victorius.[27] Most important was an Easter table, and this has survived in the codex Paris, Bibliothèque nationale de France, MS Lat. 10837 (see Figure 10.4).[28] It consists of four parts, covering the 19-year periods 684–702, 703–721, 722–759, 760–797. This demonstrates that the 95-year structure was not considered essential. Apparently, Willibrord and his companions did not find it difficult to calculate a new table every 19 years, a clear indicator of their profound knowledge. In fact, Willibrord brought not only the Easter table and his famous calendar (preserved in the same manuscript) to the Continent, but also a set of algorithms ultimately going back to Dionysius's own writings, which facilitated calculating the data of each column of the Dionysiac table.[29] The impact of Willibrord's Frisian mission on Frankish culture can hardly be overestimated. Not only did he introduce the Dionysiac reckoning

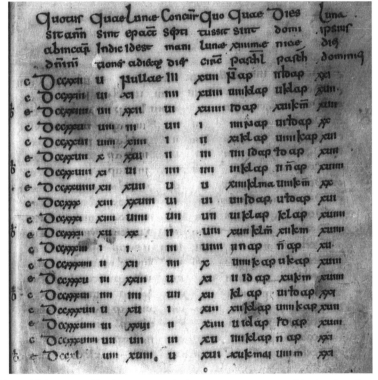

Figure 10.4   Paris, Bibliothèque Nationale de France, MS Lat. 10837, fol. 41r. The columns are: bissextile years; common and embolismic years; AD; indiction; lunar age of 22 March; weekday of 24 March; cyclic number in the *cyclus lunaris*; Julian calendar date of the Easter full moon; Julian calendar date of Easter Sunday; its lunar age.

to a fervently Victorian environment, but with this also AD dating. His calendar is the first known in the early Middle Ages; this genre soon began to immensely flourish in the Frankish Empire.[30] His scientific texts predate those extant from Francia and seem to have considerably stimulated intellectual debate, theological controversy, and scientific thought.[31] Whether Ireland, from where he set out, or Northumbria, from where he originated, is considered the origin of these achievements, is a moot point. Insular scholars of *c.* 680 to 730 laid the foundation for what is often called, in grandiose terms, the 'Carolingian Renaissance', at least for its scientific strand.[32]

Texts and textbooks

Two aspects made insular scientific knowledge particularly attractive to Frankish intellectuals: firstly, introducing the Dionysiac system in a Victorian environment meant that the Frankish clergy faced the same questions in the first half of the eighth century which the southern Irish church had tried to solve towards the end of the seventh. Thus, Frankish scholars were grateful to draw on southern Irish expertise and texts in this question. Most notably, they embraced text which were supposed to prove Dionysius's superiority over Victorius like *De comparatione epactarum Dionysii et Victorii*, which originated in Ireland in 689 and is the central document for the debate at the time.[33]

Secondly, when Dionysius was finally accepted in Francia, the details of his system had to be fully understood for teaching in the growing schools. In this context, the Dionysiac reckoning was less problematic than the Victorian one or the *Latercus*, as Dionysius accompanied his Easter table with two letters (one serving as a prologue to his table, the other was supposed to explain the 19-year cycle), he translated another instructive letter composed by Proterius in 455, and, most importantly, he attached nine *argumenta* (short algorithms) for calculating the data of the table. Especially the *argumenta* became extremely influential in subsequent centuries, establishing its own literary genre, the computistical formulary, of which Willibrord's text is just one of its earliest exponents.[34] But these formulae only helped calculate the data of the table, they did not explain the underlying system. And neither did Dionysius's letters. Quite the contrary, they posed more questions than they were able to answer.

In order to fill this major lacuna, insular scholars invented a new literary genre, the computistical textbook.[35] Its origin lies in Ireland. Working from the meagre information available (principally the writings of Dionysius, Victorius, Anatolius Latinus and Isidore of Seville) and, more importantly, outlining their own findings, three major texts were produced in southern Ireland in the period *c.* 700–725. The earliest appears to be the *Computus Einsidlensis*, discovered as late as 2006 in the Benedictine monastery of Einsiedeln in the Swiss Alps.[36] The only securely datable textbook is the Munich Computus, composed in 718/719.[37] And finally, *De ratione conputandi*, arguably the most sophisticated computistical text of the eighth century, introduced into modern scholarship by Dáibhí Ó Cróinín in the 1980s.[38] Of a fourth only fragments have survived in the libraries of Regensburg and Harvard,[39] and surely there are more important texts still hidden in the hundreds of manuscripts.

These Irish textbooks are extremely important because they make it possible to define Irish scientific thought in the late seventh and early eighth centuries, which then in turn serves as a basis for establishing the Irish contribution to Frankish computistica. In the period between *c.* 725 and 760, the Irish influence certainly was the most dominant.[40] With Willibrord's achievements, it set the foundation for Frankish scientific knowledge. But it also continued to be influential into the early ninth century, when it was gradually replaced by Bedan thought and original Frankish contributions. In fact, the period *c.* 760–820 saw an immense increase in scientific literature in Francia, though more in quantity than in quality. From the early ninth century, Bede's writings became the standard texts on the Continent.[41] Bede's computistica principally consist of two textbooks, *De temporibus* of 703 and *De temporum ratione* of 725.[42] The first provided only a basic outline of the most central issues, and on request from his brethren he produced the more detailed second text two decades later. *De temporum ratione* was to dominate computistical thought during the ninth century before it was substituted by Helperic's *Liber de computo* of 903 (although Bede's work certainly remained popular even after that).[43] Insular thought, therefore, dominated the Continental approach to science. The textbooks principally served the schools. Nevertheless, their sophistication should not be underrated, as they were extremely progressive for their time: many of the concepts discussed had never been explained before, and many definitions and algorithms were new inventions.[44] Only as the decades progressed towards the end of the eighth century did their content become standard knowledge. Then, with the dawn of the Carolingian educational reform, we witness a distinction emerging between two registers of learning: classroom teaching and advanced science. The latter register directly leads into the next topic.

Teachers and scholars

The methodology for analysing the influence of Irish scientific thought on the Continent can be defined as follows: First, it is essential to continue to study the existing manuscripts for evidently Irish treatises (and this work is still very much ongoing and new major discoveries are very likely to be made in the future); the integral use of the vernacular, Old Irish, in the otherwise Latin texts is an especially clear indicator of Irish origin. Second, comparing these texts with other contemporary computistica (Anglo-Saxon, Visigothic, Italian, Frankish), diagnostic Irish features emerge. Third, with these at hand it is then possible, in another round of manuscript analysis, to identify more Irish tracts and therefore more diagnostic features. Fourth, and more importantly, these demonstrably Irish concepts, algorithms and definitions can be traced in later continental texts, which makes it possible to assess the Irish contribution to continental scientific thought. One aspect, however, cannot be solved, namely the authorship of most of these texts. We can speculate about the region of composition, but the name and personality of the author will remain unknown. On the other hand, Irish expertise came to the Continent not only through ideas transmitted in written form, but also orally. The point is best illustrated by Notker the Stammerer in an oft-cited passage of his *Deeds of Charlemagne*, composed in the 880s:[45]

> When he [Charlemagne] had begun to rule alone in the western parts of the world, and the study of letters was everywhere almost forgotten, so that the worship of the true God was weak, it happened that two Scots [i.e. Irishmen] from Ireland came with British traders to the shore of Gaul, and they were men most wonderfully instructed in secular and in sacred texts. When they displayed nothing for sale, they used to shout to the crowds who had come to buy things: 'If anyone is eager for wisdom, let him come to us and receive it, for that is what we have for sale.' [...] When he [Charlemagne] received this answer he was filled with great joy and first he kept them both with him for a short time. Later, when he was compelled to go on military campaigns he ordered one of them, named Clement, to live in Gaul, and he entrusted to him many boys very noble and middling and wretched, and ordered that they be fed and given suitable places to live. The second, who was called <...>, he sent to Italy and granted him the monastery of St Augustine near the city of Pavia, so that whoever wished might gather there to be taught by him.

The implication is that certainly at the height of Charlemagne's educational reform, Irish scholars moved to the Continent to find employment in any of the many Carolingian monastic, cathedral or palace schools. Between the time of Columbanus in the early seventh century and that of Notker in the late ninth, roughly the period under discussion in the present volume, we actually know a number of Irishmen on the Continent by name. For some of them, like Fursa, the basic outlines of their careers are recorded,[46] while for many others we are fortunate to have their bare names, most prominently in the famous codex Bern, Burgerbibliothek, MS 363.[47] Even when biographical details survive, computistica or scientifica may not be among them. In fact, of the Irish scholars on the Continent known by name, very few can be classified as scientists.

There are nevertheless two prominent examples: Dúngal and Dicuil. In 810, six years after the death of Alcuin, who was Charlemagne's advisor and mentor in scientific matters, Dúngal was commissioned to investigate the claim made by a Byzantine embassy that the year 810 witnessed not one but two solar eclipses. Having consulted Pliny and other authorities known to him, Dúngal confirmed the Byzantine assertion.[48] It appears to be no coincidence that an Irishman was chosen for this task. A previously unknown eclipse prediction, datable to 754 (the earliest from the Latin West), has recently come to light in the manuscript Paris, Bibliothèque nationale de France, MS Lat. 6400B.[49] Its Irish authorship can be proven beyond reasonable doubt. Accordingly, Irish scholars had tackled the most fundamental scientific questions of the early Middle Ages well before Carolingian science. Dúngal should be placed in this tradition of exceptional Irish expertise. There are clear examples, therefore, that Continental scholars looked to their insular colleagues for answers to questions pertaining to the higher register of scientific learning.

Even more intriguing is the research that Dicuil produced very early in the ninth century. Like Dúngal, Dicuil is only known through his writings, which consist of two texts, one geographical, the other computistical. Of these, *De mensura orbis terrae*, his description of the known world based on late antique models, is the more famous. This is somewhat unfortunate, as it is actually his computistical *Liber de astronomia* in which he displays the full thrust of his intellect.[50] It may well be described as the most unconventional and original scientific text of the Carolingian period. His continental contemporaries found it difficult to follow his genius. The *Liber* survives in only one manuscript and seems not to have been cited anywhere in the Middle Ages.[51] One may argue, therefore, that if the Irish textbooks of the early eighth century laid the foundation of Carolingian science, Irish scientific learning of the ninth century reached such a level of sophistication that contemporary scholars found difficult to digest. The focus was on the schools, not necessarily on original thought. It may well be that Dicuil's fate would have been different had he lived a few decades later. Under the patronage of Charlemagne's grandson Charles the Bald, an exceptional group of scholars flourished, many of whom were Irish. The most notable among these was, no doubt, John Scottus Eriugena (see Chapter 12). He and his circle are particularly credited with the revival of Greek and Greek learning. To what extent they were involved in scientific studies, is a different and by no means straightforward matter. One of the major impacts in the ninth century was the wider availability of late antique authors like Macrobius, Martianus Capella and Calcidius. These texts were intensively studied during Charles the Bald's reign and helped to deepen the understanding especially of astronomical matters.[52] Generally, these works should, however, be classified as philosophy rather than scientifica, not least because of their allegorical style and their neo-Platonic viewpoint. Likewise, Eriugena is best described as a natural philosopher.

Manuscripts and monastic centres

Autographs of Irish scientifica have not survived (i.e. the original in the author's handwriting is lost). In fact, prior to the ninth century, autographs do not exist. This means that all texts discussed are transmitted in later copies, all of them in continental manuscripts. We would know virtually nothing about early medieval Irish culture had its written witnesses not made it to the Continent, where they enjoyed wide popularity. In the area of computistica, only five manuscripts in Irish script survive.[53] It is therefore necessary to study continental codices in order to identify Irish scientifica and, even more importantly, to assess their reception on the Continent. This provides us with vital information about monastic centres particularly influenced by Irish thought.

The most prominent (at least in our present context) group of manuscripts is named after the French Jesuit scholar Jacques Sirmond (d. 1651). Sirmond was a prolific writer himself who was known for his generosity in sharing manuscripts from his private collection with his Jesuit colleagues for their own studies. One codex in particular, which contains all the crucial late antique texts on chronology, provided the basis for the ground-breaking works of Denis Pétau and Gilles Bouchier (better known under their latinized names, Dionysius Petavius and Aegidius Bucherius), both entitled *De doctrina temporum*. Since this heyday of Jesuit scholarship, the manuscript appeared to have been lost. Therefore, as neither library nor shelf-mark could be assigned to it, it became known as the mysterious Sirmond manuscript. During his library tour through Europe in the 1930s, Charles W. Jones rediscovered the codex in the Bodleian Library in Oxford, where it is kept under the shelf-mark Bodley 309.[54] On the basis of Bruno Krusch's earlier research, Jones identified a number of ninth-, tenth- and eleventh-century manuscripts with close connections to the Oxford codex, which were aptly styled 'the Sirmond group of manuscripts'. Jones suspected that this so-called Sirmond material had been assembled in Ireland and argued convincingly that Bede drew on it for composing his computistical textbooks in the early eighth century. Subsequently, Dáibhí Ó Cróinín confirmed Jones's hypothesis by his discovery of a dating clause for 658 in the Sirmond manuscript which pointed to southern Ireland as the place of compilation.[55]

It must be stressed, however, that the Sirmond material is principally a collection of the most important late antique texts and tables on the subject, and includes only very few Irish computistica of the seventh century. Nevertheless, the Sirmond group of manuscripts is key to our understanding of the transmission of late antique computistical knowledge to the early Middle Ages. For the reception of Irish scientific thought on the Continent, on the other hand, we need to consider the manuscripts containing the texts discussed above. They reveal a very obvious pattern: since the days of Columbanus, Irish influence spread in certain parts of the Continent, most prominently in north-eastern France, Switzerland, Lombardy and Bavaria. One would therefore expect Irish scientific thought to be clustered in these areas, and this is exactly what happened.[56] The major centres evidently influenced by Irish scientifica are especially Bobbio, St-Gall, Regensburg and Cologne (probably owing to the north-eastern French connection).

Another approach to this question is to search for probable routes of transmission. These could potentially (though not necessarily) coincide with pilgrimage routes to Rome. Two options appear to be the most apparent, depending on whether the pilgrim set out from the northern or the southern *regiones Scottorum*. From the north, it would have led through Anglo-Saxon England (or around Britain by boat), north-eastern France, the Rhine, Switzerland, and Lombardy. This route could provide the reason for the importance of Cologne for the transmission of Irish thought, as would its proximity to Willibrord's mission, who, no doubt, kept his connections to the *regiones Scottorum*. From the south, Brittany and the Loire valley would have been the first points of contact, before again Switzerland and Lombardy served as the next stops. This certainly explains the very prominent occurrence of Irish computistica in places like Landévennec and Fleury. But the spread of Irish ideas hardly went strictly along those routes. The most common procedure was that one copy of a textbook or treatise would have been commissioned by or brought to one particular centre first, and in subsequent years, decades or centuries it would have been distributed further to, at least intellectually, connected monasteries. Therefore, the spread of texts and ideas is ideal for network analysis between monastic centres, but, as mentioned at the beginning of this chapter, this research is still in its infancy.

Notes

1. Very readable, though now outdated, is A. Borst, *The Ordering of Time: from the Ancient Computus to the Modern Computer*, trans. A. Winnard (Cambridge, 1993).
2. On the *Supputatio Romana*, see A. A. Mosshammer, *The Easter Computus and the Origins of the Christian Era* (Oxford, 2008), pp. 204–13; L. Holford-Strevens, 'Paschal Lunar Calendars up to Bede', *Peritia* 20 (2008), pp. 165–208, at pp. 173–8.
3. Padua Biblioteca Antoniana, MS I 27, fos 76r–77v; Daniel Mc Carthy and D. Ó Cróinín, 'The 'Lost' Irish 84-Year Easter Table Rediscovered', *Peritia* pp. 6–7 (1987–88), 227–42.
4. On the *Latercus*, see especially Daniel Mc Carthy, 'Easter Principles and a Fifth-Century Lunar Cycle used in the British Isles', *Journal for the History of Astronomy* 24 (1993), 204–24; Holford-Strevens, 'Lunar Calendars', pp. 178–87. The Easter dates are best accessed through B. Blackburn and L. Holford-Strevens, *The Oxford Companion to the Year: an Exploration of Calendar Customs and Time-Reckoning* (Oxford, 1999), pp. 870–5.
5. M. Lapidge and M. Herren, *Aldhelm: the Prose Works* (Cambridge, 1979), pp. 157–8; see Daniel Mc Carthy, 'The Origin of the *Latercus* Paschal Cycle of the Insular Celtic Churches', *Cambrian Medieval Celtic Studies* 28 (1994), 25–49; I. Warntjes, 'The Munich Computus and the 84 (14)-Year Easter Reckoning', *PRIA* 107 C (2007), 31–85, at 36–7.
6. For the late antique Easter controversy, see G. Declercq, *Anno Domini: The Origins of the Christian Era* (Turnhout, 2000), pp. 49–82; a more technical account is Mosshammer, *Easter Computus*, pp. 162–277.
7. Victorius's computistica are ed. by B. Krusch, 'Studien zur christlich-mittelalterlichen Chronologie: die Entstehung unserer heutigen Zeitrechnung', *Abhandlungen der Preußischen Akademie der Wissenschaften Jahrgang 1937, phil.-hist. Klasse* 8 (1938). Cf. Declercq, *Anno Domini*, pp. 82–95; Mosshammer, *Easter Computus*, pp. 239–44; Holford-Strevens, 'Paschal Lunar Calendars', pp. 192–6.
8. Dionysius's computistica are ed. by Krusch, 'Studien', pp. 59–87. Cf. Declercq, *Anno Domini*, pp. 97–200; Mosshammer, *Easter Computus*, pp. 56–106.

9. Modern scholars tend to portray Victorius as a rather limited scientist, which does not do him justice; devising an Easter table was a highly complex task, and he was the last in a prominent line of late antique scholars achieving this; nothing similar was subsequently produced before the end of the 11th century.
10. Prosper of Aquitaine's *Chronicon*, ed. Theodor Mommsen, MGH Auct. ant. 9, p. 473. For Daniel Mc Carthy's hypothesis, see his 'On the Arrival of the *Latercus* in Ireland', in I. Warntjes and D. Ó Cróinín, *The Easter Controversy of Late Antiquity and the Early Middle Ages* (Turnhout, 2011), pp. 48–75.
11. See C. Corning in this volume and the literature cited there.
12. CCSL 148A, p. 132.
13. See C. Corning, *The Celtic and Roman Traditions: Conflict and Consensus in the Early Medieval Church* (New York, 2006), pp. 19–94.
14. Cummian's Letter is ed. and trans. in M. Walsh and D. Ó Cróinín, *Cummian's Letter De Controversia Paschali, together with a Related Irish Computistical Tract, De Ratione Conputandi* (Toronto, 1988), pp. 1–97.
15. I. Warntjes, 'Victorius vs Dionysius: the Irish Easter Controversy of AD 689', in P. Moran and I. Warntjes, *Early Medieval Ireland and Europe: Chronology, Contacts, Scholarship* (Turnhout, 2015), pp. 33–97.
16. I. Warntjes, 'Seventh-Century Ireland: the Cradle of Medieval Science?', in M. Kelly and C. Doherty, *Music and the Stars: Mathematics in Medieval Ireland* (Dublin, 2013), pp. 44–72.
17. Paris, Bibliothèque nationale de France, MS Lat. 4860, fol. 147v; Vatican, Biblioteca Apostolica Vaticana, MS Reg. lat. 586, fol. 9v.
18. I. Warntjes, *The Munich Computus: Text and Translation. Irish Computistics between Isidore of Seville and the Venerable Bede and its Reception in Carolingian Times* (Stuttgart, 2010), CLXIII–CLXV.
19. I. Warntjes, 'A Newly Discovered Prologue of AD 699 to the Easter Table of Victorius of Aquitaine in an Unknown Sirmond Manuscript', *Peritia* 21 (2010), pp. 255–84.
20. The incarnation era was first introduced into Francia by Willibrord, but its theological weaknesses led to its rejection by adherents of Victorius, who followed the superior *anni passionis*; the first Frankish text to apply AD is *Dial. Neustr.* of 737, chapter 30 (ed. by A. Borst, *Schriften zur Komputistik im Frankenreich von 721–818*, 3 vols [Hanover, 2006], p. 421); cf. Declercq, *Anno Domini*, pp. 160–4 (the text of 727 mentioned there, *Prol. Aquit.* in Borst's edition, should be considered Visigothic rather than Frankish).
21. The literature on these developments is outlined in Warntjes, *Munich Computus*, pp. XXXIX–XL; additionally, Corning, *Celtic and Roman traditions*; for the reservations towards Dionysius articulated by the southern Irish followers of Victorius, see Warntjes, 'Victorius vs Dionysius'.
22. For Felix, see L. Cuppo, 'Felix of Squillace and the Dionysiac Computus I: Bobbio and Northern Italy (MS Ambrosiana H 150 inf.)', in Warntjes and Ó Cróinín, *Easter Controversy*, pp. 110–36.

23. Bede, *HE,* V.21.

24. Bede, *De temporum ratione* 65, trans. by F. Wallis, *Bede: The Reckoning of Time* (Liverpool, 1999), pp. 155–6. For Bede's Easter table, see ibid., pp. 392–404, and CCSL 123, pp. 549–62.

25. Among our earliest witnesses for the Dionysiac 532-year Easter table are the oldest three codices transmitting Bede's *De temporum ratione*: Cologne, Dombibliothek, MS 103, fos 9r–22v (Cologne, very end of the eighth century; www.ceec.uni-koeln.de); Berlin, Staatsbibliothek, MS Phillipps 1831, fos 8r–14v (Verona, very early ninth century); Kassel, Universitätsbibliothek – Landes- und Murhardsche Bibliothek, MS 2° Ms. astron. 2, fos 1v–8r (Fulda, very early ninth century; http://orka. bibliothek.uni-kassel.de/viewer/image/1327910656180/1/); cf. C. W. Jones, *Bedae opera de temporibus* (Cambridge, 1943), pp. 144–5. Earlier still are the related Münster, Staatsarchiv, MS I 243, fos 1r–12v (Northumbria, mid-eighth century); Munich, Bayerische Staatsbibliothek, MS Clm 14641, fos 32v–46r (Fulda, late eighth century; http://daten.digitale-sammlungen.de/~db/0006/bsb00065770/images/), which serve as a reminder for the potential composite nature of the earliest Dionysiac 532-year Easter tables; cf. R. Corradini, 'The Rhetoric of Crisis: Computus and Liber Annalis in Early Ninth-Century Fulda', in R. Corradini, M. Diesenberg, H. Reimitz, *The Construction of Communities in the Early Middle Ages: Texts, Resources and Artefacts* (Leiden, 2003), pp. 269–321, at pp. 278–88.

26. Warntjes, *Munich Computus,* XC–XCIII, pp. 310–11.

27. I. Warntjes, 'The *Computus Cottonianus* of AD 689: a Computistical Formulary written for Willibrord's Frisian Mission', in Warntjes and Ó Cróinín, *Easter Controversy,* pp. 173–212.

28. On this Easter table, see D. Ó Cróinín, 'Rath Melsigi, Willibrord, and the Earliest Echternach Manuscripts', *Peritia* 3 (1984), pp. 17–49, repr. in idem, *Early Irish History,* pp. 145–72, at pp. 155–6.

29. Warntjes, '*Computus Cottonianus*'.

30. A. Borst, *Die karolingische Kalenderreform* (Hanover, 1998); idem, *Der karolingische Reichskalender und seine Überlieferung bis ins 12. Jahrhundert,* 3 vols (Hanover, 2001).

31. The earliest Frankish computistical texts (Bern, Burgerbibliothek, MS 645, fos 41r–71v of, probably, 696; *Dial. Burg.* of 727) appear to be a Victorian reflex to Willibrord's Dionysiac mission; the note in the Victorian table for 700–771 cited n. 17 above is explicit that, in 740, Victorius and Dionysius had been compared for 50 years, that is, starting with Willibrord's mission in 690.

32. A representative, though not complete corpus of Frankish computistica of the period is ed. by Borst, *Schriften.* For the Irish influence on these, see Warntjes, *Munich Computus,* pp. CLIX–CLXXXIII; I. Warntjes, 'Irische Komputistik zwischen Isidor von Sevilla und Beda Venerabilis: Ursprung, karolingische Rezeption und generelle Forschungsperspektiven', *Viator* 42 multilingual (2011), pp. 1–31, at pp. 16–21.

33. This text is ed. and discussed in Warntjes, *Munich Computus*, pp. 322–6, CLII–CLVIII. See also C. P. E. Nothaft, *Dating the Passion: The Life of Jesus and the Emergence of Scientific Chronology (200–1600)* (Leiden, 2012), pp. 78–80.
34. I. Warntjes, 'The *Argumenta* of Dionysius Exiguus and their Early Recensions', in I. Warntjes and D. Ó Cróinín, *Computus and its Cultural Context in the Latin West, AD 300–1200* (Turnhout, 2010), pp. 40–111.
35. Warntjes, *Munich Computus*, pp. LII–LVI.
36. For this text, see J. Bisagni and I. Warntjes, 'The Early Old Irish Material in the Newly Discovered *Computus Einsidlensis*', *Ériu* 58 (2008), 77–105; Warntjes, *Munich Computus*, pp. CXXXIII–CLII.
37. The Munich Computus is ed. and trans. in Warntjes, *Munich Computus*.
38. *De ratione conputandi* is ed. by D. Ó Cróinín in Walsh and Ó Cróinín, *Cummian's Letter*, pp. 99–213. See D. Ó Cróinín, 'A Seventh-Century Irish Computus from the Circle of Cummian', *PRIA* 82 C (1982), 405–30; Warntjes, *Munich Computus*, pp. CXCI–CCI.
39. Harvard, Houghton Library, MS Typ 613, fol. 7r-v; Regensburg, Staatliche Bibliothek, MS Frag., 1ar–v, 1dr–1ev.
40. See n. 32.
41. On the reception of Bede's scientifica see J.J. Contreni, 'Bede's Scientific Works in the Carolingian Age', in S. Lebecq, M. Perrin and O. Szerwiniack, *Bède le Vénérable: entre tradition et postérité* (Lille, 2005), 247–59; J.A. Westgard, 'Bede and the Continent in the Carolingian Age and Beyond', in S. deGregorio, *The Cambridge Companion to Bede* (Cambridge, 2010), pp. 201–15.
42. These texts are translated in C.B. Kendall and F. Wallis, *Bede: On the Nature of Things and On Times* (Liverpool, 2010); Wallis, *Bede*.
43. Helperic's *Liber de computo* is ed. in *PL* 137, pp. 17–48. Cf. L. Traube, 'Computus Helperici', *Neues Archiv der Gesellschaft für ältere deutsche Geschichtskunde* 18 (1893), pp. 73–105.
44. Warntjes, *Munich Computus*, CLIX–CLXVIII.
45. Translated by D. Ganz, *Einhard and Notker the Stammerer: Two Lives of Charlemagne* (London, 2008), pp. 55–6.
46. Fursa's life is sketched in Bede, *HE,* III.19 (Colgrave and Mynors, *Ecclesiastical history*, pp. 268–77).
47. J. J. Contreni, 'The Irish in the Western Carolingian Empire (according to James F. Kenney and Bern, Burgerbibliothek, 363)', in H. Löwe, ed., *Die Iren und Europa im früheren Mittelalter* (Stuttgart, 1982), pp. 758–98; D. Ó Cróinín, 'The Irish as Mediators of Antique Culture on the Continent', in P. L. Butzer and D. Lohrmann, *Science in Western and Eastern Civilization in Carolingian Times* (Basle, 1993), pp. 41–52.
48. B.S. Eastwood, 'The Astronomy of Macrobius in Carolingian Europe: Dúngal's Letter of 811 to Charles the Great', *EME* 3 (1994), 117–34; idem, *Ordering the Heavens: Roman Astronomy and Cosmology in the Carolingian Renaissance* (Leiden, 2007), pp. 43–63, 175–77.
49. I. Warntjes, 'An Irish Eclipse Prediction of AD 754: the Earliest in the Latin West', *Peritia* pp. 24–25 (2013–14), 108–15.

178   *The Irish in Early Medieval Europe*

50. Dicuil's *Liber de astronomia* is ed. by M. Esposito, 'An Unpublished Astronomical Treatise by the Irish Monk Dicuil', *PRIA* 26 C (1907), 378–446. Unreliable are A. Cordoliani, 'Le comput de Dicuil', *Cahiers de civilization médiévale* 3 (1960), 325–37; W. Bergmann, 'Dicuils Osterfestalgorithmus im *Liber de astronomia*', in Warntjes and Ó Cróinín, *Easter Controversy*, pp. 242–87.
51. Valenciennes, Bibliothèque municpale, MS 404 (386), fos 66r–118r.
52. See especially Eastwood, *Ordering the Heavens*.
53. Vatican, Biblioteca Apostolica Vaticana, MS Vat. lat. 5755, fos 3–6 + Milan, Biblioteca Ambrosiana, MS L 22 sup., fos 146–7; Nancy, Bibliothèque municipale, MS 317 (356). The Vatican + Milan fragments contain some of the *Argumenta* ascribed to Dionysius and excerpts from the Calculus of Victorius of Aquitaine; the Nancy fragment contains Ps.-Dionysiac and other *argumenta*. See especially Warntjes, 'Argumenta', 66–7, 69–72, 96–105, 110–1, with further references. The Vatican + Milan fragments and the Nancy fragment may stem from the same manuscript, as David Ganz informs me, but only a full-scale study of these fragments will shed further light on this question. The other computistical MSS in Irish script are: Vienna, Österreichische Nationalbibliothek, Supp. 2698 (Vienna Bede); Carlsruhe, Badische Landesbibliothek, Aug. Perg. 167 (Carlsruhe Bede); Carlsruhe, Badische Landesbibliothek, Frag. Aug. 107; and the fragments mentioned in n. 39.
54. C. W. Jones, 'The 'Lost' Sirmond Manuscript of Bede's Computus', *English Historical Review* 52 (1937), pp. 204–37.
55. D. Ó Cróinín, 'The Irish Provenance of Bede's Computus', *Peritia* 2 (1983), pp. 229–47.
56. The following discussion is based on all manuscripts transmitting the Irish computistical texts outlined above: Munich, Bayerische Staatsbibliothek, MS Clm 14456 (St Emmeram in Regensburg, early ninth century); Einsiedeln, Stiftsbibliothek, MS 321 (647) (Strasbourg or Lake Constance?, late ninth century); Brussels, Koninklijke Bibliothek van Belgie, MS 5413–22 (northern France, second half of the ninth century); Vatican, Biblioteca Apostolica Vaticana, MS Reg. Lat. 1260 (Loire valley, ninth century); Cologne, Dombibliothek, MS 83–2 (Cologne, early ninth century); Bremen, Staats- und Universitätsbibliothek, MS msc 0046 (St–Gall, late ninth century); Padua, Biblioteca Antoniana, MS I 27 (northern Italy, early tenth century); Paris, Bibliothèque nationale de France, MS Lat. 6400B (Fleury based on a Breton exemplar, tenth century). Additionally, the only glosses to Bede based on the Irish computistical textbooks can be found Angers, Bibliothèque municipale, MS 477 (461) (Lendévennec, late ninth century); also, evidently Irish computistica not mentioned above can be found in Milan, Biblioteca Ambrosiana, MS H 150 inf. (Bobbio, early ninth century); and the early transmission of the Irish Ps.-Columbanus' *De saltu lunae* is exclusive to St–Gall (Stiftsbibliothek, MSS 250, 459, both late ninth century).

11

Irish Scholars and Carolingian Learning

Sven Meeder

One of the most curious sources for the history of the Irish on the Continent in the ninth century must be a collection of six letters in a tenth-century composite manuscript, now in Leiden's university library in the Netherlands. The letters are preserved amidst an eclectic mix of brief texts and fragments and were probably intended for Bishop Franco of Liège (852–901).[1] In three letters the respective bearers are identified as Irish and a fourth also appears to be from one of these Irishmen.[2] The letters all include pleas for the bishop's assistance in the provision of sustenance and accommodation or, in one case, for his help in the restoration of stolen property. In one of the letters a poor Irish traveller (*pauperculus Scottus peregrinus*), weary from his travels from Rome, begs the bishop for help and charity. He does so with rhetorical flourish and conviction. He eloquently reminds the reader that Christ was found among the least of the poor and that it is Christ who will admit the elect into heaven. The poor *peregrinus* furthermore cites Christ's pronouncement in the Gospel of Matthew: 'as long as you did it to one of these my least brethren, you did it to me'.[3]

As an added favour, the Irish sender asks for the letter to be returned to him as it is written in a language that is not his own. Although the letter speaks for him, he explains, he is 'neither a grammarian nor skilled in Latin speech'.[4] The Irishman's request for the return of his letter explains why the formulaic plea lacks a formal salutation: both the parchment and the text were meant to be recycled. The letter appears to have served as the pilgrim's meal ticket for the whole journey to and from Rome. Were it not for a thrifty (or inattentive) clerk at Franco's court this utilitarian letter would have probably never been preserved to us. It makes this a valuable piece of evidence: among the numerous sources for gifted Irish intellectuals on the Continent, this document sheds unusual light on the Irish presence on the Continent during one of the formative phases of European learned culture: the Carolingian revival of learning.

This beggarly itinerant Irishman with no Latin skills does not strike us as an important player in the scholarly circles of the ninth century, but his note is just as much a product of its time. The Leiden letters paint a picture of visiting Irishmen travelling throughout Europe, who were dependent on the charity of monasteries, bishops and the elite. The adamant denial that the Irish traveller is a grammarian ought to serve as a reminder to historians that not all travelling Irishmen were highly learned scholars. At the same time, the fact that the bearer of the letter makes a special effort to declare his incompetence at Latin, suggests that this was a relevant detail at the time of writing during the bloom of the Carolingian reforms. In other words, even in his day, the letter bearer appears to have assumed that people would expect Irish travellers to be grammarians. This expectation was not wholly unfounded: a good number of Irish travellers on the Continent were in fact grammarians.

The revival of learning in the Latin West in the late eighth and ninth centuries is closely linked with the efforts of *renovatio* of the Carolingian kings. The *Admonitio Generalis*, Charlemagne's capitulary from 789, is generally regarded as a reform agenda. It reveals a deep concern with the spiritual wellbeing of the king's subjects and therefore with the correct knowledge of church dogma and the correct practice of ecclesiastical rituals. It calls for schools to be set up for teaching and for the correction of religious books, for, as Charlemagne puts it, 'often, while people want to pray to God in the proper fashion, they yet pray improperly because of uncorrected books'.[5] It illustrates the strong connection recognized by the court between grammatical skills and correct worship. The primacy of the study of grammar is evidenced by the works copied for and used at the Carolingian court by its scholars, their pupils and their sponsors, even before it settled at Aachen in the 790s.[6] Charlemagne had his own teacher of grammar in the person of Peter of Pisa. Another Italian courtier, Paul the Deacon, wrote a grammatical treatise as did Alcuin, the dominant intellectual at court, whose text is based on Donatus's *Ars Maior*, a more advanced Latin textbook which was possibly reintroduced in Francia through his efforts.[7]

Scholars from far and wide were attracted and employed to further the knowledge of grammar, and grammatical handbooks were copied enthusiastically. Insular intellectuals had a significant role to play in the promotion of good grammar. The fact that Ireland had not been part of the Roman Empire granted it a special place in the western post-Roman world and this extends to the Irish approach to Latin literacy. Without a living tradition of Latin as a spoken language, the universal language for the Irish was not only the language of *the* book, but rather a 'book language': it had to be learned from written sources.[8] This explains the interest shown by Irish intellectuals in grammatical textbooks and their readiness to provide commentaries to these treatises, a sixth- and seventh-century novelty that proved its worth in the early phases of the Carolingian reforms.[9] This expertise arguably made Irish scholars particularly suited to function within the context of these reforms. The extant sources report a multitude of Irishmen finding employment on the Continent as teachers of grammar. The courtier known as Cadac-Andreas seems to have been a teacher of grammar and Bible studies (and possibly of ancient mythology) at the court of Charlemagne, where he worked with scholarly greats like Alcuin and battled with Theodulf of Orléans (see below). With his expertise in both grammar and biblical studies, Cadac-Andreas personified an ideal scholar in the formative phase of the Carolingian reforms. Both subjects were at the core of the Carolingian reforms: grammar, so as to better understand and perform the important liturgical ceremonies, but of course also to better understand the Bible.

Another teacher of grammar working at the imperial court was Clemens Scottus, or Clemens Hibernicus.[10] He features in the largely anecdotal Deeds of Emperor Charles, written by Notker Balbulus at the end of the ninth century, as one of the two Irishmen arriving on the shore of Francia in the early years of Charlemagne's reign and offering their wisdom for sale.[11] The two, 'incomparably learned in both secular and sacred writings', were quickly summoned by the king and enlisted for his ambitious programmes for education. Clemens ended up as master of the palace school, where he appears to have been the successor of Alcuin and was probably still at court in 826.[12] Fellow courtier Theodulf of Orléans paid him effusive compliments in a poem: 'A salute to Clemens, a man of highest merits, who shines brightly, decorated with such a name, and who is honest with loyalty.'[13] Among his students he could count the future emperor Lothar, as well as some monks from the great monastery of Fulda expressly sent by their abbot to study under him. In addition to teaching, Clemens also seems to have authored the *Ars Grammatica*, based to some extent on a now-lost Irish grammatical treatise on the Latin verb.[14]

As the study of grammar progressed in the course of the ninth century so did the genre of grammatical handbooks which now increasingly took the form of commentaries on late antique instructive texts such as the *Ars Maior* by Donatus, like the one composed by Alcuin. The Irish *peregrini* seem to have been at the vanguard of this development. Murethach (or Muridac; Old Irish Muiredach), arriving on the Continent in the 840s, may have written his commentary on the *Ars Maior* here.[15] His commentary depends on an Irish archetype by an earlier, unknown master, which also lay at the basis of the commentaries of Sedulius Scottus and the so-called Anonymous of Lorsch.[16] Of the three texts, Murethach's commentary enjoyed the widest diffusion, perhaps due to the functionality of the used *quaestio* method, which foreshadows the scholasticism of later centuries.[17] In addition to the commentary on Donatus's *Ars Maior,* Sedulius Scottus also penned commentaries on the *Ars Minor,* Eutyches's *Ars de Uerbo,* and Priscian's *Institutiones Grammaticae.*[18]

The Irish scholars were thus proficient in the main subjects of importance to the reform efforts of Carolingian rulers, namely grammar and the correct understanding of Latin. There is no doubt that the growth of literate culture and the interest in Latin literacy in Ireland itself, evidenced by seventh- and eighth-century texts, benefitted the emigrant scholars, and it goes a long way to account for their visibility in the sources. There seems to be enough reason to believe that by the ninth century the Irish became famous for their grammatical expertise, so much so that the poor Irish pilgrim at Liège had to clarify that he was not a grammarian. Although this certainly did not mean that the Irish had a monopoly on grammatical scholarship and much less that they were the only immigrant scholars on the continental scene.

The court of Charlemagne where some of these Irishmen arrived at the end of the eighth and beginning of the ninth century proved a very international place. Following the conquest of the Lombard kingdom in 774, scholars from Italy such as Peter of Pisa and Paul the Deacon found employment in Charlemagne's entourage. They seem to have been followed shortly by Irish scholars: Clemens and the mysterious poet who calls himself *Hibernicus Exul* appear to have arrived from Ireland before Alcuin came up from Northumbria.[19] Afterwards we find more insular men amongst the court's rank and file, including the Irish Joseph, one of Alcuin's pupils from York, who might have accompanied his master to the Continent in 782 or 786.[20] He was charged with long-distance errands by both Alcuin and Charlemagne.[21] The forceful Theodulf identified himself as a *Getulus,* a Goth, while the influential Einhard, later Charlemagne's biographer, was a Frank of modest background. The Irish Dicuil seems to have appeared on the scene in Charlemagne's later years.[22] Ethnic identity was certainly not forgotten in these surroundings, something perhaps illustrated by the fact that Paul the Deacon would later write a history of his own people, the Lombards, after his stay at court.[23]

The international scene at Charlemagne's court was partly the result of the king's own love of learning, stressed by his biographers,[24] and his desire to gather the best scholars available. Walahfrid Strabo observed this in the 840s in the prologue of a re-edited version of Einhard's Life of Charlemagne: 'Charles was, of course, the keenest of all kings in zealously searching out and supporting wise men so that they might pursue knowledge without material worry.'[25] This multi-ethnic outlook also reflected the Carolingian ideas of kingship and empire. The Royal Frankish Annals, once dubbed the 'closest thing to "official history" we have from the early Carolingian period',[26] stress the international relations of the Frankish court from the 790s onwards. Foreign visitors, among them scholars, were frequently mentioned, spotlighting the king's ability to safeguard the security of *peregrini* within the *Regnum Francorum*, a topic that also received attention in many Carolingian capitularies.[27] Within his court, Charlemagne's reputation for hospitality and his 'good name', so Einhard tells us, were of great importance in Charlemagne's dealings with foreigners. So much so that the king was very little disturbed by what Einhard describes as the nuisance of their massive presence (an endurance not all courtiers possessed, judging by Einhard's choice of words).[28] Similarly, diversity determined the very essence of empire, namely an *imperium* harbouring different peoples from all over western Europe. The aforementioned opening of Notker's Deeds of the Emperor Charles (with the arriving Irish wisdom peddlers) is well-chosen, as it combines all of these royal ambitions in just a few lines. The patronage of scholars of unequalled learning from the outer edge of the Christian world presented a powerful image that the Carolingians loved to display.

We see the emphasis, and often celebration, of ethnic diversity also in works from the court school itself. The most famous example is perhaps a literary battle in which the self-proclaimed Goth Theodulf and the Irishman Cadac were engaged.[29] This episode has long been read as an instance of ethnic tension in which Theodulf disqualifies Cadac's Irishness. More recent attention to the poetic weapons used in this fight (only Theodulf's contributions survive) shows that Theodulf is criticizing Cadac for his affected speech as he tries to mimic the sophisticated speech of the Continent. Rather than pronouncing the 'c' in Latin words consistently as 'k' according to the Irish fashion, Cadac supposedly introduced the 'soft c' in his speech.[30] He overcorrected his insular accent, however, and used a 'soft c' also at places where a 'hard c' was required. His pronunciation of the letter combination 'sc' in any word thus sounded like 's'. Theodulf mocks that, if one were to use the Irishman's pronunciation, Cadac would be *sottus* (a fool) rather than a *scottus* (an Irishman). Although it is perfectly possible that ethnic tensions sporadically produced such conflicts within the corridors of the court, this particular episode between the Goth and the Irishman seems to testify to a rather subtly different argument. Theodulf chastises Cadac for his attempts to obscure his heritage, whereas the multi-ethnic outlook of Charlemagne's empire in fact put a premium on ethnic diversity.[31] Cadac misread the social rules of the court and his venture to fit in backfired.

Cadac appears to be an exception; the extant sources at least present many immigrants from his homeland stressing and celebrating their extraction. It results in the striking phenomenon of Irishmen abroad sporting ethnic epithets. We have already encountered Clemens Scottus or Clemens Hibernicus, someone presenting himself as *Hibernicus Exul* ('an Irish exile') and of course, later in the ninth century, Sedulius Scottus, John Scottus Eriugena (the last word literally means 'of Irish birth'), and Martin Hiberniensis. While for some it is unclear whether they themselves ever used the cognomen, for others it seems evident that they did. A Greek psalter, now in the Bibliotheque de l'Arsenal in Paris, features a colophon in which Sedulius seems to use the cognomen himself: 'CHΔΥΛΙΟC CKOTTOC EΓω EΓPAΨA' ('I, Sedulius Scottus, wrote this').[32] Laon's celebrated master Martin appears to have referred to himself as 'Martinus Hiberniensis [...] exulans magister Laudunensis', if the identification of the scribe's hand with that of Martin is correct.[33] The oldest manuscripts of Eriugena's work refer to him as *Ioannes Eriugena* and to contemporaries he was known as Iohannes Scottus.[34]

The flaunting of one's Irish heritage was not only a response to the imperial ambitions of multi-ethnicity, but was certainly also meant to spotlight one's advanced level of learning. Christian scholars in Ireland from an early stage were committed to demonstrating their membership of a greater intellectual world and this also inspired Irishmen to confidently present themselves as accomplished scholars. The association of Irishness with learning was stressed by the immigrants themselves. Sedulius's description of the party of seafaring Irishmen (of which he may have been a member) seems to use 'learned' and 'Irish' interchangeably.[35] Fellow scholars appear to have feared being criticized by Irish intellectuals, if Ermenrich of Ellwangen's fear for 'javelins from a particular Irish bag' is to be interpreted as an expression of anxiety over piercing literary assessments.[36] At the same time, their reputation for scholarship provided continental critics with a place to hit the Irish where it hurt. Hence, at the close of Theodulf's poem on Charlemagne's court scholars, he delivers his last blow at Cadac citing Martial on the worthless practical education of the Irishman.[37]

In the Carolingian era, we thus see a number of elements coalesce in a continental attitude that was a priori appreciative to Irish intellectuals. The home-taught skills in Latin grammar resulted in a situation in which, in Elva Johnston's words, 'Irishness was explicitly linked with scholarly excellence in a period that self-consciously saw itself as raising intellectual standards.'[38] At the same time, the Carolingians' imperial ambitions went hand-in-hand with royal hospitality and an embrace of ethnic diversity. In addition, the acknowledgment of Ireland as harbouring Christian scholars was attractive to contemporary continental thinking for it revealed that even the remote periphery of the Western world was blessed by God's grace reinforcing the universality of Christendom, and thereby the strength of orthodoxy, defined as those tenets of belief that are held everywhere.[39] These circumstances made it rewarding for Irish intellectuals (and other Irish travellers) to boast their Irishness, even when this meant that our poor Irish pilgrim at Liège had to expressly distance himself from the association with grammatical skills. From the perspective of contemporaries, at least, this resulted in a very visible presence of Irish travellers on the Continent. Continental texts preserve various statements of uncertain sentiment about the ubiquity of Irishmen on the European mainland, such as Heiric of Auxerre's hyperbolic question at the sight of the number of Irishmen on the European mainland whether there were still Irishmen left in Ireland,[40] or Walahfrid Strabo's observation that travelling had become 'second nature' to all Irishmen.[41]

When Walahfrid and Heiric were writing, in the 830s and 860s respectively, the intellectual environment of continental Europe had already changed since the days of Charlemagne's convivial court school. With more complex political circumstances, the intellectual scene also turned more complex. The Carolingian revival of learning had spread to episcopal and monastic schools where it was maintained for the remainder of the Carolingian era. None of these can be labelled as 'Irish centres on the Continent', a term which, despite its tenacious presence in modern cultural memory, represents mere illusions and should be regarded a figment of creative Carolingian notaries. There is no evidence that monasteries such as Luxeuil, Honau or St-Gall, nor indeed other religious centres in this period, were either dominated by Irish monks or preserved a monastic identity that was defined by their Irish heritage.[42] Bishops and archbishops of the ninth century in particular were starting to emulate the example of Charlemagne's court and impressive cathedral schools were founded where international scholars found employment. Dúngal can be said to have personified the shift, moving from the sphere of Charlemagne's and Louis the Pious's courts to Pavia around 825, where he was responsible for the organization of schools.[43] Murethach worked from Metz, where he enjoyed the patronage of Bishop Drogo (a bastard son of Charlemagne). Some Irish scholars similarly gained a high position at such schools, like Sedulius Scottus in Liège and Martin Hiberniensis in Laon. Here they moved outside of the rather safely enclosed environment of the palace school and interacted on a larger scale than before with different important actors in the outside world.

Several elements seem to converge in the person of Sedulius Scottus. Together with Eriugena, Sedulius is the quintessential constituent of Irish intellectuals working on the Continent in the Carolingian era.[44] The breadth of his scholarship includes the disciplines of poetry, theology and exegesis,[45] as well as grammar. In addition he authored a mirror of princes titled *De Rectoribus Christianis,* 'On Christian Rulers', which he dedicated to Charles the Bald and which demonstrates that he was willing to advise kings and was also in a position to do so. His notebook filled with *memoranda* known as the *Collectaneum Miscellaneum* gives insight to Sedulius's practice of reading and excerpting, as well as his access to classical works.[46] The few details that are known about his personal life and his work environment must, however, be gleaned from his poems.[47] Sedulius's earliest (roughly) datable poems are dedicated to Bishop Hartgar of Liège, whose episcopacy began in 840, and to the emperor's wife Irmingard (d. 851). His arrival on the Continent is therefore generally placed sometime between these two dates. As an exponent of the next generation he did not seek employ at an imperial or royal court, but settled, at least for some time, in Liège, a bishopric in the Carolingian heartlands not far from Aachen. He describes arriving there and being drafted into Bishop Hartgar's service in similar terms as the anonymous Irishmen in the Leiden letters: he praises Hartgar for giving rest and comfort to the indigent,[48] for clothing them, and for enriching them with threefold honour.[49]

In one poem Sedulius describes Hartgar's gracious reception of three learned Irish who arrived on the Continent after a journey over a tempestuous sea. Since Sedulius refers to 'us' on three occasions, it appears that he was a member of this band of scholars. The identity of his companions remains uncertain: can any of them be identified with Fergus, Blandus, Marchus or Beuchell, whom Sedulius praises as 'four-span of the Lord, lights of the Irish people'?[50] Equally uncertain is whether the whole group stayed with Sedulius in Liège. And while we may assume that the episcopal schools were less ethnically diverse than Charlemagne's court was, it is quite uncertain if the Irishmen of Sedulius's group were the only intellectuals in Hartgar's service, or if there was something like an 'Irish colony' in existence.[51] The term 'colony' certainly carries connotations which the sources cannot maintain. Yet, Sedulius does not mention other scholars besides Irishmen at Liège and – despite the fact that non-Irishmen must have claimed positions within the cathedral – he plainly foregrounds the Irish as a select circle. In one poem he describes the Irish (*Scottigenae*) responding to the pious songs of the 'brothers' (*fratres*) praising the bishop.[52] It is possible, though, that we should read 'Irish' in Sedulius's *carmina* as a reference to men coming from the edge of the world. The allusion to the 'edge of the world' then functions as an expression of the universal praise befalling Hartgar, and others likewise. Queen Irmingard, for instance, is said to have been exalted by the 'Hebrews, the Greeks, and the Irish',[53] and in a description of a Christmas pageant probably performed in the church of Liège, the three Magi bringing Christ gifts from the East are paralleled by Irish scholars arriving from the West to bring gifts of learning.[54]

Apart from the question of the physical (exclusive) presence of Irish intellectuals at Liège's school, Sedulius is often placed within a circle of Irish scholars roaming the Continent. The basis for this perceived 'circle of Sedulius' is twofold: first, historians have noticed that some of the Irishmen mentioned by Sedulius as associates recur in other contexts, such as the Irish Marcus who is praised in Sedulius's poem and who can very well be identified with the Irish Bishop Marcus whom Ekkehart describes as settling in St-Gall with his nephew Moengal-Marcellus sometime before 872.[55] Secondly, an important group of manuscripts testify to a collaboration between various Irishmen involved in their composition and dissemination. These manuscripts are the famous bilingual Greek-Latin psalter now at Basle,[56] the bilingual St-Gall Gospels[57] and the bilingual copy of the Pauline letters in the so-called *Codex Boernerianus*.[58] They were written in the mid-ninth century by scribes writing an Irish script, with one hand appearing in multiple manuscripts, and they are similar in form and content. One of the scribes also seems to have been involved in the copying of Bern, Burgerbibliothek MS 363, a codex with a mix of didactic works including texts by Dioscorides, Servius's commentary on Virgil, Fortunatianus's *Ars Rhetorica*, texts by Augustine, a tract on rhetoric by Clodianus, poems by Horace, a passage from Ovid's Metamorphoses, a fragment of Bede's *Historia Ecclesiastica*, and poems with clear reminiscences of, or outright verbatim citations from, Sedulius Scottus's poetry.[59] The texts are copiously glossed in the margins with the names of ancient and contemporary scholars who, supposedly, wrote works pertaining to the content of the main text or whose lives could be used to illustrate a point made in the text. These names include those of continentals like Bishop Hagano of Bergamo, Hincmar of Laon, Bishop Adventius of Metz, Gottschalk of Orbais, Ratramnus of Corbie and Louis II's Queen Angelberga, but many of the names are of known Irishmen including Sedulius Scottus (mentioned over 200 times) and Eriugena (more than seventy times). It demonstrates that the Bern master must have possessed an impressive library of works by eighth- and ninth-century scholars, testifying to a lively 'republic of letters' on the Continent where the works of active scholars (insular and otherwise) were quickly shared and read.[60]

All that can be safely said is that the complex relations between these four manuscripts evince the existence of a small team of scholars and scribes, at least some of them Irish, who were very familiar with the writings of contemporary migrant compatriots. Equally evident is their knowledge of contemporary continental scholarship and their intimacy with the plots played out at the highest political ranks.[61] This tends to be the image most persistent of the activities of Irish scholars on the Carolingian Continent; they appear to be at once fiercely Irish and simultaneously firmly connected with continental intellectuals and the powerful.

An overview of the addressees of Sedulius's poems further confirms his entanglement in continental affairs: they include the bishops of Liège, Bishop Gunther of Cologne, Bishop Tado of Milan, King Charles the Bald, Empress Irmingard and Duke Eberhard of Friuli. Eriugena was well connected with the secular leadership and had a position at the palace school of Charles the Bald, where he corresponded and debated with the highest-ranking intellectuals of the day including Gottschalk of Orbais and Archbishop Hincmar of Reims. Martin Hiberniensis also appears to have been very conscious of the fact that he was operating in an international setting, with supra-national, or supra-ethnic, circumstances, demands and expectations. He adopted Carolingian minuscule as his own handwriting – with only very occasional slips into insular letter forms – which demonstrates he was keenly aware of his readership. The twenty-one manuscripts of Martin's collection include works on a wide range of subjects by Church Fathers, contemporary continental scholars, Anglo-Saxons (Bede and Aldhelm) and only a few Irish works (Laidcenn's *Ecloga* and Adomnàn's *Vita Columbae*). It reinforces the image that these men had outgrown their Irish roots and were now performing on a world stage.

When John Contreni in 1982 posed the question 'what was there specifically Irish about the contribution of Martin, John, Sedulius, and others to Carolingian life?', he conceded that one could only make a case for the statement that Martin and John's concept of the arts might have originated from Ireland, but that their lives and labours were neatly in tune with the Carolingian programmes of education and learning.[62] It is important to keep in mind that as soon as the Irish wandering scholars touched the European mainland, they were not only influencing continental culture, but were also influenced by the cultural and political contexts of their new homes. Amidst the boisterous declarations of their Irishness, these men functioned within a wholly European network of knowledge. And some functioned very well indeed. In fact, it was the premium put by the Carolingians on their continuous acts of self-identification as 'Irish' that granted these Irish wandering scholars a very visible presence in the ninth-century revival of learning and in modern cultural memory.

Notes

1. Leiden, Universiteitsbibliotheek, MS VLO 92, fols 122r–3v; the letters are edited by E. Dümmler in MGH Epp. 6 (Berlin, 1875), pp. 195–7 (no. 31); the verses added at the end of three letters are separately edited by Ludwig Traube in MGH Poetae 3 (Berlin, 1896), pp. 690–1.
2. James F. Kenney, *The Sources for the Early History of Ireland: Ecclesiastical. An Introduction and Guide* (New York, 1929), p. 601 (no. 420).
3. Matt. 25.40; MGH Epp. 6, pp. 195–6.
4. 'Non sum grammaticus neque sermone Latino peritus, sed haec epistola quasi mea lingua pro me loquitur [...] Mihi reddite meam epistolam, quia non est sermo in lingua mea': MGH Epp. 6, p. 196.
5. *Admonitio Generalis* (789), c. 72, ed. A. Boretius, MGH Capit. 1 (Hanover, 1883), pp. 52–62, at p. 60; trans. P.D. King, *Charlemagne: Translated Sources* (Kendal, 1987), pp. 209–20, at p. 217.

6. Donald A. Bullough, 'Aula Renovata: the Carolingian Court before the Aachen Palace', *Proceedings of the British Academy* 71 (1985), 267–301, reprinted in: Donald A. Bullough, ed., *Carolingian Renewal: Sources and Heritage* (Manchester, 1991), pp. 123–60, at p. 139.

7. On the Carolingian study of grammar, see Vivien Law, *Grammar and Grammarians in the Early Middle Ages* (London, 1997), esp. pp. 70–90 and 129–63.

8. On early insular literacy, see Elva Johnston, *Literacy and Identity in Early Medieval Ireland* (Woodbridge, 2013), pp. 9–26.

9. Vivian Law, *The Insular Latin Grammarians* (Woodbridge, 1982).

10. On Clemens, see Philippe Depreux, *Prosopographie de l'entourage de Louis le Pieux (781–840)*, Instrumenta 1 (Sigmaringen, 1997), pp. 155–6.

11. Notker the Stammerer, *Gesta Karoli Magni Imperatoris*, ed. and trans. Hans F. Haefele, *Notker der Stammler, Taten Kaiser Karls des Grossen*, MGH SS rer. Germ. N.S. 12 (Berlin, 1959). There are various English translations of this text, including Thomas F.X. Noble, *Charlemagne and Louis the Pious: The Lives by Einhard, Notker, Ermoldus, Thegan, and the Astronomer* (University Park PA, 2009), pp. 51–118.

12. Ermoldus Nigellus, *In honorem Hludowici* IV.403, MGH Poet. 2 (1884), p. 69.

13. '... saluta ... Maxime Clementem merito qui nomine tali Ornatus claret et pietate probus': Theodulf of Orléans, *Carmen* 79, MGH Poet. 1, pp. 508–9.

14. The edition has been in preparation for some time: Clemens Scottus, *Clementis Ars Grammatica*, ed. A. M. Puckett and F. Glorie, CCCM 40E (forthcoming).

15. Muretach (Muridac), *In Donati Artem Maiorem*, CCCM 40, Grammatici Hibernici Carolini aevi 1 (Turnhout, 1977); Bernhard Bischoff, '*Muridac doctissimus plebis*, ein irischer Grammatiker des IX. Jahrhunderts', *Celtica* 5 (1960), 40–4, repr. in Bernhard Bischoff, *Mittelalterliche Studien*, 3 vols. (Stuttgart, 1966–81), II, pp. 51–6, at p. 54–5; In a late-Carolingian manuscript from the region of Reims a gloss on the latter text reads: 'Explicit in arte Donati (*deleted*: sensus) intellectus murtac scotti': Vatican, Biblioteca Apostolica Vaticana, MS Regin. Lat. 1586, fol. 69v.

16. *Ars Laureshamensis (Expositio in Donatum maiorem)*, ed. B. Löfstedt, CCCM 40A, Grammatici Hibernici Carolini aevi 2 (Turnhout, 1977).

17. Haimo of Auxerre, who is sometimes seen as a precursor to Peter Abelard, was the disciple of Murethach, applying his master's method to biblical exegesis: John J. Contreni, 'The Irish in the Western Carolingian Empire (according to James F. Kenney and Bern, Burgerbibliothek 363)', in Heinz Löwe, ed., *Die Iren und Europa im früheren Mittelalter*, Veröffentlichungen Des Europa Zentrums Tübingen, Kulturwissenschaftliche Reihe (Stuttgart, 1982), pp. 758–98, at p. 766.

18. Sedulius Scottus, *In Donati Artem Maiorem*, ed. B. Löfstedt, CCCM 40B, Grammatici Hibernici Carolini aevi 3 (Turnhout, 1977) and idem, *In Donati Artem Minorem. In Priscianum. In Eutychem*, ed. B. Löfstedt, CCCM 40C, Grammatici Hibernici Carolini aevi 4 (Turnhout, 1977); see Law, *Grammar*, p. 144.

19. See Mary Garrison, 'The English and the Irish at the Court of Charlemagne', in P.L. Butzer, M. Kerner, and W. Oberschelp, eds, *Charlemagne and His Heritage: 1200 Years of Civilization and Science in Europe* (Turnhout, 1997), pp. 97–123, at p. 100 nn. 13–14.

20. John Marenbon, *From the Circle of Alcuin to the School of Auxerre: Logic, Theology and Philosophy in the Early Middle Ages* (Cambridge, 1981), pp. 38–9; Garrison, 'English', pp. 105–6.

21. See Bullough, 'Aula Renovata', p. 140.

22. On Dicuil, see Mario Esposito, 'An Irish Teacher at the Carolingian Court: Dicuil', *Studies* 3 (1914), 651–76, at 660–2; Pierre Riché, 'Les Irlandais et les princes carolingiens aux VIIIe et IXe siècles', in Heinz Löwe, ed., *Die Iren und Europa im früheren Mittelalter* (Stuttgart 1982), pp. 735–45, esp. pp. 736–9.

23. Paul the Deacon, *Historia Langobardorum*, ed. G. Waitz, MGH SS rer. Lang. (Hanover, 1878); English translation W.D. Foulke, *Paul the Deacon, History of the Lombards* (Philadelphia, 1907; repr. 2003).

24. Einhard, *Vita Karoli*, ed. O. Holder-Egger, MGH SS rer. Germ. 25 (Hanover, 1911); trans. Paul Dutton, *Charlemagne's Courtier: The Complete Einhard* (Peterborough, Ont., 1998).

25. Walahfrid Strabo, *Prologue to Vita Caroli Magni*, ed. O. Holder-Egger, MGH SS rer. Germ. 25 (Hanover, 1911), pp. xxviii–xxix, at p. xxviii; English translation in Dutton, *Charlemagne's Courtier*, p. 8.

26. Rosamond McKitterick, *Charlemagne: The Formation of a European Identity* (Cambridge, 2008), p. 31.

27. For instance the *Capitulare missorum generale* (a. 802), ch. 27 and 30, ed. A. Boretius and V. Krause, MGH Capit. 2 (Hanover, 1897), pp. 91–9, at p. 96.

28. Einhard, *Vita Karoli*, c. 21 (p. 26).

29. This is based on a poem copied in Paris, Bibliothèque nationale, MS lat. 7490, fol. 8v; edited by Bernhard Bischoff, 'Theodulf und der Ire Cadoc-Andreas', *Historisches Jahrbuch* 74 (1955), 92–8; repr. in Bischoff, *Mittelalterliche Studien*, II, pp. 19–25, at pp. 21–2.

30. Keith Sidwell, 'Theodulf of Orléans, Cadac-Andreas and Old Irish Phonology: a Conundrum', *Journal of Medieval Latin* 2 (1992), pp. 55–62; and Anthony Harvey, '"Battling Andrew" and the West-Brit Syndrome Twelve Hundred Years Ago', *Classics Ireland* 9 (2002), pp. 19–27.

31. On the influence of this phenomenon on so-called 'Irish foundations', see Sven Meeder, 'The Irish Foundations and the Carolingian World', *Settimane* 57 (2010), pp. 467–93.

32. Bibliotheque de l'Arsenal, MS 8407, fol. 55r. A facsimile of the manuscript is now accessible through the website of the *Gallica* project, see

192 The Irish in Early Medieval Europe

http://gallica.bnf.fr/ark:/12148/btv1b550008210 (accessed March 2015). See also Ludwig Traube, 'O Roma Nobilis: Philologischen Untersuchungen aus dem Mittelalter', *Abhandlungen der Philosophisch-Philologischen Classe der königlich bayerischen Akademie der Wissenschaften* 19 (1892), 297–395, at 344–5 (where he erroneously refers to fol. 53).

33. The Laon Annals are preserved in Berlin, Deutsche Staatsbibliothek, MS Phillipps 1830 and edited by O. Holder-Egger, *Annales Laudunenses et sancti Vincenti Mettensis breves*, MGH SS 15 (Hanover, 1856), pp. 1293–5, at p. 1294. On the scribes' handwriting, see John J. Contreni, *The Cathedral School of Laon from 850 to 930: Its Manuscripts and Masters*, Münchener Beiträge zur Mediävistik und Renaissance-Forschung (Munich, 1978), pp. 99–100.

34. Maïeul Cappuyns, *Jean Scot Érigène: Sa vie, son oeuvre, sa pensée* (Louvain/Paris, 1933), pp. 4–8.

35. 'Doctos grammaticos presbiterosque pios', 'Sophos Scottigenas', 'ternos ... sophos': Sedulius Scottus, *Carmen* 3, ed. L. Traube, MGH Poetae 3 (Berlin, 1896), p. 168; Sedulius's poems are translated into English by Edward Gerard Doyle, *Sedulius Scottus On Christian Rulers and The Poems* (Binghamton, 1983).

36. 'Inter haec etiam et cuiusdam Scotticae perae iacula uereor, ceu ex latere emissa, quae modo in partibus Ausoniae puttoni cittonias uel aliud quid incogniti cibi colligit, et, licet attrita fronte, apparebit, quando putto inde gustabit': Ermenrich of Ellwangen, *Epistola ad Grimaldum*, c. 29, ed. E. Dümmler, MGH Epp. 5 (Berlin, 1899), pp. 534–79, at p. 567; see also Johannes Duft and Peter Meyer, *The Irish Miniatures in the Abbey Library of St. Gall* (Olten and New York, 1954), p. 31.

37. Theodulf of Orléans, *Carmen* 25 *(Ad Carolum Regem)*, ed. E. Dümmler, MGH Poet. 1 (Berlin, 1881), pp. 483–9, at lines 159–234.

38. Johnston, *Literacy*, p. 49.

39. This sentiment is most eloquently voiced in the works of Ermenrich of Ellwangen, in particular his *Vita Sualonis*: see Lynda L. Coon, 'Historical Fact and Exegetical Fiction in the Carolingian Vita S. Sualonis', *Church History* 72 (2003), 1–25; For Ermenrich's *Vita Sancti Galli*, see Damian Bracken, '"Whence the Splendour of Such Light Came to Us": The Account of Ireland in Ermenrich's Life of St Gall', in Elizabeth Mullins and Diarmuid Scully, eds, *Listen, O Isles, unto Me: Studies in Medieval Word and Image in Honour of Jennifer O'Reilly* (Cork, 2011), pp. 73–86 (see for this definition of orthodoxy, pp. 74–5).

40. *Vita Sancti Germani Episcopi Autissiodorensis*, ed. L. Traube, MGH Poetae 3 (Berlin, 1896), pp. 428–517, at p. 429, lines 24–6.

41. 'Nuper quoque de natione Scottorum, quibus consuetudo peregrinandi iam paene in naturam conuersa est. . .': Walahfrid Strabo, *Vita Sancti Galli Confessoris*, c. II.46, ed. B. Krusch, MGH SS rer. Merov. 4 (Hanover and Leipzig, 1902), pp. 280–337, at p. 336.

42. Meeder, 'The Irish Foundations'.

43. Mirella Ferrari, 'In Papia conueniant ad Dungalum', *Italia Medievale e Umanistica* 15 (1972), pp. 1–52.

44. This is certainly not to say that Sedulius can be viewed as a typical Irish immigrant scholar with a 'characteristische Beitrag'; cf. Nikolaus Staubach, 'Sedulius Scottus und die Gedichte des Codex Bernensis 363', *Frühmittelalterliche Studien: Jahrbuch des Instituts für Frühmittelalterforschung der Universität Münster* 20 (1986), 549–98, at 549.

45. A recent publication on Sedulius's theological work is Michael C. Sloan, *The Harmonious Organ of Sedulius Scottus: Introduction to his Collectaneum in Apostolum and Translation of its Prologue and Commentaries on Galatians and Ephesians* (Berlin and Boston, 2012).

46. See François Dolbeau, 'Recherches sur le Collectaneum Miscellaneum de Sedulius Scottus', *Bulletin Du Cange: Archivum Latinitatis Medii Aevi* 48–9 (1988–9), 47–84; Bengt Löfstedt, 'Zum Collectaneum des Sedulius Scottus', *Acta Classica* 32 (1989), 111–17. For the edition, see Sedulius Scottus, *Collectaneum Miscellaneum*, ed. Dean Simpson, CCCM 67, 2 vols. (Turnhout, 1988–90).

47. See especially Staubach, 'Sedulius Scottus', pp. 549–62.

48. Sedulius Scottus, *Carmen* 1 (to Hartgar), p. 166.

49. Sedulius Scottus, *Carmen* 3, p. 168.

50. Sedulius Scottus, *Carmen* 34 (to his Irish companions), pp. 199–200.

51. The term 'Irish colony' is used (in quotation marks) by, for instance, John J. Contreni, 'The Irish "Colony" at Laon during the time of John Scottus', in R. Roques, ed., *Jean Scot Érigène et l'histoire de la philosophie* (Paris, 1977), pp. 59–67.

52. Sedulius Scottus, *Carmen* 6 (to Hartgar), p. 170–2.

53. Sedulius Scottus, *Carmen* 20 (to Irmingard), pp. 186–7; see also *Carmen* 39 (to Eberhard of Friuli), pp. 202–4: 'Vosque Francorum decoratis almum / Nomen et famam seritis per orbem / Scottus et Graecus celebrant ouantes / Vestra duella'.

54. Sedulius Scottus, *Carmen* 11.

55. Ekkehart IV, *Casus Sancti Galli, continuatio I*, ed. Georg Heinrich Pertz, MGH SS 2 (Hannover, 1829), pp. 74–147, at pp. 78–9.

56. Basle,Universitätsbibliothek, MS A VII 3; facsimile accessible through the e-codices project: http://www.e-codices.unifr.ch/en.

57. St-Gall, Stiftsbibliothek, MS 48; facsimile accessible through the e-codices project: http://www.e-codices.unifr.ch/en.

58. Dresden, Sächsische Landesbibliothek, Staats- und Universitätsbibliothek, MS A.145.b. On these three manuscripts, see Michael Herren, 'John Scottus and the Biblical Manuscripts Attributed to the Circle of Sedulius', in Gerd Van Riel and Carlos G. Steel, eds, *Iohannes Scottus Eriugena, the Bible and Hermeneutics: Proceedings of the Ninth International Colloquium of the Society for the Promotion of Eriugenian Studies, held at Leuven and Louvain-la-Neuve, June 7–10, 1995* (Louvain, 1996), pp. 303–20; and Bernice Kaczynski, *Greek in the Carolingian*

Age: The St. Gall Manuscripts, Speculum Anniversary Monographs 13 (Cambridge MA, 1988), esp. pp. 75–98.

59. Bern, Burgerbibliothek, MS 363; A facsimile edition was published in the nineteenth century: Hermann Hagen, *Augustinus, Beda, Horatius, Ovidius, Servius, Alii: Codex Bernensis 363 phototypice editus*, Codices Graeci et Latini Photographice Depicti (Leiden, 1897). At the time of writing, Bern 363 had not yet been included in the e-codices project: http://www.e-codices.unifr.ch/en. On the manuscript, see Bernhard Bischoff, *Katalog der festländischen Handschriften des neunten Jahrhunderts (mit Ausnahme der wisigotischen)*, 3 vols. (Wiesbaden, 1998–2014), I, p. 125 (no. 585). On the Irish 'Schülerkreis' see also Bischoff's 'Irische Schreiber im Karolingerreich', in *Jean Scot Erigène et l'histoire de la philosopie, Laon, 7–12 juillet 1975*, Colloques Internationaux du Centre National de la Recherche Scientifique (Paris, 1977), pp. 47–58, repr. in Bischoff, *Mittelalterliche Studien*, II, pp. 39–54; Contreni, 'The Irish', pp. 766–98; Simona Gavinelli, 'Per un'enciclopedia carolingia (Codice Bernese 363)', *Italia medioevale e umanistica* 26 (1983), 1–25; and Staubach, 'Sedulius Scottus'.

60. Contreni, 'The Irish', pp. 766–7.

61. That is, the backlash from Lothar II's bid for a divorce and its effects on Sedulius's correspondents Gunther of Cologne and Tado of Milan, see Staubach, 'Sedulius Scottus', 549–98, at 558–70. On Lothar's divorce, see Karl Josef Heidecker, *The Divorce of Lothar II: Christian Marriage and Political Power in the Carolingian World* (Ithaca, 2010).

62. Contreni, 'The Irish', p. 765. On the Irish concept of learning and education, see Jean-Michel Picard, 'Pour une économie du savoir à l'époque carolingienne: l'apport irlandais', *Revue du Nord: Histoire et Archéologie, nord de la France, Belgique, Pays-Bas* 391–2 (2011), pp. 721–33.

12

Controversies and Ethnic Tensions

Roy Flechner and Sven Meeder

Anecdotal evidence for anti-Irish sentiment abounds, especially from Frankish Europe. A random selection in chronological order may feature the monk Agrestius of Luxeuil making slanderous remarks about fellow Irish inmates and Columbanus's monastic rule;[1] Boniface's condemnation of bishop Virgil of Salzburg, also known by his Irish name Fergal;[2] the mocking poem that Theodulf of Orléans wrote on Cadac-Andreas, an Irish scholar at the court of Charlemagne known for his convoluted biblical exegesis;[3] or the slating comments that monks of Tours made about *peregrini* of both Irish and Anglo-Saxon origin.[4] The question that immediately springs to mind when glancing at this short list is to what extent these negative responses were really directed at Irishmen on account of their being Irish. Or should we treat each incident on its own merits and perhaps identify instances where the animosity can be attributed to other causes, like personal tensions? The present chapter will address this question by examining a number of case studies in which Irish clerics and scholars were implicated in major controversies, be they political, church-political or theological. By their very nature, controversies are public affairs that draw attention, either positive or negative, to the personalities involved. The way in which such personalities are portrayed is fodder for stereotyping, sometimes along ethnic lines, and not only reflects but also contributes to shaping the image of a people in the eyes of both contemporaries and future generations.

Columbanus as controversial figure

Our first case study comes from late sixth- and early seventh-century Gaul. We shall begin by setting the scene, describing some of the configurations of political and religious power at that period. Those were challenging times for the Gallic episcopate because Merovingian royals and Frankish aristocrats, hitherto inextricably linked to the episcopate by both kinship and patronage ties, were beginning to extend their patronage to other forms of religious devotion and organization.[5] Monastic foundations, especially those connected with the Irish abbot Columbanus, were becoming their new favoured beneficiaries.[6] These monasteries, as some historians believe, were more effective in engaging with outlying communities in the countryside than the episcopate was or might have cared to be.[7] The foundation of outlying monasteries was followed closely by the emergence of new cults of saints geared towards fostering the memory of royal or aristocratic founders, thereby adding an important religious and ideological dimension to the hereditary grip on monastic properties.[8]

It has been argued that the common cause that the Gallic aristocracy made with Columbanus's (and other monastic) foundations helped it in asserting its independence vis-à-vis Merovingian kings, especially towards the end of the sixth and early seventh century, while also benefitting from the relatively weak reign of minors in all three Frankish kingdoms.[9] As this argument goes, the patronage of monasteries marks the beginning of the aristocracy's transformation from a subordinate class that formerly relied on the king for obtaining legal immunities and lacked institutional recognition, into a more self-assured entity with stronger group identity, with the power to exercise direct control over its estates, and the ability to enjoy social and legal status that was institutionally recognized.[10] It continues to be a commonly held view that Columbanus, as well as other Irish *peregrini* who followed, 'presented the Merovingians and their aristocracy with opportunities that were not immediately covered by older patterns of monastic foundation'.[11] Although Columbanus's impact is undeniable, one should be careful not to overstate the case for Columbanus's contribution to the resurgence of the aristocracy because it can be shown that hagiography deliberately minimized the crucial role that kings, both Merovingian and Lombard, played in the foundation of Columbanian monasteries.[12] Another caveat to be made is that Columbanus might only have been the catalyst that accelerated an already-ascending trajectory of power that Gallic monasticism exhibited from the early fifth century.[13] In its earliest, fifth-century phase it was characterized by conspicuous links between monastic and episcopal authority, which at their most trivial level consisted of monks who would go on to become bishops. However, by the first half of the seventh century this growth might have been checked. It was then that formal legal steps were taken in order to loosen the monastic/episcopal link or, alternatively, simply to give formal recognition to the fact that it had already been loosened.[14]

Whereas Merovingian dynasts showed themselves to be avid supporters of Columbanus and his monasteries, the Gallic bishops appear not to have had any dealings with Columbanus's early foundations at Annegray, Luxeuil and Fontaines. Rather than choosing to stay out of monastic affairs, they might in fact have been kept out deliberately, barred from intervening in monasteries by royal guarantees of monastic immunity, perhaps similar to those that survive from later in the seventh century.[15] Columbanus's foundation at Luxeuil, and perhaps his other early foundations, might have appeared to onlookers as independent of episcopal jurisdiction or even as an alternative to the Gallic episcopal hierarchy.[16] This dispute over jurisdiction and authority appears to have been of major concern for the bishops, who responded in different ways. The condemnation of Columbanus at the synod at Chalon in 602 × 604 (on which more anon) was one of them, and it is also noteworthy that one of the two chief instigators of accusations that were brought against Columbanus at the synod, the metropolitan bishop of Lyon Etherius (d. 602) or his successor Aridius (d. 614), was also likely to have been the compiler of an important contemporary collection of canon law commonly known as the *Vetus Gallica*, which stressed that monks and their abbots should be subordinate to bishops.[17]

As we try to view the situation from Columbanus's perspective, it may be argued that Columbanian houses did not shun bishops *qua* bishops, but only *Gallic* bishops, while Irish bishops were given free access into the monastic church's holy of holies. This is supported by Columbanus's fourth letter, where we read that the altar at Luxeuil was consecrated by the Irish bishop Áed (of whom nothing else is known) rather than by a member of the Gallic episcopate.[18] One may, however, argue that Áed was preferred not for his ethnicity, but for the fact that he ministered according to the rites to which Columbanus adhered. But it so happens that these rites, and especially the observance of Easter (see Chapter 6), were identified almost exclusively with the Irish (and Britons, but they were not a factor in continental affairs at this time). Hence, religious rite and ethnic identity could have informed one another and been, perhaps, indistinguishable. Indeed, Tommaso Leso's systematic analysis of Columbanus's references to Ireland as well as his privileging of insular authorities in lieu of continental, shows that Columbanus was not only proud of his origins but also boastful about them. According to Leso: 'Columbanus wanted to

distinguish himself from the world he was living in, boldly asserting his insular origins.'[19]

The status quo between Columbanus and the bishops was
anything but a peaceful settlement. Indeed, the Gallic episcopacy is
depicted as hostile both by Columbanus and his hagiographer
Jonas.[20] In the rhetoric of the hagiography and of Columbanus's
letters, which also give us second-hand reports of the council of
Chalon and other communications with the bishops, the Easter
controversy is portrayed as a major bone of contention. But
Columbanus suspected that the debate over the correct dating of
Easter (see Chapter 6) might not have been the real reason for the
Gaul's disapproval of him but only an *occasio* 'pretext', though he
never says what for.[21] When the tension between the Gallic bishops
and Columbanus reached its climax with the condemnation of
Columbanus at Chalon, those gathered at the council went as far as
to accuse him of being a Quartodeciman heretic, namely a heretic
who observed Easter on the Jewish date of 14 Nissan.[22] In a letter to
Pope Gregory he stressed that he had already refuted the accusations
of Quartodecimanism on a previous occasion, but the bishops nevertheless persisted with their slander.[23] Columbanus was easily able to
prove that he was not a Quartodeciman but a follower of an 84-year
cycle that permitted (but did not oblige) him to celebrate Easter on
this date (see Chapter 6). The bishops, however, did not seem to care
this way or the other and continued their campaign against him.
Clare Stancliffe cautions that the bishops' accusation of Columbanus
as 'Judaizing' should not be dismissed too lightly as a ruse, but might
have been genuine.[24] According to her, the bishops might have
wished to draw clearer boundaries between Christian and Jew in
Gaul, a distinction that would have seemed superfluous to Columbanus
who came from a land devoid of Jews. In the absence of Jews, adherence to Old Testament stipulations in Ireland would not have been
associated with an actual Jewish community and would therefore
have carried less of a controversial baggage.

It is difficult to point to a single or even a single-significant factor
that dominated the vicissitudes of the relationship between the
Gallic bishops, Frankish aristocracy, Columbanus and the
Merovingian royals who eventually forced him out. Competition for
patronage was certainly a key factor as was rivalry over authority.
Both might have become fused with the debate over Easter which
appears to have acquired an ethnic dimension, dividing the Gauls
from the Irish and their followers. Columbanus might not have been
resented for his Irishness per se, but his decision to allow only an

Irish bishop to consecrate the altar at Luxeuil, would undoubtedly have reinforced the ethnic aspect of what might otherwise have been a religious or political dispute. Thereafter, as far as the Gauls were concerned, it was no longer the case that 'certain people' residing in Gaul observed a different rite, but that the Irish did. The way in which the Gallic bishops framed the rite highlights another ethnic element, which is the accusation of Judaizing, an accusation that was to haunt the Irish throughout the Middle Ages, and we find another example for this in the dealings of Boniface with an obstinate Irishman named Clemens.

An Irish heretic

At the first day of the proceedings of the Roman council of 745, the gathering of bishops and priests in the presence of Pope Zacharias declared that it considered the Irish bishop Clemens to be a servant of Satan and a precursor of the Antichrist.[25] Some days later, the council would result in a formal sentencing of the hapless Irishman in which he was stripped of his priestly functions and punished with immediate excommunication, with no prospect of penance. The case against Clemens had been brought before the council by English-born Archbishop Boniface of Mainz, who for some years had corresponded with the pope about the Irish bishop and his alleged heretical practices and teachings. The situation he described was very serious, as Boniface feared that the continued liberty of Clemens would lead to the spread of Satan's seed and the contamination of Boniface's entire flock.[26]

Clemens was convicted at a time when the Anglo-Saxon Boniface was reaping success in his efforts to obtain recognition throughout Francia as a leading authority on matters of church discipline, clerical regulation and overall Christian morality. Boniface saw the influence of his reform agenda for the Frankish church grow, while east of the Rhine his project of diocesan reorganization and foundation of monasteries was coming to completion.[27] In the years leading up to the Roman council, several reform councils had been organized in the Frankish lands, beginning with the *Concilium Germanicum*, which was convoked by the Pippinid mayor of the palace Carloman at Boniface's instigation in 742. Around the same time, Boniface must have broached the subject of the Irish heretic cleric Clemens with the pope for the first time, because our earliest source for Clemens (although he remains unnamed in the text) is a letter sent by Pope Zacharias in 743 in response to a letter from Boniface, which is now lost. The renewed attention to ecclesiastical discipline seemed to have resulted in the unmasking of many men of the cloth as false priests, adulterous deacons and lustful clerics, or so Boniface wants us to believe. His chief trouble had been two 'well-known heretics': Aldebert, a Gaul, and Clemens, an Irishman. Their errors were 'different in kind, but of equal sinfulness'.[28]

The only evidence we have for the Irish heretic Clemens is from material stemming from Boniface's circle; these are five extant letters in the collection of Bonifacian letters assembled by his successor Lull, including the proceedings of the Council of Rome.[29] In addition, there are allusions to the abuses Clemens and Aldebert were accused of in a short list of titles in the so-called *Sententiae Bonifatianae Wirceburgenses,* which possibly represents a preparatory draft for Boniface's contribution to the agenda of a synod or council.[30] Our evidence, therefore, was written or preserved by Clemens's detractors. As is often the case with purported heretics, we have no documents detailing Clemens's side or even references that he put up a defence against the allegations levelled against him. As a result, it is impossible for historians to reconstruct Clemens's teachings, actions or responses to his antagonists.

That the context in which the Irishman is portrayed is wholly determined by Boniface and the people around him is evident through the consistent pairing of Clemens with the aforementioned Aldebert. Although it is clear from the evidence that both men lived and worked in separate parts of the Frankish realms and their sins were, as Boniface admits, of a different nature, the two appear in tandem in almost all the evidence.[31] As supposed heretics, they display very different behaviour: Aldebert is described as a charismatic swindler, seducing people with false miracles, declaring himself equal to the apostles and dedicating oratories to himself for people to say public prayers that invoke the merits of St Aldebert. He distributed his own fingernails and hairs as sacred objects, claimed to know the names of the angels and boasted of having received a letter from heaven.[32] Clemens, on the other hand, strikes us as a religious teacher, whose beliefs were at odds with the most current (or at least with Boniface's) interpretations of ecclesiastical authoritative texts. At the council of Rome he was said to have argued against the Catholic Church, denying and contradicting synodal law and rejecting the writings and teachings of the holy Fathers Jerome, Augustine and Gregory. He was furthermore accused of introducing Judaism when contending that it was right for a Christian, if he so pleased, to accept the widow of his dead brother as wife. He furthermore went against 'the belief of the holy Fathers' when he taught that Christ Son of God, descending to the lower world, set free all whom the prison of hell held, believers and unbelievers, those who praised God as well as the worshippers of idols. And he declared 'many other horrible things concerning God's predestination contrary to the Catholic faith'.[33] Even the basest of sins ascribed to Clemens, that of being a lustful cleric with a concubine and having two children by her, is framed as the result of Clemens's erroneous understanding of Christian law.

The only thing that the messianic holy man Aldebert and the aberrant teacher Clemens have in common is that they were both simultaneously accused by the same man. This has led historians to believe that Boniface's combined attack served a specific purpose other than solely to keep them from harming the souls of innocent people. It appears that Aldebert and Clemens were, to paraphrase one scholar, 'useful heretics' in a larger enterprise.[34] Together, the Gaul and the Irishman represented the various guises of the abuses which Boniface wanted to be seen to be combating in the Frankish lands. The accusations are made up of well-worn commonplaces about heresy and, especially, the signs of the Antichrist. In Clemens's case these are his alleged lustfulness and his *stultitia*, which as an expression of 'false views' was a sign of the Antichrist. In similar fashion, Aldebert was made into the embodiment of the lying and deceiving agent of evil.[35] The figures of Clemens and Aldebert are employed as types, providing concrete examples for Boniface's general critique. Both personify two different stereotypical antagonists of ecclesiastical norms and hierarchy: the charismatic, spiritual leader Aldebert, and the combative theological antagonist Clemens.[36]

It is possible that Clemens's ethnicity also had a part to play in the cliché-ridden incriminations by Boniface. The accusations levelled at Clemens echo others that had already been levelled at Irishmen in the past. Of these, the allegation of 'Judaizing' stands out. As in the case of Columbanus, the root of the problem appears to have been a debate about the authority of biblical precepts, especially from the Old Testament, over other ecclesiastical authorities such as synodal acts and patristic writings. A literal reading of Old Testament passages could be invoked to allow polygamy and the marriage of a brother's widow, which are two of the offences allegedly committed by Clemens. There are indeed indications that such a literal reading was at the heart of the matter. In fact, the *Sententiae Bonifatianae Wirceburgenses* allude to the error of interpreting all written authorities literally, suggesting that this was not always deemed appropriate.[37]

While there is evidence to suggest that religious scholars in Ireland were less reticent in their use of the Old Testament in moral teaching than their continental counterparts, the accusation that Clemens 'imposed Judaism' certainly seems an exaggeration deliberately designed to cause maximum outrage. This hyperbole functions best in an atmosphere in which the alleged abuses of the Irishman Clemens answered to prejudices that Boniface's audience had about Irishmen in general and Irish religious customs in particular. The jaundiced memory of the history of Columbanus and his alleged 'Judaizing' may have fostered precisely such stereotypes of Irishmen imposing Judaism.[38]

The incorrect reckoning of Easter is also mentioned in the context of Clemens in the *Sententiae Bonifatianae Wirceburgenses* although the last Irish community to adopt the Roman date of Easter had done so several decades earlier. This Irish peculiarity by now had become a literary cliché rather than a reality encountered by continentals and this seems yet another indication that Boniface was willing to consider using received ideas about the Irish in his allegations. The by now historic error of the Irish observance of Easter was well publicized and latterly given an extra boost by the writings of Bede, whose attention to the Easter controversy within the Irish church was rather disproportionate.[39] Such subjects were of interest to Boniface, judging by the special efforts he took to acquire Bede's works.[40]

There was certainly no shortage in writings associating the Irish with improper marriage arrangements of the type reflected by Clemens's alleged behaviour. In eighth-century collections of canon law the Church Father Jerome is cited contrasting Irish marriage with Christian marriage, observing that the 'Scotti', the 'Atacotti' and the people of Plato's republic have promiscuous wives and raise their children collectively.[41] In his treatise *Against Jovinianus* Jerome iterated as a well-known truism that the Irish have no 'proper wives' but 'run riot like animals'.[42] Similarly, the charge of having 'horrible thoughts concerning predestination' may have served to conjure up thoughts in continental minds of the Pelagian heresy, whose association with Ireland was emphasized by (again) Jerome and Bede.[43]

While Boniface does not explicitly attribute Clemens's errors to his ethnicity, his accusations mirror those made about the Irish in the past. It is possible that Boniface pandered to the stereotypes that his audience had of Irish idiosyncrasies in order to present a powerful, credible image of the kinds of errors he was battling within the church. This in turn could serve as a propellant for Boniface's incipient position as a reformer of the Frankish church. The image of two archetypical heretical figures within Frankish lands, who were both outsiders (note that Aldebert was not identified as a Frank, but as a Gaul), must have helped to provide Boniface's undertaking with greater urgency and secure the attention of Frankish rulers and the pope, who was the addressee of the letters. In fact, the decision to deal with the heretics at church assemblies was modelled on late antique councils in a manner that would be recognizable to the Greek-born Pope Zacharias.[44] Although Clemens is not accused *because of* his ethnicity, his Irishness did provide Boniface with the opportunity to allude to prejudices about this particular brand of the Other as preserved in an anthology of stereotyping narratives. It appears that Boniface embraced this opportunity with both hands.

Ethnic tensions at St-Gall monastery

At ninth-century St-Gall we find Irishmen expressing their discomfort with what they perceive to be their treatment as the Other. It was the Reichenau monk, poet and diplomat Walahfrid Strabo (d. 849) who conjured up an image of a continent awash with Irish travellers with his infamous statement that the custom to travel had become almost second nature of the Irish.[45] The phrase is entered in Walahfrid's Life of St Gallus, a work completed in 833 at the request of Abbot Gotzbert of the abbey of St-Gall. His Life was one in a series: it adapted the contents and style of the oldest known Life, the *uetustissima*, and the version written by the Reichenau teacher Wetti (d. 824), also at Gotzbert's request. These works were followed by a metrical Life of St Gallus, begun by Walahfrid before his untimely death but completed by another author, and another Life that was started but never finished by Ermenrich of Ellwangen.[46] There was, in short, a remarkable interest in hagiographical stories concerning the patron saint of St-Gall in the ninth century.

While Wetti and Walahfrid mention Gallus's time in Ireland briefly, they are remarkably reticent in using words emphasizing the saint's Irish identity. In fact, when pressed, the hagiographers seem to circumvent the issue of the saint's place of birth and references to Gallus's Irishness are indirect, often in the form of words put in other people's mouths.[47] From this wealth of hagiographical text it does not appear that the Irish origin of their patron saint was a significant factor in the institutional identity of the abbey.[48]

Yet, the abbey of St-Gall, housing the tomb of a saintly compatriot and perfectly situated on the road to Rome, attracted many Irish visitors as demonstrated by narrative sources, such as Walahfrid's statement about the peripatetic second nature of the Irish. Some of these visitors will have exerted a certain amount of influence by the books they carried and left at the abbey, while others decided to remain and spent their lives at St-Gall in devotion or scholarly pursuits.[49] The abbey of St-Gall, however, was never a monastery dominated by Irish monks and at no point in this period did it house something resembling an Irish colony. As a multi-ethnic community, St-Gall was not immune to ethnic tension concerning Irishmen and other inmates as an anecdote in Walahfrid's work shows.[50]

In the second book of the Life, on his miracles after death, Walahfrid recounts a miracle performed in his own time (*nuper*), involving a sick anonymous Irish traveller (*de natione scottorum*) who, unfit to travel further, was left by his companions in the care of the monks at St-Gall. The saint appeared to this Irishman in a vision, whereupon the sick man implores Gallus to heal him: 'do not delay further in what I believe you to be about to do'. He thereby identifies the saint as one of his own people:

> For I believe that I have been kept here till now so that the glory and renown of your merits may be revealed also to the men of your own people, just like your power is most widely known among these barbarians. You yourself verily know how long I have been parted from my native soil and oppressed by the hardships of travel through bodily sickness.

The Irishman was eventually healed by the saint and decided to stay at the abbey, where he was still living a holy life when Walahfrid was writing his story.[51]

This passage confirms Walahfrid's perception of Gallus as an Irishman, or at least the anonymous sick Irish traveller's perception of the saint as one of his people. At the same time, the passage hints that the saint's reputation was not as well-known among Irishmen as among the people of Alemannia. And it betrays the existence of ethnic tension at the abbey. The most eye-catching witness to this is perhaps the use of the word *barbari*, which, although it is here probably simply used to denote non-Irish people, is laden with derogatory undertones. The passage displays some jealousy on the sick man's part due to the fact that an Irish saint performs miracles for 'barbarians' and not (or less so) for his fellow Irishmen. The Alemannic Walahfrid, who earlier in the Life picked a fight with the neighbouring Rhaetians,[52] was not one to shy away from revealing ethnic tension and there is no reason to assume his choice of words was accidental.

The sense of entitlement held by the sick Irishman described above also features in a poem added in a tenth-century continental hand to a St-Gall manuscript dating from the second half of the ninth century. Here a man sporting the Irish name Dubduin complained about the lack of respect shown at St-Gall (and elsewhere) to his countrymen, to which he seems to think they are entitled because of the Irish contribution to the conversion of England and continental Europe:

> These are the illustrious saints whom our noble island of Hibernia reared as her glorious children; whose grateful faith, virtue, honour, and blameless life hallowed these lofty palaces and beautiful houses. They strewed over the fields of England the seeds of life, whose ripe fruits you now gather into your storehouse. And we are their brothers, sprung from the same stem as they, we, whom you arrogantly despise as pitiful weaklings, you princes and puffed-up members of the world; rather should you appear as members of Christ. Here the prudent man stops – in fact Gallus himself is also buried here; the bright flame of the Irish has risen to the skies.[53]

The verses were probably copied from an earlier Irish archetype of unknown date.[54] Like Walahfrid's story of the sick Irish pilgrim, they offer a glimpse of ethnic tensions in a multi-ethnic monastery and present an image of Irish *peregrini* confidently flaunting their ethnic identity only to find that their Irishness was not celebrated at St-Gall as much as they might have hoped or expected. The fact that their disappointment was expressed at St-Gall, following what must have been an already long and arduous journey through foreign lands, suggests that their expectations were not only raised by Gallus's Irish descent but also not yet dampened by experiences on the way over. In other words, Irish travellers appear to have been met with attitudes oscillating between approbation and indifference. The latter, especially, was hard to swallow for some proud Irishmen.

A theological controversy

It is in the second half of the ninth century that we meet another proud Irishman. In the course of his career John Scottus Eriugena showed himself to be a prolific and wide-ranging scholar who translated works from Greek, wrote theology, biblical commentaries, poetry, and finally what was to become his most celebrated work: the *Periphyseon,* 'On the Nature of Things'. His scholarship, and especially his approach to logic, is generally seen to reflect great originality, but it has been remarked that he 'arrived at his approach to logic not from a wish to innovate, but out of the desire to remain true to two traditions which were opposed in their implications: the Carolingian logical tradition, based on Boethius and, ultimately, on late Greek Platonic scholasticism; and the Platonic metaphysics of the Greek Christian writers'.[55] It is this fusion of different traditions which is of interest for present purposes, and especially the question of whether and how his Irish background is reflected in his activities and, ultimately, in the controversy that he would be engulfed in.

His Irish origin is undeniable and it is confirmed by the epithet Eriugena, meaning 'Irish born', by which he identified himself as did others. As in the case of his contemporary learned compatriot, Sedulius Scottus at Liège, nothing is known of his early background. Nevertheless, speculations have been made regarding the route that he might have travelled to reach the Continent. John Contreni and Pádraig Ó Néill, for example, suggested that Eriugena might, 'like contemporary Irishmen such as Sedulius [Scottus], have first crossed to Wales, where Irish scholars would have been assured of hospitality from King Merfyn Vrych (d. 844) of Gwynedd in North Wales and his son, Rhodri Mawr, before continuing through Britain and on to Francia'.[56] This route describes not only a passage across territory but a journey through political and possibly scholarly networks which could have affected the scholarly and identity formation of the two learned Irish travellers. Indeed, the prevalent view nowadays seems to be that John, like Sedulius or Martin, the Irish schoolmaster at Laon, and perhaps other erudite *peregrini*, acquired much of their education on the Continent.[57]

It was this erudition that contributed to Eriugena's rise to fame but also to his involvement in the ninth-century controversy over the question of predestination, which was described as 'one of the most vexing intellectual and theological controversies of the day'.[58] At the centre of the controversy was the monk Gottschalk of Orbais, formerly of Fulda, whose doctrine of 'double predestination' (*gemina est praedestinatio*) divided opinions between leading clergy of the day.[59] His doctrine that God predestines the blessed to salvation and the wicked to damnation went contrary to the prevalent belief that God only predestines the elect for salvation, but not the wicked to perdition.[60] The distinction was significant because double predestination could be taken to imply that God is capable of committing evil. Among those who rejected Gottschalk's doctrine were Pardulus (d. 857) of Laon and Hincmar (d. 882) of Reims both of whom asked Eriugena, while he was teaching at the Palace School in 850/851, to refute it as heretical.[61] Instead of taking the line that Hincmar expected him to take by showing that Gottschalk was wrong to claim that his position was consistent with the teachings of St Augustine, Eriugena chose to offer an original counter thesis that stressed three points: (i) that God cannot do evil, (ii) that humans have free will, and (iii) that God's judgement is just.[62] Being no less controversial than the doctrine that it sought to refute, Eriugena's treatise, *De praedestinatione*, was condemned by the very same man who commissioned it, Hincmar. Of the subsequent condemnations only two survive which are of significant detail.[63] One, by Prudentius (d. 861) of Troyes, addresses Eriugena's treatise directly[64] whereas the other, by Florus of Lyons, drew solely on fragments from the treatise and citations from it in Prudentius's response.[65] His detractors' retorts consisted for the most part of rhetorical posturing and as such were nowhere as impressive as Eriugena's cogently argued treatise. According to John Marenbon, Prudentius and Florus 'missed no opportunity for abuse and were willing to take phrases and ideas from the *De praedestinatione* out of context if they provided an opportunity to contradict or ridicule their author'.[66] By 855 John's *De praedestinatione* was also condemned by the Council of Valence, a condemnation that was reaffirmed at the Council of Langres in 859.

It is here that we encounter an ethnic dimension in the rhetoric of the controversy, for the words that were chosen to condemn Eriugena at Valence invoke not only *his* Irish identity, but regard him as a representative of the Irish at large, whose idiosyncratic doctrines he was said to have been mouthing. In other words, rather than being the learned author of an original thesis, he was simply allowing his Irish mentality to get the better of him: 'likewise, concerning grace . . . and free will . . . we have strongly rejected the old wives' tales and the pottage of the Irish'.[67] Such defamatory ethnic identification is also a feature of Prudentius's rhetoric which did not spare personal insults, calling Eriugena a 'barbarian' because of his foreign background: 'you, a barbarian, and a man honoured with no grade of ecclesiastical dignity, and never so to be honoured by'.[68] It is interesting to note the contrast with Walahfrid's differentiation between Irish and barbarian, as discussed above.

But Eriugena's Irishness can also be seen to have been a cause for praise and wonder, as in the following extract: 'you, the one surpassing all in cleverness, Ireland has sent to Gaul in order that those things which no one could know without your help might be discovered by means of your scholarship'.[69] A penchant for exoticizing the Irish is also evident in a letter dated 23rd March 860 to Charles the

Bald from the papal librarian, Anastasius, who was entrusted with examining Eriugena's translation of Pseudo – Dionysius from the Greek: 'it is a wonderful thing how that barbarian, living at the ends of the earth, who might be supposed to be as far removed from the knowledge of this other language as he is from the familiar use of it, has been able to comprehend such ideas and translate them into another tongue: I refer to John Scotigena, whom I have learned by report to be in all things a holy man'.[70] At other times his Irishness was simply used as a descriptive identifier, seemingly with no demeaning undertones. For example, Pardulus of Laon and Hincmar of Reims addressed him by the epithet *Scottus* (*Scottum illum qui est in palatio regis, Iohannem nomine*) and so did Bishop Prudentius of Troyes, formerly John's friend and later among his fiercest detractors.[71] Indeed, despite the condemnations, Eriugena appears not to have lost patronage and continued pursuing scholarly investigations vigorously, with his greatest work, the *Periphyseon*, still to come.

The example of Eriugena in many ways epitomizes the multivalent constructions of identity that the Irish – mostly cleric scholars and typically conspicuous at times of crisis – were negotiating vis-à-vis their continental hosts. What we have seen in Eriugena's case is a complex ambiguity whereby his Irish origins could be used as a mere identifier, an exotic attribute, or a target for verbal abuse. In none of these cases, however, is there any indication that the authors in question accepted Eriugena as an equal, putting aside his foreign origins. For Hincmar, when he needed a refutation of Gottschalk, Eriugena was indeed perceived *ad hoc* as 'one of us' in regard to his doctrinal views, although Hincmar later had a change of heart. It is, however, his condemnation by the councils of Valence and Langres which, more than anything, betrays ethnic stereotyping: his originality was identified with Otherness, and in this case Otherness could conveniently be given the name Irish.

Notes

1. See Chapter 7 in this volume.
2. Boniface, Letters 80, ed. M. Tangl, *Die Briefen des heiligen Bonifatius und Lullus,* MGH Epp. Sel. 1 (Berlin, 1916), pp. 172–80, at pp. 178–9.
3. Ed. and trans. P. Godman, *Poetry of the Carolingian Renaissance* (London, 1985), pp. 158–9. See also Chapter 11 in this volume.
4. *Vita Alcuini,* c. 18, ed. Wilhelm Arndt, MGH SS 15.1 (Hanover, 1887), p. 193.
5. P. Geary, *Before France and Germany: the Creation and Transformation of the Merovingian World* (Oxford, 1988), pp. 168–77.

6. Geary, *Before France and Germany*, pp. 172–7. For Columbanus's associations with Merovingians and the Frankish aristocracy see Jonas, *Vita Columbani*.

7. For this view, which is somewhat dependent on Gregory of Tours's Histories and later seventh-century hagiography, and a critique, see Y. Fox, *Power and Religion in Merovingian Gaul. Columbanian Monasticism and the Frankish Elites* (Cambridge, 2014), pp. 3–9.

8. For the latest on these family churches see S. Wood, *The Proprietary Church in the Medieval West* (Oxford, 2008), pp. 109–39; Fox, *Power and Religion*, p. 134, and literature therein.

9. The most robust argument to this effect was made by G. Halsall, 'Social Change around A.D. 600: An Austrasian Perspective', in M.O.H. Carver, ed., *The Age of Sutton Hoo: The Seventh Century in North-Western Europe* (Woodbridge, 1992), pp. 265–78, at pp. 272–3, 277–8; Halsall, *Settlement and Social Organisation: The Merovingian Region of Metz* (Cambridge, 1995), p. 264. His evidence comes primarily from law codes that appear to recognize an independent upper stratum of Frankish society only from the early seventh century. He believes that Columbanus was a catalyst for the rise of the new class. On the opportunity that Columbanian monasticism provided the aristocracy to express its identity as a distinct group, see F. Prinz, 'Columbanus, the Frankish Nobility and the Territories East of the Rhine', in H.B. Clark and M. Brennan, eds, *Columbanus and Merovingian Monasticism* (Oxford, 1981), 73–87. For a reassessment of the relationship between aristocracy and Columbanian institutions, see Fox, *Power and Religion*, pp. 50–135. And for further insights, see Tommaso Leso, 'Columbanus in Europe: the Evidence from the Epistulae', *EME* 21 (2013), pp. 358–89, at 374–5.

10. Halsall, 'Social Change', pp. 272–73, 277–78.

11. The citation and the caveat concerning the state of Gaulish monasticism on the eve of Columbanus's arrival are I.N. Wood's in 'The Irish in England and on the Continent in the Seventh Century', The O'Donnell Lectures, Faculty of English, Oxford, 10–11 May 2012, unpublished manuscript, II.

12. I. N. Wood, 'Jonas, the Merovingians, and Pope Honorius: *Diplomata* and the *Vita Columbani*', in A. C. Murray, ed., *After Rome's Fall: Narrators and Sources of Early Medieval History. Essays Presented to Walter Goffart* (Toronto, 1998), pp. 99–120; Fox, *Power and Religion*, pp. 50–135, but for a short convenient summary see p. 43.

13. Fox, *Power and Religion*, pp. 2–9. See also Leso, 'Columbanus in Europe', pp. 374–5.

14. The most frequently cited example is the immunity from episcopal control given in Dagobert's 635 charter to Rebais, MGH Diplomata I, *Diplomata regum Francorum e stripe Merowingica*, ed. K.A.F. Pertz (Hanover, 1872) c. 15, pp. 16–18. The charter cites Luxeuil as a precedent for royal immunity from episcopal intervention, though this

example may be anachronistic. The text of the charter, its origin, significance and questions of authenticity are discussed by B. H. Rosenwein, *Negotiating Space: Power, Restraint, and Privileges of Immunity in early Medieval Europe* (Ithaca, 1999), pp. 60–74.

15. See above, note 14.

16. The evidence, as Wood, 'The Irish in England and on the Continent' II, recently argued, shows that Columbanus 'seems to have seen himself as being outside episcopal jurisdiction'.

17. By cross-referencing sources it is possible to say that it was either one or the other, but there is no certainty as to which one. See C. Stancliffe, 'Columbanus and the Gallic Bishops', in G. Constable and M. Rouche, eds, *Auctoritas. Mélanges offerts au Professeur Oliver Guillot* (Paris, 2006), pp. 205–14, at pp. 211–12.

18. Columbanus, Letter 4 (ed. Walker, p. 30, lines 6–9).

19. Leso, 'Columbanus in Europe', 363–8, quotation from 364.

20. *Vita Columbani* 1.19 (ed. Krusch, p. 189).

21. Columbanus, Letter 2, to the Gaulish Synod (ed. Walker, pp. 12–21, at p. 12 line 16, p. 18 lines 24–8). See also Walker's comment on the letter to the synod (p. xxxvi): 'Realizing that the Easter controversy was a mere pretext for an attack on his whole way of life, he relegated it to a minor position in his letter'.

22. The possibility that it was not the council of Chalon but of Sens (594 × 614) that was mentioned in Columbanus's second letter is cited with reservations in G. I. Halfond, *The Archaeology of Frankish Church Councils, AD 511–768* (Leiden, 2010), p. 236.

23. Columbanus, Letter 1 (ed. Walker, p. 6, lines 8–10).

24. Stancliffe, 'Columbanus and the Gallic Bishops', p. 206.

25. Boniface, Letter 59 (ed. Tangl, pp. 108–20, at p. 113). The Roman council is also edited as *Concilium Romanum* (*a. 745*), ed. A. Werminhoff, MGH Conc. II.1 (Hanover and Leipzig, 1906), pp. 37–44; this passage at p. 40.

26. Boniface, Letter 59 (ed. Tangl, at p. 112) = *Concilium Romanum* (ed. A. Werminhoff, at p. 40).

27. Recent books on Boniface's career are M. Glatthaar, *Bonifatius und das Sakrileg: Zur politischen Dimension eines Rechtsbegriffs*, Freiburger Beiträge zur Mittelalterlichen Geschichte 17 (Frankfurt am Main, 2004); and John-Henry Clay, *In the Shadow of Death: St Boniface and the Conversion of Hessia, 721–754* (Turnhout, 2010).

28. Boniface, Letter 59 (ed. Tangl, at p. 110) = *Concilium Romanum* (ed. A. Werminhoff, at p. 39).

29. The letters are translated by E. Emerton, *The Letters of Saint Boniface* (2nd edn, New York, 2000). The letters concerning Clemens are nos 57, 59, 60, 62, and 77 in Tangl's edition.

30. Würzburg Universitätsbibliothek, MS Mp. th. q. 31, fol. 54v. On the so-called *Sententiae Bonifatianae Wirceburgenses,* see Glatthaar, *Bonifatius*

und das Sakrileg, pp. 84–5, 117–63 (esp. pp. 134–63); and S. Meeder, 'Boniface and the Irish Heresy of Clemens', *Church History* 80 (2011), 251–80. The epilogue of the *Iudicia Theodori* in the version of the *discipulus Umbrense* might also refer to the Clementine heresy: see P.W. Finsterwalder, *Die Canones Theodori Cantuariensis und ihre Überlieferungsformen* (Weimar, 1929), pp. 333–34 (We thank Michael Elliot for this reference).

31. There is one exception: at the Neustrian Council of Soisson of 744 only Aldebert is mentioned. See *Concilium Suessionense (a. 744)* c. 2, MGH Conc. II.1, pp. 33–6, at 34. On the independence of both men, see Meeder, 'Boniface and the Irish Heresy', pp. 265–67.

32. Boniface, Letter 59 (ed. Tangl, at pp. 111–2) = *Concilium Romanum* (ed. A. Werminhoff, at pp. 39–40).

33. Boniface, Letter 59 (ed. Tangl, at p. 112) = *Concilium Romanum* (ed. A. Werminhoff, at p. 40). See also Boniface, Letter 57 (ed. Tangl, at p. 105).

34. N. Zeddies, 'Bonifatius und zwei nützliche Rebellen: die Häretiker Aldebert und Clemens', in M.T. Fögen, ed., *Ordnung und Aufruhr im Mittelalter: Historische und juristische Studien zur Rebellion*, Ius Commune, Sonderhefte 70 (Frankfurt am Main, 1995), pp. 217–63.

35. Zeddies, 'Bonifatius und zwei nützliche Rebellen', pp. 246–51.

36. Zeddies, 'Bonifatius und zwei nützliche Rebellen', p. 245.

37. *De eo quod dicunt omnem scriptum historialiter debere intellegi*, 'Concerning that they say that all literature must be understood historically': *Sententiae Bonifatianae Wirceburgenses* c. 23 = Würzburg Universitätsbibliothek, MS Mp. th. q. 31, fol. 54v. See also Chapter 7.

38. On the affairs of Columbanus reflecting back on the Irish in general, see Bede, *HE*, II.4.

39. C. Hartz, 'Bede and the Grammar of Time', *British Journal for the History of Philosophy* 15 (2007), pp. 625–40.

40. See Boniface, Letter 91 (ed. Tangl, pp. 206–8, at p. 207); and H. Schüling, 'Die Handbibliothek des Bonifatius', *Archiv für Geschichte des Buchwesens* 4 (1963), pp. 285–348, at p. 318.

41. See for instance the *Collectio Herovalliana* of the third quarter of the eighth century, printed in *PL* 99, cols. 989–1086, at 1082A, citing Jerome, Letter 69, ed. J. Divjak, CSEL 88 (Turnhout, 1981), p. 684. Thomas Charles-Edwards conjectures that 'Scotti' and 'Atacotti' refer to allied Irish confederations: see Charles-Edwards, *Early Christian Ireland* (Cambridge, 2007), pp. 158–60.

42. Jerome, *Adversus Jovinianum Libri Duo*, *PL* 23, cols. 221–352, at 296A. For the observation that Boniface's critique on Clemens's teachings on marriage may have been inspired by local, continental, customs, see M. Innes, '"Immune from Heresy": Defining the Boundaries of Carolingian Christianity', in D. Ganz and P. Fouracre, eds, *Frankland: The Franks and the World of Early Medieval Europe* (Manchester, 2008), pp. 101–25, at p. 110.

43. Jerome, *In Hieremiam prophetam libri ui*, prologue 4, III.1, ed. S. Reiter, CCSL 74 (Turnhout, 1960), II, p. 120; and Bede, *HE*, II.19. See D. Ó Cróinín, '"New Heresy for Old": Pelagianism in Ireland and the Papal Letter of 640', *Speculum* 60 (1985), 505–16; and G. Bonner, 'The Pelagian Controversy in Britain and Ireland', *Peritia* 16 (2002), pp. 144–55.

44. Zeddies, 'Bonifatius und zwei nützliche Rebellen', pp. 251–63.

45. *Nuper quoque de natione Scottorum, quibus consuetudo peregrinandi iam paene in naturam conversa est. . .*', Walahfrid Strabo, *Vita (III) S. Galli*, II.46, MGH SS rer. Merov. IV, pp. 280–337, at p. 336.

46. On the various Lives of St Gallus, see W. Berschin, *Biographie und Epochenstil in lateinischen Mittelalter*, 5 vols, Quellen und Untersuchungen zur lateinischen Philologie des Mittelalters 8–10, 12, 15 (Stuttgart, 1986–2004), especially volume III.

47. See for instance Wetti, *Vita (II) S. Galli*, I.21, MGH SS rer. Merov. IV, pp. 256–80, at p. 267; and Walahfrid Strabo, *Vita (III) S. Galli*, II.46, MGH SS rer. Merov. IV, pp. 280–337, at p. 336 (on which see below).

48. Cf. W. Berschin, 'Die karolingische Vita S. Galli metrica (BHL Nr. 3253), Werk eines Iren für St. Gallen?', *Revue Bénédictine* 117 (2007), pp. 9–30, at p. 20.

49. The most notable monks of St-Gall of Irish descent are Marcus and his nephew Moengal/Marcellus, whose story is related most fully by Ekkehart IV, *Casus Sancti Galli, continuatio I*, ed. G.H. Pertz, MGH SS 2 (Hanover, 1829), pp. 74–147, at pp. 78–9. On the various manifestations of Irish influence at St-Gall in general, see J. Duft and P. Meyer, *The Irish Miniatures in the Abbey Library of St. Gall* (Olten and New York, 1954).

50. On ethnic tensions in the multi-ethnic communities of monasteries in general, see P. Erhart, 'Contentiones inter monachos — ethnische und politische Identität in monastischen Gemeinschaften des Frühmittelalters', in R. Corradini et al., eds, *Texts and Identities in the Early Middle Ages*, Forschungen zur Geschichte des Mittelalters 12; Denkschriften der Österreichischen Akademie der Wissenschaften: Philosophisch-historische Klasse 344 (Vienna, 2006), pp. 373–87.

51. Walahfrid Strabo, *Vita (III) S. Galli*, II:46, MGH SS rer. Merov. IV, pp. 280–337, at p. 336.

52. Walahfrid Strabo, *Vita (III) S. Galli*, II.1, II.11, at pp. 314 and 321.

53. St-Gall, Stiftbibliothek MS 10, p. 3; ed. K. Strecker, MGH Poetae V.1 (Leipzig, 1937), no. 48, 527. We have emended the translation of J.M. Clark, *The Abbey of St Gall as a Centre of Literature and Art* (Cambridge, 1926), pp. 29–30.

54. See Duft and Meyer, *The Irish Miniatures*, p. 32.

55. J. Marenbon, 'Carolingian Thought', in R. McKitterick, ed., *Carolingian Culture: Emulation and Innovation* (Cambridge, 1994), pp. 171–192, at p. 189.

56. J. Contreni and P. Ó Néill, *Glossae Divinae Historiae: The Biblical Glosses of John Scottus Eriugena*, Millennio Medievale 1, Testi 11 (Florence, 1997), pp. 72–84, at p. 80, following N. K. Chadwick, 'Early Culture and Learning in North Wales', in Chadwick et al., eds, *Studies in the Early British Church* (Cambridge, 1958), pp. 93–110. Contreni and Ó Néill's study of Eriugena's career was reprinted and revised as 'The Early Career and Formation of John Scottus', -, in J. Contreni, *Learning and Culture in Carolingian Europe* (Farnham, 2011), pp. 1–24.

57. Marenbon, 'Carolingian Thought', p. 184.

58. Contreni and Ó Néill, *Glossae Divinae Historiae*, p. 77.

59. The political and theological dimensions of the debate on predestination are discussed in D. Ganz, 'The Debate on Predestination', in M.T. Gibson and J. Nelson, eds, *Charles the Bald: Court and Kingdom* (2nd rev. ed. Aldershot, 1990), pp. 283–302.

60. W. Otten, 'Carolingian Theology', in G.R. Evans, ed., *The Medieval Theologians. An Introduction to Theology in the Medieval Period* (Oxford, 2001), pp. 65–82, at p. 78.

61. Contreni and Ó Néill, *Glossae Divinae Historiae*, p. 77.

62. Otten, 'Carolingian Theology', p. 78; J. Marenbon, 'John Scottus and Carolingian Theology: from the *De Praedestinatione*, its Background and its Critics, to the *Periphyseon*', in M.T. Gibson and J. Nelson, eds, *Charles the Bald: Court and Kingdom* (2nd rev. ed. Aldershot, 1990), pp. 303–26, at p. 308.

63. Marenbon, 'John Scottus and Carolingian Theology', p. 311.

64. *PL* 115, cols 1009–1366.

65. *PL* 119, cols 101–250.

66. Marenbon, 'John Scottus and Carolingian Theology', p. 311.

67. J.-D., Mansi, *Sacrorum Conciliorum Nova et Amplissima Collectio*, 31 vols (Florence, 1758–98), V, cols 5–7, at col. 6.

68. PL 115, col.1043A; trans. J. F. Kenney, *The Sources for the Early History of Ireland: Ecclesiastical. An Introduction and Guide* (Columbia NY, 1929), p. 577.

69. PL 115, col. 1194A; trans. Kenney, *Sources*, p. 577.

70. PL 129, col. 739C; trans. Kenney, *Sources*, p. 582.

71. See, respectively, *De tribus epistolis liber* 39 (*PL* 121, col.1052A) and Prudentius, *De praedestinatione contra Iohannem Scottum* (*PL* 115, col. 1011B). References from Contreni and Ó Néill, 'The Early Career and Formation of John Scottus'.

13

The Irish and their Books

Elizabeth Duncan

The surviving manuscript evidence reveals that the Irish had a long and fruitful history of book-production.[1] Writing and literacy are thought to have been brought to Ireland with the arrival of Christianity in the fifth century, and by the seventh century a unique range of scripts and distinctive book-production methods were employed in Irish manuscripts. These distinctive features in both palaeography (script) and codicology (physical construction of manuscripts) are commonly named 'insular'. Apart from Britain and Ireland, insular script was also used in parts of Europe to which the tentacles of insular influence spread, most notably in ecclesiastical establishments founded by both Irish and English *peregrini*. Hence, the study of insular manuscripts and script-specimens bears testament to the important contribution of Irish scribes abroad and often provides vital and otherwise unchartable information on script-development. In what follows I shall consider the history of insular script and book-production from its early beginnings until *c.* 850. The focus will be on manuscripts written in an Irish context but with the understanding that because of the shared scribal practices throughout the insular world in these early centuries, it is not always possible or desirable to assess origin or influence with greater precision.

Insular features

Insular book-production is distinctive, not only in terms of its palaeography, namely features pertaining to script and its layout, but also in the manner in which manuscripts were physically prepared and constructed. In both respects insular features are easy to identify and contrast with features reflective of a continental background.

Perhaps the most immediately visible feature of insular writing is the use of triangular-shaped wedges on the tops of ascenders (vertical strokes which extend above the head-line, for example in **b** and **d)**

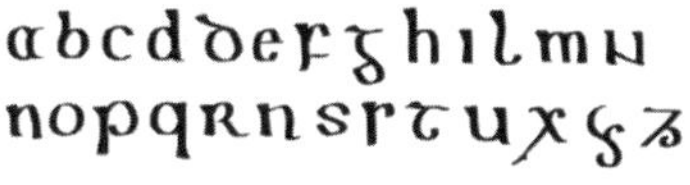

abcdᵭeꝼȝhilmн
nopqʀnsꞃτuxȝⱬ

Figure 13.1   Insular half-uncial letter forms

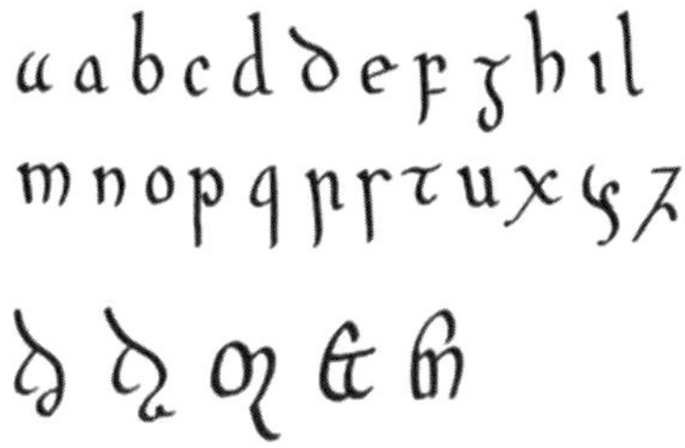

ɑabcdᵭeꝼȝhil
mnopqꝑꞃτuxⱳⱬ
ᵭ ᵭ̨ oꞇ & ᵬ

Figure 13.2   Insular minuscule letter forms

and minims (short vertical strokes running from head- to base-line, for example, in **i** and **m**)[2] (see Figures 13.1 and 13.2). Decorative techniques may also hint at an insular background. For example, the so-called *diminuendo* lettering in which consecutive letters following larger initials at the beginnings of paragraphs gradually shrink until they become the same size as the main text. The use of a multitude of small dots to decorate initials may also signal insular heritage. Another distinctive feature of insular script is the scale of its hierarchical, multi-grade system with one majuscule script (also called two-line script with letters of equal height written between two lines) and four types of minuscule script (equivalent to modern-day lower case lettering with script written on four lines with ascenders and descenders), descending in order of formality. Abbreviations and ligatures are most common in the lower grades of minuscule script and were employed to save time and space. For example, tall **e** in ligature with **t** is distinct from the equivalent ligature used in continental scripts (which developed into the modern-day ampersand). Other insular features include tall **e** used in ligature with other minim-height letters and the *tia* and *tio* ligatures.[3] Many abbreviations used in insular manuscripts were drawn from the ancient abbreviation-system of Roman-era Latin writing; however, it is notable that many were developed in the insular world and can therefore denote insular influence.[4] Furthermore, analysis of abbreviations in the early period shows evidence of distinction between Anglo-Saxon and Celtic usage, and this is one of the few ways in which insular script-specimens can sometimes be geographically differentiated.[5]

The highest grade of writing in the insular multi-grade system was Insular Half-Uncial, a majuscule script reserved for high-grade, often biblical texts. Alone in the insular script-system, Insular Half-Uncial was a straight-pen script for which the scribe held the quill at a 90-degree angle to the line of writing. For this majuscule script the scribe's intention was to keep the bulk of writing between head- and base-lines (hence the term 'two-line' script in which ascenders and descenders rarely extend beyond these two ruled lines). As Insular Half-Uncial's name indicates, many of the letters are the same as those found in Roman Half-Uncial. However, a few crucial exceptions to this give Insular Half-Uncial its own distinctive appearance, namely the use of Uncial **d**, **r** and **s** which were employed alongside their Half-Uncial equivalents.[6] The use of minuscule **n** alongside Uncial **N** in Insular Half-Uncial is also noteworthy. The highest grade of insular minuscule is Hybrid (*bastarda*) script. Like all minuscule scripts it is slant-pen, meaning the scribe held the quill at an angle to the line of writing. Although insular minuscule letter forms were employed, Hybrid shares a roundness of aspect with Insular Half-Uncial and – as its name suggests – often displays Insular Half-Uncial letter forms.[7] The following three minuscule scripts – Set (*formata*), Cursive (*cursiua*) and Current (*cursiua currens*) – can be distinguished from one another by the level of pen lift within and between letters and words. Insular Set minuscule shows the most pen lift and the scribe would have formed some letters by lifting the pen at points where one would not expect to see pen lift in Cursive and Current scripts (namely, in the letters **a**, **h**, **m**, **n** and **f**, **p**, **r**, and **s**). Cursive script is defined by its very slanted pen angle which created extremely pointed minims and descenders and commonly displays many ligatures and abbreviations. Current script shares many of Cursive's features but in this lowest grade of writing the scribe sometimes linked letters. An especially characteristic feature of Current script is the creation of the letter **u** without pen-lift.

It is not only in script that distinctive insular features are apparent but also in physical features of the construction of manuscripts. For example, the appearance and texture of insular parchment is noticeably different from continental parchment.[8] Medieval scribes used specially prepared animal skins, from cow, sheep or goat, to name but a few. Skins would have been soaked in lime water to loosen hair/wool and flesh, making it easier to scrape away debris with a knife. Skins were then stretched and dried on wooden frames and scraped further. The principal distinguishing feature of insular parchment is that hair- and flesh-sides can be nearly indistinguishable. Continental parchment does not exhibit this feature and often follicles (and sometimes hair) are still clearly visible on so called 'hair-sides': it seems that the insular method gave greater importance to removing hair and follicles to create a more consistent texture on either side of the parchment. It is also likely that both sides of insular parchment were roughened with a pumice stone to provide a textured surface. Furthermore, insular parchment is often darker in tone and it is possible that the insular method involved a light tanning process.

The general construction of insular manuscripts is also unique in early medieval practice. Medieval manuscripts were arranged in gatherings, which are known by the technical name quires, in which bifolia (folded sheet of parchment comprising two folios) were stacked, folded and sewn down their centres and then joined together with other quires to form books.[9] The standard continental practice was to prick and rule folios before folding. By contrast, the evidence from insular manuscripts shows that pricking and dry-point ruling were carried out on parchment after folding, usually on recto-sides of folios penetrating several folios at once.

Distinctively, ink used for writing text was a very dark brown – almost black – compared with that commonly found in continental European practice which tended to be a lighter shade of brown. This is likely due to a special recipe for ink developed by insular scribes using gall nuts, iron sulphate, water and gum. A range of coloured pigments were also used in insular manuscripts for decorative purposes.[10]

Origins of insular script

The precise origins of the distinctive character of insular manuscripts are – in the words of the palaeographer Elias Avery Lowe – 'shrouded in obscurity'.[11] This is principally due to the paucity of surviving, accurately datable British and Irish manuscripts from the fifth and sixth centuries. The origins of the insular script-system ultimately lie in the writing that developed in either sub-Roman Britain or Ireland in the fifth and sixth centuries, whose sources – in all likelihood – would have been Roman Cursive (lower grade script intended for rapid and fluent writing) and the majuscule pre-canonical Roman Half-Uncial.

A specimen of pre-canonical Half-Uncial survives that has an early (seventh-century) association with Ireland and which provides some context to possible script either written or circulated in the fifth- or sixth-century insular world. The so-called *Codex Usserianus Primus*, the Ussher Gospels, is preserved as Dublin, Trinity College, MS 55 (A.iv.15). The manuscript's provenance, as indicated by the presence of seventh-century glosses in both Latin and Old Irish, can be traced to the Gaelic world, defined here as comprising Ireland, Gaelic North Britain, and scriptoria on the Continent with Gaelic connections. However, the text of the gospel was copied much earlier than the glosses. The pre-canonical Half-Uncial script does not display features which would allow for a dating beyond the fifth century if written in continental Europe although a sixth-century dating could be possible if written in the insular world. Odd loops on the tops of ascenders and minims are perhaps precursors to the insular wedge; otherwise the script displays no insular features and the parchment was prepared using the continental method. However, some features indicate an insular background; for example, folios were ruled after folding, hair-sides face flesh-sides and other aspects of layout and punctuation are indicative of insular practice.[12] Wherever it was written, the likelihood that the kind of script in the Ussher Gospels was either an ancestor or exemplar to what became insular script makes it an important witness to the script-history of this period.

In spite of the obscure early history of insular manuscripts, palaeographers have not refrained from offering theories on origin and script-development.[13] On the one hand, some scholars are of the opinion that insular script originated in Ireland and subsequently spread to Britain by Irish missionary activity in Northumbria in the sixth century.[14] However, it is also possible that insular script was developed in Britain.[15] Although there is no clear way to refute or support any of these theories on origins, the earliest insular script-specimens offer some fleeting glimpses of changes underway in insular script and book-production.

The so-called Springmount Bog Tablets, now preserved at the National Museum of Ireland, were discovered in 1913 in the Springmount Bog (Co. Antrim) by a peat digger.[16] This unexpected discovery provides one of the earliest known script-specimens. The tablets, which contain parts of Psalms 30–32, are impossible to date with accuracy. Although a sixth-century dating is most favoured by scholars, a fifth-century dating is also possible. Two hands have been distinguished which look to have been imitating Roman models, including the fourth-century New Roman Cursive.[17] However, some specifically insular features are notable – although never consistently executed – and reveal at least one example of the kinds of mixed script we may imagine to have been written during the development of fully-fledged insular script.[18]

Further research on the links between stone inscriptions, which are often undatable, and book scripts is required to achieve a fuller understanding of the development of both. A stone inscription at Llangadwaladr on Anglesey in North West Wales which commemorates Cadfan, king of Gwynedd, datable to *c.* 620 × 682, provides the earliest datable evidence of early insular script in the Brittonic world and reveals a mixture of letter forms that came to be a marked feature of the higher grades of insular script.[19] The specimen does not necessarily reflect the writing found in manuscripts at this time. However, the mixed majuscules display Half-Uncial, some specifically insular letter forms, and the **ti**- and **eg**- ligatures alongside Uncial **a**. The latter form was not the common form in Insular Half-Uncial, although it is reported in early specimens of the script-type. This experimentation – if one can call it that – shows the fluidity in the development of insular script.

Our first examples of fully-fledged insular script with a specifically Irish connection are found in three closely related manuscripts: the *Cathach* of St Columba (Dublin, Royal Irish Academy, MS 12.R.33), a fragmentary bifolium of the *Historia Ecclesiastica* of Eusebius in Rufinus's translation,[20] and St-Gallen, Stiftsbibliothek, MS. 1399.a.1, containing a copy of Isidore of Seville's *Etymologiae*.[21] Only the latter manuscript can be provided with a *terminus post quem* of 636, corresponding to the date of publication of the *Etymologiae*. The close connection in script between all three specimens indicates a similar or earlier dating for the *Cathach* and the fragment of Eusebius's *Historia*. Furthermore, the parchment of all three manuscripts has been described as prepared or arranged using continental methods, suggesting that these manuscripts could have been written by an insular scribe working on the Continent.

The development of insular script and the role of continental scriptoria

By the end of the seventh century methods of insular book-production were manifestly employed across the insular world.[22] Manuscript evidence for England is the most plentiful and many datable specimens from the end of the seventh century onwards provide a clear script-chronology until the ninth century. Manuscripts surviving from the Gaelic world also originate from the seventh century, and although these cannot be accurately dated, they nevertheless provide evidence for writing in Ireland, Gaelic North Britain or scriptoria on the Continent with Gaelic connections. Before 800 there are no manuscripts surviving from the Brittonic world – defined here as comprising Strathclyde, Galloway, Mann, Wales, Cornwall, and Brittany – although stone inscriptions provide evidence for insular script at an earlier date. Population movement from south Britain to the Continent began in the second half of the fifth century and by the later sixth century the kingdoms of early medieval Brittany had been created as migrations continued. When Breton insular script is chartable from the first half of the ninth century, distinctive methods and idiosyncrasies suggest a long and separate regional practice from the rest of the insular world.[23]

Traces of insular methods and manuscripts are evident in various establishments in continental Europe during the period under discussion. Influence can be deduced in a range of ways.[24] For example, some manuscripts were written on the Continent in insular script or display other insular symptoms in their physical creation. Other manuscripts show only some insular features and were perhaps written in a local script on insular parchment or reveal other codicological methods in the arrangement of quires or prickings and rulings. Influence can also be charted by the presence of insular manuscripts that were taken abroad and used there. Even when such manuscripts no longer survive, textual critical studies can determine the influence of insular exemplars. Where it is possible to distinguish between strands of insular manuscript influence, the bulk of evidence emanates from English ecclesiastics working in the missionary fields (so-called *Missionsgebiet*), for example at centres founded by Boniface and his disciples, namely Mainz, Würzburg, and Fulda, as well as at churches founded by Willibrord at Echternach and Utrecht.[25]

The legacy of Columbanus

The evidence gleaned from extant manuscripts at some of the continental establishments is extremely important, not only because it informs us of developments at particular scriptoria but also because it offers a vital nugget of information on script-development and book-development which no longer survives elsewhere. From the Gaelic perspective, this is particularly true of the contribution documented through the life and work of the Irish abbot Columbanus (d. 615), who left Bangor in Northern Ireland in 590 for religious exile on the Continent, where he founded the monasteries of Annegray, Luxeuil and Fontaines in Gaul (at present-day Fontaine-lès-Luxeuil) and Bobbio in northern Italy. Another foundation at St-Gall in Switzerland developed from the cell of Gallus, one of Columbanus's followers.[26]

A wealth of material survives from Columbanus's later foundation at Bobbio which constitutes the bulk of dated and localized Irish insular manuscripts from the seventh and eighth centuries. Nine manuscripts containing insular script survive from Bobbio and are datable to the seventh and eighth centuries.[27] These Bobbio manuscripts are important because they comprise the earliest surviving evidence – in an Irish context – of what Julian Brown termed 'Phase I', that being the systematic employment of the multi-grade insular script-system with its distinguishing features clearly visible.

There are noteworthy similarities in script between some of these Bobbio manuscripts, in particular those between the text of Orosius's *Historia aduersum paganos*, now in Milan, Biblioteca Ambrosiana, MS D.23.Sup., and the *Cathach* (and its scribal relatives discussed above). The fact that the Bobbio Orosius was written on both insular and continental parchment is also interesting and attests another link between it and the other earliest surviving insular Irish manuscripts which seem to have incorporated continental parchment. Bobbio appears to have been a conduit of Irish influence between Ireland and Northern Italy within which insular-style manuscripts were written and developed. Insular influence on manuscripts written in the following century at Bobbio is also marked.[28] For example, eighth-century manuscripts written in continental scripts at Bobbio still display insular abbreviations and some insular influence in morphology and initials.[29]

Phase-II insular script

Around 750 we witness a distinct change in Insular Half-uncial and insular minuscule scripts towards scripts that are commonly called 'Phase II', a term coined by the palaeographer Julian Brown. The overriding feature of Phase II is discipline across all levels of book-production with regularity and order visible across all levels of book-production.[30] In the construction of books it is possible to see more regularity in the size of quires and consistency in the use of quaternions (quires constructed with four bifolia folded in two to make eight folios). Double horizontal ruling is used for Insular Half-Uncial. In terms of layout of writing on the page, text in minuscule is often supplied in two-column format and attempts at justification of line-ends are found, providing a level of tidiness distinct from

Phase I. Biblical text is laid out *per cola et commata* (meaning that lines of text were divided by clause and phrase units). In script, fewer variant letter forms were used and greater regularity is apparent in the execution of individual letters. Furthermore, a more restricted repertoire of both ligatures and abbreviations is present in Phase-II specimens in comparison with Phase-I. Insular 'Half-Uncial' has a more 'solemn, heavy style' and reveals monograms at line ends, for example, **NT** and **UNT**. The influences in Phase II lie in familiarity with Italian uncial manuscripts, elements of which were incorporated into insular manuscripts.

Phase-II scripts were used across the insular world as well as abroad in continental houses. However, many Phase-II specimens survive from Northumbria, a fact that has led scholars to actively pursue a place of origin for the development of Phase II.[31] Benedict Biscop's twin foundation at Monkwearmouth-Jarrow, founded in the last quarter of the seventh century in the diocese of Hexham is a possible contender.[32] Biscop's successor, Abbot Ceolfrith, oversaw the creation of a plentiful library which also contained manuscripts that originated from southern Europe. Furthermore, specimens of Roman Uncial and the lighter and less formal Capitular Uncial, which was developed specifically at Monkwearmouth-Jarrow, both common to this foundation, betray an insular background in lapses of usage, most notably in abbreviations, ligatures and subscript lettering.[33] This fact, combined with the stock of Mediterranean books and the survival of three Phase-II insular minuscule specimens datable to the second half of the eighth century and written at Monkwearmouth-Jarrow would seem to suggest that the twin monastery possessed the necessary fusion of learning and skill for the development of Phase II.

The Abbey of Echternach, now in German-speaking Luxemburg, was likewise a melting pot that blended insular and continental ecclesiastical culture.[34] Founded in 706 by the English missionary Wilibrord on the site of a pre-existing monastery that he took possession of in 697/8, it comprised both insular and continental members. The foundation of this abbey was directed from Ireland by Ecgberht (638/9–729) who had lived as a religious exile in Ireland from before 664 until his death at Iona. A corpus of eighth-century charters and manuscripts can be attributed to Echternach and on that basis it is evident that the use of insular script continued into the ninth century. Although much of the manuscript evidence from Echternach seems to be English rather than Irish there appear to be traces of Irish influence there.[35]

The potential importance of this continental house in the development of Phase II is further highlighted by the survival of two closely related specimens of Insular Half-Uncial. The earliest known location (provenance, distinct from origin) for the Echternach Gospels (Paris, Bibliothèque nationale, MS lat. 9389) is fifteenth-century Echternach. The Insular Half-Uncial used for the first page of these gospels is very closely related to that found in another gospel text the Durham Gospels (Durham, Cathedral Dean and Chapter Library, MS A.II.17) whose earliest known provenance is at Chester-Le-Street in the tenth century. It is possible that both script-specimens were written by one and the same scribe, or, at the very least, written by scribes trained within the same scribal milieu. Both manuscripts contain parchment prepared in the continental fashion, although the Durham Gospels also contains insular parchment. It is unknown with surety where either of these gospels was written, but as David Dumville has pointed out, the only known place in the British Isles where continental parchment was used at this date was at Monkwearmouth-Jarrow. The possibility that they were written in different locations by a travelling scribe clearly highlights the speed with which the dissemination of ideas could take place, which has no doubt influenced insular script and book-production throughout its history, not least in the development of Phase II.

The ninth century

The role and contribution of Irish scholars in the continental centres of learning that blossomed during the reforms of Charlemagne from the end of the eighth century and into the ninth is significant.[36] The Irish scholar and poet Sedulius Scottus worked at the Cathedral school of St-Lambert in Liège where he arrived between 840 and 851.[37] Like Sedulius, the work of another Irish scholar and teacher, Johannes Scottus Eriugena, who worked at the palace school of Charles the Bald, is also important for understanding the Irish contribution to medieval thought and text. Some surviving manuscripts written in insular script are associated with these two Irishmen and their scholarly circles and provide evidence for the beginnings of the next generation of insular script representing the very end of the period under discussion here.[38]

Around 850 we see the development of Late Celtic script which was used in both the Brittonic and Gaelic worlds. The script can be classified by the appearance of 'new' abbreviations and letter forms hitherto unreported in insular script: an abbreviation for *ra* which consisted of two suprascript commas often digging into the tops of letters; an abbreviation for *Nam* (**N** + cross-stroke); an adapted abbreviation for *est* in which commas, instead of points, were often employed, with the upper comma often penetrating the cross-bar; **v**-shaped **u** replaced the conventional form in some situations and was used in abbreviations for *uero* and a new abbreviation for *ut* (**u** + suprascript comma). Some other new features were imported from Caroline script (the abbreviation for *per*: **p** with cross-stroke through descender) and the majuscule **o** + **R** ligature (in which **o** and **R** are drawn as one with the right-hand side of **o** forming the back of **R**).[39]

St-Gallen, Stiftsbibliothek, MS 904 contains a copy of Priscian's *grammatica* and was written by two principal scribes although other relief and glossing hands are also apparent.[40] A marginal annotation contains a note on *satharnn samchasc* (the Sunday at the end of Summer Lent, namely the seventh Sunday after Pentecost)[41] and indicates that the manuscript could have been written in either 845 or 856.[42] It is unclear whether the manuscript was produced in either Ireland or continental Europe. However, shortly after its production, as additional texts testify, it was present among the circle of Sedulius Scottus by either the 850s or 860s. Both principal hands show features of Late Celtic script, like the syllabic *ra* abbreviation and the new-style *est* abbreviation.[43] A thorough study of all the hands in this manuscript would no doubt help to advance further discussion on the development of Late Celtic script.

The first part of Leiden, Universiteitsbibliotheek, MS BPL 67 (fos 1–7) contains Priscian's *Periegesis* in insular script and was written in 838 by a certain Dubthach, who may have worked in Sedulius's circle.[44] Folios 9–207 of the same manuscript were written later in the middle of the ninth century and contain Priscian's *Grammatica*; it is to this text that commentary attributed to Eriugena or his circle has been recorded. Wallace Martin Lindsay recorded abbreviations in this manuscript and it is interesting that some early Late Celtic features are apparent: for example, the adoption of the abbreviation for *per* and the new-style *est*-nota, which are indicative of changes underway.[45]

The full history of Late Celtic script to which all surviving ninth-century script-specimens with or without continental connections bear witness remains to be researched and published. The datable evidence provided by these manuscripts surviving in continental libraries is important because it supplies a significant piece of the palaeographical puzzle, which allows us to compensate for the fact that the latest datable manuscript written in Ireland before the development of Late Celtic is the Book of Armagh (Dublin, Trinity College, MS 52), part of which at least was written in 807, and that otherwise the earliest datable Late Celtic specimen from Ireland is the MacDurnan Gospels (London, Lambeth Palace, MS 1370), dated to before 927.[46]

Conclusion

The role of the Irish *peregrini* in the preservation and production of early insular manuscripts was significant. At each major development in the early history of insular book-production the evidence from continental houses with Gaelic links can provide important insights. Irish connections with foundations overseas did not end in the ninth century. The group of monasteries with Irish connections (the so-called *Schottenklöster*) in Germany which sprung up in the eleventh century provide evidence of insular manuscript culture: for example, the bulk of the first copy of the Chronicle of Marianus Scottus (Vatican, Biblioteca Apostolica Vaticana, MS Pal. lat. 830) was written in a descendant of Late Celtic script, so-called Gaelic National minuscule.[47] As late as the seventeenth century Mícheál Ó Cléirigh (*c.* 1590–1643), the Irish Franciscan based at St Anthony's College in Louvain, Belgium, was responsible for collecting manuscripts and texts in Ireland.[48] The Franciscans also preserved Gaelic manuscripts at St Anthony's which are now in University College Dublin.[49] Indeed, the extent to which contact between the Gaelic world and continental foundations – which occurred at various points in the Middle Ages and the early modern period – led to the survival of early medieval manuscripts and texts which may have otherwise not been preserved is intriguing. It is notable that a substantial number of extant manuscripts are now preserved in continental repositories or had earlier provenances in such collections.[50] Assessing a manuscript's provenance or origin can be an imprecise exercise and therefore gaining a full understanding of survival patterns is full of conjectures and uncertainties. Nevertheless, it is striking that a much smaller number of early medieval manuscripts survive in Irish libraries in comparison with those preserved outside of Ireland and the implication is that many simply did not survive in Ireland itself.[51] Without the manuscripts and texts which owe their survival to activities in continental Europe our understanding of early medieval Irish manuscript culture would be far less rich.

As script and book-production methods developed over time, so too the fields of insular palaeography and codicology continue to evolve. In the last decade discoveries of previously unknown script-specimens have provided fresh evidence for analysis. For example, the Fadden More Psalter was discovered in 2006 in peat at Fadden More, County Tipperary. A full study of its script is awaited in print but initial studies suggest a dating of *c.* 800.[52] Another discovery of an insular palimpsest script-specimen was made by Michelle Brown at the monastery of St Catherine's, Mount Sinai.[53] Such new discoveries add to our knowledge of all angles of early insular book-production. One imagines that the technological process called hypersceptral imaging (HSI) for retrieving erased text will also lead to discoveries of more insular script-specimens.[54] This process can also help to understand collaboration between scribes and the sequence of their writing stints.[55] Other technological advances have also made way for different kinds of examinations which are duly bringing fresh and interesting perspectives. In the field of palaeography computer programs have been developed which can assess script-specimens in various ways and are changing the ways in which specimens are examined and understood.[56] In line with these developments, recent years have also seen a surge in digital access to manuscripts which are often free of subscription charges and allow close examination through the publication of high resolution images online.[57] This fundamental change has opened up accessibility to texts in manuscript context and script-specimens to a wider audience.

The field of insular book-production is an area that offers potential for innovation and new methods of analysis and (online) presentation are providing some important insights into both palaeography and codicology. In spite of the improvements which these technological advances have made to areas of palaeographical research, much work remains to be done in the field of medieval Irish palaeography and codicology.

Notes

1. I use the term 'Irish' throughout with some caution. It is sometimes possible to be specific about a manuscript's origin and/or its scribes. The shared culture on either side of the North Channel means that the term 'Gaelic' – which includes both – lends itself to a more open-minded approach in cases where evidence of origin is wanting.
2. For descriptions of insular script, see: Bernhard Bischoff, *Latin Palaeography. Antiquity and the Middle Ages* (Cambridge 1990), pp. 83–90; T.J. Brown, *A Palaeographer's View. The Selected Writings of Julian Brown*, eds Janet Bately, et al. (London, 1993); David N. Dumville, *A Palaeographer's Review: The Insular System of Scripts in the Early Middle*

Ages (Osaka, 1999), pp. 5–8. For a discussion of the wedge and its origins, see Gifford Charles-Edwards, 'The Springmount Bog Tablets: their Implications for Insular Epigraphy and Palaeography', *Studia Celtica* 36 (2002), pp. 27–45, at pp. 30–1.

3. See Figure 13.2, above.
4. W. M. Lindsay, *Notae Latinae. An Account of Abbreviation in Latin MSS. of the Early Minuscule Period* (c. *700–850*) (Cambridge, 1915); with *Supplement* by D. Bains (Cambridge ,1936).
5. David N. Dumville, *Abbreviations used in Insular Script before A.D. 850: Tabulation based on the Work of W.M. Lindsay* (Cambridge, 2004).
6. See Figure 13.1, above and Bischoff, *Latin Palaeography*, pp. 67 and 74 for Roman Uncial and Roman Half-Uncial.
7. See Figure 13.2, above for insular minuscule forms.
8. For information on parchment preparation, see Bischoff, *Latin Palaeography*, p. 9; Kathleen Ryan, 'Holes and Flaws in Medieval Irish Manuscripts', *Peritia* 6–7 (1987–8), 243–64; Carlo Federici. et al., 'The Determination of Animal Species Used in Medieval Parchment Making: Non-Destructive Identification Techniques', in Guy Petherbridge and John L. Sharpe, eds, *Roger Powell the Compleat Binder: Liber Amicorum* (Turnhout, 1996), pp. 146–53 (see p. 151 for reports that a range of different animal species were used to create insular parchment).
9. Bischoff, *Latin Palaeography*, p. 22.
10. Michelle P. Brown, 'Pigments and their Uses in Insular Manuscripts', in Petherbridge and Sharpe, *Roger Powell the Compleat Binder*, pp. 136–45, and Appendix A for a list of pigments identified in insular manuscripts.
11. *CLA* II, p. xiv.
12. Michelle P. Brown, 'From Columba to Cormac: the Contribution of Irish Scribes to the Insular System of Scripts', *Settimane* 57 (2010), 623–49, at p. 649.
13. To my knowledge no arguments have been put forward for the chronology of insular codicological practices which may not necessarily have developed hand in hand with script.
14. Bischoff, *Latin Palaeography*, pp. 77, 83–95; *CLA* II, p. xi, IV, p. xxiii.
15. Dumville, *A Palaeographer's Review*, pp. 9–16 for a critical summary of the debate; Brown, *A Palaeographer's View*, pp. 179–241, 284–7.
16. Dumville, *A Palaeographer's Review*, pp. 31–5.
17. Charles-Edwards, 'The Springmount Bog Tablets', p. 27.
18. Among these features are *diminuendo* lettering, wedges and tall **e** in ligature.
19. V.E. Nash-Williams, *The Early Christian Monuments of Wales* (Cardiff, 1950), pp. 55–7 (no. 13) and plate VII.
20. Described by A. Breen, 'A New Irish Fragment of the *Continuatio* to Rufinus-Eusebius *Historia Ecclesiastica*', *Scriptorium* 41 (1987), pp. 185–204.
21. Dumville, *A Palaeographer's View*, pp. 19–26. The scripts of the Eusebius fragment and the *Cathach* bear very close resemblance to one another and the Insular Half-Uncial of the *Cathach* displays fully

formed insular wedges and use of the Insular Half-Uncial **a**, so-called '**oc a**' constructed in a way which resembles the letters **o** and **c** joined together. *Diminuendo* lettering and insular abbreviations have been recorded in the *Etymologiae*.

22. Dumville, *A Palaeographer's Review*, pp. 81–4 for the synopsis which follows.
23. W.M. Lindsay, 'Breton Scriptoria: their Latin Abbreviation-Symbols', *Zentralblatt für Bibliothekswesen* 29 (1912), p. 264–72.
24. Brown, *A Palaeographer's View*, p. 128–33; Rosamond McKitterick, 'The Diffusion of Insular Culture in Neustria between 650 and 850: the Implications of the Manuscript Evidence', in Hartmut Atsma, ed., *La Neustrie. Les Pays du Nord de la Loire de 650 á 850*, 2 vols (Sigmaringen, 1981), II, pp. 395–432, for a thorough discussion of the different kinds of insular manuscript evidence, albeit with an English focus.
25. Dumville, *A Palaeographer's Review*, pp. 84–5.
26. Evidence from Luxeuil is minimal compared with that from Bobbio: Julian Brown recorded the use of insular prickings and rulings in some seventh- and eighth-century manuscripts written at Luxeuil (Brown, *A Palaeographer's View*, p. 129; see pp. 128–33 for a full list from other scriptoria); a few insular palaeographical features are also reported in some specimens of local Luxeuil script in the form of wedges and *diminuendo*-lettering (E.A. Lowe, *Palaeographical Papers 1907–1965*, ed. Ludwig Bieler, 2 vols [Oxford 1972], II, pp. 396–7). The presence and use of insular manuscripts in the medieval libraries of St-Gall in Switzerland and the nearby island monastery of Reichenau in Lake Constance in southern Germany reveal some evidence of insular (Irish and English) influence at these houses but this is minimal in terms of scribal practice (Johannes Autenrieth, 'Insular Spuren in Handschriften aus dem Bodenseegebiet bis zur Mitte des 9. Jahrhunderts', in G. Silagi, *Paläographie 1981: Colloquium des Comité International de Paléographie, München, 15.–18. September 1981* [Munich, 1982], pp. 145–57).
27. According to Dumville, *A Palaeographer's Review*, pp. 27–8, Milan, Biblioteca Ambrosiana, MS S.45.Sup. was not written in insular script but does display some insular influence in script and decoration.
28. W.M. Lindsay, 'The Bobbio Scriptorium', *Zentralblatt für Bibliothekswesen* 26 (1909), pp. 293–306.
29. P. Engelbert, 'Zur Frühgeschichte des Bobbieser Skriptoriums', *Revue bénédictine* 78 (1968), 220–60; Bischoff, *Latin Palaeography*, pp. 102–3, 191–2.
30. For Phase II, see Dumville, *A Palaeographer's Review*, pp. 60–1 and Brown, *A Palaeographer's View*, pp. 179–200.
31. Dumville, *A Palaeographer's Review*, pp. 61–110 for an overview of this debate.
32. Dumville, *A Palaeographer's Review*, p. 66: Monkwearmouth founded in 673/4 dedicated in 675/6 and Jarrow – perhaps in 681 and dedicated in 685.

33. Dumville, *A Palaeographer's Review*, p. 89.
34. Dumville, *A Palaeographer's Review*, pp. 89–101, for a full discussion of Echternach.
35. Dáibhí Ó Cróinín, 'The Old Irish and Old English Glosses in Echternach Manuscripts', in Michele Camillo Ferrari et al., eds, *Die Abtei Echternach 698–1998* (Luxembourg, 1999), pp. 85–101.
36. Bernhard Maier, *The Celts. A History from Earliest Times to the Present* (Edinburgh, 2003), p. 143.
37. Michael C. Sloan, *The Harmonious Organ of Sedulius Scottus: Introduction to his Collectaneum in Apostolum and Translation of its Prologue and Commentaries on Galatians and Ephesians* (Berlin, 2012), p. 3. See Chapter 11.
38. For a discussion of three bilingual manuscripts associated with both men and containing insular script, see Michael W. Herren et al., 'John Scottus and the Biblical Manuscripts attributed to the Circle of Sedulius', in Gerd Van Riel, ed., *Iohannes Scottus Eriugena: The Bible and Hermeneutics: Proceedings of the Ninth International Colloquium of the Society for the Promotion of Eriugenian Studies, held at Leuven and Louvain-La-Neuve, June 7–10, 1995* (Louvain, 1996), pp. 303–17. W.M. Lindsay, *Early Irish Minuscule Script* (Edinburgh, 1910) also contains palaeographical information and plates of some other early continental examples. See Edward Kennard Rand, 'The Supposed Autographa of John the Scot', *University of California Publications in Classical Philology* 5 (1918–23), 135–41 and Édouard Jeaneau and Paul Edward Dutton, *The Autograph of Eruigena* (Turnhout, 1996) for important studies which distinguishes Eriugena's (Caroline) hand.
39. See Figure 13.2, above.
40. For this background, see Rijcklof Hofman, ed., *The Sankt Gall Priscian Commentary*, 2 vols (Münster, 1996), I, pp. 12–23.
41. *Dictionary of the Irish Language* (Dublin, 1983), *s.v.* 'sam'.
42. Bruno Güterbock, 'Aus irischen Handschriften in Turin und Rom', *Zeitschrift für vergleichende Sprachforschung* 33 (1895), 86–105, at p. 92.
43. Lindsay, *Early Irish Minuscule*, pp. 43–6.
44. Jeaneau and Dutton, *The Autograph*, pp. 39–40 for information about this manuscript.
45. Lindsay, *Early Irish Minuscule*, pp. 37–8: the script of this manuscript requires more research as my preliminary examinations reveal that it is unlikely that Dubthach was responsible for all the insular script in the manuscript.
46. David N. Dumville, *Celtic Essays, 2001–2007*, 2 vols (Aberdeen 2007), I, pp. 156–8 for 'The MacDurnan Gospels'; Dumville, *A Palaeographer's Review*, pp. 122–6, for 'The Book of Armagh' and an overview of the Welsh manuscripts in this period.
47. Brian Ó Cuív, 'The Irish Marginalia in Codex Palatino-Vaticanus No. 830', *Éigse* 24 (1990), pp. 45–67.
48. Maier, *The Celts*, p. 201.

49. J.T. Gilbert, 'The Manuscripts of the Former College of Irish Franciscans, Louvain', in *Fourth Report of the Royal Commission on Historical Manuscripts, Part 1* (London, 1874), pp. 599–613.

50. James F. Kenney, *The Sources for the Early History of Ireland. An Introduction and Guide* (Dublin, 1929; rev. edn by L. Bieler, 1966), pp. 9–10, reported that ten manuscripts survive in Irish libraries from before 1000 compared with fifty preserved abroad.

51. Opportunities for manuscript loss are prevalent in Ireland: Viking raids, the large scale destruction of books during the reformation and damp weather conditions are all possible causes for the apparent lack of manuscripts surviving in Ireland itself. See Richard Sharpe, 'Books from Ireland, fifth to ninth centuries', *Peritia* 21 (2010), 1–55 for a detailed discussion on manuscript loss and survival in this period.

52. For a collection of preliminary discussions, see *Archaeology Ireland* 77 (Supplement: The Fadden More Psalter, Autumn, 2006), pp. 1–15.

53. Michelle Brown, 'The Eastwardness of Things: Relationships between the Christian Cultures of the Middle East and the Insular World' in Matthew T. Hussey and John D. Niles, eds, *The Genesis of Books: Studies in the Scribal Culture of Medieval England in Honour of A. N. Doane* (Turnhout, 2011), pp. 17–49, at pp. 26–7.

54. For example, recent discoveries by Paul Russell and Myriah Williams using ultraviolet light and photo editing software on the Welsh thirteenth-century manuscript Black Book of Carmarthen (Aberystwyth, National Library of Wales, MS Peniarth 1) have led to discoveries of lost text erased by a sixteenth-century owner (correspondence with Myriah Williams, July 2015).

55. Patrick Sheil et al., 'The Ghost in the Manuscript: Hypersceptral Text Recovery and Segmentation', in Malte Rehbein et al., eds, *Kodikologie und Paläographie im Digitalen Zeitalter – Codicology and Palaeography in the Digital Age* (Norderstedt, 2009), pp. 159–74, which describes HSI as an optical imaging process which analyses reflectance properties of text and parchment in order to detect subtle differences between inks and has been used to render erased text legible.

56. Tal Hassner, et al., 'Computation and Palaeography: Potentials and Limits', *Dagstuhl Manifestos* 2 (2013), 14–35 for an overview of the kinds of systems that can be developed and used.

57. For Irish manuscripts, the exemplary resource of this kind is *Irish Script on Screen* provided by the Dublin Institute of Advanced Studies at https://www.isos.dias.ie/. The resource provided by Digipal (http://www.digipal.eu/) in which hands - predominantly from eleventh-century English manuscripts - can be easily compared and contrasted, shows the impact digitization is having as a research tool.

Conclusion

The chapters in this book address the many facets of the Irish cultural presence in post-Roman western Europe. Despite its popular reputation as a 'dark age', this period in history saw intellectuals all over Europe involved in a dynamic interaction with each other and with each other's cultural heritage. The Irish were not absent from this stage: the pages of this book are filled with evidence for the contribution of the Irish to the cultural, religious and political life of early medieval Europe. This contribution came in the shape of ideas, texts and objects (including manuscripts) from Ireland which found their way overseas where British and continental scholars would copy, alter, vandalize or (rarely) ignore them. But the most conspicuous Irish presence overseas took the form of people, most of whom were ecclesiastics, who travelled to the Continent laden with intellectual baggage from their homeland.

The presence of Irishmen in Britain and continental Europe had different manifestations in the early Middle Ages. Nevertheless, within this broad period – in which protagonists and their motives varied, and so did their legacies – two phases stand out. The earliest phase, between the mid-sixth and late seventh century, can be described as the phase of monastic foundation abroad, with personalities such as Columba, Columbanus, Fursa and Aidan settling overseas and establishing monasteries under royal or aristocratic patronage. The second phase, in the long Carolingian ninth century, saw the flourishing of Irish scholars abroad, some of whom are known by name and even attained universal renown, such as John Scottus Eriugena or Sedulius Scottus, while others, especially computists, have only left a mark in anonymous treatises. For either phase travel would have been facilitated through international aristocratic, trade, and ecclesiastical networks that enabled long-distance communication, secured safe passage, and determined the nature of hospitality offered to *peregrini* as well as the extent of integration into political, scholarly, religious and social circles that was open to them. These networks are mostly invisible in the surviving source material – always inadequately and lamentably incomplete for the early medieval period – but can be inferred by analogy to the better documented experience of Anglo-Saxon *peregrini* (see Introduction). However, some international routes and the practicalities of travelling them become more visible in the

Viking era, especially from the mid-tenth century, thanks to the archaeology of trade, as discussed in Chapter 1.

Crucial to understanding the story of Irish *peregrini* at any time is the Irish background whence these men came and where they received their training in scholarship and religion. This background was in a constant state of flux. Thus, in the earlier period, the Ireland that Columba and Columbanus left behind was one in which churches were at a relatively early (albeit successful) stage of accumulating property and political power, and establishing patterns of relationships (sometimes quite symbiotic) with secular rulers. But the homeland that Eriugena or Sedulius had left behind would have been unrecognizable to their predecessors. Parts of it were now overrun by Viking invaders and some long-standing patronage relationships were being dissolved. The disruption of such ties made the migration of certain scholars oversees not only attractive but necessary. These dynamics serve to remind us how important it is to understand the historical context within which Irish people made their way to Europe and within which they functioned.

All the contributors to this volume, without exception, demonstrate that there is still much to be gained from a greater awareness of the nature of the sources that testify to the ways in which Irish intellectual achievements made their mark on European culture. It is necessary to acknowledge our dependence on the vagaries of evidence and the choices that early medieval authors made in what to tell, how to tell it and what not to tell. The place to begin, then, is by reflecting on the types of sources that are available to us.

Sources and their interpretation

Sources can tell entirely different stories. A central division would be between narrative sources – these are usually written after the events they describe – and non-narrative sources, like letters or legal documents, which are usually contemporary. So, for example, Columbanus's letters tell a story about his career and activities which is different from that told by his biographer Jonas, who wrote a hagiography after the saint's death. Among the discrepant details in the latter are the supposed remoteness of Columbanus's foundation at Luxeuil and his campaigns to convert pagans, which are not corroborated by Columbanus's own writings. In this respect Jonas's account may be ambiguous (see Chapter 5), and he was perhaps discreetly hinting at a more thriving settlement, for which indeed there is abundant archaeological evidence (see Chapter 1).

The comparison between the Life of Columbanus and other sources is instructive for gauging the differences between hagiography, with its selective and edifying narrative, and other more mundane types of text. Thus, it is remarkable that Jonas says nothing of the Easter debate, which figures prominently in Columbanus's letters. Was the debate not as important as the historiography has made it out to be, or was it simply not crucial to Jonas's narrative agenda? Caitlin Corning in Chapter 6 suggests that 'by the time [Jonas] wrote the Life in *c.* 640, the monasteries originally founded by Columbanus had adopted the Victorian table', and since thereafter all churches in Gaul followed the same table there was little point in rehearsing an obsolete controversy and reigniting old animosities.

Nevertheless, one ought to be careful not to draw too sharp a distinction between hagiography and less 'celebratory' texts, because hagiography could have its own pragmatic agenda which would intersect with its spiritual message. Saints' Lives that lay claim to land are not uncommon and in the seventh and eighth centuries such claims could be buttressed by reliable or exaggerated tales about Irish founders (see Chapter 3).

Notwithstanding its multifaceted nature, the corpus of saints' Lives can be drawn upon as a convenient measure for comparison with other contemporary texts owing to the large number of Lives and their wide distribution. Such a comparison eventually allows us to better understand the hagiographical genre itself. An interesting comparison is between Life and monastic rule. As Albrecht Diem notes in Chapter 4, the Life of Columbanus is at variance with the surviving rule of Columbanus on matters concerning monastic routine and ideal. If one prefers the testimony of the Life then it must be concluded that the rule we have differs from that drawn up by the saint. It does not even include the practical regulations that one normally finds in such texts. Its lesser practical import can, perhaps, offer a partial explanation as to why its influence appears not to have been as strong as was once believed. Ian Wood in Chapter 5 rightly draws attention to the fact that the rule of Columbanus was 'a minor ingredient' in so-called 'mixed rules' (rules combining Columbanus's teachings with those of Basil, Caesarius of Arles, or Benedict). On the other hand, as Diem suggests, instead of quantifying the relative space that Columbanus's rule occupies in a 'mixed rule' as a whole, one may consider the quality and integrity of the text that *was* extracted from the rule. For example, the first chapter of Columbanus's *Regula monachorum* is in fact the only text cited by the *Regula cuiusdam patris* in a form that is nearly complete. This detail leads Diem to contest the validity of the classification of the *Regula cuiusdam patris* as a simple mixed rule, assembled from an eclectic mix of other monastic works. Rather, much of its material is original, albeit drawing on a thoughtful synthesis of earlier texts. It can be said to respond to Columbanus's rule rather than merely copy from it, because the *Regula cuiusdam patris* elaborates its own more 'democratic' views on abbatial power and monastic government.

Of major significance to the study of the impact of teachings authored by Irish monastic leaders on the Continent is the pattern of transmission of manuscripts containing hagiography or texts of other genres. Forms of script and codicological contexts are of interest in this respect because they demonstrate specific choices, sometimes determined by concerns for asserting identity (for example, insular script is distinct from Caroline minuscule and so on) and as such suggest something about the historical circumstances in which the manuscripts were both produced and received, as Elizabeth Duncan explains in Chapter 13. The acquisition of materials from which manuscripts and ink were made can bear witness to actual long-distance contacts across Europe, as signalled by Christopher Loveluck and Aidan O'Sullivan in Chapter 1. For example, certain minerals used for ink in Argyll must have been imported along a long and winding route from Vesuvius. Just as importantly, the context in which the minerals were found raises the possibility that they were acquired through secular rather than ecclesiastical initiative, as a gift from the political centre at Dunadd to the monastic community of Iona.

The study of text-transmission can be an effective exercise for assessing the spread and reception of Irish scientific learning, both of which can be detected by tracing citations from specific texts in continental manuscripts, as Immo Warntjes shows in Chapter 10. It is possible to infer diagnostic Irish features in computistical texts and manuscripts by careful comparison with examples from Anglo-Saxon, Visigothic, Italian and Frankish texts. This makes possible the further identification of distinct Irish material, even when the identity of individual authors remains unknown. Warntjes finds evidence of influence especially in places like Bobbio, St-Gall, Regensburg and Cologne, noting that network analysis of the intellectual connections that brought them there promises fruitful research in the future.

Yet assigning a distinctive and exclusive Irish identity to specific textual features can be a hazardous exercise within the dynamic cultural environment of early medieval Europe. The most controversial instance involves the thirty-nine works of biblical exegesis which Bernhard Bischoff famously attributed to Irish authors. The method by which Bischoff arrived at his identification is criticized in Chapter 7 by Mark Stansbury who says of Bischoff's *Symptomen* for identifying Irish exegesis: 'rather than looking at all exegesis and picking works that shared features, he started with the shared features and worked backward – he shot first, and drew the target second'. As Stansbury explains, these features were arguably not peculiar to Irish authors but were also utilized, for example, by Church Fathers. They were nevertheless seen frequently in Irish-linked texts, a fact that could easily deflect attention from others who applied them. The significance of analysing Bischoff's method, even if one accepts that it has its flaws, is that it highlights the preconceptions with which scholars could approach (not necessarily consciously) the study of Irish *peregrini* in the early medieval period.

One could challenge Bischoff's quest for Irish symptoms and Irish originality on the grounds that a closer look at cultural exchange in the early Middle Ages may actually reveal that variety and 'eclecticism' were the norm. Within this intellectual environment, Irish elements could quickly be integrated within wholly continental works. Conversely, Irish cultural expressions could be strongly indebted to continental influences. As Yitzhak Hen notes in Chapter 9, Irish liturgical originality was in fact strictly synthetic, as is shown by the Stowe Missal. The compiler of this book devised an original framework within which he placed prayers that had been cherry-picked from Gallican sources, he modified their language when this suited his purpose, and he even added new prayers. Nevertheless the core of the liturgy of the Stowe Missal, as well as of other Irish-related liturgical texts, was evidently the Gallican rite that was widespread in the early medieval Latin West. The so-called 'Celtic rite', popularized by scholars of the late nineteenth century (most notably Frederick Warren), is argued to be no more than a figment of antiquarian imagination, which actually masks the fact that the sources do not offer evidence for liturgical uniformity in Ireland itself – quite the contrary.

Understanding the sources available to us and how to interpret them is our insurance policy against preconceptions and truisms. Such truisms, espoused both by contemporaries and modern commentators, abound. Here too, the student of history needs to take into account context, in this case the historiographical context within which our understanding of the period was shaped.

Challenging narratives

Received ideas about Irish *peregrini* were formed not only as a result of certain notions that were repeated time and time again, but also as a result of the things that were left unsaid. Probably the most regrettable tendency of modern scholarship has been to discuss Irish *peregrini* with near-complete disregard to their homeland. We have attempted to redress this oversight here by examining the Irish background from an economic and cultural perspective, and its contribution to *peregrinatio*. This topic is covered in Chapters 1 and 2. Insofar as the economy is concerned, the earliest incidents of *peregrinatio* occurred during a period of population and economic growth, when agriculture was highly productive. By observing changes in the motivations of *peregrini* over time, Johnston in Chapter 2 distinguishes different stages of *peregrinatio* which correspond broadly to the two phases described at the outset. Whereas the *peregrini* of the sixth to early eighth century can be said to have been motivated by the ideal of *peregrinatio pro Christo*, over which much scholarly ink has been spilled over the years, those of the ninth century were drawn mainly by the promise of Carolingian patronage. When the phase of *peregrinatio pro Christo* is examined more closely, it is possible to identify two ways in which the Irish background can be said to have acted as a push factor that accelerated the drive to travel overseas. The first, which Kathleen Hughes was the first to point out, derives from the growing number of members of the *Céli Dé* in the eighth-century Irish church who encouraged asceticism and who may have promoted the increased use of the vernacular in scholarship, and the second, originally explored by Thomas Charles-Edwards and re-examined here by Johnston in Chapter 2, derives from the native conception of exile, which appears to precede Christianity. This conception has its roots in native Irish traditions enshrined in legal provisions that gave travel privileges to members of the elite on the one hand, but on the other hand prescribed exile as punishment. This dual legal interpretation was echoed by the Irish Christian concept of *peregrinatio* which could simultaneously be an act of ascetic mortification and an assertion of elite status. The ideal of *peregrinatio pro Christo* was therefore no mere religious cliché but a principle deeply ingrained in Irish culture.

It has often been said that, once on the Continent, the Irish who arrived in the first phase of *peregrinatio* imparted their own unique conception of monastic culture. According to this narrative, the best known of these *peregrini*, Columbanus, appeared as a 'bolt from the blue' to reinvigorate a religiously stale and soporous Francia and spark a new monastic tradition (this topic is considered in Chapters 5 and 12). This view of events, again, is based on the hagiographical record. In the present volume we have explored alternative views to the effect that Columbanus did not lay the foundations for Gallic monasticism, nor did he grant the aristocracy power *ex nihilo* over monasteries. Rather, he was arguably benefitting from an upward trend in the fortunes of Gallic monasticism, or perhaps simply taking advantage of it more effectively, as described in Chapters 3 and 12. This is not to deny the invigorating influence of the career of Columbanus, but simply to put his contribution and legacy in a contextual perspective.

The innovations that Columbanus was believed to have introduced into Gallic monasticism were supposedly continued and developed by his followers and by those who hitched their wagon to his monastic 'franchise'. The question of Columbanian monasticism, which for many has become the hallmark of Irish presence on the Continent, has been explored here from a number of angles, especially in Chapters 3, 4 and 5. The central problem, to put it crudely, is whether Columbanian monasticism is more myth than it was ever a reality. What scholars intend by the expression 'Columbanian monasticism' varies in nuance, but it can broadly be said to denote a type of monastic institution (historians disagree on how many such houses there would have been) which had Irish origins, or had been founded from another monastery that had Irish origins, or else had assumed certain characteristics of Irish monasticism in its continental guise. The checklist for such characteristics also varies, but it often includes the following: enjoying certain kinds of legal immunities and privileges, adhering to an Irish rule or a 'mixed rule', and venerating the memory of an Irish founder. Interestingly, no continuity of direct contacts with Ireland is ever assumed.

Rather than being a reality, however, Columbanian monasticism has been shown to be a historiographical construct, which can be traced back to the heady days of the nineteenth century when Irish political activists became role models for the protagonists of the Catholic revival in France. From the perspective of historical research there is little evidence to sustain the concept of Columbanian monasticism. Rather, 'what we call Columbanian monasticism was developed largely by Columbanus's Frankish successors', in the words of Wood in Chapter 5. At best – and even this is doubtful – there could have been what Friedrich Prinz labelled non-commitally and vaguely as *irisch beeinflusste klöster*, 'Irish monastic influence'. But this concept is so subjective as to be rendered almost useless as a valid category for modern scholarly analysis. As the contributions to this volume show, it is not always possible to establish 'Irish influence', let alone to sustain the concept of Columbanian monasticism, without a selective and perhaps credulous reading of sources, especially hagiography.

The other major issue with which Columbanus's name is associated is the Easter Controversy, considered in Chapters 6, 10 and 12. The debate over the dating of Easter and its implications for the formation of the Christian calendar was a central theme in the quest for universal Christian identity in the late antique and early medieval period. It was informed by a number of disciplines, to the extent that it can be framed in modern terms (and with no little anachronism) as the most interdisciplinary debate of the first Christian millennium. It exercised the minds of theologians, exegetes, authors of early canon law and of some of the greatest scientific thinkers of the period, among whom Irish computists stand out as uniquely influential, as Warntjes shows in Chapter 10.

The more practical aspects of the Easter debate in the early medieval period are best known from late sixth- and early seventh-century Gaul, from seventh-century Ireland and Northumbria, and from early eighth-century Iona. For present purposes, the Gallic phase of the debate, with Columbanus at its centre, is the most pertinent. The importance of the Easter calculation to both the Gallic bishops and Columbanus is undeniable, but Roy Flechner and Sven Meeder in Chapter 12 ask whether we ought to take Columbanus at his word when he says that divergences over the reckoning of Easter were used as a pretext by the Gallic bishops in order to discredit him rather than being the core issue that drove a wedge between them. The Easter debate was certainly a pretext by Boniface's time, when an erroneous Irish observance of Easter, as Flechner and Meeder contend, became a literary cliché and continued to be used as a means of vilifying the Irish long after they had reformed their Easter tables. For Boniface the real issue at hand was competition over patronage and ecclesiastical jurisdiction against his charismatic rivals, among them the Irish bishop of Salzburg, Virgil, and the purported heretic Clemens. Such controversial issues, along with disputes over control of land, were also prominent in Gaul during the time of Columbanus, and in Northumbria during the years that lead up to the Council of Whitby of 664, at which the question of Easter was debated. Therefore, notwithstanding its intrinsic importance, Easter could have been a rhetorical battering ram in the hands of politically-motivated detractors, just as were the unfounded accusations of Judaizing hurled by Gallic bishops at

Columbanus. These accusations continued to be thrust at the Irish throughout the Middle Ages by such influential commentators as Boniface, Bede and (with some modifications) Gerald of Wales. They included claims that the Irish adhered too closely to Old Testament teachings, or followed Old Testament marriage customs that violated canon law, or observed Easter at the same time as the Jews (*sc.* Quartodeciman heresy).

It is not only Columbanian monasticism that can be shown to be a doubtful concept (albeit one repeatedly urged and perpetuated by nineteenth- and twentieth-century scholarship) but also the notion of continental 'Irish centres', which is yet another scholarly common-place. Meeder argues in Chapter 11 that none of the episcopal and monastic schools that have emerged as part of the Carolingian revival of learning could indisputably be labelled 'Irish centres'. The expression is primarily a modern scholarly construct, but derives from concepts authored by what Meeder calls in 'creative Carolingian notaries'. According to Yaniv Fox in Chapter 3, the tendency of Carolingian authors to weave Irish figures into their texts and to emphasize or invent an Irish origin for the monasteries about which they wrote, can be attributed to two main causes, each correspond-ing to a different genre: hagiographers used Irish *peregrini* as narrative devices usually associated with particular religious practices that they were said to have introduced, and notaries recorded Irish *peregrini* as 'legitimizing agents' in their cartularies.

The ubiquity of the epithet 'Irish' in the Carolingian period is a pendant to the multi-ethnic dynamics of its revival of learning. It is an undisputed fact that the thriving intellectual life under the Carolingians drew an international mix of scholars to Carolingian royal or episcopal patrons. And although large centres or 'colonies' of foreign scholars are not securely attested in our sources, we do know of communities defined as *scholae* in Rome. Loveluck and O'Sullivan discuss in Chapter 1 the *scholae peregrinorum*, which were home to pilgrims, merchants and could also accommodate travelling scholars. According to the *Liber Pontificalis*, Rome had separate *scholae* for Franks, Frisians, Anglo-Saxons and Lombards. These *scholae* had their own discrete legal status that conferred both privileges and obligations such that they could even be called upon to provide mili-tary defence for Rome. Loveluck and O'Sullivan suggest that the Irish might have had their own *schola*, just as other peoples did.

One of the more tenacious notions associated with Irish *peregrini* is their commitment to scholarship, especially the study of grammar. The image of the travelling Irish scholar peddling knowledge is not a modern invention but goes back to the ninth century at least. Some Irish scholars rose to prominence by serving dignitaries at the highest echelons of power. Sedulius Scotus at Liège and Eriugena at Charles the Bald's palace school are the prime examples. But there are others. A famous episode related by Notker the Stammerer, discussed here by Warntjes in Chapter 10, tells of two Irishmen arriving in Gaul with British traders, with nothing to sell but their wisdom. They so impressed Charlemagne that he kept them in his company for a while and later settled them in his realm. This story is testimony to the premium put on 'Irishness' by the Carolingians (and their biographers), in particular in the context of scholarship. The Carolingian appreciation of Irishness has led to a strong presence of the label 'Irish' in the sources from this period.

Whether Irish scholars were more original than others, or whether they offered more original syntheses of previous scholarship, are questions that are being debated by modern-day historians, just as they were debated by contemporaries. Eriugena was accused by leading ecclesiastics of his day of unwarranted originality in his treatise on predestination. Historians take different views as to whether Eriugena's treatise was indeed original, whether he intended it to be original or whether it simply did not formally conform to conventions of Carolingian theological disputation.

Unlike Eriugena, Dicuil, a scientist of the first order, is said by Warntjes in Chapter 10 to have indisputably written 'the most unconventional and original scientific text of the Carolingian period'. His *Liber de astronomia* appears to have been so complicated, that it is not known to have been cited anywhere and only survives in a single manuscript copy. Whether originality, when it is present, can be directly linked to a scholar's Irish heritage is a matter of contention. In many ways, however, such an assertion is methodologically risky: the works in questions were written in a continental context, where Irish intellectuals worked for and alongside the continental elite and read and engaged with works originating from all over Europe. Their scholarship was now firmly a part of a pan-European pool of learning.

The acknowledgement that it is impossible to isolate the Irish contribution to European scholarship and the realization that other myths about the Irish in the early Middle Ages have already been debunked and continue to be debunked (for example, Irish foundations in Gaul were not in remote places, there was no seventh-century Columbanian monasticism, nor were there ninth-century 'Irish centres' on the Continent and so on) ought not detract from the fact that the Irish *did* make a genuine contribution to the cultural, religious, and political life of early medieval continental Europe. The debunking of myths does not deny the actual contribution of Irish *peregrini*. In fact, one could argue the opposite: it helps us to focus attention on the reality of their activities and allows us to regard these activities in their proper contemporary context rather than in an apocryphal context dominated by wishful thinking. There is much to be said on the many ways in which Irish achievements found their place within western European culture, where intellectuals from diverse ethnic and cultural backgrounds engaged with them. Only through a contextual interpretation of the evidence available to us, be it written or material, can we hope to gauge the role played by the Irish overseas and their enduring legacy.

Further Reading

1   Travel, Transport and Communication to and from Ireland, c. 400–1100: An Archaeological Perspective

For additional recent discussion of the connections between Ireland and her neighbours in the early medieval period, see Michael Richter, *Ireland and Her Neighbours in the Seventh Century* (Dublin, 1999); Ewan Campbell, 'The Archaeological Evidence for External Contacts: Imports, Trade and Economy in Celtic Britain, AD 400–800', in Ken Dark, ed., *External Contacts and the Economy of Late and Post-Roman Britain* (Woodbridge, 1996), pp. 83–96; Ewan Campbell, *Continental and Maritime Imports to Atlantic Britain and Ireland, AD 400–800* (York, 2007); A. O'Sullivan and C. Breen, *Maritime Ireland: An Archaeology of Coastal Communities* (Stroud, 2007); I.W. Doyle, 'Mediterranean and Frankish Pottery Imports in Early Medieval Ireland', *Journal of Irish Archaeology* 18 (2009), 17–62; A. Kelly, 'The Discovery of Phocaen Red Slip-Ware (PRSW) form 3 and Bii Ware (LR1 Amphorae) on Sites in Ireland: An Analysis within a Broader Framework', *PRIA* 110C (2010), pp. 35–88.

For the context of Atlantic Europe, also see Christer Westerdahl, 'From Land to Sea, from Sea to Land. On Transport Zones, Borders and Human Space', in Jerzy Litwin, ed., *Down The River To The Sea. Proceedings of the Eighth International Symposium on Boat and Ship Archaeology, Gdansk 1997* (Gdansk, 2000), pp. 11–20; Barry Cunliffe, *Facing The Ocean. The Atlantic and its Peoples* (Oxford, 2001).

For textual evidence on the presence of Byzantine merchant-seafarers in Atlantic Europe between the fifth to early seventh centuries, see E. Dawes and N.H. Baynes, trans., *Three Byzantine Saints: Contemporary Biographies Translated from the Greek*, (London, 1977); A.T. Fear, ed. and trans., *Lives of the Visigothic Fathers* (Liverpool, 1997).

For Anglo-Saxons mistaken for Irish travellers at Tours in the mid-eighth century, see W. Arndt, ed. and trans., *Vita Alcuini,* MGG SS 15/1 (Stuttgart, 1887), p. 193.

For further discussion of the monastery of Saint-Denis, see Michel Wyss, 'Saint-Denis (France): du mausolée hypothétique du Bas-Empire à l'ensemble basilical carolingien', in Guy De Boe and Frans Verhaeghe, eds, *Death and Burial in Medieval Europe, Papers of the 'Medieval Europe Brugge 1997' Conference* (Zellik, 1997), II, pp. 111–14 ; Michel Wyss, 'Un établissement Carolingien mis au jour à proximité de l'abbaye de Saint-Denis: la question du palais de Charlemagne', in Annie Renoux, ed., *Aux Marches Du Palais Qu'est-ce-qu'un palais médiéval? Actes du VIIe Congrès international d'Archéologie Médiévale* (Le Mans, 2001), pp. 191–200.

For further references on the monastery at Hamage and the possible Irish influences on its early phase, see Étienne Louis, 'Archéologie et bâtiments monastiques, VIIème–IXème siècles. Le cas de Hamage (France, Département du Nord)', in De Boe and Verhaeghe *Religion and Belief in Medieval Europe,* IV, pp. 55–63; Étienne Louis, 'A De-Romanized Landscape in Northern Gaul: the Scarpe Valley from the 4th to the 9th Century', in William Bowden, Luke Lavan and Carlos Machado, eds, *Recent Research on the Late Antique Countryside,* Late Antique Archaeology 2 (Leiden and Boston, 2004), pp. 479–504; Étienne Louis and Joël Blondiaux, 'L'abbaye mérovingienne et carolingienne de Hamage (Nord). Vie, mort et sépulture dans une commu- nauté Monastique féminine', in Armelle Alduc-Le Bagousse, ed., *Inhumations de prestige ou prestige de l'inhumation?* (Caen, 2009), pp. 117–49.

For further information on the river trading port at Taillebourg, in French and English, see Jean Chapelot, 'Aux origines des châteaux et des bourgs castraux dans la Moyenne et Basse Charente: entre sources écrites et archéol- ogie', in A. Flambard-Héricher and J. le Maho, eds, *Château, Ville et Pouvoir au Moyen Âge* (Caen, 2012), pp. 81–156; Christopher Loveluck, *Northwest Europe in the Early Middle Ages, c. AD 600–1150. A Comparative Archaeology* (Cambridge, 2013), pp. 195, 203.

References to trade in slaves by Irish seafarers in western Britain and the slave trade along the coasts of Atlantic Europe down to Spain include: Pamela Nightingale, *A Medieval Mercantile Community. The Grocers' Company and the Politics and Trade of London, 1000–1485* (New Haven and London, 1995), p. 9 ; Mark Horton, 'Bristol and its International Position', in Lawrence Keen, ed., *"Almost the Richest City" — Bristol in the Middle Ages,* British Archaeological Association Conference Transactions XIX (Leeds, 1997), pp. 9–17. For further references on specific Iberian products (silks and dye materials) arriving into north-western Europe as a result of trade along the Atlantic coast, from the mid/late tenth to early twelfth century, see F. A. Pritchard, 'Late Saxon Textiles from the City of London', *Medieval Archaeology* 28 (1984), 46–76; F. A. Pritchard, 'Small Finds', in A. Vince, ed., *Aspects of Saxo-Norman London 2* (London, 1991), pp. 120–278; G. Jones, V. Straker and A. Davis, 'Early Medieval Plant Use and Ecology', in ibid., pp. 347–55.

2   Exiles from the Edge? The Irish Contexts of *Peregrinatio*

The writings of Columbanus are a key source for understanding *Peregrinatio.* The standard edition and translation is G.S.M. Walker, *Sancti Columbani Opera* (Dublin, 1957). The career of Columbanus has received considerable atten- tion. Thomas M. Charles-Edwards, *Early Christian Ireland* (Cambridge, 2000), pp. 334–90, provides an overview. His writings are considered in Michael Lapidge, ed., *Columbanus: Studies on the Latin Writings* (Woodbridge, 1997) and his theological position is explicated in Damian Bracken, 'Authority and Duty: Columbanus and the Primacy of Rome', *Peritia* 16 (2002), 163–213. The saint's influence on Frankish monasticism, among other things, is the subject of the important collection of essays edited by H. B. Clarke and Mary Brennan, *Columbanus and Merovingian Monasticism* (Oxford, 1981). The most detailed study of this aspect is Yaniv Fox, *Power and Religion in Merovingian Gaul. Columbanian Monasticism and the Frankish Elite* (Cambridge, 2014).

Jonas's Life of Columbanus is another crucial source. Unfortunately, it lacks a modern edition; scholars still have recourse to Bruno Krusch, ed., *Ionae Vitae Sanctorum*, MGH SS rer. Germ. (Hanover, 1905). The influence of *Vita Columbani* is considered in Ian N. Wood, 'The *Vita Columbani* and Merovingian Hagiography', *Peritia* 1 (1982), 63–80. The context of its composition receives detailed treatment in Clare Stancliffe, 'Jonas's Life of Columbanus and his Disciples', in John Carey et al., eds, *Studies in Irish Hagiography: Saints and Scholars* (Dublin, 2001), pp. 189–220.

There is significant scholarship on Adomnán and his writings. The standard edition and translation of *Vita Columbae* is Alan Orr Anderson and Marjorie Oglivie Anderson, *Adomnán's Life of Columba* (Edinburgh and London, 1961). The translation by Richard Sharpe, *Adomnán of Iona: Life of St Columba* (Harmondsworth, 1995), is more nuanced and has an excellent introduction. Jonathan Wooding et al., eds, *Adomnán of Iona: Theologian, Lawmaker, Peacemaker* (Dublin, 2010) explores many aspects of its subject's career. The same collection contains an essay by Dan Tipp and Jonathan Wooding, 'Adomnán's Voyaging Saint: The Cult of Cormac Ua Liatháin', pp. 237–52, which is the most comprehensive treatment available of this subject.

The definition of *peregrinatio*, based on *Vita Columbani*, is ubiquitous. It is usefully summarized in Michael Richter, *Ireland and Her Neighbours in the Seventh Century* (Dublin, 1999), esp. pp. 41–7. The connection between *peregrinatio* and the Cambrai Homily is considered in Stancliffe's influential 'Red, White and Blue Martyrdom', in Dorothy Whitelock et al., eds, *Ireland in Early Medieval Europe* (Cambridge, 1982), pp. 21–46. Kathleen Hughes, 'The Changing Theories and Practice of Irish Pilgrimage', *Journal of Ecclesiastical History* 11 (1960), 143–51, identifies the Céli Dé as prime contributors to a decline in *peregrinatio*. However, Westley Follett, *Céli Dé in Ireland: Monastic Writing and Identity in the Early Middle Ages* (Woodbridge, 2006), repositions the Céli Dé on a spectrum of ecclesiastical opinion.

The origins of *peregrinatio* in the Irish legal mindset received its most important treatment in T.M. Charles-Edwards, 'The Social Background to Irish *Peregrinatio*', *Celtica* 11 (1976), 43–59. This has influenced most subsequent work on the topic. Fergus Kelly, *A Guide to Early Irish Law* (Dublin, 1988) is an excellent introduction to vernacular law. The role of the *túath*, is analysed in Francis John Byrne, 'Tribes and Tribalism in Early Ireland', *Ériu* 22 (1971), 128–66, while genealogical connections are explored in Donnchadh Ó Corráin, 'Creating the Past: the Early Irish Genealogical Tradition', *Peritia* 12 (1998), 177–208. The punishment of being set adrift is outlined in Mary E. Byrne, 'On the Punishment of Setting Adrift', *Ériu* 11 (1932), 97–102. Muirchú's account of Macc Cuill can be found in the standard edition and translation of his Life by Ludwig Bieler, *The Patrician Texts from the Book of Armagh* (Dublin, 1979), pp. 102–7.

The Christian reception and development of classical geography receives detailed treatment in Natalia Lozovsky, *'The Earth is our Book': Geographical Knowledge in the Latin West ca. 400–1000* (Ann Arbor, 2000). The location of paradise is considered in Jean Delumeau, *History of Paradise: The Garden of Eden in Myth and Tradition* (New York, 1995), pp. 42–56. Markus Bockmuehl, 'Locating Paradise', in M. Bockmuehl and G. G. Stroumsa, eds, *Paradise in Antiquity: Jewish and Christian Views* (Cambridge, 2010), pp. 192–209, provides a detailed study.

Carl Selmer, ed., *Navigatio Sancti Brendani Abbatis from Early Latin Manuscripts* (Notre Dame, 1959) has long been the standard edition of the *Nauigatio*. It has recently been joined by Giovanni Orlandi and Rossana E. Guglielmetti, eds, *Navigatio Sancti Brendani: alla scoperta dei segreti meravigliosi del mondo* (Florence, 2014), accompanied by an Italian translation. The best English translation is John J. O'Meara, *The Voyage of Saint Brendan: Journey to the Promised Land* (Gerrards Cross, 1976). Its date has been debated, ranging from the tenth century, as suggested by Selmer, to David N. Dumville's argument for the eighth century in 'Two Approaches to the Dating of "Navigatio Sancti Brendani"', *Studi Medievali* 29 (1988), 95–9. James Carney, 'Review of Selmer, *Navigatio*', *Medium Aevum* 32 (1963), 37–44, situates the *Nauigatio* in the wider Brendan tradition. Its theological significance is usefully explored in Thomas O'Loughlin, 'Distant Islands: the Topography of Holiness in the *Nauigatio Sancti Brendani*', in *The Medieval Mystical Tradition England, Ireland and Wales*, ed. M. Glasscoe (Woodbridge, 1999), pp. 1–20.

Irish monastic exploration of the North Atlantic is best attested in the work of Dicuil, which has been edited and translated by J.J. Tierney, *Dicuili Liber de Mensura Orbis Terrae* (Dublin, 1967). Archaeological data for an Irish presence in the Faroes is ambiguous. A cautious approach is adopted by Símun V. Arge et al., 'Viking and Medieval Settlement in the Faroes: People, Place and the Environment', *Human Ecology*, 3/5 (2005), 597–620. The possibilities of pollen evidence are explored in Douglas B. Borthwick and Kevin J. Edwards, 'Peaceful Wars and Scientific Invaders: Irishmen, Vikings and Palynological Evidence for the Earliest Settlement of the Faroe Islands', in John Sheehan et al., eds, *The Viking Age: Ireland and the West; Papers from the Proceedings of the Fifteenth Viking Congress, Cork, 18–27 August 2005* (Dublin, 2010), pp. 66–79. A useful collection of essays on the *papar*, the Irish who were believed to have been the earliest settlers of Iceland, is Barbara Crawford, ed., *The* Papar *in the North Atlantic Environment and History: The Proceedings of a Day Conference Held on 24 February 2001* (St Andrews, 2002).

Irish networks of *peregrini* feature in general and specialized scholarship. A useful starting point is Dáibhí Ó Cróinin, *Early Medieval Ireland 400–1200* (London, 1995), pp. 221–32. There is a more detailed analysis in the same author's 'The Irish as Mediators of Antique Culture on the Continent', in P. L. Butzer and D. Lohrmann, eds, *Science in Western and Eastern Civilization* (Basle, 1993), pp. 41–52. The best introduction to the Irish presence in northern France is the collection of essays edited by Jean-Michel Picard, *Ireland and Northern France AD 600–850* (Dublin, 1991). Fursa, in particular, is examined in Stefanie Hamann, 'St Fursa, The Genealogy of an Irish Saint – The Historical Person and his Cult', *PRIA* 112C (2011), pp. 1–41.

The importance of the medieval Irish chronicles is such that there have been two recent and important monographs: Daniel McCarthy, *The Irish Annals. Their Genesis, Evolution and History* (Dublin, 2008) and Nicholas

Evans, *The Present and the Past in Medieval Irish Chronicles* (Woodbridge, 2010).
Their lack of commemoration of *peregrini* is touched on in Elva Johnston,
Literacy and Identity in Early Medieval Ireland (Woodbridge, 2013), as is the role
of churchmen and poets as custodians of social memory. A good introduction
to social memory is James J. Fentress and Chris Wickham, *Social Memory: New
Perspectives on the Past* (Oxford, 1992).

3   The Political Context of Irish monasticism in Seventh-Century Francia: Another Look at the Sources

On Columbanus, the Columbanian movement, and other Irish *peregrini*:
A. Diem, 'Was bedeutet regula Columbani?', in W. Pohl and M. Diesenberger,
eds, *Integration und Herrschaft: Ethnische Identitäten und soziale Organisation im
Frühmittelalter* (Vienna, 2002), pp. 63–90; idem, 'Monks, Kings, and the
Transformation of Sanctity: Jonas of Bobbio and the End of the Holy Man',
Speculum 82 (2007), 521–59; B. Dumézil, 'L'affaire Agrestius de Luxeuil:
hérésie et régionalisme dans la Burgondie du VIIe siècle', *Médiévales* 52
(2007), 135–52; M. Dunn, 'Columbanus, Charisma, and the Revolt of the
Monks of Bobbio', *Peritia* 20 (2008), 1–27; S. Hamann, 'St Fursa, the
Genealogy of an Irish Saint: the Historical Person and his Cult', *PRIA* 112C
(2011), 1–41; M. Lapidge, ed., *Columbanus: Studies on the Latin Writings*,
Studies in Celtic History 17 (Woodbridge, 1997); T. Leso, 'Columbanus in
Europe: the Evidence from the *Epistulae*', *EME* 21 (2013), 358–89; W. Müller,
'Der Anteil der Iren an der Christianisierung der Alemannen', in H. Löwe,
ed., *Die Iren und Europa im früheren Mittelalter*, 2 vols. (Stuttgart, 1982), I,
pp. 330–41; D. Ó Cróinín, 'Zur frühzeit der irischen Mission in Europa', in
J. Erichsen, ed., *Kilian. Mönch aus Irland – aller Franken Patron. Aufsätze*
(Munich, 1989), pp. 49–55; D. Ó Riain-Raedel, 'Bemerkungen zum hagiographischen Dossier des hl. Gallus', in *Gallus und seine Zeit: Leben, Wirken,
Nachleben. Akten der Tagung vom 5. Bis 8. September 2012 in der Stiftsbibliotek
St. Gallen* (St Gall, in press); A. O'Hara, 'The *Vita Columbani* in Merovingian
Gaul', *EME* 17 (2009), 126–53; F. Prinz, 'Columbanus, the Frankish Nobility
and the Territories East of the Rhine', in H.B. Clarke and M. Brennan, eds,
Columbanus and Merovingian Monasticism, British Archaeological Reports,
International Series 113 (Oxford, 1981), pp. 73–87; P. Riché, 'Columbanus,
his Followers and the Merovingian Church', in Clarke and Brennan,
Columbanus and Merovingian Monasticism, pp. 59–72; M. Richter, *Bobbio in the
Early Middle Ages: The Abiding Legacy of Columbanus* (Dublin, 2008); M. Schär,
Gallus: der Heilige in seiner Zeit (Basel, 2011); C. Stancliffe, 'Jonas's *Life of
Columbanus and His Disciples*', in J. Carey, M. Herbert and P Ó Riain, eds,
Studies in Irish Historiography: Saints and Scholars (Dublin, 2001), pp. 189–220;
eadem, 'Columbanus and the Gallic Bishops', in G. Constable and
M. Rouche, eds, *Auctoritas: Mélanges offerts à Olivier Guillot*, Cultures et
Civilisations Médiévales 33 (Paris, 2006), pp. 205–15; eadem, 'Columbanus's
Monasticism and the Sources of his Inspiration: From Basil to the Master?',
in F. Edmonds and P. Russell, eds, *Tome: Studies in Medieval Celtic History and*

Law in Honour of Thomas Charles-Edwards, Studies in Celtic History 31 (Woodbridge, 2011), pp. 17–28; I.N. Wood, 'Jonas, the Merovingians, and Pope Honorius: *Diplomata* and the *Vita Columbani*', in A.C. Murray, ed., *After Rome's Fall: Narrators and Sources of Early Medieval History.* (Toronto, 1998), pp. 96–120; and B. Yorke, *Nunneries and the Anglo-Saxon Royal Houses* (London and New York, 2003).

On Pope Martin, Heraclius, and relations between the papal and imperial courts: C. Cubitt, 'The Lateran Council of 649 as an Ecumenical Council', in R. Price and M. Whitby, eds, *Chalcedon in Context: Church Councils 400–700* (Liverpool, 2009), pp. 133–147; I.N. Wood, 'The Franks and Papal Theology, 550–660', in C. Chazelle and C. Cubitt, eds, *The Crisis of the Oikoumene: The Three Chapters and the Failed Quest for Unity in the Sixth-Century Mediterranean* (Turnhout, 2006), pp. 223–42.

On Romainmôtier: G. Coutaz, 'Romainmôtier ou la succession de deux vagues de l'élan missionaire (ve–viie siècles), in J.-D. Morerod, ed., *Romainmôtier: Histoire de l'abbaye* (Lausanne, 2001), pp. 25–37; A. Pahud, ed., *La cartulaire de Romainmôtier (xiiᵉ siècle): introduction et édition critique* (Lausanne, 1998); P. Pradié, 'Saint Wandrille à Romainmôtier', in Morerod, *Romainmôtier*, pp. 39–49.

On the activities of Amandus: A. Dierkens, 'Saint Amand et la foundation de l'abbaye de Nivelles', *Revue du Nord* 68 (1986), 325–34; C. Mériaux, *Gallia irradiata: saints et sanctuaires dans le nord de la Gaule du haut Moyen Âge* (Stuttgart, 2006), pp. 63–74; I.N. Wood, *The Missionary Life: Saints and the Evangelisation of Europe, 400–1050* (Harlow, 2001), pp. 39–42.

On Audoin of Rouen and his family: E. Dobler, 'Die Sippe des Grafen Audoin/Otwin: Fränkische Aristokraten des 7. und frühen 8. Jahrhunderts in Südalemannien', *Zeitschrift für die Geschichte des Oberrheins* 149 (2001), 1–60; H. Ebling, 'Burgundofarones', in *Lexikon des Mittelalters* (Munich, 1989), II, pp. 1098–9; P. Fouracre, 'The Work of Audoenus of Rouen and Eligius of Noyon in Extending Episcopal Influence from the Town and the Country in Seventh-Century Neustria', in D. Baker, ed., *The Church in Town and Countryside*, Studies in Church History 16 (1979), pp. 77–91; J. Guérout, 'Les origines et le premier siècle de l'abbaye', in Y. Chaussy et al., eds, *L'abbaye Notre-Dame de Jouarre* (Paris, 1961), pp. 1–67; idem, 'Le testament de sainte Fare, matériaux pour l'étude et l'édition critique de ce document', *Revue d'histoire ecclésiastique* 60 (1965), 761–821; J. Jarnut, *Agilolfingerstudien: Untersuchungen zur Geschichte einer adligen Familie im 6. Und 7. Jahrhundert* (Stuttgart, 1986), pp. 41–4, 125; R. Le Jan, 'Convents, Violence and Competition for Power in Francia', in M. de Jong and F. Theuws, eds, *Topographies of Power in the Early Middle Ages* (Leiden, Boston and Cologne, 2001), pp. 243–69; G. Scheibelreiter, 'Audoin von Rouen: ein Versuch über den Charakter des 7. Jahrhunderts', in H. Atsma, ed., *La Neustrie: les pays au nord de la Loire de 650 à 850* (Sigmaringen, 1989), I, pp. 195–216.

On Dido of Poitiers and Grimoald's coup d'état: M. Becher, 'Der soge-nannte Staatsstreich Grimoalds. Versuch einer Neubewertung, in J. Jarnut, ed., *Karl Martell in seiner Zeit*, Beihefte der Francia 37 (Sigmaringen, 1994), pp. 119–147; R.A. Gerberding, *The Rise of the Carolingians and the* Liber

248   *Further Reading*

Historiae Francorum (Oxford, 1987), pp. 47–66; S. Hamann, 'Zur Chronologie des Staatsstreich Grimoalds', *Deutsches Archiv* 59.1 (2003), 49–96; Y. Hen, 'Changing Places: Chrodobert, Boba, and the Wife of Grimoald', *Revue Belge de Philologie et d'Histoire* 90.2 (2012), 225–44; J.-M. Picard, 'Church and Politics in the Seventh Century: The Irish Exile of King Dagobert II', in J.-M. Picard, ed., *Ireland and Northern France, A.D. 600–850* (Dublin, 1991), pp. 27–52.

On Millebeccus, Longoretus, and the *Visio Baronti*: J.J. Contreni, 'Building Mansions in Heaven: the "Visio Baronti", Archangel Raphael and a Carolingian King', *Speculum* 78 (2003), 673–706; Y. Hen, 'The Structure and Aims of the Visio Baronti', *Journal of Theological Studies* 47 (1996), pp. 477–97.

On personal confession and tariffed penance as an 'Irish' invention: T.M. Charles-Edwards, 'The Penitential of Columbanus', in M. Lapidge, ed., *Columbanus: Studies on the Latin Writings* (Woodbridge, 1997), pp. 217–39; K. Dooley, 'From Penance to Confession: the Irish Contribution', *Bijdragen: Tijdschrift voor filosofie en theologie* 43 (1982), 390–411; M. de Jong, 'What was Public about Public Penance? Paenitentia publica and Justice in the Carolingian World', in *La guistizia nell'alto medioevo, vol. II: Secoli IX–XI = Settimane* 44 (1997), 863–902; eadem, 'Transformations of Penance', in F. Theuws and J.L. Nelson, eds, *Rituals of Power: From Late Antiquity to the Early Middle Ages* (Leiden, Boston and Cologne, 2000), pp. 185–224; R. Meens, *Penance in Medieval Europe, 600–1200* (Cambridge, 2014), pp. 70–100.

On *laus perennis* in Frankish monasteries: A. Diem, 'Who is allowed to pray for the king? Saint-Maurice d'Agaune and the Creation of a Burgundian Identity', in G. Heydemann and W. Pohl, eds, *Post-Roman Transitions: Christian and Barbarian Identities in the Early Medieval West*, Cultural Encounters in Late Antiquity and the Middle Ages 14 (Turnhout, 2013), pp. 47–88; F.S. Paxton, 'Power and the Power to Heal', *EME* 2 (1993), 95–110; B.H. Rosenwein, 'Perennial Prayer at Agaune', in S. Farmer and B.H. Rosenwein, eds, *Monks and Nuns, Saints and Outcasts: Religion in Medieval Society. Essays in Honor of Lester K. Little* (Ithaca, NY, and London, 2000), pp. 37–56; eadem, 'One Site, Many Meanings: Saint-Maurice d'Agaune as a Place of Power in the Early Middle Ages', in M. de Jong and F. Theuws, eds, *Topographies of Power in the Early Middle Ages* (Leiden, Boston and Cologne, 2001), pp. 271–90; J. Semmler, 'Saint-Denis: von der bischöflichen Coemeterialbasilika zur königlichen Benediktinerabtei', in H. Atsma, ed., *La Neustrie: les pays au nord de la Loire de 650 à 850*, 2 vols (Sigmaringen, 1989), II, pp. 75–123; I.N. Wood, 'The Burgundians and Byzantium', in A. Fischer and I.N. Wood, eds, *Western Perspectives on the Mediterranean: Cultural Transfer in Late Antiquity and the Early Middle Ages, 400–800 AD* (London and New York, 2014), pp. 1–16.

4   Columbanian Monastic Rules: Dissent and Experiment

The most widely used introductions to monastic history are Marilyn Dunn, *The Emergence of Monasticism. From the Desert Fathers to the Early Middle Ages* (Oxford, 2000); C.H. Lawrence, *Medieval Monasticism. Forms of Religious Life in Western Europe in the Middle Ages* (London and New York, 1984); Friedrich

Prinz, *Frühes Mönchtum im Frankenreich. Kultur und Gesellschaft in Gallien, den Rheinlanden und Bayern am Beispiel der monastischen Entwicklung (4. bis 8. Jhd.)*, 2nd ed. (Darmstadt, 1988). All of these need to be read cautiously against more recent insights on the topics discussed here. An exhaustive bibliography on early medieval monasticism can be found on www.earlymedievalmonasticism.org/bibliographymonasticism.htm.

A first access to monastic rules is Adalbert de Vogüé, *Les règles monastiques anciennes (400–700)*, Typologie des Sources 46 (Turnhout, 1985) and his multi-volume *Histoire littéraire du mouvement monastique dans l'antiquité* (Paris, 1991–2008). A new assessment of the sources is Albrecht Diem and Philip Rousseau, 'Monastic Rules, 4th–9th c.', forthcoming in Alison Beach and Isabelle Cochelin, eds, *The Cambridge History of Western Medieval Monasticism*, vol. 1 (Cambridge, 2016).

Editions of the Columbanian monastic rules discussed in this article: G.S.M. Walker, *Sancti Columbani Opera* (Dublin, 1957), pp. 122–68; Adalbert de Vogüé, 'La règle de Donat pour l'abbesse Gauthstrude', *Benedictina* 25 (1978), 219–313; Fernando Villegas, 'La "Regula cuiusdam Patris ad monachos". Ses sources littéraires et ses rapports avec la "Regula monachorum" de Colomban', *Revue d'Histoire de la Spiritualité* 49 (1973), 3–36 and 135–44. I am currently preparing a new edition of the *Regula cuiusdam ad virgines*. New editions of the *Regula Donati* and the Columbanian rule fragments appeared in CSEL 98 *Monastica*, vol. 1. Translations of the Irish monastic rules are available in Uinseann Ó Maidín, *The Celtic Monk. Rules and Writings of Early Irish Monks* (Kalamazoo, 1996). Most earlier monastic rules are edited with a French translation in the *Sources chrétiennes*. For the manuscript transmission of monastic rules, see www.earlymedievalmonasticism.org.

The best introduction to the works of Columbanus is *Columbanus. Studies on the Latin Writings*, ed. Michael Lapidge (Woodbridge, 1997).

Studies on Columbanian monastic rules: Albrecht Diem, 'Das Ende des monastischen Experiments. Liebe, Beichte und Schweigen in der *regula cuiusdam ad virgines* (mit einer Übersetzung im Anhang)', in Gert Melville and Anne Müller, eds, *Female vita religiosa between Late Antiquity and the High Middle Ages. Structures, Developments and Spatial Contexts* (Münster and Berlin, 2011), pp. 81–136; Albrecht Diem, 'New Ideas Expressed in Old Words: The *Regula Donati* on Female Monastic Life and Monastic Spirituality', *Viator* 43 (2012), 1–38; A. Diem and M. van der Meer, *Columbanische Klosterregeln. Regula cuiusdam patris, Regula cuiusdam ad virgines, Regelfragment De accedendo* (Sankt Ottilien, 2016); A. Diem, 'Disputing Columbanus' Heritage: The *Regula cuiusdam patris*', forthcoming in: A. O'Hara, ed., *Meeting the Gentes – Crossing Boundaries: Columbanus and the Peoples of Post-Roman Europe* (Oxford, 2016) (with an English translation of the *Regula cuiusdam ad virgines*); B. Dumézil, 'L'affaire Agrestius de Luxeuil: hérésie et régionalisme dans la Burgondie du VIIe siècle', *Médiévales* 52 (2007), 135-152; G. Muschiol, *Famula Dei. Zur Liturgie in merowingischen Frauenklöstern* (Münster, 1994). Eoin de Bhaldraithe, 'Obedience: The Doctrine of Irish Monastic Rules', *Monastic Studies* 14 (1983), pp. 63–84.

5   Columbanian Monasticism: a Contested Concept

Little attention was paid to Columbanus or Columbanian monasticism before the nineteenth century. The main exceptions were the publications of Columbanus' works by Patrick Fleming in *Collectanea Sacra* (Louvain, 1667) and Jean Mabillon's edition of much of the relevant hagiography, in L. d'Achery and J. Mabillon, *Acta sanctorum ordinis sancti Benedicti in seculorum classes distributa, saeculum II* (Paris, 1669). Not surprisingly the saint's own works have since appeared in a better edition, by G.S.M. Walker, *Sancti Columbani Opera* (Dublin, 1957), which has a facing-page translation, while the edition by Bruno Krusch of the Life by Jonas, in B. Krusch, *Ionae Vitae Sanctorum, Monumenta Germaniae Historica, Scriptores Rerum Germanicarum* (Hanover, 1905), was a major step forward, although Krusch did not know the earliest surviving manuscript, for which one has to consult M. Tosi, *Vita Columbani et discipulorum eius* (Piacenza, 1965). There is, as yet, no full translation into English, and none of the translations of sections of the work are flawless: most of Book One was translated by D.C. Munro, *The Life of St. Columban by the Monk Jonas*, 2nd edn (Philadelphia, 1895); the chapters on Bobbio were translated by Ian Wood in T. Head, ed., *Medieval Hagiography, An Anthology* (New York, 2000), pp. 111–35; the section on Faremoutiers was translated (somewhat freely) by Jo Ann McNamara, in *Sainted Women of the Dark Ages* (Durham and London, 1992), pp. 155–75. There are translations into Italian (by Tosi, in his edition of the text), and into French by Adalbert de Vogüé, *Vie de saint Colomban et de ses disciples* (Abbaye de Bellefontaine, 1988), which cannot be recommended for anything other than its notes.

Discussion of Columbanian monasticism largely originated with A.F. Ozanam, *Études germaniques pour servir à l'histoire des Francs*, vol. II, *La civilisation chrétienne chez les Francs* (Paris, 1849), and C.F.R. de Montalembert, *Les moines d'Occident* (Paris, 1860). The other major contribution to the debate in the nineteenth century was A. Malnory, *Quid Luxovienses Monachi discipuli ad regulam monasteriorum atque ad commune ecclesiae profectum contulerint* (Paris, 1894).

In the early twentieth century little of significance was added to the work of Ozanam, Montalembert and Malnory. The best general statement in the middle of the century came with Ludwig Bieler, *Ireland, Harbinger of the Middle Ages* (Oxford, 1966). Of more historiographical significance was F. Prinz, *Frühes Mönchtum im Frankenreich* (Kempten, 1965), which set out, sometimes overenthusiastically, the networks of early medieval monasticism, not least of Luxeuil. This was refined by H. Atsma, 'Les monastères urbains du Nord de la Gaule', *Revue d'Histoire de l'Église de France* 62 (1976), pp. 163–87.

Among general histories of early medieval monasticism since Prinz the work that has argued most forcefully for the significance of Columbanian monasticism is M. Dunn, *The Emergence of Monasticism: From Desert Fathers to the Early Middle Ages* (Oxford, 2000). Albrecht Diem's *Das monastische Experiment. Die Rolle der Keuschheit bei der Entstehung des westlichen*

Klosterwesens (Münster, 2005) has much to say about Columbanus, as do numerous of his articles, the most important of which for Columbanian studies is 'Was bedeutet *Vita Columbani*', in W. Pohl and M. Diesenberger, eds, *Integration und Herrschaft. Ethnische Identitäten und soziale Organisation im Frühmittelalter* (Vienna, 2002), pp. 63–89.

Other important statements in general works are to be found in T.M. Charles-Edwards, *Early Christian Ireland* (Cambridge, 2000), and Peter Brown, *The Rise of Western Christendom*, 2nd edn (Oxford, 2003). Although Columbanus had little impact on Ireland, Charles-Edwards devotes a whole chapter to the saint and his disciples.

Few monographs have dealt with Columbanus, although Michael Richter's *Ireland and its Neighbours in the Seventh Century* (Dublin, 1999) had a good deal to say about the Irish saint, as did his *Bobbio in the Early Middle Ages. The abiding legacy of Columbanus* (Dublin, 2008), both of which set out a maximalist interpretation of the saint's impact. The most recent monograph to deal with Columbanus, which constitutes a major statement on the patronage of the monasteries and their position in society is Y. Fox, *Power and Religion in Merovingian Gaul. Columbanian Monasticism and the Frankish Elite* (Cambridge, 2014). It also boasts a very up-to-date bibliography.

Most of the significant work on Columbanian monasticism in recent years has been in articles. There is the collection edited by H.B. Clarke and M. Brennan, *Columbanus and Merovingian Monasticism* (Oxford, 1981), which marked a milestone in Columbanian studies. There are also important pieces in H. Löwe, ed., *Die Iren und Europa im früheren Mittelalter*, 2 vols. (Sigmaringen, 1982). More recent is the collection edited by Michael Lapidge, *Columbanus: Studies on the Latin Writings* (Woodbridge, 1997), which includes articles by a high proportion of the scholars who have worked on Columbanus since the closing decades of the twentieth century, among them Thomas Charles-Edwards and Clare Stancliffe.

The most sustained series of articles from a single scholar has undoubtedly been Eugen Ewig's studies on monastic immunities, which have been conveniently collected in his *Spätantikes und Fränkisches Gallien*, 2 vols. (Munich, 1976–9), II, pp. 411–583. The issue of immunities has been examined most fully in recent years by Barbara Rosenwein, *Negotiating Space. Power, Restraint, and Privileges of Immunity in Early Medieval Europe* (Ithaca, 1999).

On Jonas there have been studies by Ian Wood ('The *Vita Columbani* and Merovingian Hagiography', *Peritia* 1 (1982), 63–80, and 'Jonas, the Merovingians and Pope Honorius: *Diplomata* and the *Vita Columbani*', in A.C. Murray, ed., *After Rome's Fall: Narrators and Sources of Early Medieval History* (Toronto, 1998), pp. 99–120). Particularly important for the text of Jonas and for previous arguments about it, is Clare Stancliffe's 'Jonas's *Life of Columbanus and his Disciples*', in J. Carey, M. Herbert and P. Ó Riain, eds, *Studies in Irish Hagiography: Saints and Scholars* (Dublin, 2001), pp. 189–220. The most recent contribution has been A. O'Hara, 'The *Vita Columbani* in Merovingian Gaul', *EME* 17 (2009), pp. 126–53.

6   Columbanus and the Easter Controversy: Theological, Social and Political Contexts

Until the discovery of the *Latercus* in 1984, historians were not sure of the exact calculations used by the Irish in Columbanus's period. Older reconstructions, then, have been replaced by more accurate information. For discussion of the *Latercus* see Daniel Mc Carthy, 'On the Arrival of the *Latercus* in Ireland', in Immo Warrntjes and Dáibhí Ó Cróinín, eds, *The Easter Controversy of Late Antiquity and the Early Middle Ages*, Studia Traditionis Theologiae 10 (Turnhout, 2011) pp. 48–75; Daniel Mc Carthy and Dáibhí Ó Cróinín, 'The "Lost" Irish 84-Year Easter Table Rediscovered', *Peritia* 6–7 (1987–88), 227–42. Corrections and adjustments in Daniel Mc Carthy, 'Easter Principles and a Lunar Cycle Used by Fifth Century Christian Communities in the British Isles', *Journal for the History of Astronomy* 24 (1993), 204–24; Immo Warntjes 'The Munich Computus and the 84 (14)-year Easter Reckoning', *PRIA* 107C (2007), 31–85. For Irish support of the Victorian table see Maura Walsh and Dáibhí Ó Cróinín, ed. and trans., *Cummian's Letter De Controversia Paschali Together with a Related Irish Computistical Tract De Ratione Computandi* (Toronto: 1988).

For general studies of the Easter controversy see Bonnie Blackburn and Leofranc Holford-Strevens, *The Oxford Companion to the Year* (Oxford, 1999); Alden Mosshamer, *The Easter Computus and the Origins of the Christian Era* (Oxford, 2008); Dáibhí Ó Cróinín, *Early Irish History and Chronology* (Dublin, 2003); Bede, *The Reckoning of Time*, ed. and trans. Faith Wallis (Liverpool, 1999); Immo Warntjes, *The Munich Computus: Text and Translation: Irish Computistics between Isidore of Seville and the Venerable Bede and its Reception in Carolingian Times* (Stuttgart, 2010).

7   Irish Biblical Exegesis

Introduction

The study of exegesis in the early Middle Ages sometimes falls between two scholarly stools: the period is at the very end of patristic studies, which often takes Bede as the final father, and at the very beginning of scholarship on medieval exegesis, which tends to focus on the High Middle Ages. Charles Kannengiesser's *Handbook of Patristic Exegesis* (Leiden, 2006) is a comprehensive survey of the earlier period with up-to-date bibliography, but has its shortcomings, as pointed out in the review by L. Ayres, *Journal of Early Christian Studies* 13 (2005), 532–6. The latest work on early medieval exegesis is found in articles and edited collections, such as those by Claudio Leonardi and Giovanni Orlandi, *Biblical Studies in the Early Middle Ages. Proceedings of the Conference on Biblical Studies in the Early Middle Ages* (Florence, 2005); and Pierre Riché and Guy Lobrichon, *Le Moyen Âge et la Bible*, Bible de touts les temps 4 (Paris, 1984). Henning Graf Reventlow's *Epochen der Bibelauslegung II: Von der Spätantike bis zum ausgehenden Mittelalter* (Munich, 1994) and Magne Sæbø's *Hebrew Bible/Old Testament. The History of*

Its Interpretation. I/2: *The Middle Ages* (Göttingen, 2000) have some material on the early Middle Ages. The review article on *Epochen der Bibelauslegung*, 'Zur Geschichte der Bibelauslegung' by Ulrich Köpf in the *International Journal of the Classical Tradition* 15 (2008), 98–126, raises many interesting general questions about the history of exegesis.

Friedrich Stegmüller's inventory of the manuscript sources, *Repertorium Biblicum Medii Aevi* I–XI (Madrid, 1950–1980), remains invaluable and a searchable version is now online at http://repbib.uni-trier.de/cgi-bin/rebi-home.tcl but the interface is only in German. For the bible as book, see Richard Gameson's *The Early Medieval Bible: Its Production, Decoration, and Use* (Cambridge, 1994), as well as Richard Marsden's *Text of the Old Testament in Anglo-Saxon England* (Cambridge, 1995), which is valuable not only for the insular world.

Older surveys are still worth consulting, especially Beryl Smalley's *Study of the Bible in the Middle Ages* first published in 1941 (last revised edition (the third) Oxford, 1983) and Ceslas Spicq's *Esquisse d'une histoire de l'exégèse latine au Moyen Âge* (Paris, 1944). Henri de Lubac's *Exégèse médiévale. Les quatre sens de l'Ecriture*. Vol. I.1–2; II.1–2 (Paris, 1959–64) is often cited and offers many valuable insights, but its focus on the four senses of scripture can seem anachronistic for works of our period. It has been partially translated in *Medieval Exegesis. The Four Senses of Scripture*, trans. E. M. Macierowski and M. Sebanc, 3 vols (Edinburgh, 1998–2009).

Irish Exegesis and its Study

The early response to Bischoff's 'Wendepunkte' article included Clare Stancliffe's excellent 'Early "Irish" Biblical Exegesis', *Studia Patristica* 12 (1975) (= *Texte und Untersuchungen zur Geschichte der altchristlichen Literatur* 115, ed. Elizabeth Livingstone), 361–70, and Joseph F. Kelly's 'Catalogue of Early Medieval Hiberno-Latin Biblical Commentaries (I and II)', *Traditio* 44 (1988), 537–71; and 45 (1989), pp. 393–434.

But then two articles by Michael Gorman that were critical of the thesis provoked a vigorous response. Gorman's articles are: 'A Critique of Bischoff's Theory of Irish Exegesis: The Commentary on Genesis in Munich CLM 6302 (*Wendepunkte* 2)', *Journal of Medieval Latin* 7 (1997), 178–233, and 'The Myth of Hiberno-Latin Exegesis', *Revue Bénédictine* 110 (2000), 42–85. The response began with one article by Gabriel Silagi, 'Notwendige Bemerkungen zu Gormans "Critique of Bischoff's Theory of Irish Exegesis"', *Peritia* 12 (1998), 87–94, then continued with one article by Charles D. Wright, 'Bischoff's Theory of Irish Exegesis and the Genesis Commentary in Munich Clm 6302: A Critique of a Critique', *The Journal of Medieval Latin* 10 (2000), 115–75, and two articles by Dáibhí Ó Cróinín, '*Wendepunkte* 50 years on', *Revue Bénédictine* 110 (2000), 204–37 and 'A New Seventh-Century Irish Commentary on Genesis', *Sacris Erudiri* 40 (2001), 231–65. See also Michael Herren's 'Irish Biblical Commentaries before 800', in *Roma, Magistra Mundi. Itineraria Culturae Medieualis. Mélanges offerts au Père L.E. Boyle a l'occasion de son 75ème anniversaire* (Louvain, 1998), pp. 391–407. Gorman's articles on exegesis are collected in *Biblical Comentaries from the Early Middle Ages*, Millennio Medievale 32; Reprints 4 (Florence, 2002).

Kelly continued his work with 'Bede and the Irish Exegetical Tradition on the Apocalypse', *Revue Benedictine* 92 (1982), 393–406; 'Frigulus: An Hiberno-Latin Commentator on Matthew', *Revue Benedictine* 91 (1981), 363–73; 'Hiberno-Latin Exegesis and Exegetes', *Annuale Mediaevale* 22 (1981), 46–60; 'The Bible in Early Medieval Ireland', in David Hunter, ed., *Preaching in the Patristic Age: Studies in Honor of Walter Burghardt, S.J.* (New York, 1989), pp. 198–214.

Martin McNamara wrote a series of books and articles emphasizing the theological dimension of bible study, including, 'A Plea for Hiberno-Latin Biblical Studies', *Irish Theological Quarterly* 39 (1972), 337–53; *The Apocrypha in the Irish Church* (Dublin, 1975); 'Psalter Text and Psalter Study in the Early Irish Church (AD 600–1200)', *PRIA* 71C (1973), 201–98; *Studies on Texts of Early Irish Latin Gospels (AD 600–1200)*, Instrumenta Patristica 20 (Steenbrugge, 1990); and *The Psalms in the Early Irish Church*, Journal for the Study of the Old Testament Supplement Series 165 (Sheffield, 2000). Twenty-one essays are collected in *The Bible and the Apocrypha in the Early Medieval Church (A.D. 600-1200)*, Instrumenta Patristica 66 (Steenbrugge, 2015).

Pádraig Ó Néill has made important contributions, including 'The Old-Irish Treatise on the Psalter and Its Hiberno-Latin Background', *Ériu* 30 (1979), 148–64; 'The Earliest Dry-Point Glosses in Codex Usserianus Primus', in Toby Barnard, Dáibhí Ó Cróinín and Katharine Simms, eds, '*A Miracle of Learning': Studies in Manuscripts and Irish Learning: Essays in Honour of William O'Sullivan* (Ashgate, 1998), pp. 1–28; 'Irish Transmission of Late Antique Learning: the Case of Theodore of Mopsuestia's Commentary on the Psalms', *Texte und Überlieferung* (2002), 68–77; and *Biblical Study and Mediaeval Gaelic History*, Quiggin Pamphlets on the Sources of Mediaeval Gaelic History 6 (Cambridge, 2003).

Finally, Thomas O'Loughlin's collection *The Scriptures and Early Medieval Ireland, Proceedings of the 1993 Conference of the Society for Hiberno-Latin Studies on Early Irish Exegesis and Homiletics*, Instrumenta Patristica 31 (Brepols, 1999).

Current and Future Work

Michael Cahill's 'The Turin Glosses on Mark: Towards a Cultural Profile of the Glossator', *Peritia* 13 (1999), 173–93. The relationship between images and exegesis has been insightfully investigated by Jennifer O'Reilly in 'Exegesis and the Book of Kells: the Lucan Genealogy', in Felicity O'Mahony, ed., *The Book of Kells: Proceedings of a Conference at Trinity College Dublin 6–9 September 1992* (Aldershot, 1994), pp. 344–97; and 'The Image of Orthodoxy, the *mysterium Christi* and Insular Gospel Books', in *L'irlanda e gli irlandesi nell'alto medioevo* = *Settimane* 57 (2010), 651–72. In a similar vein are Christoph Eggenberger's 'Das Psalterbild als Exegese', in *Testo e immagine nell'alto medioevo* = *Settimane* 41 (1994), 773–800; and Lawrence Nees's 'Words and Images, Texts and Commentaries', in Colum Hourihane, ed., *Irish Art Historical Studies in Honour of Peter Harbison* (Dublin, 2004), pp. 47–69. Finally, Tomás O'Sullivan looked at the relationship between exegesis and hagiography in 'The Miraculous Production of Water from Rock and the Impact of Exegesis on Early Irish Hagiography', *Eolas* 3 (2009), pp. 19–50.

8   The Irish Contribution to the Penitential Tradition

Insular penitentials are easily available in Ludwig Bieler, ed. and trans., *The Irish Penitentials*, Scriptores Latini Hiberniae 5 (Dublin, 1963). This should be supplemented with the edition of the *Paenitentiale Ambrosianum* in Ludger Körntgen, *Studien zu den Quellen der frühmittelalterlichen Bußbücher*. Quellen und Forschungen zum Recht im Mittelalter 7 (Sigmaringen 1993). For a detailed study of the penitential of Columbanus, see Thomas Charles-Edwards, 'The penitential of Columbanus', in *Columbanus. Studies on the Latin Writings*, ed. Michael Lapidge (Woodbridge, 1997), pp. 217–39. Editions of continental penitentials, often influenced by insular material, have been published as *Paenitentialia Franciae, Italiae et Hispaniae saeculi VIII–XI*, CCSL 156 (Turnhout, 1994) and in Rob Meens, *Het tripartite boeteboek. Overlevering en betekenis van vroegmiddeleeuwse biechtvoorschriften (met editie en vertaling van vier tripartita)* (Hilversum, 1994). A more widely available, albeit somewhat dated, translation of a good number of insular and continental penitentials is John McNeill and Helena Gamer, trans., *Medieval Handbooks of Penance. A Translation of the Principal Libri poenitentiales and Selections from Related Documents* (New York, 1938).

Recent studies on early medieval penance are Sarah Hamilton, *The Practice of Penance, 900–1050* (London, 2001) and Rob Meens, *Penance in Medieval Europe, 600–1200* (Cambridge, 2014). On medieval penance and penitentials more generally, see Allen Frantzen, *The Literature of Penance in Anglo-Saxon England* (New Brunswick, N.J., 1983); Abigail Firey, ed., *A New History of Penance* (Leiden, 2008).

For an overview of the dissemination of insular penitential texts, see R. Kottje, 'Überlieferung und Rezeption der irischen Bußbücher auf dem Kontinent', in *Die Iren und Europa im früheren Mittelalter*, ed. H. Löwe, 2 vols (Stuttgart, 1982), I, pp. 511–24. More specialised studies on insular penitentials and the interface between early Anglo-Saxon and Irish penitential teachings, are Thomas M. Charles-Edwards, 'The Penitential of Theodore and the Iudicia Theodori', in *Archbishop Theodore: Commemorative Studies on his Life and Influence*, ed. M. Lapidge (Cambridge, 1995), 141–74; Roy Flechner, 'The Making of the Canons of Theodore', *Peritia* 17–18 (2003–2004), pp. 121–43.

On penance and the performance of political power, see Mayke De Jong, *The Penitential State: Authority and Atonement in the Age of Louis the Pious, 814–840* (Cambridge, 2009); Levi Roach, 'Public Rites and Public Wrongs: Ritual Aspects of Diplomas in Tenth- and Eleventh-Century England', *Early Medieval Europe* 19 (2011), pp. 182–203.

9   The Liturgy of the Irish on the Continent

The best introduction to early medieval liturgy and its sources is still Cyrille Vogel, *Medieval Liturgy: An Introduction*, trans. and rev. William Storey and Niels Rasmussen (Washington DC, 1986). See also Éric Palazzo, *A History of Liturgical Books from the Beginning to the Thirteenth Century*, trans. M. Beaumont (Collegeville, 1998); A.A. King, *Liturgies of the Past* (London, 1959). For a survey and catalogue of liturgical manuscripts, see *Codices liturgici latini antiquiores*, ed. Klaus Gamber, 2nd ed., 2 vols., Spicilegii Friburgensis subsidia 1 (Freiburg, 1968); supplemented by B. Baroffio et al., Spicilegii Friburgensis subsidia 1A (Freiburg, 1988). One should note that Gamber's analysis and typology are in many cases out of date and in need of revision according to modern scholarship.

On the liturgy of early medieval Gaul, see Yitzhak Hen, *Culture and Religion in Merovingian Gaul, AD 481–751* (Leiden, New York and Köln, 1995); idem, *The Royal Patronage of Liturgy in Frankish Gaul to the Death of Charles the Bald (877)*, HBS, Subsidia 3 (London, 2001); Philippe Bernard, *Du chant romain au chant grégorien (VIe–XIIIe siècle)* (Paris, 1996); Matthieu Smyth, *La liturgie oubliée: la prière eucharistique en Gaule antique et dans l'Occident non romain* (Paris, 2003).

The best study of the early Irish liturgy is Neil X. O'Donoghue, *The Eucharist in Pre-Norman Ireland* (Notre Dame, 2011). See also Yitzhak Hen, 'The Nature and Character of the Early Irish Liturgy', in *L'Irlanda e gli Irlandesi nell'alto medioevo = Settimane 57* (Spoleto, 2010), pp. 353–80. Some of the older studies of the Irish liturgy are still extremely useful; see, for example, Frederick E. Warren, *The Liturgy and Ritual of the Early Irish Church* (Oxford, 1881); reprinted with a lengthy new introduction by Jane Stevenson (Woodbridge, 1987); reprinted again with a short preface and updated bibliography by Neil X. O'Donoghue (Piscataway NJ, 2010); James F. Kenney, *The Sources for the Early History of Ireland, I: Ecclesiastical* (New York, 1929), rev. by Ludwig Bieler (Dublin, 1966); Louis Gougard, *Christianity in Celtic Lands: A History of the Churches of the Celts, their Origin, their Development, Influence and Mutual Relations*, trans. Maud Joynt (London, 1932; reprinted with an introduction by Jean-Michel Picard, Dublin, 1992); Mark Schneiders, 'The Origins of the Early Irish Liturgy', in Próinséas Ní Chatháin and Michael Richter, eds, *Ireland and Europe in the Early Middle Ages: Learning and Literature* (Stuttgart, 1996), pp. 76–98.

10   Computus as Scientific Thought in Ireland and the Early Medieval West

A general study of the reckoning of Easter in Late Antiquity is A.A. Mosshammer, *The Easter Computus and the Origins of the Christian Era* (Oxford, 2008). The contributions of Irish and Anglo-Saxon scholars to the study of mathematical knowledge, in particular in the area of computus, at the courts of Charlemagne and Louis the Pious are discussed by P.L. Butzer and K.W. Butzer, 'Mathematics at Charlemagne's Court and its Transmission', in C. Cubitt, ed., *Court Culture in the Early Middle Ages: The Proceedings of the First Alcuin Conference*, Studies in the Early Middle Ages, 3 (Turnhout, 2003), pp. 77–89. On the influential scientific learning – and especially computus – from Anglo-Saxon England, see F. Wallis, trans., *Bede: The Reckoning of Time* (Liverpool, 1999), pp. xv–lxxi; F. Wallis, 'Bede and Science', in S. DeGregorio, ed., *The Cambridge Companion to Bede* (Cambridge, 2010), pp. 113–26; B. Kendall and F. Wallis, trans., *Bede: On the Nature of Things and On Times* (Liverpool, 2012), pp. 20–32; Hollis, 'Anglo-Saxon Secular Learning and the Vernacular: An Overview', *Amsterdamer Beiträge zur älteren Germanistik* 69 (2012), 1–43. An aspect of the influence of Bede's scientific knowledge on an Irishman settled on the Continent is discussed in J.J. Contreni, 'John Scottus and Bede', in J. McEvoy and M. Dunne, eds, *History and Eschatology in John Scottus Eriugena and his Time* (Louvain, 2002), pp. 91–140. On the study of the natural world in Ireland and its intersection with biblical scholarship, see M. Smyth, *Understanding the Universe in Seventh-Century Ireland* (Woodbridge, 1996). The significance of the oldest known geography from Carolingian Europe by the Irishman Dicuil is considered by W. Bermann, Werner 'Dicuil's *De Mensura Orbis Terrae*', in P.L. Butzer, ed., *Science in Western and Eastern Civilization in Carolingian Times* (Basel, 1993), pp. 525–37. The *De Mensura Orbis Terrae* is edited with translation by J. J. Tierney, *Dicuili Liber de Mensura Orbis Terrae*, Scriptores Latini Hiberniae 6 (Dublin, 1967). An introduction to the *Periphyseon*, the important work by the celebrated Irishman at Charlemagne's court, John Scottus Eriugena, which combines scientific and theological thinking, is D.W. Hadley and C. Steel, 'John Scotus Eriugena', in J.J.E. Gracia and T.B. Noone, eds, *A Companion to Philosophy in the Middle Ages*. Blackwell Companions to Philosophy, 24 (Oxford, 2003), pp. 397–406. The four books of the *Periphyseon* are edited with translation by I.P. Sheldon-Williams (but book IV ed. by É.A. Jeauneau and trans. by J.J. O'Meara), *Iohannis Scotti Eriugenae Periphyseon*, Scriptores Latini Hiberniae 7, 9, 11, 13 (Dublin, 1968–95).

On the Easter controversy underlying the present chapter, see C. Corning, *The Celtic and Roman Traditions: Conflict and Consensus in the Early Medieval Church* (New York, 2006); as corrective, see I. Warntjes, 'Victorius vs Dionysius: the Irish Easter Controversy of AD 689', in P. Moran and I. Warntjes, eds, *Early Medieval Ireland and Europe: Chronology, Contacts, Scholarship* (Turnhout, 2014), pp. 33–97. The classic work on early medieval computistical thought is C.W. Jones, *Bedae Opera de Temporibus* (Cambridge, 1943), pp. 3–139; for the Irish contribution see various publications by Dáibhí Ó Cróinín collected in his *Early Irish History and* Chronology (Dublin, 2003); I. Warntjes, *The Munich Computus: Text and Translation. Irish Computistics between Isidore of Seville and the Venerable Bede and its Reception in Carolingian Times* (Stuttgart, 2010); and more nuanced I. Warntjes, 'Seventh-Century Ireland: the Cradle of medieval Science?', in M. Kelly and C.

Doherty, eds, *Music and the Stars: Mathematics in Medieval Ireland* (Dublin, 2013), pp. 44–72.

11   Irish Scholars and Carolingian Learning

For a good overview of western Europe in the Carolingian period, see Marios Costambeys, Matthew Innes and Simon MacLean, *The Carolingian World*, Cambridge Medieval Textbooks (Cambridge, 2011), which has curiously little to say about learning. For this, see John J. Contreni, 'The Carolingian Renaissance: Education and Literary Culture', in Rosamond McKitterick, ed., *The New Cambridge Medieval History, volume 2: c. 700–c. 900* (Cambridge, 1995), pp. 709–57. On the role of grammar in the Carolingian revival of learning, see the works of Vivian Law, the most relevant of which are collected in her *Grammar and Grammarians in the Early Middle Ages* (London and New York, 1997). On written culture more in general, see Rosamond McKitterick, *The Carolingians and the Written Word* (Cambridge, 1989). The position of literacy and written culture in Irish learning is discussed very lucidly in Elva Johnston's *Literacy and Identity in Early Medieval Ireland* (Woodbridge, 2013).

Anyone working on Irish scholars on the Continent will start with the now outdated but still crucial work by James F. Kenney, *The Sources for the Early History of Ireland: Ecclesiastical. An Introduction and Guide* (New York, 1929; 2nd edn), in particular pp. 486–744. Many aspects of Irish intellectual influence on continental learning are more recently studied in the contributions of Heinz Löwe, ed., *Die Iren und Europa im früheren Mittelalter*, 2 vols. (Stuttgart, 1982); Próinséas Ní Chatháin and Michael Richter, eds, *Irland und Europa: die Kirche im Frühmittelalter / Ireland and Europe: The Early Church* (Stuttgart, 1984); Próinséas Ní Chatháin and Michael Richter, eds, *Irland und die Christenheit: Bibelstudien und Mission / Ireland and Christendom: The Bible and the Missions* (Stuttgart, 1987); Próinseas Ní Chatháin and Michael Richter (eds), *Ireland and Europe in the Early Middle Ages: Texts and Transmission / Irland und Europa im früheren Mittelalter: Texte und Überlieferung* (Dublin, 2002). A discussion of insular men at Charlemagne's court is found in Mary Garrison, 'The English and the Irish at the Court of Charlemagne', in P.L. Butzer, M. Kerner, and W. Oberschelp, eds, *Charlemagne and his Heritage: 1200 Years of Civilization and Science in Europe* (Turnhout, 1997), pp. 97–123.

There has been no accessible overview of Sedulius's life and career since Siegmund Hellmann, *Sedulius Scottus* (Munich, 1906), although more recent work has produced new insights. For these, see Nikolaus Staubach, 'Sedulius Scottus und die Gedichte des Codex Bernensis 363', *Frühmittelalterliche Studien: Jahrbuch des Instituts für Frühmittelalterforschung der Universität Münster* 20 (1986), 549–98. There are a few biographical works on Eriugena, including John J. O'Meara, *Eriugena* (Oxford, 1988). For him and Martin Hiberniensis, see John J. Contreni, 'John Scottus, Martin Hiberniensis, the Liberal Arts and Teaching', in Michael Herren, ed., *Insular Latin Studies*, Papers in Mediaeval Studies (Toronto, 1981), pp. 23–44.

12 Controversies and Ethnic Tensions

There has been much recent interest in the history of alterity and 'otherness', reflecting modern society's struggle with it. For our period the work of Walter Pohl is prominent, see for instance his 'Introduction: Ethnicity, Religion and Empire', in Walter Pohl, Clemens Gantner and Richard Payne, eds, *Visions of Community in the Post-Roman World: The West, Byzantium and the Islamic World, 300–1000* (Farnham, 2012), pp. 1–23; and 'Introduction: Strategies of Identification: a Methodological Profile', in Walter Pohl and Gerda Heydemann, eds, *Strategies of Identification: Ethnicity and Religion in Early Medieval Europe*, Cultural Encounters in Late Antiquity and the Middle Ages 13 (Turnhout, 2013), pp. 1–64. Alternative views are presented in Andrew Gillett, ed., *Barbarian Identity: Critical Approaches to Ethnicity in the Early Middle Ages* (Turnhout, 2002).

The complete writings of Columbanus, including letters and texts of monastic discipline, are available in G.S.M. Walker, ed. and trans., *Sancti Columbani Opera*, Scriptores Latini Hiberniae 2 (Dublin, 1957). The standard edition of the Life of Columbanus by Jonas is *Vita Columbani discipulorumque eius*, MGH SS. rer. Germ. 37, ed. B. Krusch (Hanover, 1910), pp. 1–294. This edition artificially fuses two parts that had been transmitted independently. A translation of the first part of the Life is by D.C. Munro, *Life of St Columban by the Monk Jonas* (Philadelphia, 1895; repr. Felinfach, 1993). The literature on Columbanus is quite substantial. What follows is a selection of both recent studies and studies that are pertinent to this chapter. For Columbanus's biography and activities on the Continent, including controversies, see Dáibhí Ó Cróinín, *Early Christian Ireland 400–1200* (Harlow, 1995), pp. 199–203; Donald Bullough, 'The Career of Columbanus', in *Columbanus: Studies on the Latin Writings*, ed. M. Lapidge (Woodbridge, 1997), pp. 1–28; Rob Meens, 'Columbanus', in *Oxford Dictionary of National Biography* (Oxford, 2004) [http://www.oxforddnb.com/view/article/6002, accessed 30 July 2015]; Tommaso Leso, 'Columbanus in Europe: the Evidence from the Epistulae', *EME* 21 (2013), 358–89. On Columbanus and the Merovingian aristocracy, see F. Prinz, 'Columbanus, the Frankish Nobility and the Territories East of the Rhine', in H.B. Clark and M. Brennan, eds, *Columbanus and Merovingian Monasticism* (Oxford, 1981), pp. 73–87. Ian N. Wood, 'The Irish and Social Subversion in the Early Middle Ages', in *Irland, Gesellschaft und Kultur*, ed. D. Siegmund-Schultze (Halle, 1989), pp. 263–70, offers a brief discussion of hagiographical representations of Irish 'subversive' behaviour, consisting mainly of behaving irreverently to royalty, as Columbanus is said to have done. He compares this to similar behaviour by native clergy in Francia.

Boniface's letters are edited by M. Tangl, *Die Briefen des heiligen Bonifatius und Lullus*, MGH Epp. Sel. 1 (Berlin, 1916) and translated by Ephraim Emerton, *The Letters of Saint Boniface* (2nd edn, New York, 2000). The literature on Boniface is extensive. Recent publications on Boniface's career are Michael Glatthaar, *Bonifatius und das Sakrileg: Zur politischen Dimension eines Rechtsbegriffs*, Freiburger Beiträge zur Mittelalterlichen Geschichte 17

(Frankfurt am Main, 2004); and John-Henry Clay, *In the Shadow of Death: St Boniface and the Conversion of Hessia, 721–754* (Turnhout, 2010). Boniface's dealings with the heretics Clemens and Aldebert is discussed in Nicole Zeddies, 'Bonifatius und zwei nützliche Rebellen: die Häretiker Aldebert und Clemens', in Marie Theres Fögen, ed., *Ordnung und Aufruhr im Mittelalter: Historische und juristische Studien zur Rebellion*, Ius Commune, Sonderhefte (Frankfurt am Main, 1995), pp. 217–63; Matthew Innes, '"Immune from Heresy": Defining the Boundaries of Carolingian Christianity', in D. Ganz and P. Fouracre, eds, *Frankland: The Franks and the World of Early Medieval Europe* (Manchester, 2008), pp. 101–25; and Sven Meeder, 'Boniface and the Irish heresy of Clemens', *Church History* 80 (2011), pp. 251–80.

There have been many publications outlining the Irish influence on the monastery of St-Gall including the still entertaining J.M. Clark, *The Abbey of St Gall as a Centre of Literature and Art* (Cambridge, 1926). The most complete treatment remains Johannes Duft and Peter Meyer, *The Irish Miniatures in the Abbey Library of St. Gall* (Olten and New York, 1954), despite some outdated arguments, rephrased but not greatly altered in his later publications. Duft has been influential in identifying the tendency in literature to overestimate the Irish element in St-Gall in his article 'Iromanie – Irophobie. Fragen um die frühmittelalterliche Irenmission exemplifiziert an St. Gallen und Alemannien', *Zeitschrift für Schweizerische Kirchengeschichte* 50 (1956), 241–62. A somewhat celebratory tone is found in Michael Richter, 'St Gallen and the Irish in the Early Middle Ages', in Michael Richter and Jean-Michel Picard, eds, *Ogma: Essays in Celtic Studies in Honour of Próinséas Ní Chatháin* (Dublin, 2002) pp. 65–75. The Lives of St Gallus are discussed in Walter Berschin's five-volume *Biographie und Epochenstil in lateinischen Mittelalter*, Quellen und Untersuchungen zur lateinischen Philologie des Mittelalters 8–10, 12, 15 (Stuttgart, 1986–2004).

John Scottus Eriugena's most famous work, the *Periphyseon*, has been edited by I.P. Sheldon-Williams (books I–III) and É.A. Jeauneau (book IV) and translated by Sheldon-Williams (books I–III) and J.J. O'Meara (book IV), *Iohannis Scotti Eriugenae Periphyseon*, Scriptores Latini Hiberniae 7, 9, 11, 13 (Dublin, 1968–95). His poems have been edited and translated by Michael W. Herren, *Iohannis Scotti Eriugenae Carmina*, Scriptores Latini Hiberniae 12 (Dublin, 1993).

For his biography see John Marenbon, 'John Scottus', in *Oxford Dictionary of National Biography* (Oxford, 2004) [http://www.oxforddnb.com/view/article/24940, accessed 30 July 2015]; D. Carabine, *John Scottus Eriugena* (Oxford, 2000).

On Eriugena's biblical exegesis see G. Van Riel, C. Steel and J. McEvoy, ed., *Iohannes Scottus Eriugena: The Bible and Hermeneutics* (Louvain, 1996). The theology and political implications of the tract *De Praedestinatione* are discussed in J. Marenbon, 'John Scottus and Carolingian Theology: from the *De Praedestinatione*, its Background and its Critics, to the *Periphyseon*', in M.T. Gibson and J. Nelson, eds, *Charles the Bald: Court and Kingdom* (2nd rev. ed. Aldershot, 1990), pp. 303–26. There is also a good contextual discussion by

W. Otten, 'Carolingian Theology', in G.R. Evans, ed., *The Medieval Theologians. An Introduction to Theology in the Medieval Period* (Oxford, 2001), pp. 65–82.

For a biography of Sedulius Scottus, see Luned Davies, 'Sedulius Scottus', in *Oxford Dictionary of National Biography* (Oxford, 2004) [http://www. oxforddnb.com/view/article/50134, accessed 30 July 2015]. Not many of his works are available in English translation. A recent edition and translation of his 'mirror of princes', a practical work of political philosophy, is by R.W. Dyson, *De Rectoribus Christianis. On Christian Rulers* (Woodbridge, 2010). An older translation of the same that includes translations of poems by Sedulius is E. G. Doyle, trans., *On Christian Rulers, and The Poems* (Binghamton NY, 1983).

13   The Irish and their books

For a succinct and introductory summary of the issues surrounding the discipline of palaeography (and to some degree by association that of codicology) – albeit with reference to later Protogothic and Gothic scripts –, see Albert Derolez, *The Palaeography of Gothic Manuscript Books from the Twelfth Century to the Early Sixteenth Century* (Cambridge, 2003), pp. 1–27. Introductions to the study of Latin palaeography as a subject in its own right are essential reading for understanding the context to insular manuscript production: Edward Maunde Thompson, *An Introduction to Greek and Latin Palaeography* (Oxford, 1912); J.J. John, 'Latin Palaeography' in James M. Powell, ed., *Medieval Studies. An Introduction* (Syracuse NY, 1976, 2nd edn 1992), pp. 3–81 (a good general background to history of scripts and codicology). For useful guides to terminology in script and manuscripts: Michelle P. Brown, *A Guide to Western Historical Scripts from Antiquity to 1600* (London 1990); eadem, *Understanding Illuminated Manuscripts. A Guide to Technical Terms* (Los Angeles, 1994).

The disciplines of palaeography and of calligraphy are often treated as distinct. However, there is much that palaeographers and calligraphers could learn from one another. For an appreciation of the many practical issues which would have faced medieval scribes in the formation of letters and layout of writing see Edward Johnston, *Writing and Illuminating and Lettering* (2nd edn, London 1939), which contains intricate drawings of pen preparation, angle of writing and page layout. For a sensitive examination of the kinds of challenges which would have confronted medieval scribes the modern-day calligrapher, Timothy O'Neill (who skilfully imitates medieval Gaelic script) provides an insightful piece in 'From Fax to Vellum: Producing Manuscript Books in the 21st century', Peter Harbison and Valerie Hall, eds, *A Carnival of Learning, Essays to honour George Cunningham and his 50 Conferences on Medieval Ireland in the Cistercian Abbey of Mount St Joseph's, Roscrea, 1987–2012* (Roscrea 2012).

The standard introduction to the study of insular palaeography and codicology is Bernhard Bischoff, *Latin Palaeography: Antiquity and the Middle Ages*, transl. Daíbhí Ó Cróinín and D. Ganz (Cambridge, 1990), pp. 83–95 (where

insular script is divided into 'Irish' and 'Anglo-Saxon' and includes plates of
the insular Half-Uncial and insular minuscule alphabets), pp. 7–19 (background on writing materials and tools). Julian T. Brown, *A Palaeographer's
View. The Selected Writings of Julian Brown*, eds Janet Bately et al. (London,
1993) offers a fundamental analysis of many important aspects of both insular
script and codicology, in particular, the chapters 'The distribution and significance of membrane prepared in the Insular manner' (pp. 125–139) and
'Tradition, imitation and invention in Insular Handwriting of the seventh
and eighth centuries' (pp.179–200) as does Julian T. Brown, 'The Irish
elements in the Insular system of scripts to circa A.D. 850', in Heinz Löwe,
ed., *Die Iren und Europa im früheren Mittelalter*, 2 vols (Stuttgart, 1982), I, pp.
101–119. E.A. Lowe, ed., *Codices Latini Antiquiores. A Palaeographical Guide to
Latin Manuscripts prior to the Ninth Century*, 11 vols and supplement (Oxford
1934–71; 2nd edn of vol. II, 1972) (which contains plates and descriptions of
a wealth of antique and medieval manuscripts) provides for details of insular
codicological and palaeographical conventions (II, pp. ix–xii and pp. xiv –
xvi). For a critical and groundbreaking review of early insular palaeography
in which many accepted norms on development and history are laid out and
debated, see David N. Dumville, *A Palaeographer's Review: The Insular System
of Scripts in the Early Middle Ages* (Osaka, 1999) (pp. 57–9 for a summary of
terminology used in discussing insular manuscripts and the importance of
consistently using 'insular' in relation to script. For the earliest use of 'Insulare
Schrift', see Ludwig Traube, *Vorlesungen und Abhandlungen*, 3 vols (Munich,
1909–1920), III, pp. 95–100). For transcriptions and some images of script
used on stone inscriptions in Britain and Ireland, see R.A.S. Macalister,
Corpus Inscriptionum Insularum Celticarum, 2 vols (Dublin, 1949). Guy
Petherbridge and J.L. Sharpe, eds, *Roger Powell the Compleat Binder. Liber
amicorum* (Turnhout, 1996) contains many interesting and useful articles on
the physical production of manuscripts and conservation techniques: for
example, Michelle P. Brown, 'Pigments and their Uses in Insular manuscripts', pp. 136–45 which contains descriptions of problems determining
ingredients of inks and, in Appendix A, a list of pigments used in insular
manuscripts; Carlo Federici et al., 'The Determination of Animal Species
used in Medieval Parchment Making: Non-Destructive Identification
Techniques', pp. 146–53 is translated into English from Italian by Margaret
Hey and refers to other studies on parchment by Italian scholars.

Abbreviated forms for words and syllables employed to save space and time
are important in the study of early Insular manuscripts. The huge body of
work carried out by Wallace Martin Lindsay published as *Notae Latinae: An
Account of Abbreviation in Latin MSS. of the Early Minuscule Period
(c. 700–850)* (Cambridge, 1915) with *Supplement* published by Doris Bains
(Cambridge, 1936) covering the later period 850 to 1050, is an essential reference tool for all students of medieval manuscripts. Lindsay's work was distilled
for an insular audience by David N. Dumville and published in a useful
publication in which the distinctions between Celtic, Anglo-Saxon, and pan-
insular abbreviations are clearly laid out in tabular format: *Abbreviations used*

in Insular Script before A.D. 850: Tabulation based on the Work of W.M. Lindsay (Cambridge, 2004). Another overarching study of abbreviation-usage is Adriano Cappelli, *Lexicon Abbreviaturarum* (2nd edn, Milan 1929) and its supplement Auguste Pelzer, *Abréviations Latines Médiévales. Supplément au Dizionario di Abbreviature Latine ed Italiane de Adriano Cappelli* (Louvain, 1964). For the various marks of punctuation: M.B. Parkes, *Pause and Effect* (Aldershot, 1992); P. McGurk, 'Citation Marks in Early Latin Manuscripts', *Scriptorium* 15 (1961), 3–13, plate 1; Maartje Draak, 'Construe Marks in Hiberno-Latin Manuscripts', *Mededelingen der Koninklijke Nederlandse Akademie van Wetenschappen, Afd. Letterkunde, Nieuwe Reeks* 20 (1957), pp. 261–82.

For an overview of many of the surviving manuscripts from the period under discussion, see James F. Kenney, *The Sources for the Early History of Ireland. An Introduction and Guide* (Dublin 1929; rev. edn., by L. Bieler, 1966). For other summaries with more commentary, see William O'Sullivan, 'Insular Calligraphy: Current State and Problems', *Peritia* 4 (1985), 346–359; idem, 'Manuscripts and Palaeography', in Dáibhí Ó Cróinín, ed., *A New History of Ireland, vol. 1: Prehistoric and early Ireland* (Oxford, 2005), pp. 511–48; and Michelle Brown, 'From Columba to Cormac: the Contribution of Irish Scribes to the Insular System of Scripts', in *Settimane* 57 (2010), pp. 623–46 (focuses on manuscripts with named scribes). A number of libraries in Britain and Ireland have catalogues which specify 'Irishness' for their contents: T.K. Abbot and E.J. Gwynn, *Catalogue of the Irish Manuscripts in the Library of Trinity College, Dublin* (Dublin, 1921); Marvin L. Colker, *Trinity College Library, Dublin: Descriptive Catalogue of the Mediaeval and Renaissance Latin Manuscripts*, 2 vols (Aldershot 1991); Myles Dillon et al., *Catalogue of Irish Manuscripts in the Franciscan Library, Killiney* (Dublin, 1969); Thomas O'Rahilly et al., *Catalogue of the Irish Manuscripts in the Royal Irish Academy*, 28 fascicules and 2 index-volumes (Dublin 1926–70). For Irish manuscripts found in a few British repositories, see Pádraig De Brún and Máire Herbert, *Catalogue of Irish Manuscripts in Cambridge Libraries* (Cambridge, 1986); Brian Ó Cuív, *Catalogue of Irish Manuscripts in The Bodleian Library at Oxford and Oxford College Libraries*, 2 vols (Dublin 2001/3); Standish Hayes O'Grady et al., *Catalogue of Irish Manuscripts in The British Museum*, 3 vols (London, 1926–53). Lists of published and unpublished catalogues may be found in Paul Oskar Kristeller, *Latin Manuscript Books before 1600. A List of Printed Catalogues and Unpublished Inventories of Extant Collections* (4th revised and enlarged edn; Munich, 1993) with a supplement by Sigrid Krämer and Birgit Christine Arensmann (Hanover, 2007). Another useful resource is Leonard E. Boyle, *Medieval Latin Palaeography. A Bibliographical Introduction* (Toronto, 1984; reprinted 1995) which refers to further reading on many aspects of medieval manuscripts.

The problem of accessing images of manuscripts has been significantly ameliorated thanks to the complete or partial digitisation of many collections. The most significant of these from an Irish perspective is Irish Script on Screen (ISOS) organized by the School of Celtic at the Dublin Institute for Advanced Studies (http://www.isos.dias.ie); however, some of the older

Latin manuscripts were not incorporated in this resource and one has to rely on hard-copy publications: for example, Lowe's *CLA* contains brief descriptions and plates of many early manuscripts; J.J.G. Alexander, *Insular Manuscripts, 6th to 9th Century* (London, 1978); and John T. Gilbert and H. James, eds, *Facsimiles of the National Manuscripts of Ireland*, 4 vols in 5 (Dublin, 1874–84). For a wider-ranging survey of Irish manuscripts, see Timothy O'Neill, *The Irish Hand* (2nd edn; Blackrock, 2014; with much better plates than in the first edition and more lengthy commentary). Other digitisation projects with varying numbers of Irish manuscripts include the following: Early Manuscripts at Oxford (http://image.ox.ac.uk); E-Codices – Virtual Manuscript Library of Switzerland (http://www.e-codices.unifr.ch/en); British Library's digitized Manuscripts (http://www.bl.uk/manuscripts).

For the Late Celtic period *c.* 850 × *c.* 1000 (which includes both Welsh, Gaelic and Cornish specimens) Wallace Martin Lindsay's publications *Early Irish Minuscule Script* (Oxford, 1910) and *Early Welsh Script* (Oxford, 1912) include descriptions of some surviving manuscripts with plates. Helen McKee, ed., *The Cambridge Juvencus Manuscript glossed in Latin, Old Welsh, and Old Irish: Text and Commentary* (Aberystwyth, 2000) provides an overview and updated description of Late Celtic script along similar lines to that supplied in Dumville, *A Palaeographer's Review*, pp. 124–6. For the later history of Welsh manuscripts containing insular script, see Gillian L. Conway, 'Towards a Cultural Context for the Eleventh-Century Llanbadarn Manuscripts', *Ceredigion* 13 (1997), 9–28 and Daniel Huws, *Medieval Welsh Manuscripts* (Cardiff, 2000). In the Gaelic world, Late Celtic script developed into 'Gaelic National minuscule' *c.* 1000. The Gaelic world alone preserved this bastion of Insularity for many centuries with the last Gaelic hereditary scribe Joseph Uí Longáin dying in 1880. The history of the palaeographical development of the history of Gaelic script in the Middle Ages awaits much attention in both research and in print. For a list of surviving manuscripts from the first two centuries of its production, see David N. Dumville, *Celtic Essays, 2001–2007*, 2 vols (Aberdeen, 2007), II, pp. 83–90. For an overview of the script's initial blossoming in this same period, see Elizabeth Duncan, 'A History of Gaelic script, A.D. 1000–1200' (unpublished PhD dissertation: University of Aberdeen, 2010).

Index